WELFARE, DEMOCRACY, AND THE NEW DEAL

OTHER BOOKS BY WILLIAM R. BROCK

Lord Liverpool and Liberal Toryism

The Character of American History

An American Crisis:
Congress and Reconstruction 1865–1867

The Evolution of American Democracy

Conflict and Transformation:
The United States 1844–1877

Parties and Political Conscience:
American Dilemmas 1840–1850

Scotus Americanus:
Links between Scotland and America
in the Eighteenth Century

Investigation and Responsibility:
Public Responsibility in the United States
1865–1900

WELFARE, DEMOCRACY, AND THE NEW DEAL

WILLIAM R. BROCK

Fellow of Selwyn College, Cambridge
Professor Emeritus of Modern History, University of Glasgow

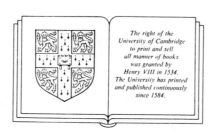

The right of the
University of Cambridge
to print and sell
all manner of books
was granted by
Henry VIII in 1534.
The University has printed
and published continuously
since 1584.

CAMBRIDGE UNIVERSITY PRESS

Cambridge
New York   New Rochelle   Melbourne   Sydney

Published by the Press Syndicate of the University of Cambridge
The Pitt Building, Trumpington Street, Cambridge CB2 1RP
32 East 57th Street, New York, NY 10022, USA
10 Stamford Road, Oakleigh, Melbourne 3166, Australia

First published 1988

Printed in the United States of America

Library of Congress Cataloging-in-Publication Data
Brock, William Ranulf.
Welfare, democracy, and the New Deal.
Includes index.
1. Public welfare – United States – History – 20th
century.   2. New Deal, 1933–1939.   3. United States –
Social policy.   4. United States – Social conditions –
1933–1945.   I. Title.
HV91.B696   1988   361.6′0973   87–20926

British Library Cataloguing in Publication Data
Brock, William R.
Welfare, democracy, and the New Deal.
1. Public welfare – United States –
History – 20th century
I. Title
361′.973   HV91

ISBN 0 521 33379 2

CONTENTS

PREFACE

In 1984 I published a book on the agencies and activities of the American states in the late nineteenth century. It was my original intention to make a similar study for the years of the Great Depression, but a preliminary survey convinced me that it would be more rewarding to limit the investigation to federal and state welfare policies, with special reference to those concerned with the relief of unemployment. They added a new element to the functions of government, transferred responsibilities that had been exclusively local to the states and the nation, and challenged traditional attitudes toward poverty and distress.

The relief of unemployment also brought to light a basic dilemma of reform in a democratic society. The new policies were initiated and largely controlled by professional social workers and welfare administrators who had been elected to no offices. The principal obstacles to humane and efficient administration were raised by elected officials and legislators: Who had the right to insist? Who had the right to refuse?

The materials for a study such as this are voluminous. Every state has a story to tell, and the papers of many men and women in public life throw light on problems and events. Selection must be made, and an author can hope no more than that his choice will be deemed judicious.

Research in the United States was made possible by a generous grant from the British Academy. In Great Britain the sources for the study of the United States in the twentieth century are greater than is sometimes imagined. The collections in the British Library, the London School of Economics, the University of Cambridge, and the Rhodes House Library in the University of Oxford were particularly useful.

Cambridge WILLIAM R. BROCK
January 1988

vii

ABBREVIATIONS

Archives, Agencies, and Frequently Used Printed Sources

APSR = *American Political Science Review.*
FDR Library = F. D. Roosevelt Library, Hyde Park, New York.
FERA = Federal Emergency Relief Administration.
LC = Library of Congress.
LC Pinchot = Library of Congress, Gifford Pinchot Papers.
NA = National Archives, Washington, D.C. (RG = Record Group).
NCSW = *Proceedings of the National Conference of Social Work;* cited with year.
N.Y. St. A. = New York State Archives, Albany.
POUR = President's Organization for Unemployment Relief.
RFC = Reconstruction Finance Corporation.
TERA = Temporary Emergency Relief Administration (New York).
WPA = Works Progress Administration.

INTRODUCTION

The focus of this book is narrow but its implications are wide. Public welfare, the latest born of government services, raises deep questions about the nature of society. Who should be given help, how, and at whose expense? Should welfare go beyond minimal aid to destitute people? Should rehabilitation, retraining, and environmental control be added to the list? Should the benefits be extended to people who are far from being destitute? And what obligations have people who support themselves for the well-being of those who do not?

Mass unemployment in advanced societies puts an edge on these questions. The unemployed suffer distress when others, over whom they have no control, fail to provide work. This situation may be attributed to international dislocation, ill-conceived national policy, or miscalculation by business leaders. As economists are seldom able to agree on the distribution of blame, the obligations of society are not easy to determine.

Whatever the theoretical problems, most national governments accept responsibility and meet the cost from taxes, to which the rich must contribute a high proportion of their income. In the United States, during the Great Depression, it was difficult to arrive at this solution because public responsibility was divided by the U. S. Constitution and further subdivided by state constitutions, and because the redistribution of wealth by fiscal policy had always been resisted. What was required was not the enlargement of existing public commitments and an increase in taxes, but fundamental changes in concepts of social obligation and government power.

The debate over poverty was not new and men continued to argue over the weight to be given to individual failings or environmental causes. The traditional attitude had been to blame able-bodied people who could not help themselves but to accept a communal obligation

1

to prevent them from dying of starvation. A distinction had always been made between paupers who were capable of work and people who were destitute because they were physically disabled, mentally incapable, or too young to work. Special programs had been set up by the states to care for people in these categories, but relief for persons outside them remained exclusively a local responsibility. This included the relief of able-bodied persons who were willing to work but could not find employment. To those for whom the states accepted responsibility there had recently been added aid for mothers with dependent children and no wage earner in the family. Some states had taken the first steps toward statutory assistance in their own homes for old people without means of support, though there was still a prevalent feeling that old people who had suffered unforeseen misfortune were best helped by private charity, but that those who had been improvident should go to the poorhouse.

The 1920s saw decided advances in institutional care, welfare administration, and social work methods. Competent observers were moderately optimistic about the future and believed that the country was set on a course of improvement in humane treatment of the unfortunate. Wise administration of public and private charity would greatly reduce, if not eliminate, avoidable destitution. If accident, illness, and unemployment could not be avoided, there would be continued improvement in bringing aid to the victims. Much was expected from organized charities, but public welfare, especially in the cities, was growing out of its primary task of relieving derelict humanity to investigate the causes of poverty and experiment with rehabilitation.

In spite of this progress America was less prepared than any other advanced country to tackle the consequences of a major depression. There was no social insurance; the federal government accepted no welfare responsibilities except for veterans; state responsibility was limited to well-defined categories; and small local governments carried the full burden of relief for the unemployed. Private charities were prepared to do as much as they could, but though their success was confidently predicted, voluntary organizations designed to help individuals and improve communal facilities could not cope with mass unemployment.

The crisis called for rapid improvisation, but ideas long regarded as taproots of American character were not easily abandoned. "Local responsibility" might be an empty slogan when so many local governments faced bankruptcy, but it was defended to the last. Public men with great experience continued to believe that private charities would meet the challenge even when their funds were running out and fund-raising campaigns no longer met their targets. In states the favorite financial expedient was to raise the ceiling on the borrowing power of local governments – thus pushing them still more deeply into debt – rather than to raise taxes to meet increasing costs.

The way in which the crisis developed, the actions taken in the worst-hit states, and the reluctant move toward federal relief are described in the third and fourth chapters of this book. At this stage it is necessary only to point out that the men and women who would have to administer the new policies, staff the new state and federal agencies, and bear the heat of the day as field representatives were drawn from a new profession. Social work had been advancing, and at its head were directors and executive officers of large charities and community chests, state welfare commissioners, and welfare directors of some large cities. There were also a few academics from the new schools of social work, which had trained most of the rank-and-file social workers (of whom many were young and a majority were women).

When relief became big government, these welfare administrators and social workers were the available experts who suddenly found themselves in positions from which they could plan policy and implement it according to professional precepts. Inevitably some mistakes were made. The methods of professional social work had been taught with a view to helping maladjusted individuals and were not wholly suitable to deal with mass destitution in a maladjusted society. Nevertheless many were willing to learn, and by good fortune there were individuals of outstanding ability at the top.

The administrators and social workers who managed emergency relief at state and national levels were a new breed in the corridors of power. They were middle class and college educated, but not from socially prominent families. They were not professional politicians, lawyers who had worked their way up the political ladder, or representatives of business interests. Their only qualification was professional competence in a field carrying little social status.

There was no precedent for federal relief. It meant that federal money was spent as never before and that professional social workers exercised surveillance over matters that had always been sheltered from scrutiny by state rights and local responsibility. The men in the lead had fairly clear ideas about the kind of change they wished to introduce, and under the banner of federal relief men dedicated to reform had a unique opportunity to introduce a new era in welfare policy.

The experiment planted in their minds the idea of a permanent, professional, and national welfare system. They argued that the facts revealed by the emergency would always exist, that the fundamental causes were nationwide, and that only the national government could supply, organize, and supervise the remedies. This dream was not to be realized in full – to the continued regret of most experts in the field – but it generated the whole modern system of social security and federal attacks on poverty.

As the federal and state relief administrators set about their tasks, the most serious impediments were presented by locally elected officials, state legislators, and some governors. The people dedicated to improvement were placed squarely in opposition to those who depended on popular choice. The first shock of mass unemployment persuaded many people that something had to be done, and there was an initial welcome for those who did it. But, as they became accustomed to the new conditions, elected officials came to resent the authority given to relief directors, and majorities in most state legislatures fought long, hard, and usually with success to avoid paying their share of relief costs. There may be lessons in this for those who talk today of the need for community politics.

Is is possible to extract from this experience a general theory to explain the expansion of public welfare? In an influential book[1] Piven and Cloward argue that "expansive relief policies are designed to mute civil disorder, and restrictive ones to reinforce work norms" and that "the historical pattern is clearly not one of progressive liberalization; it is rather a record of periodically expanding and contracting relief rolls as the system performs its two main functions: maintaining civil order and enforcing work." They accuse other writers of viewing the system as "shaped by morality" and as obscuring "the central role of relief agencies in the regulation of marginal labor and in the maintenance of civil order."

[1] Frances Fox Piven and Richard A. Cloward, *Regulating the Poor: The Functions of Public Welfare* (New York, 1971), xiii–xvii.

It is easy to select evidence to support this hypothesis. In times of economic depression there is bound to be talk of civil disorder, but it does not follow that threats of violence are the only or even the principal incentives for extending welfare. When action to combat distress is urgently needed, the possibility of violent unrest is an obvious argument to support the case for immediate relief; but it is possible to fill pages with accounts of other arguments that rely on pictures of misery, appeals to humanitarian sentiment, and stories of demoralization. On balance, a bread line was a more persuasive argument than a riot.

The following chapters include several references to threatened violence and attempts to organize the unemployed; but there is also evidence of docility, demoralization, and apathy. Communists and others tried to make the most of the opportunity, but the surprising fact is their lack of success. The most that can be said of violence as a factor in relief policy is that it may, on a few occasions, have accelerated action on lines that had already been decided. The lines themselves demand a rather different explanation.

There is no need to place too much faith in the good will of governments. Men who govern are not free agents and operate within parameters set by the culture in which they live, and the moving force in modern culture has been the scientific revelation that problems can be solved and evils prevented. This was the faith that inspired the men and women who worked on the frontiers of social welfare, and the depression allowed them to put their ideas into action on a grander scale than was ever before thought possible. It is not necessary to "view the system as shaped by morality" to believe that ideas are stronger than interests. Society changes as the result of unremitting effort and occasional opportunism on the part of minorities who start out with a hope that it can be improved. They may be moralists, scientists, utopian enthusiasts, or cool pragmatists, but all share the conviction that life can be improved by rational action.

This does not mean that those who are affected by change have no influence upon its character. As Michael Katz argues, the poor have done more on their own behalf by adaptation than by threats. "In every era the poor have created strategies of survival whose resourcefulness belies the image of passive degradation with which poor people are often portrayed."[2]

[2] Michael B. Katz, *Poverty and Policy in American History* (New York, 1983), 241.

Evidence for "strategies of survival" during the Great Depression is abundant, but this book is concerned with the formulation and implementation of new relief policies. Attention is concentrated upon ideas, the means by which they were implemented, and their legacy for the future. During the New Deal the theorists became men of action, the course of welfare history was changed, and the people were at least won halfway over. The heart of the matter is therefore the relationship between small groups working for change and the majorities voting their proposals up or down.

The history of relief during the New Deal began with hope for a national program to tackle poverty as a social disease. It ended with half measures: with a social security system that was neither generous nor comprehensive, a federal works program that was certain to be short-lived, and modest grants to supplement state care for those who were physically or mentally incapacitated. General relief was returned to the states and the treatment of poverty was often assigned to the smallest units of government, staffed by untrained officials adminstering a poor law that had not changed in essentials since the seventeenth century. These developments may have given new life to local self-government, but the fragmented character of public assistance has ruined all subsequent attempts to guarantee freedom from want.

This should not obscure the importance of what was done. After the experiment of federal relief, ideas that were unthinkable in 1930 became basic propositions in future debates. New concepts of social justice had taken root, and so rapid had been the change in national responsibility that contemporaries could hardly grasp its implications. In this as in so much else the depression and the New Deal meant that nothing would ever be the same again.

1

A VIEW FROM THE PEAK OF PROSPERITY

The Great Depression presented an unprecedented challenge to American institutions and assumptions, and in no sphere were the consequences more profound than in the treatment of poverty and destitution. To the men and women who sought quick relief for people in distress the response seemed to be exasperatingly slow; in retrospect the speed of change was remarkable. Public responsibility for the consequences of economic failure was recognized; functions that had been exclusively local were assumed by states; national agencies carried national power into areas hitherto reserved for the states; and if new ideas about the nature of poverty continued to rest on insecure philosophic foundations, old ideas were discarded.

The magnitude of the change raises perennial questions of continuity and discontinuity, of tradition and innovation, of survivals and new departures. How far were the changes, made in response to economic disaster, the acceleration of existing trends? Were they newly planted or did they grow from seeds sown in earlier years? Was there a break with the past or merely readjustment to changed circumstances?

There has been much discussion of the extent to which the New Deal was anticipated by Herbert Hoover's administration, but rather less of the relationship between the 1930s and the preceding decade. In the popular view the 1920s are still seen as the last and discredited gasp of an old order, a time of reaction and complacency, of froth and heedless optimism, the years that the locust had eaten. Yet to many intelligent contemporaries, including sharp critics of the dominant ideology, it was a time of change and opportunity, and the inauguration of Herbert Hoover as President on March 4, 1929 was welcomed as a promise that an intelligent administration would work for the betterment of national life.

Unlike his predecessor Hoover was at home with old Progressives, could appreciate the quality of intellectual debate, and had wide experience of the world. As a successful civil engineer he was accustomed to the analysis of complex problems, as a wartime administrator of relief in Europe he had shown that bureaucratic means could be used for humanitarian ends, and as Secretary of Commerce he had made a lackluster office a major force in economic policy making. It was typical of the man that early in his presidency he set up a research committee to study social trends in America and submit a report that would serve as a guide for the future. The chairman of the committee was Wesley C. Mitchell, a distinguished economist, and the members included leading authorities in every field of social science.[1]

The committee's report, in two volumes and entitled *Recent Social Trends,* included a weighty general introduction and separate chapters, each by an expert, on all aspects of national life; but it was not submitted until the closing months of Hoover's administration. The depression was then at its worst, much of the committee's work had been overtaken by events, and the report attracted less attention than it deserved; nevertheless it remains an unrivaled survey of society as seen by trained observers at the close of America's most prosperous decade.[2]

The committee members did not share the exuberant optimism that pervaded public opinion at the time of their appointment. They spent more time stressing tension and difficulty than praising the American way, but claimed that they had not exaggerated "the bewildering confusion of problems" but "merely uncovered the situation as it is." America was, they believed, in the grip of profound forces affecting all modern civilizations. Scientific discovery and technological innovation had brought about changes in economic and social organization, and these had, in turn, affected religion, family life, education, and government. Partly because of these changes and partly as a result of other long-term forces, there had been major alterations in social philosophy and personal behavior.

[1] Recent studies, more favorable to the President than earlier writers, are Joan Hoff Wilson, *Herbert Hoover: Forgotten Progressive* (Boston, 1975), David Burner. *Herbert Hoover: A Public Life* (New York, 1979), and William J. Barber, *From new era to New Deal: Herbert Hoover, The economists and American economic policy* (Cambridge, 1985). Albert U. Romasco, *The Poverty of Abundance: Hoover, the Nation, and the Depression* (New York, 1965), is less sympathetic.

[2] *Recent Social Trends in the United States: Report of the President's Research Committee on Social Trends,* 2 vols. (New York and London, 1933). Cited hereafter as *RST.*

In the introduction to *Recent Social Trends* the members of the committee drew a general conclusion:

> Many of the problems of society today occur because of the shifting order . . . of four major social institutions. Church and family have lost many of their regulatory influences over behavior, while industry and government have assumed a larger degree of control.[3]

Familiar symptoms of the consequent social malaise were crime and corruption in the cities, "forlorn government" in rural districts, and loss of confidence in the ballot. Economic power was concentrated, organized labor had declined, and there was much unprincipled manipulation of publicity and propaganda. From this evidence many people had been "led to conclude reluctantly that the emergence of some recognized and avowed form of plutocratic dictatorship was not far away."

Having outlined these apprehensions, the committee went on to point out that the disruptive forces were also capable of being used to bring about vast improvements. Familiarity with large-scale organization, the prompt application of scientific and technological advances, resistance to class privilege, and "the wholly unparalleled democratization of education" were all grounds for hope. If these developments were understood and used intelligently, democracy could survive with stronger and more unified government, better civic training, more efficient control over social and economic forces, "less lag between social change and governmental adaptation," and "more prevision and contriving spirit."[4]

Was the emphasis upon the role of government in democratic society merely a prescription for the future or was it a trend observed by the committee? Concentration on the ferment of the Progressive era and on the flood of legislation during the New Deal has often left the impression that the intervening period was one of government inactivity, save in building highways and enforcing Prohibition. The record of the federal government may seem to confirm this view, but the states tell a different story.

Between 1920 and 1931 state and local expenditure on education increased from $1,705 to $2,311 million, on highways from $1,294 to $1,742 million, on hospitals from $200 to $349 million, and on public

---

[3] *RST*, Vol. I, General Report, xiii–xiv, lxvii.
[4] Ibid, lxix.

welfare from $119 to $444 million. The very large increases in health and welfare expenditure are highly significant, and correct the impression that state and local governments served only the material interests of property owners and skilled workers. The cities accounted for much of the increased expenditure in these categories; in 1923 their total expenditure was $1,069 million, by 1930 it was $1,780 million, and of this increase public health accounted for $16 million and public welfare for no less than $84 million.[5] Behind these figures lies a story of greatly improved and expanded services for the less fortunate members of urban society.

The increasing activity of government did not escape the attention of qualified observers. In 1926 one political scientist declared that "the range of legislative interference in men's affairs, whether justifiably or not, is rapidly increasing." In 1928 another political scientist wrote that "the notion that a government governs best when it governs least has been laid aside." An authority on public administration pointed out that though the demands for better services and for government economy were logically incompatible, they had worked together for greater efficiency and stricter control. A system that had been "highly decentralized" was "rapidly tending toward a considerable degree of integration in the federal government, the states, and the cities."[6]

How did this expansion occur within the framework of the Constitution, made by men for whom suspicion of power was the first principle of political wisdom, and interpreted by judges of whom a majority treated the Fourteenth Amendment as a charter for economic freedom? The answer lies in the distinction drawn between the regulation of economic activity and the protection of health, safety, and morals. When a state intervened in economic activities, the majority of judges on the Supreme Court required clear proof that the occupation was (in the classic phrase) "affected with the public interest"; but when a state exercised its police power to regulate health, safety, and morals, it was presumed to have acted legitimately unless there was clear evidence that its action was unreasonable. The hinge upon which so many cases turned was whether legislatures had wide or narrow dis-

[5] *Historical Statistics of the United States* (Washington, D.C., 1976) Series Y 682–709; Bureau of the Census, *Historical Review of State and Local Government Finance* (Washington, D.C., 1948).
[6] *APSR* 20 (1926), 80–106. Robert E. Cushman, "Constitutional Law in 1924–5" *RST*, Vol. II, chap. XXVII; Leonard D. White, "Public Administration," ibid., 1409.

cretion in social policy. A majority of the judges believed that the Fourteenth Amendment imposed heavy shackles upon state action; but if the protection of health, safety, or morals was the issue, a somewhat different majority allowed the states surprising latitude.

Cases can therefore be cited to demonstrate either the hostility of the Court to state regulation or its sanction for the expansion of state power. Of the nine judges in the 1920s, Pierce Butler, James McReynolds, Edward Sanford, George Sutherland, and Willis Van Devanter believed that the power of states to regulate economic affairs was strictly limited by the Constitution. Chief Justice William Howard Taft was more inclined to give a state the benefit of any doubt. Oliver Wendell Holmes, often joined by Louis Brandeis and Harlan Stone, believed that these were political questions that should not be subject to judicial veto. A state should be free to legislate as it saw fit, provided that its action was not explicitly prohibited by the Constitution. However, when a law was defended as a legitimate exercise of the police power, the Chief Justice and the three dissenters were likely to be joined by at least one of the more conservative judges to make a majority to uphold the challenged state law.

In one leading case – *Federal Trade Commission v. Gratz,* decided by 7 to 2 in 1920 – the Supreme Court curbed a federal agency. The majority held that the Federal Trade Commission had no power to decide what was unfair competition, thereby reducing it to being little more than a fact-finding agency. Justice Brandeis, rightly regarded as the principal architect of the law in question, dissented in a long and closely argued opinion; but the leading conservative, Justice McReynolds, speaking for the majority, declared that the act establishing the commission "was certainly not intended to fetter free competition as commonly understood and practiced by honorable opponents in trade."[7]

In the much quoted case of *Adkins v. the Children's Hospital,* decided in 1923, the Court invalidated an order issued in the District of Columbia (under authority conferred by an act of Congress) fixing minimum wages for women. In 1925 it struck down a Kansas law making arbitration compulsory and binding in industrial disputes. Justice Van Devanter said that compulsory arbitration was "intended to compel the owner and employees to continue business on terms which

[7] 253 U.S. 421; Thomas C. Blaisdell, *The Federal Trade Commission* (New York, 1932), 43.

are not of their own making. . . . Such a system infringes the liberty of contract and rights of property guaranteed by the due process clause of the Fourteenth Amendment."[8]

The majority struck another blow for economic freedom when it invalidated a Pennsylvania law prohibiting the use of shoddy as a filling for quilts. The law was justified on the ground that shoddy was often filthy, and in a strong dissent Justice Holmes defended the right of the state to prohibit the use of a material if it had reasonable grounds for believing that only in this way could an objectionable practice be prevented. For the majority Justice Butler declared that constitutional guarantees could not "be made to yield to mere convenience." The business in question was lawful, the blanket prohibition of one material in manufacture was arbitrary, and the law was a violation of the Fourteenth Amendment.[9]

In two cases the majortiy interpreted narrowly the historic doctrine that business affected with the public interest was subject to regulation. In *Tyson v. United Theater Ticket Office* the Court invalidated a New York law declaring that the sale of theater tickets was affected with the public interest and forbidding their sale by agents at a premium of more than 50 percent. Justice Sutherland said that a business was not affected by the public interest merely because a legislature decided that it was, and that if the law was allowed there could be no limit to legislative price fixing. Tickets for "lectures . . . baseball . . . and every possible form of amusement, including the lowly merry-go-round with its adjunct the hurdy gurdy," might be regulated by similar laws. If one accepted the premise that there ought to be some limit to price control, the decision in the Tyson case might be defended, but even on this basis the decision in *Williams v. the Standard Oil Company* was dubious. A Tennessee law gave the State Finance and Tax Commission power to fix the price of gasoline, but Justice Sutherland, speaking again for the majority, declared that a business was not affected with the public interest unless it was "devoted to the public use and granted in effect to the public." The fact that many members of the public purchased gas did mean that it was devoted to public use. The Court also invalidated others parts of the law – sale permits, licenses, and the prohibition of rebates or price discrimination – on the ground that all were adjuncts to unconstitutional price fixing.[10]

[8] 267 U.S. 512.
[9] *Weaver v. Palmer Bros. Company*, 270 U.S. 402.
[10] 273 U.S. 418; 278 U.S. 235.

An Oklahoma law of 1915, declaring cotton gins to be public utilities and therefore subject to regulation survived judicial scrutiny, but an additional proviso of 1925, making it mandatory for the state to license gins run by cooperatives, was struck down on the ground that it denied equal protection to private operators. In a dissent Justices Holmes and Stone argued that it was within the power of a legislature to decide that cooperators should be given special treatment.[11]

The tolerance normally shown for health regulations did not save a Pennsylvania law preventing persons who were not registered pharmacists from owning drug stores. Justice Sutherland noted that the state already had a law requiring all dispensers of drugs to be qualified, but could find no merit in its extension to owners. In this case the law may have been inequitable – it was intended to protect small druggists rather than the public – but Sutherland invalidated it as an unconstitutional invasion of rights guaranteed by the Fourteenth Amendment. In a dissent Justice Brandeis questioned the wisdom of the law, but thought that there was no constitutional barrier to its enactment.[12]

In these cases legislative discretion fought a losing battle. "Even now," said Holmes in one of his numerous dissents, "it seems to me not too late to urge that in dealing with state legislation . . . we should avoid with great caution attempts to substitute our judgment for that of the body whose business it is, in the first place [to decide] questions of domestic policy that are fairly open to debate." To this a majority of his fellow judges might have replied that no individual rights were safe if they could be restricted whenever a majority in a state legislature claimed that the public interest made it necessary to do so. As McReynolds said, "rights guaranteed by the Constitution cannot be so lightly treated; they are superior to this supposed necessity."[13]

Yet even the stoutest defender of rights guaranteed by the Fourteenth Amendment knew that some actions infringing private rights must be allowed, and that a line was hard to draw. In the Oklahoma cotton gin case, Sutherland went out of his way to make it clear that the original act was constitutional, thus recognizing the right of a state to protect the livelihood of one group of producers. In the Pennsylvania pharmacy case, one reason for invalidating the law was that the state already had an effective (and constitutional) law regulating the sale of drugs.

[11] *Frost v. Corporation Commission of Oklahoma,* 278 U.S. 215.
[12] *Liggett Company v. Baldridge,* 278 U.S. 105.
[13] *Schlesinger v. Wisconsin,* 270 U.S. 230.

In *Kresge v. New York* the issue was whether the state could forbid the sale of spectacles unless they were prescribed by a licensed physician or qualified optometrist. The owner of a leading chain of drug stores challenged the law, and a persuasive argument was advanced that the sale of simple convex lenses at a low price was popular particularly with old people, who had difficulty in reading and merely wanted to enlarge the print. Justice Holmes, speaking for once for a unanimous Court, used his favorite argument to uphold the law. There were, he said, advantages in offering inexpensive glasses to those with failing eyesight and no complicating factors, but they should be balanced against the need to ensure that eyesight was not damaged by using spectacles sold without a test by a qualified person. When there were arguments on both sides, "the balancing of the considerations of advantage and disadvantage is for the legislature, not for the courts."[14]

A Minnesota law required an applicant for a license to practice dentistry to submit to an examination by a state board. The Court found no difficulty in upholding a further law requiring an applicant to submit a diploma from a college in good standing before admission to the examination. The argument that this was discrimination between persons and contrary to the Fourteenth Amendment was brushed aside without calling on the state to argue the law's legality. In a more surprising decision, with Holmes again speaking for a unanimous Court, a Nebraska law fixing the legal fees charged in workmen's compensation cases was upheld. In a flanking attack on the free contract theory, Holmes observed that many who claimed compensation "need to be protected against improvident contracts, in the interest not only of themselves but of the public."[15]

Legislative discretion seemed to be stretched still further when a New Orleans streetcar company contested an order by the city requiring the demolition of a viaduct, and its replacement by grade crossings, without offering compensation. Justice Butler held that the city, acting as an "arm of the state," had "wide discretion in determining what precautions in the public interest" were "necessary or appropriate"; nor was enforcement of a legitimate exercise of "police power" deprivation of property without due process of law. Compensation was not mandatory because anyone who accepted a streetcar franchise did so in full knowledge that the business was subject to regulation.[16]

[14] *Kresge v. Ward,* 279 U.S. 337.
[15] *Graves v. Minnesota,* 272 U.S. 425; *Yeiser v. Dysart,* 267 U.S. 540.
[16] *New Orleans Public Service Company v. New Orleans,* 281 U.S. 682.

Prohibition could produce striking invasions of property and privacy, but the Court found little difficulty in upholding actions to enforce it. In Pennsylvania liquor legislation had preceded the national act by many years. A law of 1915 permitted the use of liquor in private residences but it was repealed in 1917, and the sheriffs were empowered to seize liquor, wherever found, without compensation. In *Samuels v. McCurdy* the plaintiff sued a sheriff for the recovery of liquor seized under this act, alleging that the law was ex post facto, that the liquor had been legally acquired under the earlier act, and that there had been no attempt to sell or distribute it. In a dissent Butler said that the law as applied was plainly "oppressive and arbitrary," but the Chief Justice, speaking for the majority, unequivocally upheld the law and the sheriff's action. The law was not ex post facto because it proscribed no penalty for a past action but only for continuing to hold liquor after its passage; the object of Prohibition was to prevent the use of liquor because of its demoralizing effect on society, and the legislature was justified in ordering the seizure of private stocks; nor need compensation be given because anyone purchasing liquor (even under the earlier law) did so in full knowledge that it might be denied the protection normally given to property.[17]

State courts followed or anticipated Supreme Court decisions. In a case raising similar points to *Samuels v. McCurdy,* the Supreme Court of Ohio upheld a law requiring the destruction of animals infected with tuberculosis, refusing compensation unless the owner had complied with the quarantine laws and basing compensation (when paid) on low valuations. The court approved the purpose of the law and the need to destroy private property when health was at risk. It held that this action did not take private property for public use (which would have required mandatory compensation), but abated a public nuisance (which had never qualified for compensation under common law). If the legislature chose to offer compensation, it was in the nature of a gratuity and need not be related to market values. "Statutes of this nature," said the Court, "providing even drastic measures for the elimination of disease, whether in human beings, crops, stock, or cattle, are in general authorized under the police power."[18]

In 1928 the Supreme Court of Massachusetts declared that the power of the state to designate certain things as public nuisances was

[17] *Samuels v. McCurdy,* 267 U.S. 188.
[18] *Kroplin v. Truax,* 119 Ohio 610.

virtually unlimited, and property so classified could be seized at any time without compensation. The case involved the manufacture of alcohol, but the Massachusetts judges took the broad view that neither the Declaration of Rights in the state constitution nor the Fourteenth Amendment of the federal Constitution contracted the broad bounds of the police power. The same court adopted a strict interpretation of the contract clause of the federal Constitution when a water company claimed that its contract to supply water to Boston had been impaired by subsequent legislation. State Chief Justice Rugg said that the fallacy in this argument was the assumption that "the exercise of the police power depended upon the express or implied consent of the persons affected." Any contract was entered into in the knowledge that "the interests of the public are paramount, and private considerations are subsidiary where the public health and safety are at stake, irrespective of the assent or dissent of property owners."[19]

The "police power" had come to include general responsibility for security, health, safety, public morals, and welfare. For over a century, and especially since the Civil War, the courts had sanctioned the wide sweep of state authority when laws protected or promoted these social objectives. They had justified factory legislation, the enforcement of safety standards, workmen's compensation laws, the prohibition of child labor, limitation of women's hours of work, and a whole range of activities loosely described as public welfare.

In 1928 Ray A. Brown, a constitutional lawyer from the University of Wisconsin, reviewed cases involving use of the police power to protect health and safety in the *Harvard Law Review*. He pointed out that *Adkins v. the Childrens' Hospital* stood alone as the only unrepudiated decision in which a law, defended as a health measure, had been struck down. In this case the Court's hostility to wage fixing had outweighed testimony that the health of women suffered when wages were abnormally low, but on numerous other occasions, laws justified on health grounds had been upheld even when they imposed drastic restraints on employers and owners of property.[20]

[19] *Reale v. Judges of the Supreme Court of Massachusetts*, 163 N.E. 893 (the action was against the judges because they were responsible for issuing an order, on application of the police commissioner, for the abatement of a public nuisance); *Loring et al. v. Commissioner of Public Works of Boston*.

[20] *Harvard Law Review* 42 (1928–9), 866–98. Ray A. Brown, "Police Power: Legislation for Health and Personal Safety." For a review of the extension of state activities in the late nineteenth century, see my *Investigation and Responsibility* (Cambridge, 1984); court opinions are examined in Chapter 3.

Brown also argued that neither the majority nor the minority of the Supreme Court justices had developed a consistent doctrine defining the limits of police power, and the record of individual judges was of little help in predicting their decisions when specific issues were presented. This inconsistency had almost become a part of the court's tradition. In twenty-one years on the Court, the late Justice Brewer, usually regarded as the stoutest opponent of interventionist legislation, had participated in forty-six cases involving police power and had ruled against the state law in only nineteen. Justice Peckham, who had spoken for the majority in the notorious case of *Lochner v. New York,* which condemned a New York law forbidding night work in bakeries, had nevertheless upheld the use of police power in twenty-five out of forty-one cases. The judge who came closest to consistency was the veteran Holmes, who had supported police power in one hundred and ninety out of two hundred and twelve cases; but his contention that legislative discretion must not be curbed by judicial extrapolations from the Constitution was offered as a guideline, not a rule. Brown's conclusion was that "In applying the vague phrases of the fourteenth amendment, the logical approach is rendered almost impossible by the lack of any articulate major premise."[21]

Uncertain doctrine and confusing precedents meant that in each case the points for decision became practical rather than systematic or legal. Were health, safety, or morals really endangered? Or was this claim a shield for some other purpose? Was regulation or prohibition an appropriate remedy for the ill complained of? Was the infringement of individual freedom too great to justify the means used to achieve an acceptable end? Thus the Court had taken precisely the position Holmes deplored, by considering questions that were political rather than judicial, but the cumulative result had been to widen the domain of legislative discretion. In some instances this had produced decisions that anyone concerned with protecting the weak would regret, but over the years it had lead to a steady enlargement of the area in which the states could and did regulate the lives of their citizens. Prohibition had produced the most dramatic results, but the trend had been clear long before the passage of the Eighteenth Amendment. A single decision might check movement in one channel, but the tide had continued to rise. If a social evil became apparent and the

[21] Brown, "Police Power," 871.

remedy was within legislative grasp, it was unlikely that the courts would long delay its application.

Since the Civil War, there had been three principal phases in the growth of state activity. The later years of the nineteenth century witnessed the establishment of key agencies setting the pattern for future development: boards of charities and corrections (or, in some states, of state charities), boards of public health, bureaus of labor statistics, and railroad commissions. These were the parent bodies of state departments of public welfare, health, labor, and transportation. Three quite different methods of constituting these agencies had been adopted. Boards of charities and correction and of public health were normally appointed and unpaid, with salaried secretaries as full-time executives; bureaus of labor normally consisted of officials serving long terms under an appointed commissioner; railroad commissioners were elected in many states and appointed in others, but usually for short terms and with a proviso that the commission must be bi-partisan. In addition to the four principal agencies (which appeared under varied designations in most states), there were bureaus, boards, or commissions (appointed or elected in many different ways) to regulate such matters of local significance as forests, fisheries, mines, livestock, and dairy products. Thus no clear or uniform pattern of state administration had evolved and, in the numerous agencies of the states, amateurs and experts, short-term volunteers and long-serving professionals, members appointed by governors with or without legislative confirmation, men elected on party tickets and changing with each administration, or enjoying bipartisan support and surviving many elections, shared responsibility for state government. The pattern was untidy, and so was the mass of legislation generated by all this activity. Many laws were ineffective or ill-conceived, but in sum they represented a determination to regulate social forces left by earlier generations to chance or divine providence.[22]

The second phase, beginning about 1890, is usually associated with progressivisim but is better understood as a logical sequel to the first period of growth. The national government tentatively assumed limited responsibility for policing the economy with the Interstate Commerce Commission and antitrust laws. Between 1900 and 1914 the

---

[22] Brock, *Investigation and Responsibility,* Chap. 1, passim.

new powers were refined and strengthened, and new national responsibilities were assumed with a food and drug law, a Federal Children's Bureau, and a Federal Trade Commission. In the states the main thrust of these years produced civic reform, significant advances in public health, and the gradual conversion of voluntary boards into full-time professional bodies. Lay boards often continued as adjuncts to professional agencies – sometimes with purely advisory functions but often with control over the general direction of policy – and faith in the efficacy of voluntary, unpaid bodies would continue into the New Deal period, even though it meant reliance on men and women who were well-to-do, middle-class, and middle-aged, with time to devote to such pursuits.

The third phase, beginning with the First World War and continuing to 1930, was a period of consolidation but also of innovations opening new fields of public responsibility for those who could not help themselves. States financed and supervised aid for widows with dependent children. They enacted workmen's compensation laws and recognized, for the first time, a public interest in fair play in industrial relations. Some states also set up old-age pension schemes, though with limited effect, as in most cases their adoption by counties was optional.

Many of these changes took place out of the public eye and attracted little publicity beyond the circles of those who administered the programs or benefitted from them, but together they presented proof that old attitudes were dying out. In 1923 Alfred E. Smith, newly elected governor, declared that in New York they were "long past the period when workmen's compensation and enlightened labor laws were looked upon as paternalistic," and promised an administration "actively responsive to the needs of the human units that make up [the state's] citizenship." New York was no more a typical state than was Al Smith a typical governor, but his successful administration earned him the Democratic nomination for President in 1928. In that year a political scientist could declare, without fear of contradiction, that "the assumption by the states of factory inspection, food examination, disease control, and agricultural experimentation" meant that limited government was no longer the American way.[23]

---

[23] Significantly, the *Survey Graphic* (newly founded organ of the Progressive social workers; see note 45) welcomed the address as a major turning point in New York's social policy [2(4), 1923, 419–20].

In 1929 the Federal Bureau of Labor Statistics circulated to all states copies of some public lectures organized by the New York Department of Labor to explain its work. James A. Hamilton, the state industrial commissioner, gave a general account of the department's functions. It enforced labor laws, administered the workmen's compensation law, inspected factories and other places of work, investigated the condition of women in industry, inquired into the causes of strikes and lockouts, maintained a voluntary arbitration service, enforced orders affecting places of work, provided employment offices, investigated the general condition of labor, and prepared proposals for legislative action. As an executive department, it issued rules for carrying the laws into effect, directives for specific industries, regulations for safety, health, and fire protection in factories, and licenses for carrying on dangerous or unhealthy occupations.[24]

In a quasi-judicial capacity the department heard and determined all claims for workmen's compensation. This duty was particularly onerous: During 1927, 518,297 industrial accidents were reported, 173,535 claims calendared for hearings, and 187,368 cases (including some held over from the previous year) decided. Every claim was considered by a referee, who made an award after a hearing. A dissatisfied party could appeal on questions of fact to a state compensation board or on questions of law to the State Supreme Court. In 1927 the referees made awards in over 182,000 cases, of which only 12,000 were appealed. Payment of claims was guaranteed by a requirement that employers must insure against liability with the state insurance fund or an approved private company.[25]

The factory laws were enforced by inspectors, working under a Bureau of Inspection, who made sure that employers were aware of the law, drew their attention to specific shortcomings, issued orders if necessary, and, as a last resort, initiated prosecutions. In 1927 169,240 orders were issued to factories to remedy faults and 110,938 to mercantile establishments, with 166,240 and 110,172 compliances. The greatest number of orders to factories dealt with unsafe machinery but in mercantile establishments the sanitary arrangements were most often at fault. The inspectors also issued orders relating to buildings under construction, places of public assembly, mines, and quarries. In

---

[24] United States Department of Labor, *Activities of a State Department of Labor* (Washington, D.C., 1929).

[25] Ibid. (reprinting a lecture by James A. Hamilton, Commissioner of Labor, New York).

total 314,636 orders were issued during the year, or over 1,000 every working day. If the notion still persists that American capitalism was little regulated at this time, these figures may serve as a corrective.[26]

New York was large and wealthy, but its public services were exceptional only in their range and professionalism. Other states had taken the same road, and by 1930 America was more governed than at any earlier period. The monthly catalog of state government publications was evidence of the trend, listing 380 titles in 1900 and 714 by 1929. Another indicator was the increasing number and self-conscious professionalism of government officials. By 1929 there were no fewer than 400 national and regional associations of public officials.[27]

Much of this activity took place within state boundaries, but the regulation of food and drugs provided an example of coordination by the federal government of a nationwide program. Many states had been active in this field before the first federal law in 1906, but it then became the responsibility of the national government to prevent the interstate transportation of harmful food, drugs, and medicines. State cooperation was essential for the success of federal intervention, and the result was an upward surge in state activity. By 1917 most states had their own food and drug commissions with power to issue regulations and orders, conduct hearings, and make binding decisions. Appeals could be made, but pending their outcome trade in a condemned food or drug must cease. This was an early and important example of what may be regarded as an iron law of modern administration: Federal intervention increases state responsibility.[28]

In 1898 the Michigan food and drug commission prosecuted in fifty-three cases and secured only eight convictions; by 1923 the prosecutions were far more numerous and invariably successful. In 1922 inspectors of the Minnesota dairy and food commission visited 878 towns, 279 mills, and 1,865 stores and warehouses, and put a stop to the sale of many unsatisfactory food and dairy products. In 1923 the Oregon food and drug commission claimed to have analyzed 17,882 specimens during its twelve years in existence, and it then launched an intensive campaign against impure narcotics, beverages, and ice cream. The following year, it initiated 495 prosecutions and published the names of convicted offenders. In all states, the drive against harm-

[26] Ibid.
[27] Charles E. Merriam, "Government and Society," *RST,* II, 1496.
[28] See Leonard D. White, ed., "National, State and Local Cooperation in Food and Drug Control," *APSR* 12 (1928), 910–28, for this and the following paragraphs.

ful products was stimulated by scientific advances that led, in turn, to more sophisticated laws and tougher enforcement.

In spite of all the effort that went into food and drug law enforcement, and the considerable success achieved, it encountered the difficulties surrounding all forms of social regulation in America. State commissions normally directed the food and drug agencies set up by most large cities, but criminals evading the law were resourceful and well organized. In rural districts, popular ignorance and political obstruction were greater problems than organized crime. Food and drug processors and merchants were careful to keep their fences repaired by large contributions to party funds, and enforcement officers wre likely to find innumerable obstacles mysteriously placed in their path. These difficulties do not alter the fact that an active public service, affecting directly or indirectly the lives of every citizen, had come into being.

Public welfare had its place in the spectrum of expansion, and was evidence of a fundamental change in social attitudes. Howard W. Odum, who covered the subject in *Recent Social Trends,* declared:

> Within a few decades the changes in the field of public welfare or the social welfare function of government have been so numerous and so radical as to transform the whole field in method and give it a new place among the social forces now remaking the nation.

The most widely adopted novelty was a mothers' aid program which gave assistance to widows or deserted wives with dependent children. Sympathy for war widows helped to secure its rapid passage in most states. Its significance was that for the first time states accepted financial responsibility for the direct relief of individuals outside institutions.[29]

New names for old functions were symptoms of change. In most states, Boards of State Charities or Boards of Charities and Correction became Departments of Public or Social Welfare and Superintendents of the Poor became Commissioners of Public Welfare. In the more thickly populated counties, overseers of the poor were renamed public welfare officers and poor houses became county homes. The changes were not universal but were sufficiently common between 1921 and 1927 to demonstrate the acceptance of new responsibilities for those

---

[29] *RST,* II, 1224–73; Howard W. Odum, "Public Welfare Activities," 1224.

who could not help themselves. The centralization of welfare administration was also an important aspect of change. By 1930 there were single departments of public welfare in twenty-six states; in seventeen, major welfare functions covering the whole state were shared between two or more departments, and at least forty-four agencies with statewide responsibilities had come into existence since 1917.[30]

Both the rapidity of change and the constraints within which it operated were demonstrated in the history of old-age pensions. By 1931 pension laws had been passed in twelve states but were statewide and mandatory in only three (New York, California, and Wyoming); elsewhere adoption was optional for counties and only 137 out of 461 had done so. Even where old-age pension plans were operative, the record was unimpressive, and in the counties reporting in 1930, the ridiculously small number of 10,307 old people had received an average of just over $166. It was clear that eligibility tests were severe, that many indigent old people were rejected or discouraged from applying, and that those who were successful were not given enough to cover the basic needs of the most frugal existence. However, in this as in other welfare matters, New York pointed the way ahead. The state's mandatory law did not come into operation until January 1931, but by June $888,247 had been spent in helping 34,437 old people. The average was still low and many more old people still depended on private charity; but public responsibility for the well-being of the aged was now an accepted function of the state.[31]

In earlier years, state care had been limited to those who could not help themselves – the blind, physically handicapped, mentally deficient, insane, and orphaned or abandoned children – and was restricted to institutional care. Much effort in the 1920s went into improving these institutions, but mothers' aid and old-age pensions marked the first entry of states into outdoor relief, and with less publicity other forms of outdoor relief grew in volume and became com-

[30] Ibid, 1234. The new names were: Department of Social Welfare – California, New York, Maine. Department of Public Welfare – Connecticut, Florida, Georgia, Idaho, Illinois, Kentucky, Louisiana, Maryland, Massachusetts, Nebraska, New Hampshire, New Mexico, North Carolina, Ohio, Rhode Island, Vermont, Virginia, West Virginia. Department of Welfare – Minnesota, Pennsylvania. Department of Institutions and Agencies – New Jersey. Department of Institutions – Tennessee. The new name was adopted in Illinois in 1917 and in New Jersey in 1918; in all the others between 1920 and 1932 (a majority before 1928).
[31] *Annual Report of the Secretary of Labor, 1931.* (Washington, D.C., 1931), 95. Further details in ibid., 1932 and 1933.

mon in larger cities. Between 1923 and 1929 public outdoor relief in sixteen cities rose from $11,640,000 to $18,989,000 a year. Mothers' aid accounted for a good deal of this increase (rising by 41.5 percent), but general outdoor relief to those in distress increased by 110 percent even during this period of unparalleled prosperity. In the sixteen cities, the first full year of the depression saw outdoor relief, excluding mothers' and veterans' aid, leap from $6,733,000 to $13,553,000.[32]

Public welfare had also been taking over ground previously cultivated by private charities. A survey carried out by the Federal Bureau of Social Statistics in 1928 revealed that in the fifteen largest cities, 71.6 percent of all relief came from public funds. The director of the survey concluded: "Whether we like it or not, government is already in the field of social work in a big way – on a scale so colossal in fact, that even the enormous efforts of the private societies seems dwarfed by comparison." Porter R. Lee, delivering the presidential address at the National Conference of Social Work in 1929, claimed that social work was not only "a developing force in a changing world" but that its inspiration – formerly the charitable impulse of individuals to help those in distress – had become the conviction that welfare was a function of government.[33]

Public welfare gained ground but not without effort. If governments were required to act, public men, voters, and elected representatives must first be convinced. In the nineteenth century, social conditions and social ills had seldom become political issues; in the twentieth, they could not be kept out of the political arena. The rising level of expenditure meant that taxes and public debts had to win public approval, and state constitutions often required a direct popular vote before bonds could be issued or new sources of revenue approved.

A member of the Social Work Publicity Council of Cleveland gave an account of a campaign to win a popular majority for a bond issue to pay for a new hospital. The first step was to identify civic, church,

---

[32] Anne E. Geddes, *Trends in Relief Expenditure, 1910–1935* (Washington, D.C., 1937), 20ff; *NCSW 1929*, 514–22; A. W. McMillen (director, Registration of Social Statistics, University of Chicago), "Some Statistical Comparisons of Public and Private Family Social Work." The share of public and private agencies in the major cities ranged from $1.44 public and 24 cents private per capita in Detroit to 15 cents private in New Orleans (where there was no public relief). In Chicago it was 53 cents public and 91 cents private; in Cleveland, 35 and 28 cents. The contribution of public relief to total relief was 98 percent in Detroit and 63.6 percent in Chicago.

[33] Odum, "Public Welfare," *RST*, II, 255; Porter R. Lee, *Social Work as Cause and Function and Other Papers* (New York, 1937), 3. (Also *NCSW 1929:* Presidential Address.)

and business groups that might be willing to help, and to provide speakers for their meetings. The campaigners then printed and distributed posters, placed advertisements in the newspapers, and hired an airship to carry trailing banners over the city. Articles were planted in the newspapers, and students from Case Western Reserve Medical School were recruited to distribute leaflets in downtown stores. These efforts won a two to one majority for the bond issue. The new facilities enabled the city to benefit from the most recent research in tuberculosis and mental health; but without intensive publicity and a well-planned campaign, apathy among the voters would probably have handed victory to the opponents of increased public expenditure.[34]

When action by a legislature was required, effort had to be sustained over a long period and outside opinion built up to persuade enough members to promise support and to surmount procedural obstacles, which the opposition was certain to exploit. In New York an attempt to secure ratification of the federal amendment prohibiting child labor failed despite success in winning support from prominent individuals who were ready to testify at legislative hearings. The resolution to ratify was lost several times in committee, without the full legislature being given an opportunity to vote. A minimum wage law for women, drafted to find a way around *Adkins v. the Children's Hospital,* had better luck. Its supporters concentrated upon winning public support and then ensuring that the legislators felt its strength. "It was a hard fight," said one of the campaign organizers, "a dogged uphill fight, which would never have succeeded had not public opinion been so thoroughly mobilized and articulate that the legislators were never for one minute left in doubt as to what the folks back home thought."[35]

This was a notable victory but those who had won it, knowing that state statute books were littered with well-intentioned measures that no one troubled to enforce, could not relax. The Bureau of Women in Industry was the enforcement agency for the New York minimum wage law, but it had to win cases in the courts if it was to have any teeth. In its first year, between one-quarter and one-half of the convicted employers were given suspended sentences, and by 1933 almost three-quarters of those prosecuted escaped with this derisory penalty.

[34] Virginia R. Wing, "Arousing Voters to Action," *NCSW 1929,* 620ff.
[35] Dorothy Kenyon, "Technique of Utilizing American Political Machinery to Secure Social Action," *NCSW 1936,* 412–20.

Another publicity campaign would be necessary to prevent the judges from nullifying the law.

The road reformers had to follow was rough but not impassable. Moreover the intrusion of social policy into political controversy helped to educate the public and prepare the ground for further changes. The case had to be presented with skill, all the arts of publicity employed, and legislative victories consolidated by further vigilance; but when the next round was fought, the vital premises were already familiar to the public. This meant that as time went on, it might be possible to overthrow bastions that had been thought impregnable only a short while before.

A typical case history of reform was the struggle in New York to improve the institutions where the destitute were lodged. In 1923 an official report condemned the administration of the poor law as "inefficient and unbusinesslike" and recommended that counties rather than townships should be the units responsible for administration. No action was taken. The next step was for private individuals to mount their own investigation, and in 1926 an unofficial report revealed intolerable conditions in the poor houses and public infirmaries. The response to this report provided momentum for the cause of reform, and in 1929 its advocates were able to draft and secure the passage of the most important piece of poor law reform since colonial times. It was followed in 1930 by an Old Age Security Act, which has been described as "one of the milestones in social legislation."[36]

Change had usually to be achieved step by step, rather than as part of one comprehensive measure. Poverty was still thought of as evidence of individual failure, and it was necessary, at each stage and for each instance, to prove that the law and the institutions were also at fault. Public welfare was not yet seen in the same light as highways, education, or health. The rights of those in need were never self-evident, and in addition to ignorance and apathy, there were opponents who claimed to speak with the voice of economic or biological science. As one speaker in 1928 told an audience of social workers: "Every one of you finds in his own community a solid block of opinion hostile to social work, an opinion that bases its hostility on the popularization of alleged science." Relying upon the crude notion that disease and

---

[36] David M. Schneider and Albert Deutsch, *The History of Public Welfare in New York State* (Chicago, 1941), 283. For instructions to social workers on how to lobby, see pp. 355–6.

pestilence eliminated only the unfit, these people argued that social work contributed to the deterioration of the race.[37]

In the public eye, the greatest strides during the decade were taken in private rather than public welfare, and most notable was the rise of community chests in many cities. These were basically fund-raising organizations, but they became nerve centers for charitable enterprise. Acting for combined charities, mounting a single campaign, and distributing the proceeds to the participating organizations, the chest trustees had to approve objectives, decide priorities, and possibly set conditions before funds were allocated. In 1930 the executive officer of one successful chest explained that "the primary purpose of the community chest" was no longer merely to raise and disburse funds "but to serve more and more as a channel for social agencies and the community in the development of a social program."[38]

The first community chest in a large city was established in Cleveland in 1914; it set an example that was widely copied. By 1924 they were found in 180 cities and raised an estimated $48,850,000; by 1930, 363 raised over $75,000,000. They were more common in the Midwest and West than in the East, where old and wealthy charities felt less need for combination and set more value on independence.[39]

Though the community chests conducted campaigns that were intended to stimulate giving in every social class, they depended heavily on wealthy donors. In the larger cities, between one-third and two-thirds of the sums raised came in donations of $1,000 or over, and 65 percent of the total might come from a tiny fraction of donors. Nor were all wealthy men prepared to give generously; and a small number with a social conscience carried the principal burden.

Dependence on wealthy donors meant that control was normally vested in men whom they trusted to handle the money. These were often local bankers, whose eyes were inevitably fixed on the flow of cash and for whom "the gift itself was more important than the social need toward which it contributed." A different point of view usually prevailed among the trained social administrators and workers whom

[37] Presidential Address by Sherman Kingsley, "Who Needs Social Service," *NCSW 1928*, 12.
[38] Robert W. Kelso, "The Community Chest and Relief Giving," *NCSW 1930*, 233–8; Lucius B. Swift, "The Community Fund and Relief Giving," *NCSW 1930*, 239–41.
[39] *RST*, II, Chap. XXIII, Sydnor H. Walker, "Privately Supported Social Work," 1205.

the chests employed. Starting with the identification of need, they assumed that the resources should be made available to meet it, and rejected the idea that funds should be limited by the good will of the rich and allocated by men without firsthand experience in the field. Without denigrating the good intentions of chest organizers, the professional social workers moved tentatively to the position that welfare should be directed by men and women trained for the job. These ideas became convictions as the depression lengthened and assumed greater importance as social workers who had worked with the community chests were called upon to organize state and later federal relief programs.[40]

In the early days of the depression many people, including President Hoover, hoped that evidence of increasing distress, vigorous campaigning, official exhortations, and determined efforts to spread the contributions would generate a surge in the income available for relief. There was indeed an increase, but largely from the lower-income groups. Office and factory workers often pledged a day's pay a month, but the share of large donors did not increase significantly. When the contributions were already large, it was unreasonable to expect a great deal more in hard times, and those who had resisted earlier appeals did not respond in large numbers. It would be unjust to ignore private efforts, which raised very large sums in these dark days, but experience proved that there was a limit to what could be done in this way.

Many regular donors were attracted by projects that left a permanent imprint on the community, such as hospitals, clinics, homes for deserving old people, and "character building" activities such as youth clubs, scouting, and recreational programs; but money poured into the relief of destitute persons seemed to make no long-term contribution to communal well-being. The understandable reluctance to commit chest funds to unemployment relief had major consequences. In order to assure donors that their money was well spent, chest administrators insisted upon investigating each case, and it often became more important to avoid supporting the idle or those with other resources than to identify need. Or, in order to save money, community chests pressed public welfare to take on more cases, and, if the local resources were inadequate, asked for outside aid. As the depression touched new depths, many chest officials came to the fore in pressing for state and federal participation in relief programs.

---

[40] Robert W. Kelso, "Banker Control of Community Chests," *Survey Graphic* XXI, no. 2 (May 1932), 117–19, 158.

In a sense, therefore, the community chests were sowing the seeds of their own decline. They advanced the cause of professionalism in social work but also showed up the deficiences of programs that depended for their funds upon those willing to give. They expended their efforts on selected objectives rather than tackling the problem of poverty as a whole, and the flow of money into the chests, rather than the needs of those in distress, determined the character of the program.

The logic of the situation was apparent even before the onset of the depression. In 1929 John A. Brown, secretary of the Indiana Board of State Charities, told the National Conference of Social Work:

> The governmental policy of leaving humanitarian functions to private agencies has been superseded by a movement toward the regulation, supervision, and administration of many features of social welfare work. There is a growing tendency to place upon the state and its political divisions many functions that were formerly private. The government justifies its position and activities in the field of social welfare on the principle that the chief function of government is the promotion of human welfare.

In the history of workmen's compensation, old-age pensions, mothers' aid, care of the handicapped and infirm, and the whole range of measures to ensure safety in places of work, Brown saw "a constant urge for government to take over additional welfare functions." Two years later, Harry Lurie, the very able director of the Bureau of Jewish Social Research in New York, explained to the same conference the fallacies of reliance upon private charity to relieve distress. The underlying assumption was that distress was not the concern of the whole community but rather of those who were disposed to be charitable, but the democratic theory was that all were responsible for the condition of society. The generous few should not be asked to bear the burden that all should share.[41]

These arguments did not mean that public welfare should eliminate private charity. People who advocated a dominant role for public agencies also claimed to discern a historical relationship between the two that should continue. Dedicated individuals identified social evils; private charities took up the challenge, experimented with methods of relief, and devised remedies; but once the pioneer days were over, governments must take over and all citizens must pay their fair share of the cost.

[41] John A. Brown, "The Organization of State and County Welfare Departments," *NCSW 1929*, 523–30; Harry L. Lurie, "The Drift to Public Relief," *NCSW 1931*, 211–22.

Who were the individuals or organizations that took the initiative in promoting welfare legislation? Half a century before, the answer would have been clergymen (especially those influenced by the social gospel); wealthy men who took up philanthropy as a retirement occupation; members of the voluntary boards charged with responsibility for state institutions; doctors who served on state, county, or city health boards; and private individuals (many of them women) who were stirred to action by firsthand contact with conditions in the slums or among the very poor. They would indeed have been a fair sample of the people whom later generations would denigrate as "do-gooders."

In the 1920s this impression lingered on. In 1922 an article in the *Atlantic Monthly,* by Mrs. Cornelia Cannon characterized the people active in social work as well-intentioned but impractical and unlikely to influence policy. This brought a reply in *Survey* by Julia and Hilton Rainey suggesting that Mrs. Cannon attend a meeting of the National Conference of Social Work and meet

Commissioners of charities and correction, psychologists, health officers, industrial investigators, institution heads, expert case workers in varied agencies public and private, research authorities from the foundations, the staff of schools of civics and college departments, the editors of sociological magazines.

Professional experience, official responsibility, and academic expertise had "broken out of the uncongenial and archaic enclosure" that Mrs. Cannon had labeled "private philanthropy," and their influence was "sweeping into every department of our commercial lives and government."[42]

Ten years later, the Raineys' picture could have been painted in even stronger colors. The developments in public welfare and in the allied fields of health, workmen's compensation, safety regulation, and factory inspection had greatly strengthened the official element, and the community chest movement had added significant experience in the organization of welfare work. Social reform had built up its own momentum, with insiders as the driving force.

The point must be made but qualified. Social work was a new profession with a status far below that of lawyers, doctors, or even teachers, and its workers in the field were overwhelmingly women. In 1923 Roy

[42] Julia Houston Rainey and Hilton Howell Rainey, "Social Certainties," *Survey Graphic* I (July 1922), 429–35, 482.

E. Bowman of the Columbia School of Social Work sent a questionnaire to newspaper editors as part of a project to discover the public attitudes toward social work. Thirty-six did not trouble to reply, forty were hostile to social work, thirty-two were indifferent, and twenty-eight sent replies that could not be classified. Only twenty positively approved of social workers and their methods. Of the few who bothered to add comments, fifteen gave social workers credit for bringing immediate relief to those in distress but thought that this was of little lasting value to the individuals or the community; four described their work as merely palliative; three thought it had temporary use in bringing social facts to light; and only six regarded it as having great and permanent value. Among the unfavorable comments, thirteen used the words "impractical" or "visionary," four thought that social workers were "paternalistic," and five thought that they relied too much on taught techniques and too little on personal understanding. Some disparaging comments allowed for the sincerity and good intentions of social workers but went on to give them labels such as "ill-fitted novices" and "ninety percent sentiment" or to complain that they "slobbered over and made a mess of the work."[43]

Among most good citizens, the attitude toward social work was one of indifference and tolerance without enthusiasm, rather than outright hostility, but some were always ready to proclaim that no able-bodied person deserved help. The ingrained belief that destitute people were responsible for their own misfortunes was not easily erased, and though a community was obliged to ensure that no one starved, there was no call to do more than this out of taxpayers' money. Genuine cases of undeserved misfortune might safely be left to organized charities or generous neighbors. Reports of dire poverty in the larger cities were discounted in the belief that most of the poor were black or foreign born and that city politicians were always trying to get money out of honest rural voters.

Relief clients sometimes resented the investigation into their lives that current social work theory demanded. Aid in known cases was appreciated, but social workers as individuals won little respect. There was one revealing little story of a group of delinquent girls, gathered to receive advice from social workers, who gave their reactions after the meeting. They appreciated what was being done for them but concen-

[43] *NCSW 1923*, 482.

trated on "the indifference of social workers to the decrees of Dame Fashion and their excessive plainness."[44]

Although rank-and-file social workers carried little weight, the development of public and private agencies had brought into being a class of welfare administrators who exercised considerable influence as state commissioners of public welfare, city welfare directors, and executive officers of large charities or community chests. They distributed large sums of money, brought pressure to bear on state and local governments, and enlisted the support of business, professional, and fraternal associations. Together with representatives from the schools of social work, established in several universities, and social scientists interested in public administration, industrial relations, and social justice, they were the men and women who spoke most often at the National Conference of Social Work and took the lead in regional or specialist meetings. In the 1920s, most of them still talked mainly to fellow professionals, but their reports provided social work with a backbone of published data, and some of them acquired political skills in getting what they wanted from usually reluctant legislatures. Many would later be found at the head of state relief programs or in key positions in the Federal Emergency Relief Administration.

The journal *Survey,* edited by Paul Kellogg, was the organ for professional social workers, especially for those of them with reform ambitions. It adopted a popular format and was written largely in nontechnical language. A sister journal, *The Survey Graphic,* was intended to interest a wider readership in the problems of social work with articles that were vigorously written and usually provocative.[45]

Many welfare administrators, most speakers at the annual National Conference of Social Work, and all contributors to *Survey* agreed that far more ought to be done to relieve distress in a humane but systematic way, but they presented no coherent program. Years after the publication of Mrs. Cannon's article, attacked by the Raineys, her conclusion, that "as yet they have offered us no fundamental basis for the work of human improvement," was still justified. There were divisions and some difference in emphasis between representatives of public and private welfare, no agreement on the role of government, and much argument over the best methods to adopt. At the root of the contro-

---

[44] Lucia Johnson Bing, "What the Public Thinks of Social Workers," *NCSW 1923,* 486.
[45] For the *Survey* and *Survey Graphic,* see Clarke A. Chambers, *Paul U. Kellogg and the Survey: Voices for Social Welfare and Social Justice* (Minneapolis, 1971), chap. 7.

versy were two opposing views on the function of social work: For some, its primary purpose was to adjust individuals to society; for others, it was the means by which society recompensed individuals for its failure to provide them with a livelihood.

In 1923 Howard W. Odum, looking at the problem as an academic student of social work, speculated on the causes for the barren state of social theory. He wrote that in earlier historic periods ideas for social improvement had been generated by the churches, intellectuals, professional administrators, and capitalist entrepreneurs, but little had been stirring since the ferment of Progressivism had died down.

Odum thought that church leaders had become frightened by the implications of the social gospel, and the radical young theologian, Reinhold Niebuhr, agreed that critics were "justified in regarding the church, as a whole, as a hindrance to the ethical reorganization of public life." Odum found academics and intellectuals indifferent to social problems and impatient with those who sought improvement. Social scientists, whose theoretical pursuits should have interested them in change, were often the most obstructive.

The professors of economics have stood afar off or passed by on the other side. The professors of sociology, too, have sometimes taken the unreasonable position of judging social work as a whole from certain parts and individuals, and have come to erroneous conclusions without sufficient evidence, or without being willing to make the actual contribution suggested by their criticism.

As for state and local officials, it was all too common for them to treat the ideas of social workers as embarrassments, and politicians were suspicious of anyone who came between them and the voters. Some enlightened employers had introduced good welfare schemes, but their aim was to preserve existing arrangements, not to change them.[46]

Orthodox economists, many sociologists, and business leaders accepted a modified version of individualism. The men who had learned when young from William Graham Sumner and other less talented exponents of Darwinian social theory were now at the head of the establishment in learning, the professions, and business. In this social philosophy the classes owed nothing to each other, and attempts to counteract the "natural" operation of the economic system produced consequences that their authors had not anticipated, inhibited

[46] Howard W. Odum, "The Scientific Journal of Social Interpretation," *NCSW 1923,* 487–92.

enterprise, and laid up trouble for the future. This philosophy was qualified only by a recognition that short-term calculations were not invariably the best guide to future benefits. Enlightened individualism should take into account all of the relationships in a complex society (or as many of them as the individual could grasp) and include them in the calculus of gains and losses. This line of argument approved welfare schemes set up by employers while condemning compulsory insurance managed by the government and still more a dole that encouraged people not to compete in the labor market.

Conventional wisdom had its critics. In giving the presidential address to the National Conference of Social Work in 1927, John A. Lapp took "Justice" as his title, delivered a slashing attack on "the heathen doctrine of the survival of the fittest," and deplored the damage done by this "philosophy of the jungle." Every investigation conducted scientifically had shown that poverty resulted from "social injustice or avoidable causes," and even in time of prosperity "a great army, one in every ten of the population, marches in the valley of the shadow of poverty." The unhappy paradox was that although government alone could provide the remedy, there was "a concerted movement to break the confidence of the people in their government as an instrument for human betterment."[47]

Lapp turned the evidence of increased expenditure on public welfare against those who used it. Between 1913 and 1922, expenditure on the protection of persons and property had doubled, that on health and sanitation had risen from 7 cents to 20 cents per capita, on highways from 14 cents to 42 cents, and on education from $1.30 to $2.07. Welfare expenditure, which had been rising steadily to 90 cents per capita in 1913, rose by only 10 cents in the next ten years, and this included reformatories and other correctional establishments. Municipal governments had become more honest and had increased their expenditure on civic amenities, but they had shied away from frontal attacks on slums and urban poverty. Middle-class voters might be shocked by tales of dirt and deprivation, but their will to act was held in check by their respect for the business interests that might be upset by reform. Lincoln Steffens the veteran muckraker of "the shame of the cities" and recently much influenced by Marxism, declared that if middle-

---

[47] John A. Lapp, "Justice," *NCSW 1927*, 3–23.

class voters could see "the economic roots of the evils which they deplore, they would rise and defend those roots."[48]

Socialist theory was not needed to make the point that poverty, as a disease of the whole society, affected every member of it, and that it was in everyone's interest to reduce it; but even social workers, trained to adjust the maladjusted to the environment, failed to see the situation in this light. It was often the pride of their profession that social work methods succeeded where traditional poor law officials failed in weeding out scroungers, malingerers, and cheats who had hidden resources or a family able to support them.

The philosophic dilemma presented by the choice between public and private treatment of poverty was apparent in the career of Robert W. Kelso, a rising star in the social work firmament destined to play an important part in the development of federal relief. In 1922, as the very young president of the National Conference of Social Work, he tackled the underlying social theory and argued that though puritan individualism, once the dynamic force in America, could no longer play the same part in an urbanized and industrialized society, a convincing substitute had yet to be found.

Dimly we have been groping for a truer basis in our philosphy of conduct. Necessity has been the mother of our invention, and the invention is this: that we have made social relationship the basis of our law, and social necessity the driving force in its development.

Social policy had grown pragmatically from isolated responses to specific needs, but Kelso maintained that their cumulative effect had been to introduce a new and as yet unrecognized revolution. Public welfare departments were "the seat of a great seismic disturbance." The heart of the matter was that "the auditing of doles is giving way to departmental conferences on the adequacy of relief."[49]

Yet in a book entitled *Poverty,* published by Kelso seven years later, puritan individualism was dominant. Though critical of inadequate relief, Kelso stressed the need for rigorous investigation of every case to save public money and avoid the demoralization associated with relief too easily obtained. He gave the example of one Pennsylvania

---

[48] Ibid., 10–11; *Survey Graphic* XX (1931), 14 (contribution by Steffens to a symposium on municipal reform).

[49] Robert W. Kelso, "Changing Fundamentals of Social Work," *NCSW 1922,* 6–13.

poor district in which the investigation of 605 applicants for relief had found 299 of them to be fraudulent. "Wherever special investigations have been made of outdoor relief a discovery that it was administered through an unsupervised system of local doles has been tantamount to finding it thoroughly pauperizing." A public dole, he argued, inevitably gathered up "all the human dregs," along with the "ordinary poor" who might otherwise have supported themselves. A dole – that is, a fixed payment to people who claimed to be out of work or in distress – fostered antisocial forces, discouraged thrift, and encouraged fraud. Anyone seeking general remedies for poverty should prohibit alcohol and advocate birth control to "cut off defective strains." This took one back to poverty caused by weakness in character and to relief given only when the worthiness of the applicant had been established and all his means of support exhausted.[50]

Was it the task of social work to change society or to support it by dealing with the casualties? This question would continue to be asked without receiving an answer that commanded general assent. In practice, the advance of public welfare between these poles of opinion made less difference than might be supposed. Radical reformers could not escape the need to look at individual cases, and when existing law made it impossible to do justice to individuals, cautious pragmatists were drawn into the fight to change it. In 1929 the fundamental change that John Lapp would have preferred was as impractical as the hope that every able-bodied person seeking relief could be restored to the labor market. The difference between the two approaches would become significant when long-term strategy was at issue and ends had to be defined; but in 1929 small gains, made step by step, were all that anyone expected.

Even social workers who believed that their business was not to promote social change, but individual well-being, were faced with difficult choices. All agreed that investigation of each case was essential and that surveillance should continue after relief had been given; but if the main purpose of investigation was to establish need, how should it be measured? Was a man living in poverty, but just above the subsistence level, in need? If he had been prudent enough to accumulate small savings, must he exhaust them before qualifying for relief? If there were wage earners in the family, should they be required to support a dis-

---

[50] Robert W. Kelso, *Poverty* (New York and London, 1929), 239, 244.

abled or unemployed member? If a person in distress owned a house, must it be sold? Should relief take rent into account?

The word "client" – in universal use among social workers – was itself revealing. It stressed the diagnostic and counseling role and implicitly endorsed the view that the individual in distress was a maladjusted person. The experience of most social workers before 1930 was with the disabled, indigent aged, temporarily unemployed, and men and women who for temperamental or other reasons were unable or unwilling to play their part as wage earners. The most humane social worker had to qualify compassion with the knowledge that the "dregs" of the population included people who avoided work whenever possible, took whatever they could get, and had a reputation for incorrigible idleness. How much of a social worker's time should be spent weeding out these people, ensuring that they got no more than the minimum, or sending them to the poor house? Social workers prided themselves on bringing relief to those in real need and in helping the maladjusted to adjust, but if they wanted to get credit from the public, they had to prove their ability to detect the frauds, malingerers, the work-shy. Out of this situation social workers had distilled much conventional wisdom that would be thrown into total disarray by the advent of mass unemployment.

The idea that a dole demoralized the recipient was common, persistent, and rested on the assumption that a person on relief was getting something for nothing. Only a few suggested that a man who had worked and paid taxes was a creditor of society when there was no work to be had. The idea that a person on relief was taking money that was not his own was often coupled with the idea that relief must be earned by work (and preferably by work that was physically demanding and psychologically humiliating). In the public mind, it was assumed that work for relief was a penalty for idleness or improvidence, not a remedy for unemployment, and that insistence upon it was somehow less demoralizing than a straightforward payment to those in need. The logic of these propositions was seldom examined.

Social workers often complained that relief was inadequate, but what was adequate relief? Was it enough to avert starvation, or should a person who had fallen on evil times through no fault of his own be enabled to maintain something approaching the living standard to which he had been accustomed? Should relief also take care of the children to ensure that they were clothed, properly fed, educated, and given medical attention? In prosperous times, private charities had often filled the gap between the minimum given by public welfare and what was necessary to preserve self-respect and safeguard the children's future; when the depression struck private charities were overwhelmed, and the question of what was meant by "adequate" was addressed more and more to public welfare. The answers were always difficult to find because there was never enough money to go round.

Social workers were sometimes criticized for complaining about conditions that they expected someone else to remedy. "The trouble with social workers," said one experienced politician, "is that they never get away from the home plate; always raising a loud howl about conditions – but why don't they burn the midnight oil and tell us what to do about it?" William Hodson, a leading New York welfare administrator, urged social workers not to shy away from political action. They should identify their friends in politics, use their weight in elections, assert their claim to advise on social policy, secure the appointment of suitable people, and be always on the alert to promote public welfare by political action.[51]

The advice was easier to give than to take. The kind of publicity campaign that was necessary to win support from normally indifferent citizens has already been described; and this was not the kind of effort that could be expected too frequently from busy men and women. In the last resort, most issues would have to be settled by state legislatures, which were not – in the opinion of well-informed critics – the ideal bodies for dealing intelligently with complex matters. In his influential college textbook on American government, Charles Beard questioned their efficiency and denigrated their membership. They were, he said, little more than "miscellaneous assemblies of citizens, chosen independently, subjected to local influences, often with little experience in public affairs, busily engaged in making a living, eager to get things done and get home." The ordinary legislator was not corrupt and was often genuinely desirous of serving the public good, but lacked the knowledge, experience, and power to accomplish much.[52]

---

[51] *NCSW 1923*, 486 (Mrs. Lucia J. Bing). Also, "There are three things the matter with the social worker: (1) She is always a woman, (2) the breach is too wide and she can't jump the gap, (3) she is too young, and when she talks to the old woman about bringing up the kids, she can't make any impression." William Hodson, "The Social Worker and Politics," *NCSW 1929*, 103–12.

[52] Charles A. Beard, *American Government and Politics*, 9th ed. (New York, 1946), 601 (earlier editions contain similar judgments).

In New York, New Jersey, Rhode Island, and South Carolina, the legislatures had regular sessions once a year; in all other states, the meetings were biennial. A governor might call a special session, but this was not popular unless the need was clear. All of the states save Nebraska had bicameral legislatures, with senates that were smaller and usually more influential than the lower houses. In both houses most of the work was done in committees and debates were perfunctory, though there were plenty of procedural motions by which opponents could delay or wreck a measure. In most states, sessions were either of fixed length or the adjournment date was agreed at the outset and adhered to, and because many measures did not emerge from committee in their final form until the last few days, there was a frantic scramble to get bills through. In the rush, many bills, upon which time, effort, and publicity had been expended, fell by the wayside. Summing up the failings of state legislatures, Charles Beard wrote:

Broadly speaking legislative procedure in the American states is characterized by confusion and drift, no matter how strong the party organization may be. There is no one person or group of persons responsible in law and fact for formulating a program of measures to be laid before the legislature when it meets. . . . No one is responsible for a legislative program; no one is responsible for expediting business; no one is reponsible for searching all the bills, for bringing unity into the grist of laws, for eliminating disorder, conflict, and favoritism.[53]

If legislatures had been judged by output, their efficiency would have been vindicated. One calculation, which advanced no claim to statistical accuracy, was that between 1906 and 1926 over 850,000 bills were introduced in the forty-eight state legislatures, and that about 220,000 had become law. The quality of much that found its way into the statute books might be guessed from the conditions under which many bills were passed. In 1923, 217 out of the 253 acts of the New Jersey legislature were passed in the last three weeks of an eleven-week session; the Illinois legislature sat for five months but did not pass 295 of the 380 successful bills until the last week. In 1925 the Ohio legislature met on January 5 but passed no bills during its first month; 185 were passed between March 1 and 23; then, after a lull, 23 bills were passed on the last day of the session and 34 more repassed over the governor's veto. Similar stories could be told of all other states. There was no way

---

[53] Ibid., 609.

of estimating how many laws were impractical or poorly drafted, or of knowing how many worthwhile proposals sank without a trace.[54]

The best plan for individuals or organizations with a measure to promote was to get it referred to the right committee and then to approach its members directly. This initial task could be more difficult than it might appear because the number of committees was often bewildering. In 1924 there were sixty-two standing committees in the Illinois lower house and fifty-one in the Senate; in addition, dozens of special committees were set up during a session on every conceivable topic. Because committee membership was prized by most legislators and cost the party leaders nothing, there was a tendency to expand their size. The Illinois house judiciary and appropriation committees both had forty-four members in 1924. In practice, most of the work was done by the chairman and two or three experienced members; the others might be able to obstruct, but anyone who got the ear of the committee's in-group had won half the battle.[55]

Once the backers of a measure had got it into the right committee and won the good will of influential members, luck might be with them. Committees usually welcomed people with factual information (because bulky reports testified to their industry), would probably arrange hearings if time permitted, and might agree that the evidence should be published to arouse interest outside the house. In this way, it was possible for men who knew the ropes to advance their favorite reforms; but every major change meant a sustained campaign, extending perhaps over several years, and much adroit maneuvering as it approached the final stage.

The moral was that leaders in welfare administration would have to learn the art of lobbying, and that the lack of systematic organization made it possible for groups with determination to win a voice in the legislative process. Beard qualified his verdict on state legislatures by remarking:

All in all our legislatures seem to represent with a fair degree of precision the politically active elements of the population. Their members spring from the people and are in close touch with all the interests, prejudices, and customs.

[54] Ibid., 610 [citing W. E. Dodd, *State Government* (New York, 1928), 203, 613; John Mabry Matthews, *American State Government* (New York and London), 198–9; Howard White, "Can Legislatures Learn Anything from City Councils?," *APSR* 21 (1927), 95–100].
[55] Leonard D. White, "Our Legislative Mills," *National Municipal Review* XII 712ff.

Every miscellaneous group in society except as a rule industrial workers has its spokesman in one or both houses.

Participation in the legislative fray meant that proposals for welfare reform had to take their chance in competition with all of the other interests seeking legislative action. There was no overarching commitment to providing the best possible welfare standards, and it might be particularly difficult to win support when rural districts were overrepresented and the needs most evident in the cities. Highways, public health, and schools had more obvious appeal. Even so, experience in the 1920s had proved that measures to improve the treatment of the destitute could be carried along with the tide of expanding public action.[56]

The question underlying this chapter is, how far would welfare services have continued to expand if the depression had not occurred? Was discontinuity the essential condition for decisive change, or would a harvest of improvement have been reaped had economic collapse been averted? The question is not likely to receive a conclusive answer, but it is worthwhile to speculate upon the possibilities, and to begin by realizing that in all fields the mood of 1929 was forward looking and reasonably optimistic that modern society could find a way to solve its social problems. Professional observers of welfare policy looked back on a period of change and growth; though still critical of current practice, they were confident that improvement would come if men of good will kept up the pressure.

Constitutional obstacles could be surmounted, and the courts were normally sympathetic to any reasonable exercise of state police power except when it was overtly linked with wage and price fixing. Workmen's compensation, mothers' aid, and a host of measures to ensure health and safety at places of work had emerged unscathed. The enforcement of Prohibition had set the precedent for sweeping powers to deal with anything designated as a public nuisance. Old-age pensions had suffered setbacks in some state courts, but in others they had been approved; the Supreme Court had yet to consider the broad principle of pensions for the indigent aged, but there seemed to be no reason why it should not be approved.

---

[56] Beard, *American Government*, 600–1.

There had been striking advances in the organization of both private and public welfare (especially in some large cities). Institutional care was being improved, but more was also being spent on outdoor relief. Discussion of the relationship between public and private relief was moving to the conclusion that private agencies should be pioneers and should hand over to public welfare when the need and the best means of meeting it had been demonstrated. In both private and public welfare the momentum seemed difficult to halt.

The men and women who took the lead in social work were better organized than ever before. Their discussions had brought into the open a difference of opinion between those who looked forward to fundamental changes in the social, economic, and intellectual environment and those who believed that the role of social work was to diagnose and treat individual failures to adjust to the environment; but the theoretical importance of this division did not prevent cooperation in working for immediate improvement. Each year the meeting of the National Conference of Social Work unfolded new ideas and unveiled new prospects.

Social work was itself going through a process of self-examination leading, in some instances, to important changes in attitude. Many social workers had been accustomed to think that a personal relationship with their clients was more important than finding them material means of support; relief might be necessary, but only to bridge the gap until treatment was complete. As one of them, taking a detached view and with child care as his main concern, said in 1933:

We developed the atmosphere of case work in which most of us were trained with no sounding of the slogan of adequacy of relief. We gave friendship in place of bread; we separated mothers and children; people did not need alms – they needed friends. We became specialists in organizing love for the needy – they did not like it very much and the bystanders were frequently humorous, often cynical – and some went beyond this.

By 1930 there was, however, a good deal of criticism of the idea that talking things out was the best form of relief and growing support for the idea that people who had fallen on evil days should be given financial help, to enable them to live decently, without having to give account of themselves to inquisitive social workers. Complaints about the inadequacy of public relief and the excessive paternalism of private charities were becoming common.[57]

[57] J. Prentice Murphy, "Certain Philosophical Contributions to Children's Case Work," *NCSW 1933*, 75–90.

It was a formidable task to get measures adopted by state legislatures, but men and women who were prepared to put up with frustration and delay could get things done. The principal obstacle was indifference rather than hostility; public welfare was not perceived by the voters as an integral and essential function of government – in the same class as roads, schools, and public health – but as a necessary but unwelcome operation to deal with failures. Despite much evidence to the contrary, it was thought that prosperity would banish poverty, leaving only the misfits to be saved from starvation. On the credit side were great improvements in state institutional care, enlarged welfare responsibilities in many cities, old-age pensions in several states, and the reform of the New York poor law in 1929.

All this activity bred qualified optimism about the future of social welfare, reflected in *Recent Social Trends,* and forecasting moves to make existing old-age pensions statewide and mandatory, introduce pension laws in more states, extend home relief (following the precedent of mothers' aid) to the short-term unemployed and sick, and more state supervision of local authorities. It was expected that private charities would pull out of direct relief (except for topping up public relief for individuals of good character) and concentrate on medical, recreational, and character-building services. Other states might follow the lead of New York in modernizing the poor law, and though changes of this magnitude would take at least a generation, social reformers hoped that before long, states would expect uniform standards and procedures in welfare administration, and require the employment of trained social workers in key positions. Payments for rent and medical attention would become normal for persons in distress who had been stable members of society. States might also take steps to help communities impoverished by the failure of businesses or the closure of mines.

Social workers were guarded in their response to the suggestion that enlightened individualism would persuade more employers to launch private welfare schemes. A principal argument for such plans was that they kept together a skilled labor force, but this implied that several years of service would be required to qualify for benefits, which would lapse if a worker moved to another job. Employers would give something extra to favored workers but do nothing to alleviate poverty, and the most that could be hoped was that they would take some pressure off public welfare by looking after a limited number of employees when they were sick or old. More respect was given to mutual schemes for sick and unemployment benefits, run by the labor unions and other voluntary associations, but the character of organized labor at this time meant that most beneficiaries would be skilled men who had been able to afford the dues when employed. More and more, the proponents of a frontal attack on poverty put their faith in public action.

This sketch of the prospects from the vantage point of 1929 is necessarily speculative, but the ground is firmer when deciding what no one expected and very few wanted. Before the depression no one talked seriously of federal relief, and it is difficult to imagine that anything short of this catastrophe would have made it politically feasible. Some professional experts believed that the states should organize social insurance, but few had a good word to say for the various forms of compulsory insurance run by European governments. No one suggested that the federal government might organize and help to pay for a national program of old-age pensions or unemployment insurance.

If it was difficult to foresee federal participation in welfare programs, it was even more difficult to imagine that the primary responsibility of local governments for poor law administration would be loosened. Leaders in welfare reform were agreed that the law governing local poor relief was antiquated, that local officials usually knew nothing of modern social work, and that there could be no lasting improvement in the treatment of poverty until the system changed. Yet the tradition of local responsibility was so deeply rooted that nothing seemed likely to weaken its hold.

State welfare had grown by removing easily identifiable groups from local poor law administration and placing them in state institutions. The indigent insane had been the earliest group to be segregated in this way, and were followed by the blind, mentally deficient, physically incapacitated, and children without parents or means of support; but the initiative in committing persons to state care lay with the local authorities, and there had never been a suggestion that states should take from local governments the duty of "caring for their own" (in the conventional and much used phrase). It was rare for counties to do more than provide poor homes, almshouses, and infirmaries for chronic cases without means of support, and the normal administration of poor relief was exclusively in the hands of officials elected in the smallest political subdivisions – towns, townships, and poor districts. This was as most Americans thought it should be, and any change would rouse a legion to defend "local responsibility."

The depression and mass unemployment brought the principle of local responsibility to the center of the political stage. Were officials elected for short terms the best people to administer relief? Was the poor law that regulated their actions humane and efficient? What was to be done when a unit of local government had no money to spend on relief? What if there was wealth enough in the community, but officials and voters were equally determined not to increase revenue for relief by raising taxes? Was there something wrong with the whole system of local self-government, which demanded first state and then federal intervention?

These questions touched deeply sensitive nerves in the American political system and must be examined in depth; the next chapter will therefore consider local government and the poor law as they existed in the 1920s. Whatever professional critics might say, local government was, in popular estimation, the seed bed of American democracy. If the depression brought it to the verge of ruin, more would be at stake than the functions of county commissioners, boards of supervisors, township trustees, and overseers of the poor; however pressing the case for centralization, many Americans would consider that the erosion of local responsibility had inflicted fatal injury upon self-government.

Appendix 1: The National Conference of Social Work

Frequent references will be made to papers published in the *Proceedings* of the conference, and a note on its character and procedures is therefore appropriate. The conference began as the National Conference of Charities and Correction and changed its name in 1917. It met annually, usually in May, in a different large city each year. The president held office for a year, and his or her principal duty was to open the proceedings with an address, which normally offered a broad interpretation of problems and policies. There were four or five other plenary sessions with addresses by leading personalities in social work or public life, but most of the work of the conference took place in sections dealing with specific aspects of social work. Other national associations, such as the Association of Social Workers and the American Public Welfare Association, often held meetings at the same place and time.

Donals S. Howard, of the Russell Sage Foundation, reviewed the 1938 *Proceedings* in the *Social Service Review* (13, 548–50) and took the occasion to explain their compilation. All of the papers published had to be delivered at the conference so that the Program Committee had primary control over what was published, but the presentation of a paper did not guarantee publication, and in 1938 about half of the papers were excluded. Records of discussions following papers were not usually printed, partly to save space but more often because the chairmen of sections did not furnish usable summaries of what had been said. Howard regretted the omission because points made in discussions "would enable readers to evelute somewhat more realistically material presented in prepared papers." Despite rejections and the omission of discussions, the 1938 *Proceedings* ran to 754 pages and nearly a quarter of a million words.

Howard's account of the way in which papers were selected for publication is worth quoting in full.

Publication of the *National Conference Proceedings* is a joint, co-operative effort in which many people participate. Papers are first read and evaluated by the chairman of the section of committee before which they were presented. Then they are again reviewed and graded, this time by members of the Conference staff. Papers are then referred to the Editorial Committee, and to be included in the *Proceedings* must meet certain criteria established by the committee. Though each committee is privileged to establish its own criteria, those of the first committee have been adopted from year to year with but slight change. According to the criteria now being applied papers must

contain new data of practical value to the membership of the Conference; present an interpretation of social work or any of its aspects which is not now available; have important local significance of a kind which is of application or importance elsewhere; present material from a field outside social work in a way which makes clear the significance of this material for social work; or have definite historical significance important as a matter of record.

Although the criteria place heavy emphasis upon new material, allowance is made for repetition 'within a reasonable period' of important material that has already appeared in the *Proceedings*. Therefore, *Proceedings* covering a period of years are more likely to yield a true picture of the state of social work during the period than one year's *Proceedings* would do for one year.

Howard concluded that "in spite of all limitations . . . the *Proceedings* have, from year to year, become an indispensable record of what social workers think and do about creating more and better opportunities for larger numbers of people." One might also add that during the New Deal years, regular appearances of speakers from the federal relief and works administrations (especially Aubrey Williams and Josephine Brown) give an insight into the way in which the government sought to win over the people who had to do the work in the field.

Appendix 2: Personalities

Notes on some frequent contributors to the *PROCEEDINGS* of the National Conference of Social Work and others prominent in the profession (in alphabetical order).

EDITH ABBOT. b. 1876. University of Nebraska; graduate work at the University of Chicago and the London School of Economics (where she was much influenced by Beatrice Webb); joined the staff of the Chicago School of Civics and Philanthropy (which became part of the School of Social Service Administration at the University of Chicago in 1920), lived at Hull House, and gained personal experience in settlement work. In 1924 she succeeded Sophonisba Breckinridge as dean of the school, a position she held for eighteen years. She founded and was for many years editor of *The Social Service Review,* contributing papers herself and writing most of the lengthy comments that appeared in each quarterly issue. She spoke on several occasions at the National Conference of Social Work and was its president in 1937. She also contributed to the *Survey, New Republic,* and *Nation.* Among her many scholarly works, the two-volume *Public Assistance* (select documents with introductions and comment) is of permanent value. Her unremitting efforts, positive views, many publications, and persuasive rhetoric made her the most influential advocate of welfare reform of her time.

GRACE ABBOTT. b. 1878. University of Nebraska and University of Chicago. In 1908 she became director of the newly formed Immigrant's Protective League and lived at Hull House. Her work brought her into close contact with the problems of the poorest families in Chicago. In 1917 she was persuaded to join the Federal Children's Bureau to administer the first Child Labor Law and became head of the bureau in 1921. The Supreme Court declared the Child Labor Law unconstitutional in 1922, and Grace Abbott became the foremost advocate of the child labor amendment. Her publications persistently documented the plight of exploited children. In 1930 she won a much publicized fight to save the bureau, and she carried out investigations on child malnutrition and loss of education as a result of the depression. She served on the Council of Economic Security, and was president of the National Conference of Social Work in 1927, but her official position limited her contributions to public debate. In 1934 she resigned from the Federal Children's Bureau because (in her sister's opinion) "she wanted greater freedom ... to speak and write freely about social or political problems," but her health had also been weakened by over-work and she died in 1939 after four happy years as professor of public welfare at the University of Chicago. The fullest account of her life is her sister's moving and eloquent tribute in the *Social Service Review* 13, 351–407.

JACOB BILLIKOPF. b. 1883 in Russia. Parents emigrated to America. Attended the University of Richmond, Virginia, and the University of Chicago. He was employed by various charitable organizations (mainly Jewish) in Ohio, Wisconsin, Kansas City, and Philadelphia (where he became executive director of Jewish Charities). In 1931 he was a member of the Philadelphia Committee of One Hundred on Unemployment. He held many honorary and advisory offices with national philanthropic and charitable associations, and was a trustee of *The Nation* and of *Survey*.

WILLIAM HODSON. b. 1891. Attended the University of Minnesota and Harvard Law School but did not pursue a legal career. He began his professional career in social work in Minnesota, but in 1922 was appointed director of the division of child welfare for the Russell Sage Foundation and moved to New York; two years later, he became director of the foundation's division of social welfare. In 1933 he became Commissioner of Public Welfare for New York City. His frequent papers at the National Conference of Social Work were distinguished by their intellectual quality and foresight. He was president of the conference in 1936. He was active in pressing for federal relief in 1931–2 and was a key witness in the hearings conducted by Senator Robert LaFollette. He was an early advocate of federal programs for old age, unemployment, and health insurance. His entry in the *Dictionary of American Biography* (Supplement 3) observes that "his position on social measures was always substantially in advance of that of the main body of social workers." He was killed in 1943 in an air crash while on government work concerned with the welfare of troops overseas.

PAUL U. KELLOGG. b. 1879 in Kalamazoo, Michigan. Attended Columbia University. In 1903 he became editor of *Charities* (in 1909 the name was changed to *Survey*). He directed the *Pittsburgh Survey,* a pioneer venture in modern urban sociology (six volumes published, 1910–14). He was a member of an advisory committee on social security for the federal government in 1933–5. The *Survey* was the principal organ for the propagation of new ideas in social work. A companion journal, *Survey Graphic,* was popular in style and aimed to interest a wider audience in social work.

ROBERT W. KELSO. b. 1888 in Washington, Illinois. Attended Harvard University and Harvard Law School. He was secretary of the Massachusetts State Board of Charity from 1910 to 1920 (latterly also Commissioner of Welfare). From 1921 to 1929 he was the executive director of the Boston Council of Social Agencies. In 1922 he was president of the National Conference of Social Work. In 1929 he became director of the St. Louis, Missouri, Community Fund until his appointment, in 1932, as a field representative reporting on the relief situation for the Reconstruction Finance Corporation. He continued in this capacity under the Federal Emergency Relief Administration until 1935, when he joined the faculty of the University of Michigan.

SHERMAN C. KINGSLEY. b. 1866. Attended Knox College and Harvard University. From 1917 to 1921 he was director of the Welfare Federation of Cleveland, and from 1921 to 1934 executive secretary of the Welfare Federation of Philadelphia. In 1927 he was president of the National Conference of Social Work.

HARRY L. LURIE. b. 1892 in Latvia. Attended the University of Michigan, was a member of the faculty from 1922 to 1924, and then held other temporary academic assignments, teaching and researching social work and policy. From 1930 to 1935 he was director of the Bureau of Jewish Social Research in New York City. Under his direction the bureau became a major center for research in urban sociology.

2

LOCAL RESPONSIBILITY

Government

After a lifetime of public service, experience of revolution in two countries, two terms as President, and frequent occasions to reflect on the political structure of nations, Thomas Jefferson declared that the establishment of small political units was "the most fundamental measure for securing good government, and for installing the principle and exercise of self-government into the fiber of every member of our commonwealth." He maintained that the township of New England was "the wisest invention ever devised by the wit of man for the perfect exercise of self-government and for its preservation." Nor need administrative efficiency be sacrificed to promote political training, for "in government as well as in every other business of life, it is by subdivision of duties alone, that all matters, great and small, can be managed to perfection."[1]

Alexis de Tocqueville agreed that the secret of just government was the proliferation of self-governing political units, and asserted that without them a nation might possess the forms of free government but lack the spirit of liberty. Half a century later, James Bryce reaffirmed Jefferson's praise for the New England town and its town meeting. Of all of the forms of local government, it was the "cheapest and most efficient . . . the most educative to the citizens who bear a part in it." In one short sentence, Bryce summed up a great American tradition: "The Town meeting has been not only the source but the school of American democracy." A twentieth-century American was not

---

[1] Jefferson's comment comes from a letter to James Cabell written on June 17, 1814. See C. M. Wiltse, *The Jefferson Tradition in American Democracy* (Chapel Hill, N.C., 1935), 131.

inclined to question the verdict of the two most distinguished foreign interpreters of his country's institutions.[2]

Faith in local government did not require much knowledge of its operation. In 1917 one of the earliest political scientists to study county government described his subject as "the dark continent of American politics," and the phrase was repeated by most subsequent writers on local government. In the same year, a writer in the *National Municipal Review* declared:

Over all the operations of county government lies a great pall of silence and an utter absence of public opinion. If you should attempt to poke around in this darksome cave with a lantern, you will find that as soon as your light illuminates something interesting the flame is extinguished.

Rural counties might be mysterious, but when laws and institutions evolved in earlier days for simpler societies provided for great cities and their surrounding suburbs, self-government became meaningless. An account of 1933 described its exasperating complexity in Chicago:

The average citizen does not see the irrational character of the existing organization of the government ... under which the needs of the metropolitan community are attended to very ineffectually by a multiplicity of jurisdictions of various nature and size, and with no central authority capable of taking care of them in an effective and consistent manner."[3]

It might be true that local government educated those who were involved in it, but twentieth-century commentators wondered whether the lessons were worth learning. When Americans used the word "politician" in a derogatory sense (as they often did), they had most in mind the local officials in city wards, townships, or counties seeking patronage and spoils, favoring friends, juggling contracts, and acknowledging some obligation to their party but none to the community. Civic reformers, students of public administration, and almost every issue of the *American Political Science Review* produced abundant evidence of local incompetence.

The functions of local government had been shrinking through the transfer to the state of tasks that had to be performed efficiently or

---

[2] Tocqueville's remark is in *Democracy in America,* Part 1, Section 5; James Bryce, *The American Commonwealth,* Vol 1. chap. XLIX (concluding paragraph).

[3] Henry S. Gilbertson, *The County: The Dark Continent of American Politics* (New York, 1917); Richard S. Childs, "Ramshackle County Government," quoted in John M. Matthews, *American State Government,* (New York, 1924) 631; *APSR* 27 (1933), 329, in a comment on Charles E. Merriam, Spencer D. Parrott, and Albert Lepawsky, *The Government of the Metropolitan Region of Chicago* (Chicago, 1933).

humanely, or where failure might have serious political implications. There had also been moves to shift some administrative responsibility from the smallest units – townships and districts – to the counties, and what remained was often not enough to stimulate the imagination or encourage participation. In 1924 John A. Fairlie, an authority on public administration, wrote:

Local government in the rural areas has consisted for the most part in the administration of justice, the maintenance of primitive roads, the support of small elementary schools, with some provision for poor relief; such functions have continued to be carried on in much the same way, and on about the same scale, as before and immediately after the Civil War.

Could anything put new life into the system? In the same year as Fairlie's critical assessment, the Democratic party's platform called for "a revival of the spirit of local self-government essential to the preservation of the free institutions of our republic," but a cynic might read this as a protest against zealous enforcement of Prohibition in areas where it was unpopular. Neither major party was likely to set out upon the troubled sea of local government reform. The system gave the parties cheap patronage for a host of followers, and business gave tacit support to inefficient local governments that were easy to influence and provided a shield against state interference.[4]

Whatever the merits of local government, the number of units was astonishing. In 1930 there were 3,099 counties (including the parishes of Louisiana), of which 3,053 had organized governments; 16,366 incorporated cities and villages; 20,262 towns and townships (of which the majority were rural); 127,108 school districts; and 8,580 special districts with functions not assigned to other local governments. The distinguishing features of all of these units were separate and normally elected governing bodies, exclusive rights (subject to state law) to issue ordinances and executive orders, and the power to levy taxes to perform their statutory duties.[5]

[4] James A. Fairlie, "Reorganization in Counties and Townships," *Annals* 113 (1924), 187–8.
[5] The most comprehensive account is in William Anderson, *The Units of Government in the United States* (Chicago, 1934); see especially Table 2 (p. 11). Lane W. Lancaster, *Government in Rural America,* 2nd ed. (Princeton, N.J., 1952), is excellent in its range of material and informed judgments. For older but useful reviews of the characteristics of local government, see Kirk H. Porter, *County and Township Government in the United States* (New York, 1922), and the sections on local government in John Mabry Matthews, *American State Government* (New York, 1924) and W. Brooke Graves, *American State Government,* 3rd. ed. (New York, 1946).

LOCAL GOVERNMENT IN NEW YORK

Counties

BOARD OF SUPERVISORS
Members: from each township the Town Supervisor,
from each city ward, one representative
The Board appointed: a Clerk, an Attorney, a
Superintendent of Highways, other minor officials

The following were elected and were not under the authority of the Board: County Clerk, Treasurer, Welfare Commissioner, County Judge, District Attorney, Sheriff, and Coroner.

Townships

TOWN BOARD
Members (all elected): Town Supervisor, Town
Clerk, three Justices of the Peace
The Board appoints: Health Officer, Welfare
Officer, other local officers.

The following were elected and did not come under the authority of the Town Board: three Tax Assessors, Tax Collector, three School Directors, Highway Superintendent.

There were counties in every state, but in New England they were divisions for the jurisdiction of the courts, with few administrative duties. There the towns were the all-purpose units of local government, and it had not been the custom to give separate governments to small cities and villages within their boundaries. Outside New England a town was usually called a "township." In the South they were few and unimportant, and counties were the principal units of local government; some functions might be delegated to separate districts, but these were never autonomous and were always subject to the counties. In the South there were, however, a large number of incorporated cities and villages with their own governments. The mid-Atlantic states borrowed something from both systems: In New York the counties controlled a wide range of local activities, but the townships had their own governments and, for the functions assigned to them, were not subject to the counties (see the chart "Local Government in New York").

There were also a large number of cities that came under neither county nor township. West of the Appalachians there were a number of variations. Where New England settlers had predominated in the early days, there were usually townships, but on the New York rather than the New England pattern; where southern migrants had prevailed, there were at first no townships. Most midwestern and western state constitutions allowed counties to go over to township organization if approved by popular vote, and many had done so.

Where townships existed, the township meeting was usually a statutory body, required to meet at least once a year; but outside New England (and even there in some districts), it had become a meeting to give formal approval to measures already decided and was attended mainly by officeholders. It was aptly described as "the ghost of a one-time democratic institution." In some suburban townships there had been attempts to revive the meeting as a residents' association or the country club in legislative session.[6]

In areas settled before the nineteenth century, counties, towns, and townships might have historic roots and natural boundaries. Elsewhere they were more likely to be artificial creations: the result of lines drawn across blank maps by surveyors, with little regard for natural features of future economic ties. In the Midwest, where township boundaries derived from the first grid pattern survey of public lands, they were often known as "congressional townships." Of the county, Bryce had said: "It is too large for the personal interest of the citizens: that goes to the township. It is too small to have traditions which command the respect or touch the affections of its inhabitants: these belong to the State." His judgment was influenced by what he knew of New England or of townships that were vigorous in his day; later commentators would endorse what he said of the county but point out that most townships were administrative units, with little to engage the interests or affections of their citizens. In this they compared unfavorably with school districts, which had been set up to serve communities or groups of communities in a matter that was of vital concern to a majority of the people.[7]

A special district was an autonomous political unit, with power to tax and issue regulations having the force of law and to perform func-

---

[6] Porter, *County and Township Government,* 311.
[7] Bryce, *American Commonwealth,* Part 1, Chap. XLIX. Sect. 5.

tions not easily assigned to one county or township. Typical examples were flood control, irrigation, forest management, park, and pest control districts. They might be created to coordinate work spread over several counties, to avoid constitutional restraints on local taxing power, or to rescue an important responsibility from the morass of routine local administration. These were laudable objectives, but the willingness of state legislatures to create special districts during the twentieth century had added greatly to the complexity of the political scene. The existence of so many special districts was also a tacit admission that the traditional forms of local government could not cope with the problems of a modern society.

William Anderson, a political scientist who carried out a survey of local government between 1932 and 1934, found that "the mere task of counting and classifying" special districts was "excessively difficult." State legislatures and administrations often lacked clear records of what had been done, and had failed to keep abreast of what these children of their creation had been doing. Some had ceased operation after a brief spell, some were moribund, and others had gathered functions remotely linked to their original purpose. The expansion of a special district's activities often resulted from sincere dedication to the work of improvement by men who saw no harm in exceeding their powers so long as the purpose served was good. Anderson found one mosquito control district that had first, and correctly, set about draining swamps; from this it launched a conservation program for the restoration of rivers and ponds; not content to stop at this point, it went on to provide recreational facilities with several parks and a wildlife sanctuary.[8]

Confusion was greatest in some of the metropolitan centers, where conurbations spread into two or more counties, swallowed up old townships (which nevertheless retained their separate political identities), and created a demand for new school and special districts.

---

[8] Anderson, *Units of Government,* Table 5 (p. 24), lists special districts by state and function. A great discrepancy between the census figures (column 1) and Anderson's revised figures (column 2) illustrates the difficulty of classification; they coincided in only three states. In Illinois the census said 1,673 and Anderson 2,439, but in a majority of states the census recorded the higher figure by including special districts that existed on paper but had ceased to function. Anderson's total for the United States was 8,580, of which the great majority were classified as water control, irrigation and conservation, and rural roads and bridges.

Growth made worse the already confused relationship between city and state.

In 1933 27 separate governments shared responsibility for Chicago and its inner suburbs. Cook County, covering the greater part of the metropolitan region outside the city limits, contained 30 townships, 89 incorporated cities and villages, 195 school districts, and 56 park districts; with other special districts, the total was 419 for the county. Parts of the metropolis spread into other counties, and if their governments were taken into account, the grand total of independent political authorities for the Chicago region was an incredible 1,642, with 150 police forces, 343 health agencies, and 11,000 school districts. It took much time and effort to sort out the different responsibilities; correspondence with the state on debatable problems filled 26,000 typescript pages in the city's legal department, and over 10,000 opinions were filed. In exasperation, a would-be civic reformer wrote:

> The city is kept in the dark not only with respect to its specific powers and its legal status, but it is, in addition, governed by a rather indefinite, disorderly and confusing body of law wrought out of vestigial charter remains, a general cities and villages act, charter amendments, miscellaneous and special provisions, and legal and judicial proceedings designed to discover just what its phantom charter really permits it to do.

In the five densely populated counties of New Jersey that formed part of the New York metropolitan region (Hudson, Essex, Union, Bergen, and Passaic), no fewer than 140 municipalities crowded into an area 20 miles by 35. A total of 140 separate governing bodies levied taxes, maintained police departments, provided government services, administered poor relief, and legislated for health, safety, and welfare.[9]

Local government in rural America offered fewer complexities, yet criticism was equally severe. In 1927 an officially commissioned study of local government in Virginia was "particularly impressed by the scattered, disjointed, and irresponsible type of organization that exists in all counties." In each county the governing body was the board of supervisors, with one member elected from each magisterial district for four years; also elected, for varying terms, were a county clerk, a county attorney, a county treasurer, a sheriff, two revenue commis-

---

[9] Albert Lepawsky, *Home Rule for Metropolitan Chicago* (Chicago, 1935), 119; Commission to Investigate County and Municipal Taxation and Expenditure, *First Report* (Trenton, N.J., 1931), 47.

sioners, fifteen justices of the peace, and for each district one constable. The circuit judge, appointed by the legislature, appointed the county surveyor, a superintendent of the poor, three members of the board of elections, and ten members of the county board of welfare. In each school district the school board consisted of six elected trustees who came under the general direction of the state board of education appointed by the governor.[10]

The county board of supervisors was responsible for roads, bridges, and public buildings. It levied taxes for general purposes including poor relief, but the county almshouse and other institutions came under the jurisdiction of the superintendent of the poor. Outdoor relief was the responsibility of locally elected overseers of the poor. The authors of the report were struck by the independence of all officials – responsible only to those who had elected or appointed them – and the total absence of any chain of command. They wrote:

The present county government has no responsible head; it is without a chief administrative officer and the board of supervisors controls through appointment only a small part of the county administration. Authority for carrying on the administrative work of the county at the present time rests with many individuals. The voters of the county have very little power in the determination of county policies. It is true that they elect a number of administrative officers besides members of the board of supervisors, but this serves only to dissipate authority and to increase the difficulty of securing effective and economical county government. In fact there is nothing to commend the present form of county government in Virginia. In many of the counties it is grossly political, careless, wasteful, and thoroughly inefficient.

This pattern of indictment was repeated in other states: no central direction, officials responsible to no one, except nominally to those who had elected or appointed them, the will of the people nullified by dispersed authority, inefficiency, waste, and offices treated exclusively as rewards for political service.[11]

In North Carolina the county commissioners had originally provided all-purpose local government, but over the years their powers had been whittled away by supplementary and ad hoc boards, some of which had been so long in existence that it was often assumed that they

---

[10] New York Bureau of Municipal Research, *Report on a Survey for the Governor and his Committee on the Consolidation and Simplification . . . [of county government in Virginia]* (Richmond, Va., 1928), 5.

[11] Ibid., 6.

COUNTY GOVERNMENT IN PENNSYLVANIA

VOTERS

COUNTY BOARD		
Members:		
Three	Controller (of	Judges of the District
Commissioners	finance)	Court (3)
Appointed:	Auditors	Appointed:
Chief Clerk	Treasurer	Board of
County road	Surveyor	Viewers
caretakers	Sheriff	Board of Assess-
Inspector of	Coroner	ment and Tax
weights and	District Attorney	Revision
measures	Clerk of Courts	Trustees for
Staff of county	Other minor officials	county workhouse,
institutions		reformatory, and
Board of Health		other institutions
Board of Parks and		
Recreation		
Other minor		
officers		

The Commissioners, together with the appropriate elected officials, were ex officio members of certain boards (e.g., Salaries, Pensions, Prisons, Law Revision)

Poor relief was administered by Poor Boards elected in each Poor District (which might include more than one township). The county was responsible for maintaining a workhouse, a reformatory, and a tuberculosis hospital, but there was no county welfare officer.

were required by the state constitution. In fact they all derived from legislative enactments and could have been repealed in the same manner. The most important were education, highways, welfare, and election boards. In counties of over 30,000 it was mandatory for the commissioners to appoint a superintendent of public welfare, who then took his instructions directly from the state board of welfare, without reference to the commissioners.[12]

The North Carolina constitution placed little restraint on the power of the legislature to create new boards and agencies, but if the county commissioners wished to innovate, they first had to promote a bill in the legislature and then, if it involved additional expense, to submit the proposal to a popular vote. Although the county commissioners were bound strictly by precedent, no consistency was required from the legislature. What was enacted in one session could be repealed in the next. Thus the concentration of power in the legislature produced in North Carolina confusion similar to that caused in Virginia by the constitutional diffusion of power.

The county boards in the South were small. The average number of commissioners was six, and thinly populated counties might have as few as three. This made decisions easy to arrive at if the commissioners, or a majority of them, were agreed. In Pennsylvania the county boards were also small, but had no authority over a number of elected officials. The county board appointed a number of executive officers, but others were appointed by the circuit judges (who were elected). In midwestern states every township had the right to elect a commissioner; in counties without townships, a number proportionate to the population could be chosen. This meant that county boards were large and business was difficult to transact. Officials who were separately elected were not responsible to the board, and those whom the commissioners appointed could safely ignore them. Michigan county government – typical of the region – was described as "a miscellaneous collection of officials, boards, and commissions" and was, in the words of an experienced state official, "the most refined and elaborate system of passing the buck that existed anywhere."[13]

Criticisms of county government abounded, but were often inspired by the hope that, if reformed and invigorated, counties could become effective units of local administration. They were large enough and, in populous regions, could raise enough revenue to provide efficient services. If overall responsibility could be vested in a single executive head, the voters would know where praise or blame should be fixed, and the general direction of policy would be determined at elections. Townships offered no such possibilities.

---

[12] Paul W. Wager, *County Government and Administration in North Carolina* (Chapel Hill, N.C., 1928), 23ff.

[13] Arthur W. Bromage, "Local Government in Michigan," (quoting a remark by an unnamed state officer), *APSR* 27 (1933), 82.

In Michigan the townships were described as "unnecessary, costly, and wasteful," and political scientists offered similar verdicts in many states:

The vast majority of townships are condemned on every count. They are lacking in social unity, too small in area and population, and too weak in taxable resources to become vigorous units of government. There is not a single function now performed by the township which would not be better performed by other units.

Township officers were elected biennially, and seldom served long enough to acquire useful experience of government. Busy men were not normally willing to do more than what they regarded as a fair stint, and small-time politicians wanted their turn in office and objected to long tenures. The administrative apparatus was usually primitive, estimates of needs were often wildly inaccurate, and accounts were kept badly or not kept at all. In Michigan it took trained investigators six months to make even an approximate estimate of the financial situation in seventy-five of the state's townships.[14]

As in the counties, a number of township officials were directly elected and not subject to the town board. Normally they included tax collectors, assessors, and justices of the peace (though in some states the justices were ex officio members of the board). Overseers of the poor were sometimes elected and sometimes appointed by the board.

For revenue the townships depended upon property taxes, and were normally prohibited by the state constitution from taxing income or personal wealth. Revenue was therefore inelastic and shrank in hard times as the value of property fell. The amount that a township received depended upon the assessors, who were elected for short terms, needed no qualifications for valuing property, and might be subject to local pressure. In thinly populated regions assessment was seldom a full-time occupation, and low pay justified the assessor in devoting most of his time to his own business. A rural assessor might have a shrewd idea of the value of agricultural property, but when it came to factory or business premises, he might be at sea, and the easiest way of getting through the work was to accept the owner's assessment unless it was obviously absurd. In many states assessors were

---

[14]Arthur W. Bromage and Thomas H. Reed, *The Organization and Cost of County and Township Government* [*in Michigan*] (Detroit, 1933), 95.

under no supervision, even though their valuations were also the basis for county taxation; the courts would hear appeals against high assessments, but there was often no way of correcting valuations that were too low.[15]

Methods of collection varied. In the South, with no townships, both assessment and collection were county responsibilities; but local assessors might be appointed with no more attention to their qualifications or supervision of their work than in other parts of the nation. Outside the South, a county collector might receive all taxes collected by the townships and remit their share, or the township might simply deduct what it was owed and send the rest to the county. In some states, a collector was remunerated by a fee on the taxes collected and by a higher fee for recovering arrears. In New York, with a fee of 1 percent for taxes collected normally and 5 percent for the recovery of taxes from delinquents, there was no incentive to press for early payment.

The fiscal system was so clearly inefficient and inequitable that by 1930 moves to improve it had been made in several states. All states except Delaware, Texas, and Idaho had set up tax commissions; in twenty-six states the commission could order reassessments, but in only twelve could the commission anticipate events by prescribing the methods to be used and in only four could an incompetent assessor be removed. In some states, assessment had been taken from the townships and assigned to the counties, with full-time, salaried staffs. Fiscal reformers maintained that there was still a long way to go. They regarded New Hampshire, with a system little changed since colonial times, as the most backward. New York was praised for having the most modern system of state administration but condemned for its continued reliance on blatantly inefficient township assessment. Ohio had centralized administration in the counties but continued to rely exclusively on a general property tax. Reformers continued to press for centralized control of both assessment and collection, state commissions with real authority, counties acting as their agents, and a wider tax base drawing revenue from personal income and assets as well as from property. The pertinence of their criticisms would become apparent when the full burden of relieving the distress caused by unemploy-

---

[15] National Industrial Conference Board, *State and Local Taxation of Property* (New York, 1930), 52, 91 (Table 23), and, for the following paragraph, 11, 52–5.

ment fell upon the governments least able to carry it from existing revenue and least able to increase the yield from taxes.

The shortcomings of the townships were significant because they still had essential functions in addition to the assessment and collection of taxes. Their justices of the peace and constables upheld the law, punished minor offenders, and sent others for trial to higher courts. They looked after local roads and bridges, cleaned the streets, maintained public lighting, and ordered the removal of public nuisances. The township might act for the State Board of Health by enforcing sanitary laws and regulations for dangerous and unhealthy occupations. It received complaints and referred them, at its discretion, to the county or state.[16]

The depression would highlight the responsibility of the townships (or, where they did not exist, of poor districts and poor boards) for the relief of distress. Formal responsibility was with the whole board, but its overseer of the poor or poor master decided who should be committed to county or state institutions or be given direct relief, what labor should be demanded from applicants, how much should be given, and in what form. Usually there was no way in which an indigent person could make a formal appeal against an overseer's decision, and complaints to the board might be disposed of without a hearing. The State Department of Welfare normally kept its hands off relief outside of its institutions and did not supervise general relief in the localities. No procedures were laid down for assessing claims, investigating cases, or seeking out people who were destitute but reluctant to apply for relief. Thus the problem of extreme poverty was shut away in local communities, to be dealt with arbitrarily by officers on the lowest rung of the ladder of government. Humane and assiduous overseers there certainly were, but in general their competence could not be greater than that of local officials as a whole.

The quality of the persons elected to local office was a frequent cause of complaint. In rural areas farmers were always in the majority, and they might be joined by merchants, bankers, real estate dealers, and an occasional physician or lawyer. This might represent fairly the social structure of rural society (though it was often asserted that the men who sought election were not the best representatives of their respec-

---

[16] Lancaster, *Government in Rural America*, 67. His comments on local functions, which appeared in the first (1937) edition, were repeated in the second (1952) edition with no change in substance.

tive occupations), but it meant government by amateurs with limited experience. When a young social worker took over as relief director in a Michigan county, she found that the fourteen supervisors from the one modest city included the manager of a small factory, a house painter, two salesmen, an insurance man, a cobbler, a laborer, and a pool room operator; eight farmers, one merchant, one store clerk, and three with no settled employment represented the rural areas. Only two members of the entire board had attended high school, and less than a quarter had gone beyond elementary grades at school; few had good local reputations, and four had been on relief. The poor law commissioners were a barber, a farmer, and a small merchant; the county relief agent was a house decorator. Criticism might savor of elitism, but she doubted whether men with these backgrounds could handle relief during the Depression, and experience justified her fears.[17]

In Kentucky there were 490 justices of the peace in 84 of the counties, and all were ex officio members of their county's fiscal court (which performed the same functions as the county board in other states), of whom 327 had held no previous judicial or administrative office, 10 had no formal education, 368 had not progressed beyond common school, only 30 had attended high school and 14 college. There were 363 farmers, 29 merchants, 2 lawyers, and 17 with no regular occupation. The office was elective and much sought after, but once elected, fewer than half of the justices played any part in the courts of law. The attraction of the office was its status and the influence that went with it.[18]

Whatever their qualifications, a prodigious number of persons were engaged in local government. A memorandum submitted to Governor Franklin D. Roosevelt by the Institute of Public Administration described the 15,000 county and township officers in the state of New York as a "regular army of occupation." There was an even larger number of appointed executive officers. Excluding New York City and the counties of Westchester and Nassau, there were about 11,000 collectors of taxes in 911 townships, 461 villages, and 9,000 school districts. They were employed to gather only about one-sixth of the property taxes; the remainder was collected by some 200 city and county officers. The traditional system performed, at great cost for small

---

[17] Louise V. Armstrong, *We Too Are The People* (Boston, 1938; rpt. New York, 1971), 297.
[18] J. W. Manning, "Justices of the Peace in Kentucky," *APSR* 27 (1933), 90.

returns, a service that could be provided more cheaply and efficiently by a centralized administration; but the "army of occupation" and the host of officials dependent upon it formed a powerful political interest group resolutely opposed to change.[19]

Local officials did not stand alone. Patronage and control of party nominations played an essential part in political management, and powerful voices in the inner political circles were opposed to any reduction in the number of offices; but the line could not have been held without popular support for the existing forms of local government. People might have little respect for the majority of local politicians, ignore proceedings of county supervisors or town boards, and allow elections to pass without registering a vote, but their instinctive reaction was to spring to the defense of a government that they could call their own. Whatever critics might say, they would remain suspicious of more remote authority even though it promised greater efficiency and lower costs.

Not all political scientists joined their colleagues in condemning this attitude as timid, poorly informed, and irrational. A sensitive study of local government in North Carolina concluded that most county commissioners were "honest and public-spirited, conservative, limited in social vision, but politically shrewd." Few of them made any money out of their office, and the chairman of the board was expected to spend at least half of his time on county business. In character and disposition they were true representatives of "a rural people, a rural-minded people.... Conservative, individualistic, skeptical, close-fisted, yet withal ... ambitious, loyal, stable, and dependable."[20]

Some years later, Lane Lancaster, a leading authority on rural local government, reached somewhat similar conclusions in a nationwide survey:

County boards reflect rather well the qualities, aspirations, and points of view of their constituents – which is all that representative government can be expected to do.... It is probably within the mark to say that board members are normally honest and well-intentioned but not very well-informed or in close touch with developments in public administration.

There was force in this judgment, but emphasis on the representative character of local government meant that a more general cause must

---

[19] Institute of Public Administration [of New York City], "Memorandum submitted to Governor F. D. Roosevelt," 1931 (Albany, New York State Archives), 46–7.
[20] Wager, *County Government and Administration in North Carolina.*

be sought for its limitations. It was not that it failed to implement the popular will but that it implemented it all too well.[21]

In 1937, after all the storms that broke over local government during the depression years, a study of rural communities in different parts of the country found that "the vast majority of these municipalities have enjoyed honest though not always efficient government" and that people retained their confidence in it. Local government was judged largely by its success in making small improvements at minimum cost; satisfaction was assured if they did no more than pave roads, maintain sewers, lay out or extend parks, construct swimming pools, and facilitate other leisure activities. Local government was not expected to be bold or experimental, but to keep pace with the rising expectations of people who enjoyed high earnings, increased leisure, travel by automobile, and (thanks to the radio and mass circulation magazines) knew more than ever before about what the rest of the country was doing. Nor were their expectations confined to things that made an immediate impact; education and publicity had done much to increase awareness of public health, and efforts by counties and townships to safeguard water supplies and combat disease were recognized as normal and necessary.[22]

In 1933, at a Chicago conference on local government, one speaker reminded the assembled experts that it was a "locally treasured thing." A representative of the American Farm Bureau said that in many areas there was opposition to consolidation, a general belief that government ought to be close to the people, and "a strong inclination to hold to the township." In Wisconsin, one speaker pointed out, every township chairman was a member of the county board and formed a built-in majority against any reduction in the powers of the smaller unit, and in this they enjoyed widespread support.[23]

---

[21] Lancaster, *Government in Rural America,* 57.

[22] Edmund de S. Brunner and Irving Lorge, *Rural Trends in Depression Years: A Survey of Village-Centered Agricultural Communities* (New York, 1937), 287; Leonard D. White, an authority on public administraiton, wrote: "The day of isolation has passed, both for cities and states as such and for the individual official." It might not be possible to speak with such confidence of remote rural districts, but the same influences were at work. "Public Welfare and Relief Administration," *APSR* 27 (1933), 444.

[23] Social Science Research Council, New York City, "Conference on the Reorganization of the Areas and Functions of Local Government: Resume of Proceedings (at the Unviersity of Chicago), May 7–8, 1932" (mimeograph). Participants included William Anderson, Frank Bane, John A. Fairlie, Charles E. Merriam, Leonard D. White, and George Works – probably the strongest team that could be put together on local government and welfare.

If the local units often gave satisfaction to the voters on whom they depended, state governments were often criticized. Rural voters were suspicious of a legislature in which city voices might carry too much weight; city voters did not want to see too much power in the hands of a rural majority; and the vagaries of state legislatures were familiar to anyone who read the newspapers. The study of North Carolina's local government concluded that the legislature was largely "responsible for the chaos which exists." The record showed:

Offices are created and filled, other offices abolished, changes made in the membership of administrative boards, and bond issues authorized; and in various other ways the county is made the victim of legislative interference. What is done one year may be completely overturned two years later.

The recommendations of academic experts and municipal reformers commanded no more respect than the bungling performance of legislatures. Lane Lancaster, himself an expert, detected in enthusiastic proposals based on a study of statistics "a note of evangelism" that threw doubt on their objectivity; and he wondered whether men and women in the "intimacy of a rural neighborhood" were not better judges of what was required than "the distant bureau chief."[24]

The conservatism of rural voters was anticipated, but urban voters showed little more enthusiasm for change. There were successes in the number of cities where boss rule was repudiated, new forms of municipal government adopted, and services improved. Cincinnati was a notable example. Reformers broke the power of a long-established Republican machine and turned Cincinnati from being the worst to the best governed city in the United States. Reform succeeded because the scandalous neglect of city services provided visible evidence of misgovernment, and because reform leaders not only put their whole energies into a campaign that led to the election of a reform mayor, but also kept up the momentum after the first victory had been won. Too often reform movements in other cities failed because the leaders slackened their efforts after an early success and the voters lost interest.[25]

---

[24] Wager, *County Government and Administration in North Carolina,* 29–30; Lancaster, *Government in Rural America.* But Lancaster also described (p. 306) the "almost religious, fierceness" with which reform was resisted.

[25] Murray Seasongood, *Local Government in the United States: A Challenge and Opportunity* (Cambridge, Mass, 1933), passim. The author had been a reform leader and Mayor of Cincinnati.

In Chicago a move to bring the inefficient city transit system under municipal control was backed by many civic and business organizations and approved by a large majority in the City Council. A referendum was mandatory, but the many complaints of high fares and poor services encouraged the belief that the change would be widely supported. To the dismay of the reformers it was lost by over 100,000 out of the 557,000 votes cast. It was said that suspicion of the "city hall crowd" and the unpopularity of a prohibitionist mayor explained this astonishing setback for reform; but it was rather dislike of any change initiated from above that persuaded a majority of the voters to save an even more unpopular transit company.[26]

In Philadelphia an independent investigation of organized crime had uncovered links with the Republican party machine led by William Vare. Reformers took this opportunity to present a bill to the state legislature in 1929 proposing a city manager form of government for Philadelphia and proportional representation in elections to the city council. It took just five minutes for a committee of the state Senate to kill off the bill and prevent it from being put to the legislature, but this victory for the opponents of the bill was possible because the voters had shown little interest in its success.[27]

In the same year, local government reform suffered an even more spectacular defeat in western Pennsylvania. Allegheny County contained the city of Pittsburgh and had long presented a series of knotty administrative problems. During the 1920s, a plan took shape to consolidate government in the city and county, and a constitutional amendment was carried that permitted Pittsburgh, three other cities, sixty-six boroughs, and fifty-two townships to combine in a federation transferring some powers to a central government while reserving others to the existing local governments. A bill on these lines was prepared, but as soon as the details were known, "the politicians of Allegheny County girded themselves to oppose it." In legislative proceedings some of the proposed powers of the new combined government were whittled away, but the measure passed with police and health centralized, a metropolitan water authority set up, new public utility districts formed, and changes made in the assessment of taxes. A referendum was required, and it went to the people in June 1929

---

[26] "A Referendum Goes Wrong," *Survey Graphic* VII, No. 2 (May 1925), 179.
[27] *APSR* 23 (1929), 731.

with endorsements by both political parties, the League of Women Voters, the Pittsburgh chamber of commerce, the allied boards of trade, and other associations and prominent individuals. Opposition was led by the aldermen in most cities and boroughs, many justices of the peace and minor politicians, the association of volunteer firemen, and the city of McKeesport. It failed to win the necessary two-thirds vote for adoption, and years of effort were thrown away.[28]

Two states not usually in the vanguard of progress presented a welcome contrast for reformers. In Virginia the masterful Governor, Harry Byrd, succeeded where others had failed in reorganizing the state administration. In North Carolina the state took control of education and highways and rationalized the central government. Byrd reduced to three the number of state elective offices, abolished a number of small departments and bureaus, and concentrated executive authority in his own hands. He sponsored measures for the state to take control of highways, exercise greater control over schools, and increase expenditure on education. They were adopted in all but four counties, and the rationalization secured, among other things, the elimination of five hundred separate highway districts. The governor was also given power to send special police to districts where local officials were negligent or unable to control disorder. Thus, in Jefferson's own state, the autonomy of local government was substantially reduced; but Byrd had no intention of touching his own power base in the county courthouses, and when a report condemned county administration and proposed drastic reforms, he refused to submit it to the legislature and ignored its recommendations.[29]

Rationalization of state administration went further in North Carolina, and in 1933 the *American Political Science Review* considered that the state had made "the most thorough examination . . . and the most extensive changes both in state and local government of any state in recent years," though the basic structure remained unchanged. The example commended itself to political scientists because it owed much

[28] Rowland A. Egger, "City/County Consolidation in Allegheny County, Pennsylvania," *APSR* 23 (1929), 725.

[29] James E. Pate, "Recent Proposals for Reorganizing County Government in Virginia," *APSR* 23 (1929), 131ff., and "Local Government in Virginia," *APSR* 27 (1933), 34–7. For Byrd, see Edward T. Younger, ed., *The Governors of Virginia, 1860–1978* (Charlottesville, Va., 1982), 239–44, and, for a contemporary view of his administrative reforms, Robert H. Tucker, "Progress in Virginia toward Simplification and Economy in Government," *APSR* 20 (1926), 832–6.

to the work of one of their number, Paul W. Wager, and to academics from Chapel Hill.[30]

Things were also on the move in other states. In 1929 a New Jersey report had recommended the reorganization of state administration, a state office for drafting bills, a single-chamber legislature, the transfer of highways to the state, and the consolidation of city and county governments in urbanized areas; but immediate action had not followed. In Maine a proposal to reorganize sixty-five state agencies into nine major departments had been approved in part. New Hampshire had made it possible for cities to adopt the city manager plan, and action on major proposals for the reorganization of state government was awaited. In Arkansas a report on reorganization was under consideration, and in Georgia extensive changes in state administration had been made by executive order. In Illinois a massive report on local government awaited consideration, and there had been two studies of metropolitan government in Chicago, which unfortunately ended with diametrically opposed recommendations.[31]

Attention was focused on New York, where major administrative reforms – matured for many years – had been put into effect in 1927. They had been preceded in 1925 by a constitutional amendment removing obstacles to change in the state government, and Governor Al Smith had then set up a State Reorganizing Commission under a man whose opinion carried as much weight as that of anyone in the United States – Charles Evans Hughes, former governor, presidential candidate, Secretary of State, and future Chief Justice of the Supreme Court – and in 1926 its proposals became law, with little change in substance. The major functions of the state were concentrated in eighteen departments of which one, the Executive Department, exercised general control over policy and finance. For the first time, the governor was in a position to exercise effective control over all aspects of state policy, though, by a curious oversight in drafting, he could not head the department until there had been a further change in the law.[32]

It was now the turn of local government in New York, and in January 1931, Franklin D. Roosevelt chose his inaugural address as Gov-

---

[30] From a survey of reforms completed or under consideration published in *APSR* 27 (1933), 322.

[31] Ibid., 317–21, 324. For an earlier review of administrative reform, see Walter F. Dodd, "Reorganizing State Government," *Annals* 93 (May 1924), 161–72.

[32] Finla G. Crawford, "Administrative Reorganization in New York State," *APSR* 21 (1927), 349–59.

ernor to announce that "Local government in its present form has out-
lived its usefulness. . . . Due to the indifference of the electorate it has
been allowed to remain archaic in design and inadequate to the needs
of modern society." In an editorial comment, the *New York Times*
declared that "the deficiencies of the cities, suburbs, and smaller rural
units stand out stark against the comparative efficiencies of state government." Across the nation "the bloated city tax bill and the shiftless
county official and the township that has outgrown its clothes are
familiar spectacles all the way west to the Pacific." Much the same had
been said for several years by obscure political scientists, but now it
was said by a leading newspaper in praise of an initiative by the governor of the nation's wealthiest state.[33]

A memorandum, intended to initiate reform, was soon submitted to
Roosevelt by the Institute of Public Administration. Its proposals were
radical. All town governments and special districts should be abolished
and their functions transferred to the counties, which should be
strengthened to make them "less subject to partisan politics and geo-
graphic log-rolling." Thinly populated districts should be brought
directly under state control; small counties consolidated and, where
necessary, county boundaries redrawn to ensure a more equitable
spread of resources and burdens. Some county functions should be
transferred to new and larger districts under state control.[34]

For people who had long been critical of state and local government,
it seemed that a new day was about to dawn. The reorganization of
state governments, with authority concentrated in the governor and
delegated by him to responsible heads of a limited number of major
departments, would follow in a majority of the states. The redistribution of functions between state, county, city, and other small units on
rational lines would be the next step. If the smallest units were not
abolished, they would be confined to strictly local duties.

Even in New York these hopes were not to be realized, and it may
be that a great movement for the reform of state and local government
was aborted by the depression. Instead a system of government that
was, in Roosevelt's words, "archaic in design and inadequate to the
needs of modern society" faced the greatest social crisis in American
history. The burden of relieving distress caused by mass unemploy-

[33] *New York Times,* January 2 and 4, 1931.
[34] See note 19, this chapter.

ment fell upon local governments unequal to the task and guided by the principles of a poor law derived from the seventeenth century.

"To Care for One's Own"

In all states, the basic law for the administration of relief was derived directly from the English law of 1601. Its basic principles were that no one should starve, that the responsibility for giving relief should be clear and inescapable, and that able-bodied persons who refused to work and depended on others for support should be subjected to severe penalties. It made communities responsible for the care of their own poor while arming them with power to deal harshly with idlers, vagrants, and rogues. It coupled a genuine concern for the "deserving poor" with a conviction that able-bodied people must work to support themselves and their families. People who became layabouts in their own communities or refused to live a settled life might be given relief, but only in ways that stigmatized them as social outcasts. In a small rural community, everyone knew who were "deserving" and who deserved punishment; but in larger communities, or when vagrants were numerous, it became necessary to stress deterrence rather than humanity. The simplest rule was to assume that all indigent persons were the authors of their own misfortune and then to make exceptions in favor of those who had fallen on evil days as a result of illness, old age, or chronic infirmity.

If a community was responsible for the relief of its own indigent people, it was important to establish who they were. The laws of settlement, adopted in seventeenth-century England, were grafted on to colonial law, and laid down the length of time necessary to reside in a locality to become eligible for relief. Destitute persons (or "paupers," as they were usually called in America) who failed to qualify in the place where they became destitute could be sent back to the last place in which they had had a legal settlement. This might be rough justice for habitual wanderers, but it created much trouble for people who sought to better themselves by moving to another district but became sick, could not find work, or failed to make a new farm pay.

The basic principles of the poor law remained unchanged in the nineteenth century, but its administration was influenced by the new system adopted in England in 1834. The guideline was that people who could not support themselves, and were not supported by relatives or private charity, should be committed to public institutions such as almshouses, poorhouses, infirmaries, or workhouses. Relief in the home or "outdoor relief" was the exception, not the rule. The fear that idle persons might live in comfort at public expense was met by the rule that life in institutions must be more unpleasant than that of the poorest independent person. In the later nineteenth and early twentieth centuries there were frequent complaints about the conditions in public institutions (which were, with some exceptions, maintained by counties or the larger cities), and some improvements were made; but reform was curbed by the belief that it would be wrong to make anyone too comfortable, too well fed, or too well cared for in these places. The horror with which poor people regarded the poorhouse was an important element in social discipline. The harshness of the system might be mitigated in individual hard-luck cases, but an overseer of the poor was always mindful of his duty to prevent anyone from enjoying idleness at the public charge.

Another logical conclusion was derived from these principles. As relief must never appear to reward idleness, it was customary to demand work from the able-bodied poor before relief was given. The deterrent purpose was served if the work was physically hard, dirty, and humiliating; its usefulness was of secondary importance. Work provided by the poor relief authorities was a penalty for becoming a charge on public funds, not a means of rehabilitation.

Because the essence of the system was the social discipline it imposed, those who were publicly known as idle, incorrigible, or perverse must be seen to suffer; but there were always others whose misfortunes won public sympathy, and local opinion could usually be trusted to distinguish one from the other. When the facts were public knowledge, why was it necessary to investigate individual cases? The local poor masters or overseers were likely to regard the investigation demanded by the new breed of social workers as a waste of time, and to rely on the applicant's local reputation. Too often this meant that generous treatment depended upon a recommendation from a friend of the overseer, a prominent citizen, or a political boss.

Unease at the treatment given to people who had fallen on evil times was often met by the assertion that if destitution was not the result of idleness or crime, it was evidence of weak character or moral infirmity. This belief had been reinforced by genetic theories of hereditary personal defects. There had long been a debate over the external causes of poverty, but for most ordinary Americans, a bad social environment was not the cause but the consequence of depravity; and in any random sample drawn from the very poor, there were always enough people of weak character and vicious habits to justify the theory. The idea that an able-bodied man could be reduced to destitution through no fault of his own was hard to accept, and in prosperous times it was generally believed that unemployed men and women could always find work if they made an effort.

These assumptions about the causes of poverty implied that paupers could not be trusted with money. When outdoor relief was given, it was usually in the form of a grocery order, and was often made out for the specific items judged to be essential and valid only at named stores. The practice was defended as a way of preventing a dissolute father or mother from indulging themselves at the expense of their children, but it was also a fruitful source of patronage in the hands of an overseer of the poor. Even though the grocery orders might be for small amounts, enough of them (with payment guaranteed) could be of great value to favored storekeepers.

It was often assumed that genuine cases of hardship would be relieved by private charity, which might begin near the home with kindly neighbors or become the responsibility of a church, a labor union, a masonic lodge, a service organization (such as Rotary, Lions, Eagles, or Kiwanis), or one of the large organized charities. Private charity did not carry the same stigma as public relief, because it was assumed, often correctly, that a person helped in this way was of good local reputation or had been investigated and found to be deserving by the officials of a philanthropic organization. It was a further though illogical step to argue that private charity helped people to help themselves but public relief demoralized them. This belief achieved its most popular and widespread form in ritual denunciations of the dole – or regular cash payments to people out of work.

Criticisms that applied to the whole system were contained in a study of the poor law in Ohio. Written in the light of experience in the early days of the depression, it demonstrated the failure to cope with the casualties of industrial society:

The magnitude of the problem of relief . . . has focused attention in Ohio upon defects of the legislative provision for the poor, chief of which is local administration, without any relation to, or supervision from, the central authority, namely the State Department of Public Welfare. Under the present plan, instead of one standard for the care of the destitute, there are as many standards as there are townships in the state.

County commissioners and township trustees shared responsibility for relief in Ohio, but the commissioners had no authority to direct the methods used or the level of relief given. No trained social workers were employed, and in the quality of its service public relief was forty years behind the private agencies. There was no state policy, guidance, or power to supervise. "There is in Ohio today, as there was in 1790, a township standard of relief administration."[35]

These words were written when the state had at last agreed to provide some emergency funds for the relief of the unemployed and a federal relief program was in operation. It was admitted that local responsibility was no longer a viable principle when coping with the effects of depression, but in other respects things remained unchanged:

Administration of poor relief through local units, vigorous settlement requirements, and the county almshouse are as much part of Ohio's relief plan as they were more than a century ago. . . . Notwithstanding state and federal funds for outdoor relief, the poor are still largely at the mercy of the township trustees, the almshouses, and the "principles" of 1601.[36]

What was required was not an emergency program but root and branch reform. In other states, all who had given serious thought to the question agreed that economic disaster proved the need for permanent reconstruction.

The laws of settlement were inextricably tied to local responsibility and underlined the conviction of local officials that their principal duty was to keep paupers out. Local responsibility meant that much time was spent in efforts to determine whether a destitute person had a settlement, and, if possible, in making some other locality pay the cost of relief. If no immediate solution was apparent, the easiest course was to get the pauper out of the township and bid him to go and pester some other poor master.[37]

---

[35] Aileen Elizabeth Kennedy, *The Ohio Poor Law and Its Administration* (Chicago, 1934), 109.

[36] Ibid.

[37] For a general survey of the poor law, see James Leiby, *A History of Social Welfare and Social Work in the United States* (New York, 1978). Accounts of the poor law in various states reflecting the experience of the depression include David M. Schneider and Albert Deutsch, *The History of Public Welfare in New York State, 1867–1940* (Chicago, 1941); Sophonisba P. Breckinridge, *The Illinois Poor Law and Its Administration* (Chicago, 1939); Margaret Creech, *Three Centuries of Poor Law Administration in Rhode Island* (Chicago, 1936); and A. E. Kennedy, *Ohio Poor Law*.

The suffering inflicted on unfortunate individuals was documented in many cases that reached the courts, and many examples, collected by Edith Abbott (dean of the School of Social Work at the University of Chicago) for her work on public assistance, came not from some dark age of the past but from the enlightened 1930s. In some cases the courts reached decisions that were fair and showed a decent concern for unfortunate individuals, but in others they endorsed the mean spirit encouraged by the law; and whatever the outcome, the circumstances illustrated the callousness of actions local officials felt bound to take. Moreover, litigation normally took place only when two or more localities refused to accept responsibility or when a physician or surgeon sued for his fees. Thousands of instances in which the destitute person was the only sufferer never reached the courts.[38]

In a Nebraska case the court reached a sensible decision, but it came after months of argument. The son of a destitute father became critically ill and was taken by a kindly neighbor to the nearest hospital, over the county boundary, where an emergency operation saved his life. His county of residence refused to pay the medical costs on the ground that treatment out of the county had not been authorized. The court decided that when life was in danger, departures from normal procedure were justifiable and the county must pay. The California courts took a narrower view when a pauper, under treatment in his county's general hospital, was moved (with permission from the county board of supervisors) to the University of California hospital in San Francisco for an emergency operation on the brain. The county auditor refused to pay the bill on the ground that the supervisors had no authority to contract for the care of a patient outside the county and was upheld by the state appeals court. The court observed: "Charity is commendable, but it should not be conferred at the expense of others over whose funds the donors have no legal control." This left the hospital to carry the cost of an operation that no humane surgeon could have refused to perform.

In a particularly distressing case in North Dakota, an unfortunate individual paid the price. A farmer who had never been on relief moved from Hettinger County to Stark County, but before he was able

---

[38] For this and the following paragraph, see Edith Abbott, *Public Assistance* (Chicago, 1940), 478–506. She gives many details and examples, drawn from court cases, of the laws of settlement in operation. Several of these cases were heard in 1934 and 1935, showing that poor law practice had not been changed by the depression. For details of the laws in force, see Harry M. Hirsch, *Our Settlement Laws* (Albany, 1933).

to make his new farm pay, he was forced to ask for assistance in caring for his crippled son. Stark County thereupon instituted proceedings to have him removed to Hettinger, but Hettinger then sent him back to his farm in Stark. The Stark County court then ordered the crippled child to be hospitalized at the expense of Hettinger and confirmed the removal order for the father, who ended up destitute and without a farm. This action was upheld by the state supreme court on the ground that care for crippled children was "in the nature of poor relief" and therefore came under the laws of settlement.[39]

What was striking about so many cases arising from the laws of settlement was the willingness of local authorities to spend time and money on litigation to avoid the payment of comparatively small sums. The legal costs, which had to be met from local funds, must have often exceeded by far the saving that the county or township authorities hoped to achieve. When the issue was between counties or townships in different states, the proceedings could be even more protracted and difficult, with the added complication that the laws of settlement, and especially the time of residence required, varied from state to state.

With all its imperfections, however, the poor law was an advance on systems that left to charitable individuals exclusive responsibility for the relief of distress. The communal obligation might be observed in a manner designed to humiliate the recipient, but it incorporated the principle that a community had an obligation to its weakest members; without this, it would have been impossible to develop more general theories of social responsibility. Some voluntary systems had worked in the past, but only where local churches were strong, demanded contributions from property owners, and insisted that it was morally reprehensible to refuse. This system had once prevailed in Scotland, but even there it had broken down in the face of mass poverty in urban districts.

The idea that relief was best administered by men on the spot with intimate knowledge of the circumstances had merit. Indeed, the case made by social workers always began with the assumption that relief should be administered person to person, and not by applying rules laid down by a remote official. The existing system did not fail because of the intimacy of its administration, but because the men in charge

[39] Abbott, *Public Assistance*, 488–91.

did not know what to look for, were influenced by local prejudice, and (in spite of their supposed knowledge of local conditions) frequently knew little about the causes of the distress they were expected to relieve. It was not local administration but incompetent administration that came under fire.

The great weakness of the poor law lay less in its basic principles than in the failure to adapt to altered conditions. There had been a tide of change, beginning in the second half of the nineteenth century, but it had seemed to reach a high water mark and to advance no further. There had been consolidation and improvement, but no breakthrough to allow state governments to supervise the relief of poverty in all its aspects. The states had assumed responsibility for some categories of dependent persons and placed them in centralized institutions. The guideline was that the category must be large, readily identifiable, and in need of care that a small community could not provide. The most obvious examples were the insane, blind, physically disabled, and children who had been orphaned or abandoned. In the twentieth century, widows with dependent children had been added to the list, and for the first time states gave assistance outside institutions. The states had also set up schemes for workmen's compensation. This was not poor relief, but it took men disabled by industrial injuries off the relief rolls. The poor law was not unchanging, but further change could come about only by ending the exclusive control of general relief by local government.

The public welfare laws had been modified in most states without touching the fundamental principle of local responsibility for relief of destitution. In a majority of states, counties were required to maintain adequate poorhouses and infirmaries, and in many it had become mandatory for counties to appoint welfare officers and superintendents of the poor. In some states the eligibility for relief had been defined and redefined, and the circumstances under which medical treatment could or should be given at public expense had been clarified; but the most numerous amendments affected the laws of settlement. In nearly all instances random complaints had been met by piecemeal legislation, and the cumulative result defied analysis.

Lack of uniformity and obscurity were serious indictments of the poor law. Law officers of the states spent hours or days trying to interpret the law and reconcile its conflicts; local officers, with neither legal nor social work training, were defeated by its complexities. The applicant for relief had little chance of understanding his rights and had to be content with what an ill-informed overseer told him. Eligibility for relief, the level at which it was given, and the division of responsibility between county and township varied from state to state and even from county to county in the same state. In the detailed application of the law, townships might set their own rules, which might differ from those of neighboring townships. Even if the law of a state seemed clear, local officials used their discretion in deciding how it should be applied; an inconvenient law could usually be ignored; and some laws were so antiquated that no one thought of observing them.

In 1929, when New York reformed its poor law, no fewer than 130 statutes, many dating back to the first state constitution in 1778 and confirming colonial practice, had to be repealed. In Ohio the volume of opinions delivered by the attorneys general indicated "the maze and the fog in which uninformed, unprepared, and untrained poor law officials were expected to provide lawfully for the destitute." From 1861 to 1934, Kansas passed 123 laws clarifying or amending the poor law, and, as might be expected, obscurities and inconsistencies abounded. "In this state, as in every other," said one commentator, "an extraordinary number of court decisions plus many and sometimes variant opinions of attorneys general have made confusion worse confounded and increased the difficulty of interpreting the law."[40]

No reforms broke down the distinction between categorical and general relief. The responsibility of the state to care for those who could not help themselves was recognized, and improvements continued to be made in the institutions that performed this service; but the poor who did not fit into one of the "helpless"categories remained the exclusive responsibility of local government. The possibility of moving to a system in which all welfare would come under the supervision of state agencies, with power to allocate funds according to need, seemed remote.

The separation of categorical from general relief was made clear in a 1925 decision by the Supreme Court of Pennsylvania, which invalidated the state's 1923 Old Age Assistance Act. This act had appropriated money, administered by a state commission and local boards set up for the purpose, to give pensions to people over seventy who had

---

[40] Josephine Chapin Brown, *Public Relief, 1929–39* (rpt. New York, 1971). Kansas: 7; New York: ibid., quoting from Elsie M. Bond, "New York's Public Welfare Law," *Social Services Review,* September 1929; Kennedy, *Ohio Poor Law,* 104.

very low incomes but were not destitute, disabled, or senile. The opinion, delivered by Justice Kephart, took no account of evidence presented by the State on the social benefit of old-age pensions – this was for the legislature, not the court, to consider – and declared the law invalid because the state constitution forbade appropriations for charitable or benevolent purposes to any person or community. The state had relied upon the precedents set by pensions for state employees and the financial assistance already given to nondenominational charitable institutions caring for indigent, infirm, or mentally defective persons; but the court held that the first was deferred payment for services rendered and the second was a way of providing for those who could not help themselves. The Old Age Assistance Act appropriated public money to persons who had performed no service for the state and were not helpless.[41]

The court then rejected the argument that the act was an extension of the existing duty of government to relieve the poor. The word "poor," as used in all previous laws, described "those who are destitute and helpless, unable to support themselves, and without means of support," but under the 1923 act "the fundamental basis of poor laws (indigency or inability to work) had been swept aside as to certain persons, and for it is substituted an age limit for persons having property less than $3,000 a year and an income less than $365 a year." In the opinion of the court, this attempt to extend the meaning of the word "poor" to include persons with property and income made it clear that the act was not a poor law as understood by law and tradition.

The Pennsylvania judges knew that cases might arise that escaped the classification they had established, but they believed that relief could safely be left to poor directors in their districts without the intervention of a state commission or local pension boards. Justice Kephart quoted with approval a dictum of the lower court affirming the principle of local responsibility:

The system provided for poor districts, poor directors and overseers, and for the relief of paupers as a matter of *local* concern. Those who framed the Constitution so understood it, and no word is contained in the Constitution with reference to it. The system was left untouched. If there had been any purpose to change the system, some word indicating that purpose would have been found in the Constitution. . . . The conclusion is therefore irresistable that an

[41] *Busser et al. v. Snyder*, decided February 2, 1925, 128; *Atlantic Reporter*, 80.

indirect appropriation from the state treasury to any person cannot be sustained on the theory that it is a discharge of the inherent obligation of the state to take care of its paupers.

This was a strong hint from the State Supreme Court that though it had invalidated the law because it assisted people who were not "poor," it might also find difficulty in upholding a future act that dropped the property and income clauses but retained the centralized administrative machinery.

The most serious implication of the decision was that relief given to a person who was not completely destitute was unconstitutional. A poor director who gave relief to save a poor person from destitution might be on the wrong side of the law and be sued by any taxpayer for misuse of public funds. The purpose of poor relief was to save people from starvation, not to enable them to keep what little property they had. Thus an old person who had been prudent enough to save, though not to accumulate enough to live on, might be in a worse position than a feckless person who had saved nothing for old age. The paradoxical result (typical of the old poor law) was that even with the very low level of care in county institutions, it cost more to keep elderly people in an almshouse than to pay out a modest sum to allow them to continue living in their own homes.

If there were good reasons for paying money to enable someone of good character to live decently in old age, then it was for private charity, not public welfare, to find the means. From this it might be deduced that the same prescription applied to anyone who had fallen on evil days but was not disabled or destitute, and this reasoning persuaded many Americans that the relief of unemployment must be, in the first instance, the responsibility of charitable individuals and associations.

It would not have been difficult for the Pennsylvania judges to find a way around the constitutional obstacles they treated as insurmountable. Historically, it was easy to distinguish the kind of partiality that the state constitution had intended to outlaw from measures covering the entire state and applicable to a new category of easily identified persons. Other states were more fortunate in their legal drafting or in having judges more sympathetic to the extension of public welfare to people who lived in poverty but were not destitute. Indeed, even the Pennsylvania Supreme Court would shortly find it possible to accept state aid for relief of the unemployed, albeit by the bare majority of

4–3; but in the meantime, the court had expressed a view that was widespread and the starting point for much discussion of social policy. It held that public assistance by the state should be confined to persons who were not able to help themselves, and that this rule should be strictly interpreted. People who were helpless had a claim on the state, but not those who were merely weak, poor, or old. Beyond that, relief must depend upon the discretion of local officials (who were supposed to know their community and the individuals who lived in it) and these officials should bear in mind that "poor" had traditionally meant "destitute," not (to use a word adopted since their day) "deprived." This reasoning ensured that the first response of many Americans, including the Hoover administration, to the depression was to exhort private charities to bear the burden and reject the expansion of public welfare as a remedy.

Leaders of the social work profession did not accept the premises underlying this conclusion. They might be divided in their basic attitudes toward poverty, but faced with the inequities, lack of uniformity, and amateurism of the poor law, they were unanimous in demanding reform. There remained doubt about the role that government should play but growing support for greater centralization of relief. States must supervise and counties must administer; townships and poor districts – if they continued to exist – should be under firm guidance from above. John Lapp was only slightly ahead of his time when he declared in 1927: "Government is the only agency that can effectively protect human beings in their essential integrity. . . . Legislation is the means by which conditions favorable to justice may be created." By 1931 a writer in *Survey* was sure of wide support when she claimed that "government can no longer be thought of as a mere police agency, a protective institution, but as a system of public services whose scope and function are limited only by the demands of the community and its capacity to pay for what it wants."[42]

By "government" these social administrators did not mean ramshackle local government as practiced in the United States, but state agencies directing and supervising reformed county commissions or boards set up with a particular task in mind. In a 1927 paper to the National Conference of Social Work, Louise Cottrell, of the University

---

[42] For Lapp see page 34; Loula D. Lasker, "Whither City Goverment?" *Survey Graphic* 20 (October 1931), 7.

of Iowa, outlined the "organization needed to support and free the local worker for undifferentiated case work" – that is, for the administration of general relief. She argued that the minimum organization required was a strong state agency, county programs endorsed by the local officials responsible for public relief, a county governing board, local advisory committees, and cooperation by township officials and volunteers." She thought that the state agency could be private or public and might have no formal authority, but it was difficult to see how a private agency without power to command could perform the tasks she had outlined.[43]

It was not enough to make laws and then leave their implementation to local authorities. Grace Abbott, a forceful voice in the debate over the future of social policy, wrote in 1927: "Our greatest failures have been our failures to put into actual operation over a whole state a program which a state law makes universal in its application." Examples were laws setting up juvenile courts that were on the statute books in most states, but covered more than 75 percent of the population in only three and less than 25 percent in ten. There were statewide mothers' aid laws in forty-two states, but the population covered ranged from 98 to less than 5 percent. Once a policy decision had been taken and embodied in law, it should be mandatory and enforced.

The principal functions of a state agency should be to give publicity to social problems, guide the county agencies, help in training and placing social workers, and keep in close touch with county boards and agents in the field. There was a warning that division of responsibility in the field would weaken the effort. For routine administration "the county was the logical and the simplest unit for work" in rural districts, and the temptation to set up new local boards or committees when new tasks were assumed by the state should be resisted. "Local social forces which need to be cemented for the common good are driven further apart through the efforts of various local cliques each trying to outstrip the other in winning public support." Where divided loyalties already existed they should be shaken off, and everyone concerned with welfare and relief should "unite in real teamwork to study the county as a whole."[44]

In *Recent Social Trends,* Howard W. Odum argued that greater cen-

---

[43] Louise Cottrell, "Organization Needed to Support and Free the Local Worker for Undifferentiated Case Work," *NCSW 1927,* 118–22.
[44] "Developing Standards of Rural Child Welfare," *NCSW 1927,* 26–37.

tralization, whether welcome or unwelcome, was the natural response to growing awareness of social evils and the realization that many of them could be prevented. Opponents of enlarged state authority often claimed that the protection of local government was their primary concern; but experience, said Odum, had shown that state intervention stimulated local interest and that state activity in local areas improved administration in the communities. State intervention did not weaken local government but armed it against its critics.[45]

Present practice and future hopes would shortly be put to the test. Professional criticism of the welfare system, which had left politicians unimpressed and the general public uninterested, moved suddenly to the head of the political agenda. In this crisis, the men who had thought about the problems of relief administration were called upon to say what should be done, and many of their leading representatives were placed, for the first time, in positions where they could influence state and national policy. Confrontation with the idea of local responsibility as understood in America was inevitable.

[45] "Public Welfare Activities," *RST*, Vol. II 1224–73.

3

THE IMPACT OF DEPRESSION

Contemporaries could not be blamed for the failure to foresee the unprecedented length and severity of the Great Depression triggered by the stock market crash of November 1929. The depression of the 1870s was ancient history and could be attributed to the malfunctioning of an immature economy. The older men in public life could recall the year 1893, when business activity was at a peak in January and fell steadily to its lowest point in June 1894, when the recovery that then began was complete by December 1895. Unemployment had not become serious until the depression had run for seven months and began to pick up four to five months later. In 1907 there had been a peak in January, the trough was reached in June 1908, but recovery took business activity to a new peak in January 1910. Industrial unemployment was severe only in the twelve months beginning in October 1907. The depression of 1920–1, though sharp, had been even shorter.[1]

Drawing upon this experience, a reasonably pessimistic analyst in the spring of 1930 might have predicted a severe depression touching bottom in the spring or early summer of 1931 and ending early in 1932. Was the pattern likely to be distorted by the unprecedented losses sustained in the Wall Street crash? "Blood letting" was a phrase much on the lips of those whose business it was to know; unwise speculation and the erection of towering financial structures on insecure foundations were blamed; the losses were supposed to have left untouched the underlying strength of the economy. Early in 1930 and throughout the year, businessmen, bankers, politicians, and professional economists looked forward to eighteen tough months, with better times ahead. In its New Year issue the *New York Times* greeted

---

[1] The "profiles" of earlier depressions are derived from Arthur F. Burns and Wesley C. Mitchell, *Measuring Business Cycles* (Washington, D.C., 1946).

1931 with the confident assertion that "nobody in or out of Wall Street entertains the least doubt of eventual and complete reversal of the present economic trend."[2]

Not until the summer of 1931 did it become clear that something was wrong with this forecast. The downward slide had reached the point at which signs of recovery should have been visible, but the truth is revealed in an index of factory employment later prepared by the Federal Bureau of Labor Statistics (the average for 1923–5 was the base, and the figures were seasonally adjusted):

	Jan.	Mar.	May	July	Sept.	Nov.
1930	100.6	97.7	95.7	91.2	87.7	85.3
1931	82.4	81.1	80.7	79.2	76.0	72.6
1932	71.8	69.9	65.3	61.9	64.4	66.2
1933	64.9	62.2	67.1	77.4	82.8	81.2

Relying upon precedent, the upturn might have been expected, at the latest, by September 1931, and it was at this point that opinion veered from trust in old and tried remedies to demands that new expedients be tried.[3]

A monthly index of industrial employment published at the time by the New York Department of Labor and based on the average of 1925–7 reveals how glimmers of hope quickly gave way to further gloom. In October 1929 the index stood at 100.4; by March 1930 it was down to 82, but a modest recovery brought it to 86.7 in July; there was a slight but not alarming fall to 84.6 in September, but a further fall in October – normally one of the best months of the year – caused dismay. A minor recovery was recorded in January 1931, but this was followed by a sharp downturn. This was still within the parameters of the expected pattern, and a slight upward movement in the late summer

[2] *New York Times,* January 1, 1931. Studies of the government's response include Harris G. Warren, *Herbert Hoover and the Great Depression* (New York, 1967); Martin J. Fausold, *The Presidency of Herbert Hoover* (Lawrence, Kan., 1985); Albert U. Romasco, *The Poverty of Abundance: Hoover, the Nation, and the Depression* (New York, 1968); and Jordan A. Schwartz, *Interregnum of Despair* (Urbana, Ill., 1970). Two readable general accounts are Geoffrey Perrett, *America in the Twenties* (New York, 1982) and Robert S. McIlvaine, *The Great Depression* (New York, 1984).

[3] Bureau of Labor Statistics, *Employment and Payrolls* (Washington, D.C., 1940); *Historical Statistics of the United States 1789–1945* (Washington, D.C., 1949), Series 3, Appendix.

seemed to confirm predictions of recovery; but in October 1931 the index dropped three points, and even optimists began to realize that the times were out of joint.[4]

This chronology explains the response. So long as the depression followed the expected pattern, little attention would be paid to radical proposals. Social work leaders seized the opportunity to demonstrate the relevance of improvements that they had advocated for several years, including less autonomy for townships and poor districts, stronger county relief administration, greater professionalism, adequate standards, and more guidance from state departments of public welfare; but until the later months of 1931, few of them saw any need for a massive injection of state and still less of federal money into the system. Politicians, businessmen, and leaders of organized labor did no more than call for increased charity, sensible planning of industrial activity, and prudent waiting on events. Indeed, President Hoover, so often blamed for inaction, was somewhat ahead of public opinion in setting up a federal organization to obtain information, give publicity to successful private efforts, and exhort others to follow these examples.

Of the remedies available from the stockpile of ideas, the most popular was "stabilization of employment." It was argued that manufacturers would be doing themselves and their workers a good turn by building up stocks while business was slack, thus readying themselves to meet the expected surge in demand that would soon follow. The idea made the strongest appeal to employers who wanted to keep a skilled labor force together, but not if it meant keeping large numbers of unskilled men on the payroll. Another popular idea was "work sharing," which meant keeping the full number of workers but reducing the number of hours. This would keep workers and their families off relief, but with earnings at a very low level. Another expedient, addressed particularly to householders, was to make work by getting their houses painted or their gardens cleaned up. This advice might be extended to state and local governments, which were urged to get on with public works that had been projected but not yet begun.

By the fall of 1931 it was becoming clear that local resources were running out, that private charity had reached a ceiling, and that sta-

---

[4] Compiled from figures published by the New York Department of Labor in its monthly *Industrial Bulletin*.

bilizing, sharing, or making employment were short-run palliatives manifestly incapable of preventing further decline. It was at this juncture that interest in more radical change emerged from social work conferences and academic debate to become a force in politics.

In the fall of 1930, President Hoover set up a committee on unemployment to collect information, monitor the situation, and encourage voluntary action. A year later it was converted into the President's Organization for Unemployment Relief (POUR) with Walter Gifford, president of the American Telephone Company, at its head. Its major task was to stimulate voluntary activity, but implicit in its brief was the need to demonstrate that local and private resources were sufficient to weather the storm and thus rebut the case for federal action. POUR welcomed the establishment of local relief committees, but under no circumstances would it demand their creation.

In the first phase of the depression, the challenge of unemployment was met in the states without expectation of federal assistance, but the methods then adopted were to be of critical importance for the future by demonstrating what could and could not be done using the existing arrangements for relief. In several states the pressure for state aid, and with it some measure of state control over what was done, became irresistible, and reluctant legislatures were forced to appropriate money and create new agencies to handle it. As hopes for early recovery receded, the states were forced to reckon with the possibility that unemployment would remain at a high level for years to come; but unwillingness to face this future caused the word "emergency" to be tagged on to most state relief measures. Against the short-term view that most public men found it wise to adopt, many people interested in social work insisted that the ineffectiveness of local responsibility for relief had been so fully proven that a permanent and fundamental change must take place. Thus the battle lines of relief policy – centralization, professional methods, and adequate financial resources – were drawn before federal intervention became practical politics; but hardly were the issues defined before influential people were expressing their conviction that only the federal government could provide the answers.

Varying circumstances and traditions ensured that there would be many different responses to depression and unemployment, but most fell into one of four categories, which can be labeled (somewhat anachronistically) as "conservative," "moderate conservative," "liberal," and "radical." Conservatives resisted all interference with existing relief administration; moderate conservatives admitted that emergency aid for the most distressed communities was justified but insisted that its administration must remain in local hands; liberals saw the crisis as an opportunity for long overdue changes, which often included centralization of relief administration in the counties under the supervision of a state agency; radicals went further, demanding a comprehensive welfare program administered by the state, with counties acting as executive agents employing trained social workers.

The conservative position was often buttressed by statements that distress was exaggerated, that individuals who made the effort could find work, and that a dole would make matters worse. It was strongest in rural areas not yet affected by depression, in small cities without major industries, and among business leaders. In many states locally elected officials put up a strong fight against the erosion of their powers. Moderate conservatives were likely to come from similar backgrounds, but from areas where depression was more keenly felt and local resources were clearly inadequate. Liberals were strongest in the larger cities and industrial districts, where unemployment was high. Radicals were a minority composed mainly of social workers, public welfare officials, and their academic allies.

In every state, finance presented unusual difficulties. If more money had to be found, how should it be raised: by borrowing, by gas or sales taxes, or by taxing income? If a legislature reached the point at which an increase in taxation could no longer be postponed, the most favored expedients were sales and gas taxes. Sales taxes were regressive, as they took a disproportionately high share of lower incomes, thus requiring the poor to support the very poor. Gas taxes were more equitable and easy to collect, but their yield fell as the depression deepened and their effect on food prices again meant that the poor contributed a higher proportion of their income than the rich. The last measure to which any legislature turned its attention was a graduated income tax, which alone would have been capable of raising sufficient revenue and of making a modest step toward the redistribution of wealth. It was to be expected that the best funded and most articulate pressure groups would enlist in the fight against this tax, and in several states they held unbeatable hands because amendments to the constitution would be required before its enactment. Thus most states failed to find ways of increasing their revenue commensurate with the crisis, and some of the wealthiest states were the first to claim that their resources were exhausted.

When opposition to increased taxation was so strongly entrenched, the only remedies – if more money for relief had to be found – were to raid other funds or to borrow. If a raid had to be made, health and welfare services were usually the victims rather than politically sensitive highway and education funds. If loans had to be contracted, the first expedient was usually to raise the limits on borrowing by cities and counties rather than to increase the state debt. Thus units with the weakest resources were forced to mortgage their future by borrowing at high rates. If state bonds were authorized, they were seldom accompanied by realistic provision for meeting future interest charges.

The struggle over relief brought to the surface the long-standing tension between rural areas and small cities, on the one hand, and the great metropolitan centers, on the other. The depression would reveal stagnant pools of rural poverty, but these were mainly in remote and thinly populated areas carrying little political weight, whereas representatives from the more prosperous agricultural areas dominated the state legislatures. They were fully aware of falling prices and farm debts, but this made them all the more determined to resist increases in taxation. Many of their constituents were short of money, but few were unemployed. The speaker of the Illinois assembly, himself a representative from the heavily urbanized Cook County, explained:

Members who come especially from agricultural counties and the smaller counties in the state felt that they could take care of their own situation and they said to us in Cook county, mill counties, and the other large industrial centers: "You take care of your own people, We can take care of ourselves, and there is no reason why we should put a tax on the people."

A rural member who voted for higher taxes would be committing political suicide, and few were prepared to recognize that their intransigence also helped large employers who drew their wealth from cities and industries but lived in country or suburban areas beyond the reach of city tax collectors.[5]

Space does not permit a review in detail of the course of events in every state, but some deserve examination because of their importance in the development of relief policy, because they illustrate special dif-

[5] FDR Library, Hopkins Papers, Container 42. State Speaker Shannahan at a hearing before the Board of the Reconstruction Finance Corporation, September 3, 1932.

ficulties or because they demonstrate movements in public opinion. New York, as the wealthiest and most populous state in the nation, the most progressive in developing new relief policies, and the home state of both the future President and the future federal relief administrator, must be considered first.

New York was in several ways the state best prepared to meet the depression. It had a recently formed Department of Social Welfare and the best state Department of Labor in the country. Governor Al Smith had been strong, effective, and deeply concerned with urban problems. The state's charitable organizations were old, well organized, and well funded, and New York probably had a higher proportion of public-spirited businessmen – prepared to give their services to civic and charitable causes – than any other state. The state administration was in good shape after a thorough overhaul that had become effective in 1927. The only weak spot seemed to be the government of New York City, where a lightweight Mayor, Jimmy Walker, was the front man for the Tammany political machine, which was notoriously sluggish in promoting social improvement.

Of first importance in facing the depression was the Public Welfare Law of 1929. It replaced the old poor law, secured uniformity by repealing many local and special laws, reduced the power of the townships and increased that of the counties, replaced elected overseers of the poor by appointed public welfare officers, and simplified the law of settlement. Even more important than the detailed reforms was the spirit in which the law was framed. It declared:

It shall be the duty of public welfare officials ... to provide adequately for those unable to maintain themselves. They shall, whenever possible, administer such care and treatment as may restore such persons to a condition of self-support, and shall further give such service to those liable to become destitute as may prevent the necessity of their becoming public charges.

Adequate relief, rehabilitation, anticipation and prevention of destitution. The formula might have been drawn up by a committee of the National Conference of Social Work. There had not been time for the implications of the new attitude to filter down to the localities, but its principles would appear in all state measures dealing with unemployment.

If the depression severely damaged New York's welfare services, it might be expected to create havoc in other states with large cities and numerous industries, but the activist tradition in New York also promised the most telling remedies. The crisis would indeed generate measures that none could ignore and many would wish to imitate, but it was also highly significant that by the fall of 1931 New Yorkers with much experience of relief problems were converted to the principle and convinced of the necessity of federal relief. In reaching this conclusion they did not repudiate the New York policies, but rather sought to adapt them for use on the national stage.

As in other states, it was the plight of the largest cities that brought home the lesson that even the richest communities could not care for their own. At the outset, New York City faced the depression with confidence, for nowhere were private charities wealthier, better organized, or more fully prepared to face the emergency. The two largest – the Association for Improving the Condition of the Poor and the Charity Organization Society – had won international renown as pioneers in welfare work, and their efforts were supplemented by influential Catholic and Jewish charities and several others serving denominational or ethnic groups. The strength of these voluntary associations meant that a clause in the city charter forbidding public expenditure on outdoor relief caused little comment.

In September 1930 the Charity Organization Society set up an emergency employment committee under Samuel Prosser, chairman of the Bankers' Trust Society, to raise funds and organize work relief. By the end of the year, it claimed to have raised $8,000,000 and found employment for 26,000, but the work projects were costing $400,000 a week and running ahead of contributions. By the end of July 1931, the Prosser committee was almost out of funds and the demand for relief showed no sign of slackening. A new fund-raising campaign was then headed by Harvey Gibson, chairman of Manufacturers' Trust, and got off to a good start, with $31,000,000 raised by the end of the year, twenty-six employment offices in operation, and work found for 32,000. It also had the distinction of being the first agency to do something for unemployed artists and musicians. All of this effort came to a sad end when the Gibson committee ran out of money early in 1932 and was forced to close down all of its projects.[6]

Meanwhile pressure had been building up on public welfare. Wil-

---

[6] Romasco, *Poverty of Abundance*, 150–5; William W. Bremer, *Depression Winters: New York Social Workers and the New Deal* (Philadelphia, 1984), 31–5, 66–8. Bremer's valuable study is based on an intensive study of materials relating to social work in New York.

liam Hodson, director of the City Welfare Council and a man with a great reputation among social workers, initiated a work relief program that won support from Mayor Jimmy Walker, praise from the *New York Times,* and authorization from the state legislature for a bond issue to finance relief. By April 1931 the Commissioner of Public Welfare was presiding over a vigorous work relief program, and in September the charter restraint on home relief was overruled by state legislation. In spite of these efforts, the familiar cycle of falling revenue and rising demand was soon repeated. In January 1932 bankers refused the city more credit unless expenses were cut, and all the relief bureaus were forced to close. Fortunately, by this time, the city was able to seek help from the country's first state relief agency.[7]

As early as April 1930, Governor Franklin D. Roosevelt appointed a Governor's Committee on the Stabilization of Industry. It reported in November, and in January 1931, in his annual message to the legislature, Roosevelt recommended its conversion into a state relief commission. Though the consequences of the depression were less visible in the upstate cities than in New York City – with its huge bread lines and desperate apple sellers on every block – conditions were atrocious and less had been done to grapple with the situation. Only Buffalo and Rochester had made efforts to secure trained investigators, and in January 1931 a survey found that most city governments had "failed to recognize the need for adequate administration of public relief." A joint legislative committee began hearings, but as no action had been taken by August 1931, Roosevelt again took the initiative and proposed the establishment of a state relief agency and an appropriation to aid hard-pressed communities.[8]

---

[7] In March 1931 Roosevelt sent a message to the legislature requesting urgent action, but at this stage he was thinking of insurance and public works rather than direct relief. "Any nation worthy of the name should aim in normal industrial periods to offer employment to every able-bodied citizen willing to work. An enlightened government should help its citizens to insure themselves against the evil days of hard times to come"; but relief by means of a dole was "contrary to every principle of American citizenship" (*New York Legislative Documents, 1931,* Doc. 80, March 25, 1931).

[8] *New York Legislative Documents, 1931* Doc. 108, "Message of the Governor recommending legislation relative to unemployment, Aug. 28, 1931." He recommended the creation of a Temporary Emergency Relief Administration with an initial appropriation of $20,000,000 and said that his proposal was "based on the theory that the distribution of relief of the poor is essentially a local function" and that state aid should "encourage local initiative by matching local effort." The money for relief was to be raised by a graduated tax on personal income, with a single person with an income of over $100,000 paying $1,162, because "it seems logical that those of our residents who are fortunate enough to have taxable incomes should bear the burden of supplementing the local government and private philanthropic work of assistance."

Roosevelt knew that his action would shortly receive powerful support in a report on conditions in forty cities jointly prepared by the State Board of Social Welfare and the New York Charities Aid Association. The report found that relief was inadequately funded. In several cities there had been long-standing agreements that private charities would supplement grants made by city welfare, but when the huge demand for relief compelled them to reduce this form of aid, cities had not increased their relief payments, with a drastic reduction in the level of assistance as the net result. City officials insisted that as there had been no deaths from starvation, no increase in payments was necessary. This was a strict interpretation of the obligation to keep people alive and no more.[9]

The report claimed that state grants would be ineffective if administered by local officials. State aid must be accompanied by state direction, local administration must be taken out of the hands of discredited officials, and poor boards must be compelled to employ trained social workers. Work relief must provide useful employment at reasonable wages and must not be treated as a penalty imposed upon those who applied for assistance. The report suggested:

The state could wisely require administration of work relief by citizens' committees, with definite requirements to ensure the effectiveness of work relief as a relief measure. In many places, administration of home relief is at present so inadequate that the provision of additional funds by the State would not necessarily insure reasonably adequate relief if administered by the local Departments of Public Welfare under their present practices and policies.[10]

In an editorial the *New York Times* praised the report and said that even when local officials recognized that unemployment was a long-term problem, they had not realized "the inadequacy of their preparations or the consequences of continued inactivity." The *Times* gave no specific endorsement to state regulation, appointed boards, and the mandatory employment of trained social workers – but it offered no objections.[11]

Action in the legislature took the form of two bills. The first, known as the "Dunnigan bill," followed the lines of Roosevelt's recommendation, with an appropriation for relief, a new state agency to admin-

---

[9] *Welfare in Forty Cities,* Report by a Joint Committee of the State Board of Social Welfare and the State Charities Aid Association, prepared by a staff of field workers. Albany, August 1931, passim.
[10] Ibid.
[11] *New York Times,* editorial, August 24, 1931.

ister it, and local administration centralized in the counties; the second, called the "Wicks bill," was a weaker measure providing for no separate agency, continuing township responsibility for relief, and making grants directly to them. In some alarm, Homer Folks, secretary of the State Charities Aid Association and doyen of New York social workers, telephoned Roosevelt to express his decided preference for the first bill, which offered "greater opportunity to raise the standards of the entire relief operation, and to give it unity, consistency, and effectiveness." Local improvement could, he said, be effected only by the "leverage of the State." Roosevelt needed no urging to throw his weight behind his own proposals, and after extended debate a compromise measure (embodying the principal features of Roosevelt's plan, though confusingly named the Wicks Act) passed on September 23.[12]

The act established a Temporary Emergency Relief Administration (TERA) with three members and an appropriation of $20,000,000. It also declared that home relief should be sufficient to cover food, fuel, clothing, shelter, and medical attendance and allowed the city or county welfare commissioners to claim from the state 40 percent of their outlay on these items. The whole cost of approved work projects was to be carried by the TERA.

In some important respects, the Wicks Act fell short of what social workers wished. It set up no regular machinery for state supervision. Cities and counties could avoid regulation by refusing state aid, though the most anarchic implications of local autonomy were avoided by requiring townships to comply once a county had adopted the act. In spite of these limitations, the Wicks Act was a new departure in state policy, and was rightly described as a landmark in American history.

The spirit that inspired and would guide the TERA was in some respects more important than its formal powers. In an unusually philosophic message Roosevelt asked, "What is the State?"

---

[12] A transcript of the telephone call from Folks is in FDR Library, Roosevelt Papers, Governor's Files (Unemployment), September 14, 1931. Bremer (*Depression Winters,* 81–2) points to serious differences of opinion between Folks (representing the views of the State Charities Aid Association) and Roosevelt. Folks wanted the existing Department of Public Welfare to be given responsibility for unemployment relief, local work bureaus separated from general relief administration, and obligatory use of professional social workers. Roosevelt insisted on a "temporary and emergency" agency but conceded on separate work bureaus and on stronger professional requirements. Bremer discounts Roosevelt's claim that the bill put his own proposals into effect and describes the outcome as "a major stunning victory" for social work reformers. This conclusion overstates the case. The initiative was Roosevelt's, and he felt his way toward a workable system within the guidelines he himself had set.

It is a duly constituted representative of an organized society of human beings; created by them for their mutual protection and well-being. "The State" or "the Government" is but the machinery through which such mutual aid and protection is achieved. . . . Our government is not the master but the creature of the people. The duty of the State toward the citizen is the duty of a servant to its master.

It was a common error, he said, to suppose that unemployed people had forfeited their right to enjoy the benefits of civilized society; it was rather, in their time of personal crisis, that they had the strongest claim upon the state to which they had formerly contributed taxes and the fruit of their labor.[13]

The novelty and importance of the TERA was emphasized by its members after a year in office. It was, said its first report, "one of the greatest social and legal experiments ever undertaken." Never before had a great commonwealth accepted responsibility for the sustenance of all of its people. Its creation opened a new era and was (in the words of the State Attorney General):

The first enactment under which a State, as such, has accepted liability for the support of its population viewed not as wards but merely as men and women unable temporarily to accommodate themselves to the social scene without at the same time placing such men and women in the position of recipients of a bounty or a dole.[14]

To head the new agency, Roosevelt chose Jesse L. Strauss, president of R. H. Macy & Co., with Philip Wickser of Buffalo and John L. Sullivan, president of the New York Federation of Labor, as the other two members. For the vital post of Executive Secretary Roosevelt chose Harry L. Hopkins, a young social administrator, who was destined to play a great part in national affairs. From the first, it was a hard-working body. Strauss was in the office every day; Wickser on two or three days a week, even though it meant a journey from Buffalo; and Sullivan, though much occupied with union business, was readily available for consultation.[15]

---

[13] *Legislative Documents* (1931), No 108, "Message of the Governor . . . August 28, 1931."

[14] TERA, *Emergency Unemployment Relief Laws of New York* (Albany, October 1932), Introductory statement by members of the "Administration" and statement by John J. Bennett, State Attorney General. For a general survey of the work of the TERA, see *Five Million People – One Billion Dollars: Final Report of the TERA* (Albany, 1937).

[15] FDR Library, Roosevelt Papers, Governor's Correspondence (Emergency Relief File), Hopkins to FDR, January 11, 1932.

A meeting of social and welfare administrators was called to receive a briefing on the new policy. Governor Roosevelt explained that the act had two objectives: to go beyond the precept that no one should starve to ensure that no one became destitute, and to "avoid the mistakes that have been made in some other nations – such as the British dole." This signaled a break with the old idea that relief need only be given at a subsistence level, and a determination to base relief upon proven need and avoid the idea of a right to a fixed amount of public assistance. Roosevelt concluded his short address by saying that "if we do not make good in solving this temporary problem, then we must admit that there is something wrong with our government." Strauss told the assembled social workers that although the provision of relief for those in need or unemployed was primarily a local government obligation, the TERA expected them to keep a close watch on what was being done locally and to take action or make recommendations when necessary.[16]

Roosevelt included in his address one point that was not welcomed by social workers and would cause the TERA a good deal of embarrassment. He said that although money must go where it was needed, there was an obligation on communities that did not require aid not to ask for it. This placed the onus for deciding what level of relief should be given precisely where social workers believed that it should not lie – with the local officials – and would give them an excuse to hold relief at the minimum level and discourage applications. To counteract these impressions, Strauss found it necessary to draft a proclamation, which Roosevelt then issued, that stressed the need to bring relief to those who needed it but were reluctant to apply. Relief was "in no sense charity," because the unemployed received no more than their due "as taxpayers of the State." "Society," said the proclamation, "will have failed in its obligations if it allows them to suffer through no fault of their own." To an outside observer, it must have seemed that the line distinguishing the TERA policy from a dole was being so finely drawn as to be almost invisible.[17]

The Wicks Act required the TERA to reimburse the localities for 40 percent of their home relief costs, but TERA was allowed to define the conditions that must be satisfied before payment was made, and a

[16] Remarks to social workers by Roosevelt and Strauss in N.Y. St. A., Governor's Correspondence (Emergency Relief File), October 29, 1931.
[17] Ibid. (and Strauss to FDR, n.d. [early 1932]).

clause (intended to limit its discretionary power) became a means of enforcing uniform standards. Localities could not claim for obligations already imposed on them by law (notably old-age assistance and mothers' aid) or for distress not caused by unemployment. Genuine efforts must have been made to utilize local resources. The TERA would repay only expenses incurred for food, shelter, clothing, fuel, light, heat, medicine, and medical attendance, but the restriction implied that a relief client was entitled to these items. All cases must be investigated with home visits, interviews with recent employers, and an assessment of what relatives could do to help. Significantly, investigation was to include individuals who were believed to be in need but had not applied for relief. Again, in laying down the conditions that would qualify for reimbursement, the TERA was actually placing new obligations on local officials. They were also required to employ sufficient staff for relief administration and at least one trained social worker for every hundred cases. Finally, there must be no discrimination on grounds of race, religion, or political affiliation.[18]

The TERA could exhort and sometimes insist, but there were limits to what could be done, especially when the words "temporary" and "emergency" in its title indicated a short life. With conditions as they were in the fall of 1931, the immediate problem was to prevent further deterioration. Douglas P. Falconer, an Associate Director of the TERA, described the facts that had to be faced when the new agency commenced operation:

Public Welfare administration in the State had been almost entirely a local concern until the adoption of the Wicks Act. While there are creditable exceptions, on the whole the administration has been very poor; relief has been inadequate, offices poorly equipped and poorly run, and the general public almost entirely uninformed and indifferent.

The two years preceding the passage of the act had brought "almost complete disorganization and collapse" in many communities. Under these circumstances, it was difficult to refuse repayment when the money had been honestly spent, even though the conditions had not

[18] TERA, *Unemployment Relief Laws of New York; Rules Concerning Home Relief* and *Rules Governing Work Relief* (Albany, November 1931). Some local units were slow in taking the steps necessary to satisfy TERA requirements. On November 7, 1931, Strauss told Roosevelt that thirty-seven counties and seven cities had not yet done so, and that they included the city of Lackawanna, which had made a special plea for aid to the Governor (N.Y. St. A., Governor's Correspondence, Emergency Relief File).

been met and local officials were suspected of incompetence. In home relief the standards set by the TERA were benchmarks to measure progress rather than directives for the immediate transformation of local administration.[19]

When dealing with unsatisfactory local authorities, the TERA faced a dilemma that would become familiar in all relief programs: If money was cut off for failure to give adequate relief to the unemployed, the first to suffer would be the unemployed themselves. When townships failed to employ trained staff and claimed that they could not afford to do so, the TERA might have to accept inefficiency or foot the bill itself. In January 1932 Roosevelt asked for information that would enable him to answer complaints that excessive salaries were being paid by the TERA to local superintendents of welfare or relief. The reply from the TERA was that it had been impossible to tackle chaotic conditions without trained staff paid salaries commensurate with their responsibilities. Most trained men had been paid from local funds, and the cost had been reduced by using volunteers or people on loan from business; but in a few instances the TERA had come to the aid of poor townships and paid the salaries.[20]

The TERA had much tighter control over work relief. Its authority was unconditional; all counties and cities had to appoint Emergency Work Bureaus, which then came under direct TERA control. Projects submitted by the bureaus had to be approved and must not include work covered by normal appropriations; wages must be paid in cash or by check at the prevailing rates; each application must be investigated and priority given according to need.

It was the common experience of all relief agencies that their efforts appeared to lengthen the relief rolls. Unsuspected distress was revealed when the TERA insisted that investigation should include people in need who had not sought assistance. Urban destitution had been widely discussed, but extreme poverty in rural districts came to light as soon as it became known that state money was available. In addition, the economic climate worsened, more people ran out of savings,

[19] Douglas P. Falconer (associate director, TERA) to Strauss, January 28, 1932 (N.Y. St. A., Governor's Emergency Relief File).

[20] Ibid. The occasion for the letter was a memo from Roosevelt to Strauss requesting information about the employment of 100 supervisors at $2,000 each and of many assistant directors and superintendents of relief at "very high pay for local work of the usual kind."

and unemployment climbed the social ladder to include more skilled and professional men.

Past failures and present deficiencies were brought together in a gloomy report presented by Strauss to the legislature after the TERA had been in operation for less than six months:

Conditions throughout the State are, so far as one can judge from available reports, deplorable despite the fact that nearly ten percent of the State's population are beneficiaries under the Wicks Act. Such aid as has been given through home and work relief appears to be either inadequate or, at best, minimal.

He said that despite efforts to improve home relief, it was still administered incompetently in many communities by welfare commissioners who might be elected or appointed but were always untrained and often inexperienced. Work relief was handled a little better because the local committees were usually "composed of persons of superior intelligence and higher caliber."[21]

The TERA had to spend a great deal of time dealing with abuses of power by local authorities. One such case (with political repercussions that brought it to Roosevelt's attention) was in Rockland County. The county board of supervisors had set up a work relief bureau, appointed a prominent local man, Edward Wells, to head it, and appropriated $100,000. The TERA responded by making a grant of $30,000 to pay wages on work projects. At this stage, local political rivalries set the supervisors against the bureau; they decided to use the TERA money for general purposes, and the county treasurer refused to accept drafts to pay relief wages. Wells applied to the courts for a writ mandamus to compel the treasurer to release the money, and the supervisors responded by dismissing him. Strauss refused to recognize the legality of their action, continued to deal directly with Wells, and sent a sharp reminder that the work bureau was set up to relieve unemployment, not to become "a football in local politics." Trivial in itself, the incident showed that incompetence and outdated methods were not the only obstacles to conscientious relief administration.[22]

In his annual message for 1932, Roosevelt drew attention to inefficiency in local governments. He said that many of them had been

---

[21] *New York Legislative Documents,* 1932, No 97., 3–4; also an advance copy in N.Y. St. A., Governor's Correspondence (Emergency Relief File), February 23, 1932.
[22] N.Y. St. A., Governor's Correspondence (Emergency Relief File), July 7, 1932.

"guilty of great waste, of the duplication of unnecessary improvements, and of thoroughly unbusinesslike practices." The legislature did not follow the Governor's recommendation that a full-scale inquiry into local government be launched, and Roosevelt set up his own commission to do the job.[23]

Meanwhile the powers of the TERA had to be strengthened, and Philip Wickser drafted a number of amendments for incorporation into the act extending its life: The distinction between home and work relief should be less rigid; the TERA should have power to give both without waiting for local requests; the State should have its own work projects, as well as those initiated locally; and rather than wait for adoption by the counties, the TERA should have immediate power to apply the act unless a county was prepared, by a recorded vote, to refuse all state aid. More control from the center should not mean less local effort, and Wickser suggested that local taxpayers should be assured that they would get their fair share of state funds, provided that they played their part.[24]

With the extension of the TERA, Strauss thought that he could no longer give enough time to it and was replaced as chairman by Harry Hopkins. His success in office would make him an obvious choice when the future President looked for a man to head the federal program, thus establishing a direct link between what had been done in New York and what would be done in the national agency. Upon both Hopkins would impress the indelible stamp of professional social work in which he had made his whole career.

The TERA had set about its task with missionary zeal. As Executive Secretary and then as Chairman, Hopkins decided that the work was not complete when funds had been allocated. Complete reform of the whole public welfare system was the ultimate goal; the relief of distress caused by unemployment the opening campaign. Although some believed that the TERA was a temporary shelter against storms of exceptional severity, insiders saw it as the beginning of a movement that should not be halted. Central to the new attitude was a conviction that the work must be done by public agencies and not left to voluntary

---

[23] *New York Times,* January 2, 1931.
[24] N.Y. St. A., Governor's Correspondence (Emergency Relief File). Among other things, he proposed that one-third of the appropriation go to localities on a population basis, one-third as a ratio of local relief expenditure, and one-third for statewide work projects.

efforts. Public welfare, which had been the poor relation of social work, took the lead in official thinking, and as private funds ran out, many who been active in private charitable work also concluded that effective relief must be public relief.

One New Yorker with much experience in private philanthropic administration made this plain to the National Conference of Social Work in 1932. Henry L. Lurie, executive director of the New York Jewish Charities, declared that the "focal center" of social work was shifting to public welfare, and it had been the fatal error of the POUR to concentrate on private philanthropy when 60 percent of relief was already in the hands of local governments. Even if private campaigns had reached their targets, they would still have left public welfare to carry the major part of the burden. As the depression lengthened, governments were being urged to accept commitments that went far beyond the range of private philanthropy, and the future would lie with public agencies. Social work was winning recognition as a "well-defined activity of government" and must become "largely a government function."[25]

Lurie's next point was that because government was necessarily involved, voters must be educated to accept and pay for "new and desirable forms of public responsibility for dependent families." It would not be enough to set up new agencies without fundamental changes in social philosophy.

Nothing short of a new approach to the whole problem of poverty and the formulation of a modern and comprehensive public program will be sufficient to cope with the overwhelming problems into which our functions and responsibilities are leading us.

In this spirit, the leaders of social work in New York and elsewhere had next to ask themselves whether the federal government was not the only authority capable of devising such a program and providing the necessary leadership for a radical change in public attitudes.

Even without philosophic reflection on social responsibility, events were driving practical men to similar conclusions. Tighter control by the TERA, with greater and better-judged efforts by local authorities, had brought about notable improvements in relief administration and given hope to thousands of families in distress; but in spite of these

[25] Henry L. Lurie, "Developments in the Public Welfare program," *NCSW, 1932,* 253–65.

successes there remained the problem of financing relief in densely populated areas. In July 1932 the TERA told the Governor that available funds would not be enough to meet even the statutory reimbursement of 40 percent of home relief costs; it also presented a gloomy forecast of rising unemployment, acute distress, depleted private funds, shortfalls in local tax revenue, and relief standards below the desirable level. By October it was admitting that in New York City and many upstate districts "limited funds have made it impossible to assist all the families known to require aid, or to give each family the amount needed," and that in many parts of the state "adequate or satisfactory Home Relief or Work Relief is not being given, and better results are impossible with present funds." The New York TERA could hardly have been more intelligently and forcefully led; if it failed, who could succeed?

More constructive lessons could be learned. The creation of the TERA was an admission that some social problems could not be solved by local responsibility. Its refusal to make even statutory reimbursements unconditional had shown how local welfare administration might be modernized by pressure from above. The allocation of some funds at the discretion of the TERA had enabled it to give aid where it was most needed, and implied the right to collect information both by formal reports from the localities and by informal assessments from its own field representatives. Without achieving complete success, the TERA had tried to define responsibilities and establish a chain of command so that they could not be evaded. It had proved that even if government could not yet do everything that was needed, it was far ahead of the voluntary organizations.

Innovation in New York appeared the more striking when it was set beside the tale of opportunities missed in the neighboring state of New Jersey. The poor law had been revised in 1924, but local officials had been left free to choose their own methods. Some adopted the most modern approach to public assistance, others retained nineteenth-century principles unchanged. An attempt to make overseers of the poor qualify for office by passing an examination had been watered down to a requirement that they must be literate and understand the poor laws to the satisfaction of the local governing body.

However, the impetus for reform was still alive, and the strain that the depression placed on local government provided an opportunity for completing the work begun in 1924. In 1931 a plan was presented for centralizing administration in the counties and for the State to pay a proportion of relief expenditure (three-quarters for the temporarily unemployed, half for dependent children, and one-quarter plus administrative costs for old-age assistance). The State would become wholly responsible for the relief of persons without settlement.[26]

Centralization entailed abolishing the ancient office of overseer of the poor, eliminating or consolidating the smaller local units, and giving county officials the right to direct relief administration. It was also a fair guess that the financial responsibilities proposed for the State would soon be followed by state regulation. These proposals encountered a determined defense of the existing system in the name of local responsibility. Though it was argued that many local units were too small and poor to afford professional services, the opposition was able to cripple the proposal by an astute amendment requiring local units to refund to the county the whole cost of temporary relief. Ostensibly designed to prevent local governments from dodging their obligations, the effect of the change was to put the counties in charge of relief operations without contributing to their cost. This divorce of executive from fiscal responsibility damned the measure. In popular referenda all but two counties voted it down, and of the two, only one put it into effect.

Victory had been won in the name of local responsibility but the local units were soon in deep financial difficulties, and by the late summer of 1931 many were fast running out of money. A report on the situation, ordered by Governor Morgan F. Larson, found (as might have been expected) that needs were greatest where resources were weakest, and that everywhere financial stringency made it impossible to plan systematically for relief. Larson called a conference of prominent citizens to discuss the situation and in October issued an executive order creating the New Jersey Emergency Relief Administration (NJERA). This was subsequently ratified by the legislature, with an appropriation of $10,000,000.

The first intention was to limit the NJERA to financial administra-

---

[26] For a comprehensive account, see Douglas H. McNeil, *Seven Years of Unemployment Relief in New Jersey: A Report Prepared for the Committee on Social Security* (Washington, D.C., 1938). The history of emergency relief was also summarized in *Emergency Relief in New Jersey: Final Report . . . of the Emergency Relief Administration* (Trenton, N.J., 1936).

tion, but when some local units raised no funds for relief, the state agency had no option but to take complete control. Other hard-pressed units petitioned the State to take similar action, and by June 1932 the NJERA was administering relief directly in 128 localities. Other units continued to raise their own funds and retain administrative responsibility; but frequently their revenue proved to be insufficient to satisfy needs, and application for assistance had to be made to the State. The NJERA then claimed the right to decide how the money should be spent. Thus the State moved slowly and ungracefully toward centralization, but there remained ample opportunity for friction and for perpetuating the diversity in standards and methods that had long been the bane of New Jersey's relief administration.

In Pennsylvania the depression brought on a clash of principles and personalities that nullified much well-intentioned effort and produced a result or which all should have been and many were ashamed. Pennsylvania had inherited a system of local government that found few defenders except among the officeholders and politicians dependent on patronage. In 1925 a survey sponsored by the American Philosophical Society of Philadelphia reported that there were too many elective offices filled by party nominees without qualifications for the job, that county administration was incredibly confused, and that townships were "antiquated in methods, equipment, and treatment of personnel." Some townships were so small and poor that they could not afford typewriters, adding machines, or even telephones. Although acknowledging the theoretical merits of local self-government, the report found evidence of few in Pennsylvania. This was not merely academic fault finding. The report declared that failure to provide "the standards of service which our people have come to expect" threatened the survival of the system.[27]

When government was weak, public welfare was certain to be chaotic if not callous. At no point in the state administration was welfare considered as a whole, and departments dealt separately with various matters coming within their sphere. Locally, relief was the responsibility of poor districts, which were separate from the other local government units and unsupervised. Local welfare and health agencies often ignored directives from the state departments to which they were

---

[27] *Transactions of the American Philosophical Society,* New Series XXV (1935); *Report of the Pennsylvania Local Government Survey,* 7, 163.

nominally responsible, and there was little cooperation between them. In Allegheny County the responsibility for public health was divided between county commissioners, the city of Pittsburgh, and more than one hundred local units, and State Board of Health did little more than issue advice, which was seldom followed. General relief in the Pittsburgh metropolitan region was administered without coordination by the city and by poor districts in five counties.[28]

During the depression the failure of poor relief became a public scandal, and in December 1933 a grand jury investigated and condemned its administration in the state. It found 424 poor districts, each with its own board, and 920 directors or overseers of the poor, who often failed to consult their boards or each other.

The general pattern of poor relief . . . is administration by elective boards and salaried directors. Since technicians rarely find their way into public office through popular election, it is not surprising that a negligible number of poor directors have had any technical training or preparation for poor relief administration. While the poor boards have the power to employ trained relief workers, almost none of them avail themselves of this provision of the law, and even when "investigators" are employed they may have no perceptible qualification for the skilled administration of public relief.

Written in the third year of the depression, these words reveal the enormous difficulties faced by Pennsylvanians who sought to relieve the distress caused by economic failure.[29]

The Governor who faced these difficulties, from his inauguration early in 1931, was Gifford Pinchot. With a reputation made famous in Progressive annals, he had been nominated as a Republican against opposition from the state party leaders and had won the election at a time when the tide elsewhere flowed strongly for the Democrats. Bitterly opposed to party machines, suspicious of big business but not conspicuously friendly to organized labor, scrupulously honest, somewhat self-righteous, and a moralist in politics, Pinchot was not a man to be deterred by opposition or to accept equivocation and delay.

Pinchot's approach to the problems of depression was distinguished by imagination, a willingness to experiment, and determination to get

[28] Philip Klein and collaborators, *A Social Study of Pittsburgh* (sponsored by the Citizens' Committee for the Social Study of Pittsburgh and Allegheny County) (New York, 1938), 386.
[29] Copy in Library of Congress, Gifford Pinchot Papers (cited hereafter as LC Pinchot).

relief to the people who needed it; but his political achievements were meager. He was a Governor without a party, in constant dispute with Republican legislative leaders, unwilling to ally with the Democrats, and lacking the magic touch that might have rallied opinion behind his policies. Among those who soon made their opposition clear were the Republican leaders in Philadelphia, a large majority of business-men, and local politicians who lobbied at Harrisburg to prevent any weakening of their control over relief.[30]

Pinchot was also persona non grata with the Hoover administration. In the fall of 1930 he had written to the President, calling for a special session of Congress to consider remedies for distress; in office he was an outspoken advocate of federal relief, and in a circular letter to other governors he unsuccessfully solicited support for it. His commitment to state and federal relief programs did not endear him to the POUR, which was busy collecting evidence that local government plus private charity could weather the crisis.

In his own state, Pinchot took the initiative. While still a candidate, he had appointed his own committee on unemployment, and con-verted it into an official body after his inauguration. It did not report until August 1931, but in the meantime he called the legislature into special session to consider the extent of distress in the state and take appropriate steps to remedy it. He recommended an appropriation for relief, an increase in taxes to pay for it, and centralized administration under the Department of Public Welfare or a new state agency; but the legislature was not going to be hurried, and set up its own committee to collect evidence.

The legislative committee received a report from Dr. Theodore Appel, State Secretary for Health, which dealt with health in the state but was indirectly a severe indictment of local relief administration. Appel found conditions good in fifteen counties with a total population of 745,000, but not more than fair in twenty-seven with a total of 1,413,000. In the more populous counties, conditions were deplorable,

---

[30] The history of the depression in Pennsylvania is covered in Thomas Goode and John F. Bauman, eds., *People, Poverty, and Policies* (Lewisburg, Pa., 1981), especially David D. Housley, "The Rural Dimension," which contains material not otherwise easily available; and Richard C. Keller, "Pennsylvania's Little New Deal" in John Braeman, Robert H. Bremner, and David Brody, eds., *The New Deal*, Vol. 2 (Columbus, Ohio 1975), 54–76. A contemporary account is Arthur Dunham, "Pennsylvania and Unem-ployment Relief," *Social Service Review* 8 (1934), 245–88.

with great distress in fourteen, poor welfare organizations, little money for relief, and much evidence of malnutrition. In ten counties with a total population of 1,250,000 there was great privation, few remaining resources for relief, and serious undernourishment. Outside major cities, private charities were weak and county funds completely inadequate.[31]

The committee heard even more depressing evidence from Mrs. Alice Liveright, whom Pinchot had appointed Commissioner of Public Welfare. She reckoned that relief was well organized in only nine counties and that two of them were overwhelmed with applications. In seven counties, relief was satisfactory in the cities but poor in rural districts. Local inefficiency had made it impossible to obtain information in thirty counties, but independent evidence indicated that conditions were very bad in nineteen of them. In the state as a whole, one out of every four able-bodied workers was unemployed and the level of relief had fallen. In twenty-eight counties the number on relief had doubled since 1929, but relief expenditure had increased by only 36 percent.[32]

The committee also heard from Thomas Kennedy of the United Mineworkers who said that the situation in five coal-mining counties was so bad that even a massive appropriation for relief would not bring a remedy and that the legislature ought to apply for federal assistance. The committee hoped to learn that private charity could meet the painful gaps revealed in public relief; but Jacob Billikopf, long prominent in Philadelphia's charitable activities, said that unprecedented efforts in fund raising had led to the unequivocal conclusion that private philanthropy was "not capable of coping with the vast tragedies of this situation."[33]

There was indeed evidence that private efforts were often frustrated by uncooperative local governments. Pierce Williams, sent to observe

---

[31] LC Pinchot, Container 2531 (Health), Appel to Pinchot, August 24, 1931.

[32] *A Public Hearing on Statewide Unemployment Relief before Members of the General Assembly, November 24, 1931* (Harrisburg, 1931), 26ff. Mrs. Liveright's evidence and the criticisms she made in her *Biennial Report of the Department of Public Welfare* for 1932 did not endear her to some legislators, who retaliated by blocking confirmation of her appointment by the state senate at two regular and two special sessions. It was not until December 1933 that she was confirmed, and then only because her name slipped through in a long list of unopposed minor appointments.

[33] Ibid., 34, 45.

conditions on behalf of the POUR, made a detailed report on events in Allegheny County. Prominent local people had taken the lead in forming the Allegheny Emergency Association (AEA) to pay the wages for public work if local communities provided supervision and materials, but many local authorities interpreted the offer as a way to cut their own expenditure. In Pittsburgh all individuals on city relief had been transferred to the payroll of the AEA, which was then forced to use part of its funds for general relief because the city had stopped payments. The AEA claimed to have given direct relief to 4,000 families between February and August 1931, paid wages for 6,737 men on public works, and promoted many work projects that would not otherwise have been undertaken; but in August it ran out of funds and suspended its projects. It promised to make even greater efforts in a new fund-raising campaign, but even if it reached its target, it would do no more than employ 15,000 men three days a week for sixteen weeks at $3.00 a day, and would have to limit its efforts to people already on relief so that those who had recently run out of savings would get nothing.[34]

Pierce Williams believed that the whole effort had been misdirected. A realistic estimate of what had been achieved was that city and county authorities had economized at the expense of private contributors by spending fifty cents where they should have spent a dollar. He said that the sequence of operations should have been to ask the county and the cities to commit all they could to planned programs of public works, earmark private funds for general relief, and pay for work projects only when this need had been met – but never for work already undertaken by the local authorities.[35]

Neither pressure from the Governor nor evidence of muddle and distress persuaded the legislature to accelerate their deliberations. The final outcome was known as the Talbot Act and fell far short of what Pinchot had recommended. It appropriated money for relief but imposed no new taxes, so that the choice lay between borrowing, cutting into reserves, and economizing on other expenditure, and it made the Department of Public Welfare responsible for distributing the money, but without power to regulate its use. Poor directors and overseers, without supervision from the state or county relief agencies,

---

[34] NA RG 78 (POUR files), Williams to Croxton, November 9, 1931.
[35] Ibid.

would continue to do as they wished. Pinchot sent a stinging message to explain why he had allowed the bill to become law without his signature:

The bill . . . is about the worst and most slipshod measure I have ever had to handle. . . . It was conceived in politics and born in hatred, and the last thing its sponsors were concerned about was relief of the unemployed.

He did not veto the bill because opposition to increased taxes, combined with defense of local autonomy, made a better law impossible, and the Talbot Act would at least get some relief to the unemployed. Even then there was further delay because the act was challenged in the courts, and did not become effective until it was upheld by the Pennsylvania Supreme Court in April 1932.

In operation the Talbot Act fulfilled Pinchot's worst expectations. The Department of Public Welfare was told of relief refused because of personal animosity, grocery orders drawn only on stores where the poor director had a financial stake, relief withheld until useless and humiliating tasks had been performed, and relief denied to men who refused to hand in their car license plates. Some recipients had been forced to sign away their right to compensation for injury and others forced to post bonds to repay relief money in spite of a ruling by the state Attorney General that "the Talbot Act . . . did not make an appropriation to the poor boards to enable them to engage in the business of lending money."

Mrs. Liveright, whose business it was to evaluate this evidence, concluded that in most counties poor relief was administered with "inadequate knowledge and understanding of the conditions in families of the unemployed." Even where the poor boards were honest and well-meaning, unnecessary inconvenience was caused by cumbersome administration:

In several counties people had to walk many miles to make application, had to wait in crowded rooms with other discouraged people, and to return again and again to beg for help. The lack of intelligent community organization added great hardship to the lives of self-respecting people who in the past made a contribution to the wealth of Pennsylvania.

In all this there was nothing new. The poor boards simply continued to operate in their accustomed ways without recognizing that mass unemployment, unprecedented distress, and state aid made any difference.[36]

Gifford Pinchot had long been convinced that federal aid must be the solution, and experience in the state forced others to draw the same conclusion. Prominent among the converts was Jacob Billikopf, who delivered a paper to the National Conference of Social Work in 1931 on "What have we learned about unemployment?" He argued that the exhaustion of private funds, the impossibility of restoring them by private contributions, and the paralysis of local government made state action imperative, and if states could not do enough, the federal government must intervene. He sent a copy of his speech to Walter Gifford, who was a personal friend, asking him to consider the argument carefully as a counter to continued reliance on voluntary effort. He also enclosed a copy of a letter to Silas Strawn, president of the United States Chamber of Commerce, explaining that he had refused to join a delegation to the White House, organized by John Dewey, to press for federal action, because the time was not yet ripe; but

as the days go by, it is becoming increasingly evident that, whatever our conception of the functions of the States be, when people are hungry, when men and women are being evicted from their homes, lofty definitions become meaningless and deluding.

The writing on the wall was clear and read "Federal relief if depression continued."[37]

Two lesser but important conclusions were drawn by some Pennsylvanian welfare administrators: Cash payments were better than grocery orders, and work relief was often an expensive way of doing very little. In Philadelhpia cash relief became normal. As for work relief, Sherman C. Kingsley, a welfare administrator in Philadelphia, said that the city had spent nearly one and a quarter million dollars on work projects in 1931 (of which between 7 and 10 percent went for overhead) to provide unemployed men with three days work a week on projects of doubtful value.

---

[36] For a review and assessment of relief legislation in Pennsylvania, see "Unemployment Relief in Pennsylvania, September 1931–December 1935," in *Third Annual Report of the Executive Director, State Emergency Relief Board* (Harrisburg, 1936). Of the first Talbot Act, the report noted (p. 4) that it specifically rejected a plan "of permanently relieving the localities of a responsibility which would be met far more adequately, humanely, and uniformly by state measures. . . . Nowhere was a consistent public relief policy apparent."

[37] Copy in NA RG 78 Box 190.

Two midwestern states were crucial in the development of relief policy. In Illinois Chicago and in Michigan Detroit were great metropolitan centers with desperate social problems resulting from the depression and depended on state governments dominated by rural legislators. In both states, there was desperate poverty: in coal towns in Illinois, steel towns in Michigan, and, in both, rural regions left behind by progress in the 1920s. In southern Illinois there were slow-moving agricultural districts depressed by a fall in demand for their produce, and in northern Michigan, forest areas had been abandoned by the once dominant timber companies. Between them the two states contained most varieties of destitution spawned by the depression, though it was the plight of the great metropolitan centers that attracted most attention.

The reputation of the Illinois Department of Public Welfare might have given the State a leading place in the development of relief services. Modesty had never been the most evident of the department's virtues, and in 1922 its report declared that "it is generally conceded, and it is true, that Illinois is leading all other states of the Union in the management of its charitable institutions." Since its earliest days the Board of State Charities, parent of the department, had rejected the idea that pauperism was caused exclusively by personal failings and had pressed for an attack on poverty on a wide front. The 1922 report explained the principles that had since guided the department:

Social wrongs and evil environment are known to be among the causes contributing to delinquency and the attending crime. It is therefore . . . a duty of the department, representing the people of the state, to make extended research into these causes, and having ascertained them to advise, and to direct, through local community organizations, preventive measures.[38]

In 1928, in a retrospective view of earlier reports, the department hailed them as an "epic portion of the most remarkable movement in the world today," and though the term "public welfare" was of recent origin, "the very course of civilization could be traced through the ages by the development in governmental care for those citizens who are no longer able to care for themselves." It said that the agencies performing this task were as essential to modern society as public schools, and through them society repaid a debt to inmates of institutions who were there "solely because, somewhere along the line, civilization

[38] Illinois Department of Public Welfare, *Fifth Annual Report,* 84–9.

failed in her duty towards herself." All honor was due to private charities, which did work of "untold benefit to humanity" but they could never, "in the nature of things, assume the gigantic proportions of the work done by State and Nation."[39]

The majority of the citizens of Illinois may have been unaware of the views expressed by their Department of Public Welfare, and many would have repudiated its interventionist philosophy if they had understood its implications; but the well-organized, trained, and confident social administrators and workers gathered in the Department of Public Welfare formed an asset that ought to have been exploited as the state plunged into depression. As well as professional experience, the department's social philosophy, expressed in its reports, pointed the way to an early and comprehensive attack on the distress caused by unemployment; but the traditional separation between indoor and outdoor relief penned this expertise behind conventional barriers. State public welfare had never extended to outdoor relief, never provided for transients, and always limited its formal responsibility to institutional care. The relief of able-bodied but indigent persons had always been a local responsibility, and both the official and popular instinct was to keep it there. Thus Illinois is a leading example of failure to use social work expertise at the time when it was most needed.

Local arrangements for welfare were less impressive than for the state institutions. In some counties there were limited funds for the relief of the blind and dependent children, and in a few, relief administration had been centralized; but standards varied greatly, and many poorer counties had successfully resisted the humanitarian enthusiasm of the Department of Public Welfare. Despite a half century of enlightened effort, backed by the authority of the State, some county institutions remained in a primitive condition. In 1930 one of the department's inspectors reported that a poor farm was a disgrace to its county: It had worn out bedding, impure water, poor food and little of

---

[39] Ibid., *Eleventh Annual Report*, 7–8. For a general survey and assessment of relief measures, see David J. Mawer, "Unemployment in Illinois during the Great Depression," in Donald F. Tingley, ed., *Essays in Illinois History* (Carbondale, Ill., 1968), 120–32. Contemporary accounts are Frank Z. Glick, "The Illinois Emergency Relief Commission," *Social Service Review* 7 (1933), 23–48, and Wilfred S. Reynolds, "Organizing Government Agencies for Unemployment Relief," ibid., 365–74 (from Proceedings of the American Public Welfare Association).

it, no modern plumbing, and useless fire extinguishers. When inmates died, they were buried on the grounds in unmarked graves, which "might be expected in an institution where so little respect is shown for the living." It need hardly be added that counties maintaining such low standards of institutional care failed when confronted with mass unemployment. The few counties where relief had been centralized were located mainly in the more prosperous parts of the state: in the remainder, all responsibility for outdoor relief fell upon the townships.[40]

The delay in introducing centralized agencies to deal with unemployment was inexcusable in the light of long experience with irremediable poverty in the mining communities. In the majority of cases, absentee mine owners had drawn off profits and paid taxes on their real estate but not on their incomes. The miners had their benefit funds, the unions helped the sick and injured, and merchants helped by extending credit in hard times, but voluntary effort and local taxes were manifestly insufficient to meet the needs of communities in which so many were out of work or earned too little to support their families. Yet successive administrations and legislative sessions had failed to remedy (or in many cases to consider) this endemic poverty.

Though coal communities presented the most hopeless picture of chronic poverty, Chicago attracted most attention in the worsening economic climate. About half the population of the state lived in the city or in its suburbs, satellite cities, and industrial districts. Outside the city limits, Cook county was the major administrative unit, with a larger population and budget than many states. Next to New York, Chicago was the most cosmopolitan city in the United States, and in addition to very large numbers of Irish, Italians, Poles, and other East Europeans, it had received a steady influx of black and white migrants from the South. Its crime record had won international notoriety, and the frequency of violence in its streets was a portent of serious disorders if the volatile and alienated masses suffered serious deprivation. Throughout the depression, this danger was never far from the minds of state and city authorities and served as a counterweight to the inevitable opposition to financial aid for Chicago in the rural counties.

---

[40] Sophonisba P. Breckinridge, *The Illinois Poor Law and Its Administration* (Chicago; 1939) 35–49.

In the state as a whole, the fragmentation of responsibility complicated moves to counter depression. Of the 102 counties (other than Cook County) 86 were divided into 1,463 townships; the other counties were organized on the southern plan, without townships but with county governments and subordinate districts. There were also 263 cities and 857 incorporated villages and towns, all with their own elected governments. A professional survey of local government encountered an "impenetrable maze" when trying to analyze local expenditure. Officially recorded information was "fragmentary and misleading," and it was impossible to estimate how much went unrecorded. Though the county was supposed to be a unit of government, it was no more than "a territorial subdivision in which an aggregation of independent officers and agencies have jurisdiction." Township government had remained unchanged since territorial days. Overseers of the poor were appointed by the town officers, but once in office, they were under no regular supervision.[41]

In October 1930, Governor Louis Emmerson set up an Unemployment and Relief Commission, which quickly found itself enmeshed in the tangle of local responsibility. A state official was assigned to each county to help with its inquiries, but it proved to be almost impossible to obtain trustworthy information about local conditions. Detailed investigation was largely confined to Cook County, but the paucity of data did not deter the commission from bringing in the optimistic report that, with the exception of Cook County and possibly some coal-mining communities, local authorities could carry their own relief burden. A later investigation revealed the hollowness of this conclusion. During 1930 the number of families on relief in Illinois increased from 12,220 to 47,300; by the end of 1931 it was 145,000, with the trend still upward. Cook County did indeed account for over half the total, but there was a formidable increase in other parts of the state.[42]

By 1931 conditions in many coal-mining communities were desperate. County funds were fully committed to institutional care and mothers' aid, local taxes were unable to meet the cost of unemployment relief, and fund-raising campaigns sponsored by churches and unions did little more than scratch the surface. An extreme but not a typical

[41] Griffenhagen and Associates, *Local Government in Illinois* (Chicago, 1928), passim.
[42] NA RG 78, Box 80, Secretary, Governor's Commission on Unemployment and Relief, to Porter R. Lee (POUR), January 6, 1931. The final report of the committee is in ibid., March 31, 1931.

example was recorded in one city where the local campaign raised less than one-quarter of its target, and all that could be provided was 20 cents a week for families in dire need. In many smaller communities, where almost everyone was poor, it was hardly worthwhile to attempt to raise funds. By 1931 the distress had spread from coal-mining to many other districts, and more counties felt obliged to contribute to general relief in the hardest-hit communities.[43]

The first attempt by the legislature to tackle the problem made the confusion worse. Ostensibly to avoid constitutional restraints on county taxation, a measure known as the Finn Act ended county contributions to general relief. The acid comment of a later official report was that "insofar as it was the purpose of the 'Finn' bill to enable rural townships to avoid assuming the burden of supporting the poor concentrated in urban townships, that bill was a successful piece of legislation." It also ensured that the heaviest burdens would fall upon the townships with the weakest resources.[44]

The Finn Act was passed too late in the year for annual town meetings to approve new taxes, and for six months the only way to find money for relief was by raiding other funds. Not until December 1931 did the legislature authorize special town meetings to deal with the situation; but even when townships agreed to raise more money for relief, the net effect of the Finn Act was to reduce the available resources at the time when they were most needed. To make the situation more confusing, some counties refused to adopt the Finn Act and continued to administer relief centrally, and in most counties newly organized relief committees tried to coordinate public and private efforts without executive powers or money to spend.[45]

The best that the Unemployment and Relief Commission could do was to compile a manual for the use of these local committees. It recommended that money derived from local taxes be used primarily for the aged and children in need, and for the relief of distress caused by unemployment only if there were unexpended balances. Private donations must make good the shortfall. The commission suggested a scale of contributions – with $500 as the minimum to be expected from wealthy individuals – but did not encourage fund-raising events or

[43] Malcolm Brown and John N. Webb, *Seven Stranded Coal Towns* (Washington, D.C., 1941), 124–6.
[44] Arthur P. Miles, *Federal Aid and Public Assistance in Illinois* (Chicago, 1941), 10–11.
[45] NA RG 78, Box 80, Rowland Haynes to Wayne Rummer, September 1, 1931.

sales of work, which led people to think that they had done their bit by making minor purchases. All this was of little help to communities where no one had any money and organizers of voluntary efforts had already admitted defeat. Whatever the commission might recommend, it was mandatory for local governments to relieve resident paupers (including the destitute unemployed). They could not transfer statutory duty to voluntary agencies, and the only way to find the money was by borrowing in anticipation of future taxes, thus piling up more trouble for the future.[46]

The commission proceeded nevertheless on lines suggested by the President's Organization for Unemployment Relief, winning praise for its efforts. In November 1931 it assured Walter Gifford that there were no Illinois counties without relief organizations, and that although some special measures would be necessary in Cook County, all of the others would meet their obligations during the coming winter. Conditions were severe in four counties, but the commission claimed that their needs would be met by a levy of one day's pay on state employees.[47]

The men and women with actual experience of relief were telling a very different story. In October 1931 the Illinois Conference on Public Welfare, attended mainly by social workers and administrators, passed a resolution calling for "federal funds to aid all those communities unable to relieve the human suffering resulting from the present crisis," and this call was endorsed by the State Board of Welfare Commissioners. The levy on state employees was dismissed as a feeble gesture, and in the event it raised no more than $183,000 for the whole state.[48]

When the legislature met on January 5, the Chicago and Cook County representatives pressed for action; but after spending time on

[46] Copy in NA RG 78 (POUR files). Among other pieces of advice, the manual said that "as a general rule it is undesirable [for private charities] to supply food and other supplies to needy families" in their homes, though it might be done in a few instances when a family was "very sensitive and unwilling to become known as relief families." In other words, home relief might be given to "respectable" families who had never been on relief; Rowland Haynes (POUR field representative) to Wayne Rummer (POUR), September 1, 1931.

[47] NA RG 78, Box 80, Willoughby G. Walling, Commissioner of Public Welfare, to Hoover, November 9, 1931; ibid., W. R. Abbots (POUR representative in Illinois) to Gifford, November 19, 1931.

[48] On January 5, 1932, the Chicago Conference of Baptist Ministers passed a resolution stating that it was a duty of government "to provide at public expense a normal living for all for whom such a living is not otherwise available" (copy in NA RG 78, Box 80).

matters not connected with relief, the majority carried a resolution to adjourn until February 2, though it was known that Chicago relief stations would have to close on February 1. After hurried conferences with the city authorities and the State Relief Commission, Governor Emmerson recalled the legislature. After hectic scenes in the lower house as opponents fought to prevent legislation, a bill to create the Illinois Emergency Relief Commission (IERC) with an appropriation of $20,000,000 was passed on 6 February 1932. Characteristically, the money was raised mainly by bond issues and without increasing taxation.

Michigan presented a sharp contrast between metropolitan and rural society. Detroit, with its huge automobile industry, had been the boom town of the 1920s, drawing in migrant workers from all parts of the country, spawning associated supply industries in smaller industrial centers, and building up the fortunes of millionaire owners and highly paid managers. Several of the smaller cities had built up industries, many of which were dependent on Detroit. Away from the industrial and urban areas, the state contained much good farming land but also sparsely populated counties with poor agriculture, isolated iron- and copper-mining communities, and worked-over timber forests.

The inevitable tension was made worse by personal hostilities. Governor Wilbur Brucker had limited vision and opinions that were conservative even for a Republican dependent on rural and small-town support, but he spoke for a majority of his party and could expect backing from some of the state's wealthiest employers. Mayor Frank Murphy of Detroit had outstanding ability and would end his career on the United States Supreme Court after serving as Governor of the Philippines, Governor of Michigan, and Attorney General of the United States. Brucker was certain that the State could survive the depression without departing from the principle of local responsibility, and with little or no increase in state taxes; Murphy insisted that more money must be found for Detroit and, as nothing was forthcoming from the State, became an early advocate of federal relief.[49]

[49] Sidney Fine, *Frank Murphy: The Detroit Years* (Ann Arbor, Mich., 1975), is a masterly study of depression in the city. Brucker had won the governorship in 1928 by the comfortable margin of 483,990 to 357,664 (continuing a sequence of Republican governors beginning in 1917). In 1932 he was defeated by William A. Comstock and also failed to win election to the U.S. Senate in 1936. He was Secretary for the Army from 1955 to 1960.

Outside Detroit, public welfare was primitive. Even when the depression had run for a full five years, a study of local government found that

Michigan has retained the practices authorized by the territorial laws enacted prior to the admission of the State to the Union. By a profusion of ill-defined and vague enactments, indicating an imperfect understanding of the problem, the legislature has attempted to deal with the problem of poverty.

Relief was administered by 260 local units, of which some were townships and some counties. In the townships, the supervisors had absolute power to determine "whether the poor receive sufficient help or get along on a bare minimum." In the counties, things were better managed; but in some the same study found that "the sole idea in giving relief was to give the least possible amount and only when absolutely necessary," and only four counties employed trained social workers. In spite of tight-fisted parsimony, much money was wasted because lack of investigation allowed people to remain on relief who ought to have been taken off the rolls. Little effort was made to rehabilitate people who might have been capable of supporting themselves, and "the townships pay year after year for the support of families that contribute nothing to the community except a new baby as often as physically possible." Yet in Michigan, as in other states, stout defense of an inefficient system could be expected.[50]

Almost two years of the depression had passed before Governor Brucker set up a State Employment Commission in the fall of 1931, and its brief was to depart as little as possible from existing practice. Relief was, said the Governor, "traditionally, and properly so, a function of local government," and its administration should remain "in hands intimately familiar with the problems of the locality where it is dispensed." The commission was "to stimulate the sense of personal responsibility, to facilitate the operation of local public and private agencies, [and] to coordinate local effort." The possibility of innovation was suggested only in the instruction that the commission was "to consider especially the problem of those communities where all other agencies are known to be unequal to the task which confronts them,"

---

[50] Isabel Campbell Bruce and Edith Eickhoff, *The Michigan Poor Law: Its Development and Administration* (Chicago, 1936), 31. For details of relief adminsitration, see Opal V. Matson, *Local Relief to Dependents* (for the Michigan Commission of Enquiry into County, Township, and School District Government) (Detroit, 1933).

but this did not imply that federal aid might be sought. Brucker declared that "Michigan ranks among the wealthiest states in the Union, and should by all means be able to care for her own unfortunates," and he told the President that the State would accept this responsibility.[51]

The State Employment Commission followed these guidelines. It recommended but did not insist upon the establishment of county committees, and it left their membership to local choice. The chairmen of these county committees were ex officio members of the state commission, giving the rural counties a controlling majority. The tasks of the county committees were to find employment, initiate work projects, and seek cooperation from employers, churches, fraternal organizations, and other influential bodies; but they were not to countenance the notion that every person out of work had a claim on public funds. The commission was resolutely "opposed to the principle of the dole."[52]

The Dickinson County committee was regarded by the Commission as a model of its kind, and the POUR was invited to view it as an example of what should be done nationwide. The county was in the Iron Mountain region, had a population of 30,000, and property assessed at $25,000,000. The Ford Motor Company, which owned the iron mines and steel works, was the largest employer. In spite of recent prosperity, the county was as hard hit by the depression as any district outside Detroit, but the county committee was resolved "to care for its own." In a public statement it declared:

There is little distinction between the position of a State which appeals to the Federal Government for direct aid and the County which appeals to its State for direct aid, and the individual unemployed who applies to the Poor Commission for relief. Each of these cases is in principle the dole.

The county committee intended to stimulate local effort, not to document a plea for outside help.[53]

---

[51] Governor Brucker intended his speech to be a definitive statement of policy. He sent a copy to the POUR (NA RG 78, Box 183) and incorporated its substance into his reply to Governor Gifford Pinchot's circular letter to governors (LC Pinchot, November 25, 1931).

[52] NA RG 78 (POUR), Box 183 J. Walter Drake (temporary chairman, State Employment Commission) to Walter Gifford, November 18, 1931.

[53] NA RG 78, Box 184, January 2, 1932.

The Dickinson committee compiled a register of the unemployed, made it known that no applications for help from unregistered persons would be considered, investigated individual cases, and classified them according to need, occupation, skill, and availability for work. It organized a county works program and claimed that it was making the best possible use of available unemployed labor. As a result of this activity, local communities were faced with a growing number of requests to provide materials and pay the wages of men on work projects, but the county committee was firm in its insistence that these costs must be met and asked: "Can anyone show why these bodies are not as well able to finance this burden as the State or the Federal Government?"

The POUR representative who visited the county was somewhat less impressed. He regarded it as "a good example of how engineering techniques may be applied to the successful systemization of relief programs," but he thought that the prospects were bleak. Falling property values were cutting the yield from taxes; the unemployed had little chance of finding permanent work unless new industries moved in; the county committee had had little success in persuading employers (especially Ford) to spread work; and some of the unemployed, discouraged and perhaps alienated by the committee's hard line, had moved away and taken their problems to other counties. A note in the POUR file said that the county was so closely tied up with the Ford Motor Company that it would be unwise to make this report public.[54]

The city of Jackson, an industrial and railroad center with much unemployment, was also commended by the State Commission. City funds had been almost exhausted, but "not believing in a dole system or increase of taxation," the Mayor and the Chamber of Commerce had joined forces to set up an emergency welfare committee "to care for all the needy and indigent families . . . [by] asking each employed individual to pledge one day's pay a month." The committee took over the city's welfare department, obtained an appropriation of $35,000 to cover operating expenses, set up a commissary for the distribution of food, investigated all cases of need, and drew up a dietary budget as a guideline in allocating relief. All of the money received was spent on food, clothing, fuel, and shelter, and none on administration. Finally,

[54] Ibid.

"to eliminate the dole every male was required to give labor for civic projects as a condition for receiving relief."[55]

Whatever limitations in outlook were illustrated in Dickinson County and Jackson City, the men who led their relief efforts deserved credit for initiative and energy; but their example was of little relevance for Detroit. The city was unusual in the extent to which it had depended on public relief with little aid from private charities, and its welfare department was well organized, employed a full complement of social workers, and had a reputation for efficiency. In normal times about 4,000 families were on relief, but by February 1931 the figure had risen to 40,000, costs had escalated, and the city faced a financial crisis. In common with other urban centers, Detroit could not tax the income drawn from the city and had to rely upon property taxes, of which modest homeowners contributed the largest part. As Mayor Frank Murphy said: "If we were free to devise our own tax laws, it would not take us very long to solve the problems in Detroit." Lacking this power, where was the money to come from?[56]

In January 1932, Murphy told a committee of the United States Senate that from the beginning of the depression to July 1931, Detroit had spent between fourteen and fifteen million dollars on relief, and the bankers then gave notice that the city's credit would stand no more unless expenditure were cut. With great reluctance the city had to set about pruning the relief rolls, first dropping childless couples, then families with one child over sixteen, and then people with relatives who might help. By the end of 1931 the city was operating on what Murphy described as "a survival basis." Relief was available only to families with no income at all, and for them at a rate of no more than $3.00 a week plus 75 cents and some free milk for each dependent child. Meanwhile the number of unemployed was rising, and among those on relief were forty-five ministers of religion, thirty bank tellers, some lawyers, doctors, dentists, artists, and musicians, and a large number of veterans. The financial crisis not only pressed thousands down to subsistence level but also threatened the foundations of civi-

---

[55] Ibid., January 26, 1932. Jackson City was an industrial and railroad center with about 50,000 inhabitants. It claimed its place in history as the city at which the Republican party was founded.

[56] 72nd Congress, 1st Sess., Subcommittee of the Senate Committee on Manufactures, Hearings on Federal Aid for Unemployment Relief, 277–84.

lized life as expenditure was drastically reduced on civic improvements, urban transit, health, safety, police, and museums.[57]

Some companies in Detroit had their own relief programs, but normally these benefited only employees with very long service and touched only a small minority of the unemployed. Nor was there much hope that wealthy employers might come to the rescue. Senator James Couzens, a former Ford partner and himself a very rich man, had offered to donate a million dollars if others contributed a further nine million, but Murphy explained that "four efforts were made and conferences were held with the people representing large fortunes in Detroit to come into this plan. They declined." One may sympathize with men who refused to pour money into a bottomless relief pit, but what did this imply for the hope that private benevolence or enlightened self-interest could find a way through the crisis?[58]

The pattern of response to the depression in California was similar to that of other populous states, though it was better equipped than some because its welfare services had been brought together in 1927 under a newly constituted Department of Social Welfare. In 1929 an old-age pension law had been passed, with half the funds contributed by the State and administration centralized in a Division of Old Age Security in the Department of Social Welfare. The gap between institutional and outdoor relief had not been bridged, but in several counties the administration of general relief had been centralized and, by 1934, in almost two-thirds of them. San Francisco stood apart from these developments; it had no public outdoor relief and left it wholly to private agencies. In Los Angeles there was public relief, but its administration would later attract much criticism from federal investigators.[59]

The trend toward coordinated administration might well have continued, but it was slowed down by the legislative timetable and brought almost to a halt when it encountered opposition similar to that met in

[57] Ibid., 280.
[58] Ibid., 283. Senator Couzens had also been Mayor of Detroit and had therefore had firsthand experience of the city's difficulties. A contemporary account is William J. Norton, "The Relief Crisis in Detroit," *Social Service Review* 7 (1933), 1–10.
[59] For the creation and aims of the department, see State Department of Social Welfare, *First Biennial Report, 1927–8*, 4; for the old-age pension law, see *Third Biennial Report, 1930–2*, 19–22. James Leiby, "State Welfare Administration in California, 1930–1945," *Southern California Quarterly* 54 (1972), 303–18, is a good general account.

other states. In November 1930 the Governor appointed a Committee on Unemployment, and in 1931 the legislature appointed a State Unemployment Commission to study the situation and make recommendations at the next regular session; but this meant no further action until 1933. When it eventually came to consider a report from the commission, the legislature agreed to make loans to counties and cities but rejected the recommendation "that the Department of Social Welfare be given supervision over agencies furnishing unemployment relief with the object of maintaining standards and avoiding waste and duplication." In other words, at this late stage, California had reached the same point as the discredited Talbot Act of Pennsylvania.[60]

The principle of state regulation had already been accepted to deal with the problems presented by the entry into California of thousands of desperately poor people. This put a severe strain on local resources, particularly in the cities to which the unemployed transients gravitated. Acting upon a recommendation from the State Employment Commission, and in response to pressure from the city mayors, the Governor initiated a labor camp program that broke decisively with the principle of local responsibility. The camps were under the direction of a State Labor Camp Committee, and though the initiative in recruiting men for the camps and the administrative costs at that level had to come from cities and counties, the money to run the camps came from a state emergency fund, the highway fund, and the resources of various state departments. It was also significant that help was sought and obtained from the United States Army, Navy, Forest Service, and Park Service.

Twenty-eight forestry and two highway camps were in operation during the winter of 1931-2. The figures might seem impressive, but the total number given work did not exceed 4,000. The influx of migrants into the state was estimated at nearly 1,000 a day, so the labor camp program did no more than nibble at the transient problem; its importance lay in setting precedents and breaking with tradition, rather than in finding solutions. The State had been forced to recognize a limit to local responsibility, to introduce a measure of state control, to draw upon state funds, and indirectly to accept federal aid. In retrospect, migration into the state can be seen as the principal factor

[60] James Leiby, "State Welfare Administration," passim; *Report of the State Unemployment Commission* (Sacramento, Calif., 1931).

pressing California toward acceptance of federal relief and regulation on a large scale, and as a striking demonstration of the truth that the depression knew no state boundaries.[61]

In the early summer of 1932 Rowland Haynes, a staff member of the POUR, compiled a general report on steps taken by the states to counter unemployment. Most states had set up agencies to deal with unemployment; in a majority the members were prominent citizens and unpaid, though some employed trained staff. In a few cases, the work was being done by older state departments rather than by ad hoc bodies. Some of the agencies controlled funds that had been appropriated for relief, but the majority were limited to the stimulation and coordination of public and private efforts. Among the state agencies with money to distribute, a few had discretionary power to allocate aid in proportion to need, but it was more common for them to be bound by formulas that might take into account the population, the past relief expenditure, and the number of unemployed.[62]

The POUR did not encourage central direction, and in September 1931 its policy had been officially defined as based on the assumption that "unemployment relief to be effectively carried out ... must be dealt with by each local community." Haynes was not too happy with this statement as a permanent rule and pointed out that some degree of control could invigorate relief in the localities, and that the decision to commit state funds implied an obligation to see that they were used properly. State relief agencies had usually given priority to setting up county committees, and this in itself had often had a salutory effect. Haynes quoted one Michigan social worker as saying that "the mere creation of these groups had centralized the relief problem in the counties and put new energy into it." One result had been to furnish more information about local practice and thus to stimulate demands that it be improved.[63]

When state money was available for relief, some local authorities simply transferred their normal cases of dependency to the unemployment rolls, and others used it to pay for public works that should have formed part of their usual commitments. These practices had led some

[61] *Review of the Activities of the State Relief Administration of California* (Sacramento, 1936), 21–30.
[62] NA RG 78 (POUR), Haynes to Gifford.
[63] Ibid.

states to exercise more control over local expenditure; others limited aid to matching grants after approving what had been done; and in three states, local expenditure was investigated in detail before reimbursements were made. On the other hand, control was normally confined to the approval of the purpose and to satisfactory accounting, and was seldom used to lay down administrative guidelines or relief standards. If local officials were prevented from using the money improperly, they still retained absolute control over who should get relief and at what level. Nowhere was there any procedure for reviewing or reversing local decisions on applications for relief.

The trend toward state regulation, and the way in which the issues were being argued in the largest cities and most populous states, demonstrated how far events had overtaken the policy of the President and his POUR. If they were genuinely concerned with preserving local responsibility, it would have been wise to press embarrassed states to adopt measures to serve that end. Local finances should have been strengthened, local administration improved to answer its critics, and local authorities urged to forget that the unemployed were paupers. Above all, it would have been wise to recognize that voluntary effort had done all it could, and that public welfare was now in the front line and required all the reinforcement it could get.

In the fall of 1931 the keynotes of administration policy were sounded in a report prepared by the Russell Sage Foundation, and circulated by the POUR, on the tactics to be adopted during the desperate winter months. Every community should recognize its responsibility, "strengthen its own defenses," refrain from alarmist publicity, encourage local business to provide work, and persuade bankers to underwrite the credit extended by stores to unemployed families. Voluntary efforts aimed at providing relief or work should be encouraged, but to supplement, not supplant, existing private and public agencies. There was no harm in all this good advice, nor was there anything new. It was contrary to administration policy to urge states to act, and there was therefore no suggestion that additional funds should be raised from taxes or that state and county departments of public welfare should adopt new powers to place resources where they were needed and require the adoption of modern social work methods.

The President chose February 12, 1932 – Lincoln's birthday – as an appropriate occasion to make clear his own commitment to enlightened individualism. The long-term solution to the problem of unemployment in an industrial society was for employers to develop welfare programs for their own work force, and in the short run for all to contribute generously to voluntary relief schemes. It was in every employer's interest to develop a healthy social environment, and a generous contribution to a community chest was as much sound common sense as benevolence. In the future, insurance and welfare should become normal functions of management, community chests should look after able-bodied people outside these schemes, and public welfare departments in the cities and the traditional authorities in rural districts should look after those who were unemployable. In an implied rebuke to states that had passed emergency laws and created relief agencies with power to allocate funds, he said that the more that states took over, the less would individual effort be encouraged and the greater would be the threat of centralism. New Individualism might take time to build, but the edifice would rest on firm foundations.

To many of his hearers, the President's remarks seemed to be out of touch with reality. The efforts made by organized charities and community chests had been prodigious, but they had failed. The emergency relief administrations that had been created in several states – reluctantly, so far as many political leaders were concerned – had resulted from real distress, not imagined situations. The strongest pressure for outside help came from the metropolitan and industrial districts – the fine fruits of American capitalism – and was endorsed by a very large majority of the men and women who had had actual experience of relief administration. One might not like the facts, but they were the facts to be faced. Events were in the saddle and rode mankind; and when Hoover spoke, the question was not whether states would draw back from the brink of "centralism" but whether Congress would pass a federal relief law.

4

FEDERAL RELIEF

There was no serious discussion of federal aid before the winter of 1930–1. In Congress ten bills, of which the majority favored federal grants for relief in the worst hit areas, to be administered by the Red Cross (following the precedent of federal aid for victims of drought, earthquakes, or other disasters), sank without a trace. In the unlikely event that a bill of this type passed Congress, it faced a certain veto. Hoover did not rule out the possibility of federal aid in the last resort, but the reports reaching the POUR were almost unanimous in claiming that states and localities could get through on their own resources.

Men and women in close touch with relief work in the cities moved more rapidly to welcome outside help. The reaction of the more cautious among them is evident in speeches made to the National Conference of Social Work in 1930 and 1931 by C. M. Bookman, director of social agencies and of the Community Chest in Cincinnati. In 1930 he gave an account of the work of private charities in the city and stressed the importance of voluntary action, provided that it was well organized. A year later his concern was with the limitations of voluntary effort. In Cincinnati about one-third of the unemployed were by then dependent on relief and absorbing all the resources and energies of the agencies. Bookman said that the men and women in this depressed third were not the dregs of society but "peaceable, home-loving folks who seemed to be fated to do the drudgery of the world for food, clothing, and shelter with a few simple pleasures"; their needs would not diminish, others would join them as savings were used up, and opportunities for casual work contracted." His conclusion was that "arrangements must be made without delay to enlist local government support sufficient to maintain the modest relief programs to be found in our cities." This was a long way from asking for federal aid, but it was certainly an admission that private philanthropy had reached the end of the road.[1]

In an article published in the 1931 *Annals of Political and Social Science,* Jacob Billikopf of Philadelphia argued that even if good times returned, the shadow of prolonged depression would reach far into the future. In 1929 a University of Philadelphia study had found a surprising 10.4 percent of the labor force unemployed, but most of them found jobs within a few weeks. The unhappy novelty of the depression was that the period without earnings lengthened, with psychological consequences that could not be ignored. "No amount of private charity, on however grandiose a scale it be conceived or executed, can succeed in preventing or effectively mitigating the ever-spreading demoralization that results from unemployment." Billikopf predicted that the bleak present would give place to an even bleaker future as undernourished infants grew into weak adults, children removed early from school joined the ranks of the unskilled, and hardship caused broken homes. Only delinquency and crime would flourish, and the legacy of the depression would be social ills that private charities could not remedy. The inference was that modest sums spent now from the public purse would avert crippling expenses in future years.[2]

Billikopf's message was made explicit in a paper presented to the National Conference of Social Work in 1931. What could be expected from local government? In Philadelphia the private charities had made an urgent plea to the city for money in order to keep their relief operations afloat, but the answer from the Mayor was that though his heart went out to the poor he would "rather be just than generous," and had no authority to spend the city's funds on relief. The State had then allowed the city to borrow $3,000,000, but even if the full amount were raised it would soon run out. Philadelphia might not be typical, but even in the cities with a more flexible attitude there were acute shortages. What then must follow? In a warning addressed to the assembled social workers (but which he also circulated to a large number of influential people, including the chairman of the POUR), Billikopf said:

We will be guilty of great duplicity, we will be betraying the interests of millions of unemployed who expect us to articulate their needs if, in our vast

[1] C. M. Bookman, "An Attempt to Meet an Unemployment Emergency," *NCSW 1930,* 314–17; "Community and Unemployment Needs," *NCSW 1931,* 384–99.
[2] Jacob Billikopf, "The Social Duty to the Unemployed," *Annals* 154 (1931), 65–72.

enthusiasm to fill our community chests, we should give the impression, directly or even inferentially, that all a community has to do is to raise its chest quota, and the unemployed will be provided for.... As a result of the policy of drift, and the utter lack of mastery in directing it, our government will be compelled, by the logic of inescapably cruel events ahead of us, to step into the situation and bring relief on a large scale ... a scale commensurate with the vast importance and the tragedies of our problems. Private philanthropy is no longer capable of coping with the situation.[3]

Stirred by this and other appeals, the leading lights of the National Conference of Social Work decided to muster support for federal aid. William Hodson of New York wrote an open letter to the President in which he called for a comprehensive review of local resources to ascertain whether they could do what was expected of them, and for federal relief if they could not. A favorable response was neither expected nor received, and the real purpose of the letter was to open a public debate. In October 1931 a group of welfare administrators formed a cumbersomely named Social Work Conference on Federal Action on Unemployment, with fifty-seven members drawn from public and private bodies in twenty-eight states and fifty cities, and a steering committee to consider proposals and plan action.[4]

Opinion in the Social Work Conference ranged from strong advocacy of federal aid to fervent opposition, but the steering committee was able to agree that an authoritative inquiry, bringing together evidence from all parts of the country, was the essential preliminary to further action. At this point, the initiative from social workers converged with a move in Congress initiated by Senator Edward Costigan of Colorado, and on November 7 a meeting took place in Washington between members of the steering committee and Costigan, Senator Robert M. LaFollette of Wisconsin, and Representative David Lewis of Maryland. It was agreed that LaFollette, as the senior of the two Senators, should get the Senate Committee on Manufactures to appoint a subcommittee on federal aid, with himself as chairman.

---

[3] Jacob Billikopf, "What Have We Learned about Unemployment," *NCSW 1931*, 25–50.

[4] The account of the movement among social workers in support of federal aid given by Joanna C. Colcord, "Social Work and the First Federal Relief Program," *National Conference of Social Work, 1943*, 382–94, corrects that given by Josephine C. Brown in *Public Relief, 1929–39* (New York: rpt. Octagon Press, 1971). Colcord was in close touch with the people who were active in this movement. A recent and full account is in William W. Bremer, *Depression Winters: New York Social Workers and the New Deal* (Philadelphia, 1984), using additional material from the papers of Harry Lurie.

Walter West, secretary of the Assocation of Social Workers and a convinced supporter of federal aid, undertook to round up useful witnesses and to suggest the order in which they should be called.

The LaFollette subcommittee was to be of crucial importance, but less in accelerating federal action than in determining the direction it should take. LaFollette was an experienced and sympathetic chairman who knew in advance the kind of report that he intended to write, Costigan was a skilled trial lawyer who cross-examined witnesses with great effect, and no senator tried to discredit the testimony received, but the effectiveness of the subcommittee depended on the selection of witnesses and the order in which they were heard. For this, credit was due to the backstage work of Walter West. A majority of the witnesses (including no fewer than twenty social workers) were people with first-hand experience of the problems; they were given the opportunity to speak at length, but they stuck to facts and avoided speculation. The cumulative effect was an authoritative account of what was actually happening in the troubled cities from people whose evident concern was to help those in distress. A senator opposed to federal relief paid tribute to the quality of the witnesses when he said, "it is a rare thing for a group of people to come before us with facts and arguments, and seeking not their own benefit but that of other people."[5]

William Hodson led off with a formal analysis of the relief problem: In addition to the physically disabled, mentally retarded, emotionally disturbed, permanently diseased, and chronically maladjusted – always present and always requiring care – there were a large number of people who were in precarious employment and particularly vulnerable in hard times. Some in this second group would require relief in the mildest recession and many more as conditions worsened. A third category required relief in a deep and lengthy depression and consisted of people who were normally fully employed and had "never before sought charity or assistance in any form." They usually had savings and there was therefore an interval between loss of employment and application for relief, but as time went on the number seeking relief rose sharply. Their appearance on the relief rolls raised issues that had never been considered so long as the majority on relief were drawn from the first two caregories. The most important new question was whether relief should aim to preserve self-respect or merely to

---

[5] 72nd Congress, 1st Session. Committee on Manufactures, Subcommittee on Unemployment Relief, *Hearings on s.174 and s.262, 1932.*

allow survival. These were the inescapable facts, said Hodson, and they remained the same whatever the source of funds – private or public, local, state, or federal.[6]

Walter West pointed out that there was nothing new about public relief; that federal relief would be no more than another way of doing what had been done for centuries; and that there was no logical distinction between relief from an overseer of the poor or from an agent of the federal government. The only point at issue was to decide which could perform most efficiently.[7]

Was private charity capable of providng the relief that was needed? J. Prentice Murphy, executive director of the Children's Bureau of Philadelphia, thought it was incapable of doing so: Many small communities had no organized charities or community chests; in large cities their funds were running low; and even if they had funds, private contributors should not be called upon to carry exclusive responsibility for performing a duty that was "basic to our common law." Allen T. Burns, director of the National Association of Community Chests and Councils, dealt authoritatively with the practical limits of private charity. Most organized charities had not come into existence to relieve the poor but to support hospitals, clinics, child care, youth training, and "provision against the misuse of the immensely increased leisure time." Over the years they had accumulated standing commitments, and though they had willingly done what they could, Burns estimated that only a third of their income could be spent on relief. To expect more was wholly unrealistic, for years of experience had taught directors of community chests that "they played a minor part in relief" and that 70 percent of the money would have to come from public funds.[8]

What were the actual conditions in large cities? The answer given by Frank Murphy, Mayor of Detroit, was the most telling testimony received by the LaFollette subcommittee. Detroit had won reknown for its enlightened and generous welfare administration, but the depression had driven the city government to make successive cuts in relief until many in need got nothing, and no one got enough. Normal civic services had suffered as relief bit further and further into the city budget and raised a mountain of debt. The yield from local taxes could

[6] Ibid., 13
[7] Ibid., 67.
[8] Ibid., 43–50 (Prentice Murphy), 127 (Burns).

not be increased, and some of the richest employers in the nation had refused to help the metropolis from which they drew their wealth. In this situation, was not federal aid justified both morally and legally? "Each one of us," said Murphy, "is a citizen of two sovereignties," but both masters taught the same lesson. "The Constitution of our country, as well as the constitutions of the states, suggests that our order of government is set up for the promotion of the general welfare."[9]

Governor Gifford Pinchot of Pennsylvania used the opportunity to launch a moral onslaught on both local responsibility and dependence upon voluntary contributions. He argued that relief was a burden all should share and that only the federal government could distribute it equitably. The foundation of a just policy was the assumption that "the right to work for a living is part of the right to live," and society had an obligation to support those for whom it could find no work. The moral question was not who should pay but who was entitled to avoid payment. In Pennsylvania and nine other states, there were constitutional limits to what could be raised from state taxes, and "if the burden of unemployment relief is to fall where it rightly and justly should, then there is no way of escaping an increase in the higher brackets of the Federal income tax."[10]

Pinchot believed that reliance on private charity and insistence on local responsibility were shameful evasions of this obvious conclusion. As it was, pressure was put on wage earners to contribute a day's pay a month but rich employers escaped by living outside the hard pressed localities.

Local relief is the cry of that particular plan. It is vicious for several reasons. One of them is that it takes money from the little fellow . . . [and attempts] to get by without increasing income taxes, without letting the big fellows come in to carry their load.

He went on to argue that there was enough money in the country to give all the relief that was needed; the problem was to transfer it from those who had too much to those who had nothing. The solution should not be difficult to find; distress was local but its causes were national; the remedies could not be local and ought to be national.[11]

[9] Ibid., 277–84.
[10] Ibid., 211–20.
[11] Ibid., 217.

The farce of local responsibility in bankrupt communities was exposed by John Lewis of the United Mine Workers, who described the plight of isolated mining towns where there were no community chests, few men of wealth, impoverished local governments, and benevolent funds dependent on miners' contributions but long since exhausted. The Governor of Indiana had telegraphed to the President that Indiana would look after its own, but Lewis wondered what he intended to do about the 60,000 miners in his state facing destitution or whether he even knew of their existence.

Interspersed with evidence from leading public figures was that of many officials and social workers on the front line, who provided evidence enough to discredit comforting assurances. Perhaps by accident but probably by design, Walter Gifford, chairman of POUR, was called late in the hearing, so that his generalizations stood in sharp contrast to the detailed evidence of extreme distress already given. Gifford was as close as the subcommittee could get to the President; LaFollette and Costigan were not going to let him get away with imprecise information and untested assumptions, and in cross-examination, Costigan seized the opportunity to demonstrate that government policy was based on ignorance of the facts.

Gifford did not make things easier for himself by defining the function of the POUR in a way that implied that statistics were unnecessary. It "was not to do anything other than encourage the States to do this work; in other words, responsibility was to be left squarely with the States, counties, and communities." Without giving details, Gifford said that, subject to the passage of laws in four or five states where they were necessary, "each State will care for its own who must have help this winter." He thought that private contributions would probably exceed public expenditure (a proposition already dismissed by several witnesses). He offered the thought that "should such community and State responsibility be lessened by Federal aid, the sincere and whole-hearted efforts of hundreds and thousands of volunteers engaged in both raising and administering the relief funds would doubtless be materially lessened."

On what evidence were these predictions based? Costigan asked how many were unemployed. Gifford did not know. What was the situation in districts and towns without community chests? The POUR had no reliable information. What was the state of unemployment in rural areas? The information was not available. Was unemployment rising or falling? What proportion of relief was being distributed by private and public agencies? If all of these facts were unknown, what were the grounds for the POUR's optimism?[12]

Gifford clearly thought this questioning unfair. He was not the professional head of a government statistical bureau, but the voluntary and unpaid head of an agency whose main tasks were to encourage voluntary effort and to keep the President informed on the state of affairs as seen by responsible people in the states. To prepare himself for questioning, he had relied mainly on telephone calls to governors. In some instances he had heard from directors of community chests in large cities and (where they existed) from chairmen of state relief agencies. The POUR had not been given the staff to carry out investigations in the field, and for most states the data in the POUR files was meager. All of this was true, but what Costigan brought out in his questioning was that there had been no drive from the top to uncover the facts and no serious effort to use information available in the Bureau of Labor Statistics, the Bureau of the Census, or the well-organized statistical services maintained by several states. The impression conveyed, and which Costigan intended to convey, was that the administration was more interested in slogans – "local responsibility," "caring for one's own" – or ritual condemnation of the dole than in finding the facts and facing them. Gifford did not help his case by saying that government policy would not have been changed if all the missing information had been available.[13]

The next move was to prepare legislation, and a draft bill, which LaFollette would present to the Senate, was prepared by the social work steering committee. The major points were that federal aid should be available for both home and work relief, grants should be made to states that applied, a small federal relief board should be created to direct policy, and administration would be by the Federal Children's Bureau. The bill proposed an appropriation of $375,000,000, of which 40 percent would go to states in proportion to their population and the remainder would be allocated according to need. Every state would be required to set up its own relief agency (or designate an existing department for that purpose), submit an account of all private and

[12] Ibid., 227; Albert U. Romasco, *The Poverty of Abundance: Hoover, the Nation, and the Depression* (New York, 1968), 165.
[13] *Hearings 1932*, 311–13.

public relief expenditure since 1929, employ an adequate number of trained social workers, and draw up plans for looking after transients. The bill declared that it intended "to secure to the several states control of the administration of this act," but the federal agency would have to ensure that the conditions had been met and assess the need before allocating over half of the money.[14]

Discretionary grants, the right of the central agency to lay down conditions, and the implicit assumption that society had an obligation to support the unemployed owed much to the example of New York; and, apart from the choice of the Children's Bureau as the federal relief agency, the bill also anticipated most features of later New Deal legislation. Thus the work done by a small number of social workers in initiating the first serious move for a federal relief program, organizing hearings, and drafting the measure was of great historical significance.

The Children's Bureau was selected as the central relief bureau because it was an existing federal agency with extensive experience of social work. Thus it would meet the criticism that federal relief meant expensive additions to the bureaucracy while placing administration in professional hands; nevertheless the suggestion was not a happy one. The bureau had done excellent work in exposing the evils of child labor and child neglect, but its function had been to explore, advise, and make public the worst abuses. It was not an executive agency and had had no experience in handling large sums of money. Its head, Grace Abbott, was intelligent, persistent, outspoken, and greatly respected by social workers, but her qualities had not endeared her to employers or to many state officials. In a male-dominated society, additionally, it was unwise to suggest that a female social worker be given the right to inquire into the way in which states managed their affairs and to decide what grants they should receive.[15]

In addition to evidence from the hearings, LaFollette had conducted his own survey of conditions in 810 cities in all parts of the country, and revealed an extraordinary variety both in the effects of the depression and the steps taken to assist the unemployed. Asked how much unemployment had increased since December 1930, 115 cities reported increases of 50 percent, 115 of between 50 and 100 percent, and 85 of over 100 percent. Inquiries on finance and relief standards

---

[14] For an account and analysis of the proceedings in Congress, see Jordan A. Schwartz, *The Interregnum of Despair: Hoover, Congress, and the Depression* (Urbana, Ill., 1970).
[15] Grace Abbott: see Chapter 1, Appendix 2.

revealed wide variations: 127 cities reported no appropriations for relief, 105 had made no increase, but 187 reported increases – in 76 of them of over 100 percent. In 168 cities all relief was given by private charities, but there was no private relief in 27 and under 25 percent in 68. In Massachusetts and Wisconsin the average given in cash or grocery orders was $9 a week for each family; in Mississippi it was $2.50; the average in 461 cities was $6.07, but in the cities of two of the most industrialized states, Pennsylvania and Ohio, it was $5.50 and a little over $4.00, respectively.[16]

The promise of federal intervention made it certain that some southern senators would spring to the defense of state rights. It was not federal money they rejected, but the conditions that would accompany it. A substitute bill offered by Hugo Black, Thomas Walsh, and Robert Bulkeley proposed an appropriation for highway construction to be distributed to the states without requiring matching grants. They agreed that there should be an appropriation for relief of 375 million dollars, but proposed to distribute it all on a population basis, to be used "within each state under rules and regulations adopted by the State authorities." The only proposed check on expenditure was a requirement that governors should submit quarterly reports, but no action was suggested if these reports were unsatisfactory, and this was the only form of federal oversight.

Senator Hugo Black, later to be a liberal justice of the Supreme Court, made the major speech in support of the substitute bill. If the original proposal had been a simple resolution to give federal money for relief, he would have found no difficulty in voting for it, but the issue now raised was state rights versus the federal government. Distribution on a population basis would, he said, still benefit most the hardest-hit states; but dropping discretionary grants would remove the ground for federal investigation of conditions in the states and the possibility that politically sensitive large cities would get more than their fair share.[17]

Vigorous opposition was expected from orthodox Republicans, led by Simon Fess of Ohio; it could be voted down, but the belief that it reflected White House views persuaded some waverers to look for a weakened measure to avoid a veto. Others who were prepared for

[16] *Congressional Record,* 72nd Congress, 1st Sess., 3673ff.
[17] Ibid.

some degree of federal control did not wish to see it vested in the Childrens' Bureau. The position of the influential New York Democrat, Robert F. Wagner, was also uncertain. In the preceding two years, he had introduced various measures to counter unemployment and may have resented LaFollette's assumption of leadership in the fight for federal relief. Wagner favored loans rather than grants to the states and wanted to base allocations on the number of unemployed shown in the 1930 census, favoring eastern states that had felt the earliest effects of the depression on the ground that those who had been longest in the storm had the strongest claim.

These differences of opinion stacked the cards against the passage of an unamended bill, but because most Democrats and many progressive Republicans favored federal relief in some form, a majority could have been knitted together to support a compromise. The substitute bill with stronger safeguards against the misuse of federal money might have been adopted, loans instead of grants might have been accepted, and mild regulatory powers might have been given to the Department of Labor; but LaFollette and his social work advisers were resolved to stand out for their bill and nothing less. The substitute meant sacrificing the hope of using federal power to press for higher and uniform standards; loans would burden states with debt charges but leave them with a moral right to do as they wished with money they had undertaken to repay; allocations based on the 1930 census would work against industrial regions hit late by the depression and rural districts where farmer occupiers were not unemployed but could not make a living.[18]

The Black–Walsh–Bulkeley substitute was voted down by 48–31, but on the following day its supporters joined with conservative Republicans to kill the LaFollette bill by 48–35. Fifty-six senators (including pairs) had supported federal relief in one form or another, but the voting was so confused that there was no obvious formula for a compromise. A stalemate ensued during which numerous proposals reached the floor but none got beyond perfunctory debate. Meanwhile, in the House of Representatives, Speaker Jack Garner was pushing forward proposals for a massive program of federal public works to provide employment. He carried a bill to build or rebuild post offices across the nation, and the Senate passed it in July – to meet with a

[18] Ibid.

veto and a stinging message from the President that the bill was "not unemployment relief but the most gigantic pork barrel bill ever proposed to an American Congress."[19]

The situation was one familiar in congressional history. Six months of a session had gone by and nothing had been done. If there had been an economic upturn in the spring, the whole plan for federal relief would have died, and Walter Gifford could have consoled himself with the thought that he had been correct in his prediction that the states could get through without federal aid; but things did not improve, and as the weeks went by pressure mounted on Congress to do something. Everyone was tired, but ready to welcome anything that looked positive and might command a majority.

In this mood, Senator Robert Wagner took up the task of patching together the bits and pieces of rejected measures, adding a few new ingredients, and presenting the majority with a bill on which they could unite in July without publicly disavowing principles proclaimed with such confidence in February. His first attempt passed both houses but was killed by a veto; his second survived to become law as the first Federal Emergency Relief and Reconstruction Act.[20]

The act authorized federal loans, not grants. It made the recently created Reconstruction Finance Corporation, or RFC (which commanded business support), the agency for allocating and distributing loans. The initiative would have to come from governors of states in applying for loans, and once received, the funds would be wholly under state control; but until that time, there was a measure of federal oversight. Governors would have to certify that all state and local funds were exhausted, and the RFC would have to verify these statements before agreeing to a loan and deciding how much it should be. If loans were made to cover short periods, the governor would have to apply repeatedly and the process of investigation would begin again, with the added responsibility of finding out how the previous loan had been used. Thus federal agents acquired the right and duty to inquire

---

[19] Schwartz, *Interregnum of Despair,* 154, gives the following analysis of the votes: fifteen Democrats for both bills, five Democrats against both; twelve Democrats against the LaFollette–Costigan bill but for the Black–Walsh–Bulkeley substitute; thirty Republicans against both bills. Seventeen members of both parties did not vote on the original bill, and thirteen did not vote on the substitute.

[20] Romasco, *Poverty of Abundance,* 224–6; Schwartz, *Interregnum of Despair,* 172.

into matters that had hitherto been jealously guarded as state pre-
serves, and the importance of this innovation cannot be rated too
highly.

Social workers could see some serious faults in the law. It focused
on what states could afford, not on what they ought to spend. A corporation set up to finance industry and dominated by bankers was not
the ideal body to investigate distress, and there was no suggestion that
experienced social administrators should be added to their number.
The requirement that governors must certify that state and local
resources were exhausted before receiving a loan was in the spirit of
the old "pauper's oath," by which an applicant for relief had to swear
that he had no income, no assets, and no relative able to support him;
it might also be interpreted to mean that relief must be cut to bare
subsistence before aid could be sought. Once a loan had been given, a
state became wholly responsible for its use, and there was no hint that
the RFC might use its power to raise standards or insist on the employment of trained social workers. These fears were substantiated by an
early statement from the RFC that the sole purpose of the act was to
supplement the efforts of local authorities.

Not all these fears were justified. The RFC took seriously its duty to
investigate conditions in the states applying for a loan and appointed
Fred Croxton, an experienced social administrator, to head its relief
division. Its field representatives, though too few in number to do a
thorough job, were trained social workers, executives of large charities,
or academic experts on social problems. They included Robert Kelso,
Sherrard Ewing, Rowland Haynes, and A. W. McMillen, who would
all hold key positions in relief administration under the New Deal. If
the RFC had no mandate to reform relief administration, it left to its
successor files bulging with evidence of what was wrong.

The federal government was in the field of relief and would never
again withdraw. Even during the year of RFC relief loans, the advance
of federal power was far greater than its original supporters had imagined. By the time Hoover left the White House, federal loans were paying eight out of every ten dollars spent on unemployment relief, and
their repayment was recognized as fiction rather than realizable fact.

The very first application for an RFC loan, submitted before the
final passage of the act, was from Gifford Pinchot on behalf of Pennsylvania, but the response was slow and scrutiny of the claim exacting.

The story is worth telling in some detail as an illustration of RFC methods and as a further chapter in the troubled history of relief in Pennsylvania.

On 2 August, Pinchot presented the case in person to the RFC board. He said that one and a half million were unemployed in the state, and that in the preceding twelve months $41,000,000 had been raised and spent on relief. Questioned by members of the board, he was forced to admit that only $10,000,000 had come from state revenue and $3,000,000 from the Pennsylvania relief loan, and that the legislature would not increase taxes. He blamed the legislature and the Philadelphia authorities for the situation, but the RFC took the view that whoever was to blame, a state as rich as Pennsylvania ought to do more. The chairman, Alex Pomerene, closed the meeting by saying that the board thought that the State and its political subdivisions "had not done their full duty with respect to furnishing funds for relief purposes."[21]

In the following weeks, this conclusion was reinforced in confidential reports from Robert Kelso and Pierce Williams, the RFC field representatives; and in a memorandum for the board, Fred Croxton noted that Pennsylvania had applied for a loan to cover six months when most states had asked for three, and recommended that it should not be granted because the information was incomplete and local resources were not yet fully utilized.

Robert Kelso reported that there was no doubt about the extent of distress in Pennsylvania, but that almost everywhere relief administration was faulty and funds were insufficient. At Williamsport he found that relief was being organized by an energetic group of young businessmen, but that the poor boards refused to cooperate and used the opportunity to push their normal commitments on to voluntary agencies. In Luzerne County an unofficial emergency committee worked closely with the poor boards, but with 20 percent of the population on relief, it faced insuperable difficulties; in Fayette County things were even worse, with one-third of the population out of work; and in Clearfield County private charitable funds had run out. In coal-mining communities, the employers had often looked after the unemployed as long

---

[21] There are papers and memoranda on Pennsylvania's application in FDR Library, Hopkins Papers, Box 42.

as possible but could no longer do so; nor could local resources take their place.[22]

Kelso thought that the State was not spending enough money, and what did get through was not reaching those who needed it most. Some poor boards had used the Talbot Act money to pay off old debts, had done little to relieve distress, and "could not be counted on to do anything for the emergency situation." The local atmosphere was often "charged with hostility on the part of official bodies toward each other," but it was rumored that they were nevertheless organizing "for the purpose of controlling the actions of the next legislature in the relief measures it may enact."[23]

Weak administration and wretched standards of relief might be excused or at least understood in communities where mines or steel works had closed and extreme poverty had preceded the depression; the same could not be said of the great city of Philadelphia. In a disturbing conversation, Sherman Kingsley, director of the private Philadelphia Welfare Fund, told Kelso that the city had not done enough, and had even failed to refund to private agencies $1,000,000 owed for relief normally charged to public funds. The city maintained that it could do no more because $6,140,000 was owed in uncollected taxes; but it had authority to borrow $2,000,000 (in anticipation of revenue) for emergency relief, and had refused to do so. Conditions at the relief centers were shocking. People waited in long lines to be interviewed, and those who waited in vain were given tickets for another day that might be two or three weeks ahead.[24]

Kelso's concluding verdict on Pennsylvania was that in spite of its splendid record in charitable work, long experience of industrial conditions, and foreseeable difficulties in declining mining communities, the State was "about as tardy as the new western states in getting into action." The plain truth was that "the people of this state are not making as much effort as they could make in the relief of their needy people."[25]

The knowledge that there would be no RFC loan until Pennsylvania had done more for itself at last persuaded the legislature to take effec-

[22] NA RG 69, Kelso to Croxton, November 29, 1932.
[23] Ibid.
[24] Ibid., September 12, 1932.
[25] Ibid., November 29, 1932.

tive action. In September 1932 it set up the State Emergency Relief Board (SERB), with an appropriation of $12,000,000 raised by a sales tax. The new agency was bipartisan, and though the Governor was a member ex officio, he had no casting vote. It was given power to create state organizations bypassing the poor boards, and proceeded to set up county relief boards to take complete charge of unemployment relief, settle the proportion between direct and work relief, and designate the agencies to handle funds locally. The first appointments to county boards were made by the SERB from among citizens of good standing, and the boards themselves would submit lists of persons recommended for appointment when vacancies occurred.

The bipartisan requirement was intended to prevent the SERB from falling into the net of party patronage, but it did not prevent Pinchot from using it as a major instrument in his relief policy. He took a close interest in the first appointments to county boards and conducted much correspondence to ensure that suitable people were placed on the county lists for appointment to vacancies. He also wrote personally to the first nominees, explaining their duties and urging them to accept.[26]

The great novelty in the new policy was that the entire responsibility for relieving the able-bodied unemployed was taken away from the poor boards and given to new county agencies over which the state government exercised a measure of control. Success would depend upon the quality of the people willing to serve on the county boards and upon their willingness to cooperate with the SERB and with each other. Inevitably there were difficulties. Mrs. Alice Liveright reported that in Lackawanna County the board was weak and she submitted names to be added to it. In one county it was difficult to get people to serve so long as a certain state senator continued as chairman. The Governor undertook to remove him but nothing was done, and some weeks later the chairman got back at his critics by reporting that his board was working well.

---

[26] There are many papers relating to the duties of and appointments to county boards in LC Pinchot (relief and county files, 1932). On September 15, 1932 Pinchot wrote to William Gallagher of Clearfield County pressing upon him the need to serve on the relief committee; this was one of several similar letters. On another occasion, Pinchot wrote to a county relief director, saying that a person recommended by Mrs. Pinchot would be "ideal" and requesting him to submit the name to the SERB. Mrs. Liveright, the Secretary for Welfare, also took a close interest. For instance, on November 2, 1932, she told Pinchot that the Lackawanna board needed "a good deal of strengthening." She had already submitted some names and added three more possible candidates for two vacancies.

No one claimed that the SERB had solved the relief problem, but things were on the move in most parts of the state; but unfortunately, Philadelphia was an exception. The SERB had ruled that localities must pay the administrative costs for relief distribution, but this was ignored by the city. On October 21, 1932, the SERB sent the Philadelphia city council a copy of a resolution confirming that administrative costs must be paid and requesting an immediate reply. None was received for over a month, and Edwin R. Cox, president of the council, then replied with a definite refusal. He said that Philadelphia was $20,000,000 in debt because of tax delinquencies and falling revenue, and that the current budget had been thrown out of gear when bankers demanded immediate repayment of $6,000,000 the city had expected to spread over two years.

This reasoning may have convinced the city council, but meant that if relief operations were to continue, someone else would have to pay. In other states, rural counties had objected to paying taxes for the benefit of the cities; in Pennsylvania the largest city refused to pay its share. Indeed, given the choice between halting relief and paying administrative costs, the city might prefer the former. In his reply, Cox included a personal note:

While on the subject of unemployment relief (now being borne by State and National funds), I am of the opinion that this is the dole, but in another form. How long is it to continue? What of private charity? Is it to be eliminated, or is the burden of assisting our helpless unemployed to be passed directly to the taxpayer?

This ignored the opinion of everyone concerned with private charitable work that contributions had reached a limit, the fact that relief operations in Philadelphia had been twice suspended for lack of funds, and the view of impartial observers (including the RFC representative) that distress in poorer parts of the city was extreme.[27]

Gifford Pinchot's anger exploded in several drafts of a letter (composed but not sent) in which he expressed his outrage:

That Philadelphia, with an annual budget of about $20,000,000, cannot find half a million dollars to carry out the most vital, immediate, and imperative duty which rests upon it, is simply unthinkable. So far as I am aware, Phila-

---

[27] Numerous papers relating to this and allied disputes with the city are in LC Pinchot. The letter from Cox was dated November 30.

delphia is the only large city in America which is doing nothing whatever for its unemployed.

He decided, or was persuaded, that recrimination was best avoided, and sent a formal acknowledgment with one added sentence; "What I think about the position of the city as to its unemployed may just as well be left unsaid."[28]

Philadelphia also failed to provide a shelter for homeless men. When a correspondent suggested that one should be set up by the SERB, Pinchot replied that almost every other large city maintained such a shelter and asked why Philadelphia should be the exception:

I suppose it is going to be necessary to supplement the disgraceful failure of the City authorities and the rich people of Philadelphia, and do the work, which, under every consideration of self-respect and respect for the City, ought to be done by the City and its people, But if the SERB does it, it will be done with a complete understanding of the unspeakable shortcomings of the City.[29]

Pinchot's disgust with Philadelphia was heightened by the fact that he was fighting on the other front with the RFC. The decision on the loan was still deferred, and on September 8, he wrote a furious letter to the RFC complaining of "cruel and unnecessary" delays. He said that he had complied with all the conditions laid down in the act, only to be confronted with a further demand for a monthly account of all relief expenditure in every county during the past twelve months. Even if the information had been readily available, he thought the request unreasonable. On taxation, despite his personal opinion of the legislature, he took a state rights line and argued that it was not for the RFC but for the people to decide how they should tax themselves.[30]

In November, Pennsylvania finally got a loan of $5,500,000. This was much less than had been requested and was accompanied by a warning that "until the state of Pennsylvania and/or its various political subdivisions have taken additional action to meet the emergency needs of the people," the RFC was unlikely to consider further applications with favor.[31]

[28] Pinchot to Cox (draft), December 1932.

[29] Pinchot to William T. Plummer, October 18, 1932.

[30] FDR Library, Hopkins Papers, Box 42, Pinchot to Alex Pomerne, September 8, 1932. Kelso said that Mrs. Livewright treated all requests for further information as unreasonable; Pinchot was friendly and pleasant but impatient.

[31] Ibid., Pomerene to Pinchot, November 7, 1932.

By the spring of 1933 it was clear that more must be done, and the Governor used all the pressure at his command to procure a generous appropriation backed by realistic fiscal measures. Still the legislature dallied, and showed every sign of stalling as long as possible or even of adjourning without making an appropriation. On March 30, Pinchot wrote to Karl de Schweinitz, acting chairman of the Philadelphia County Relief Board, asking him to use his influence to get things done:

The relief situation is getting steadily worse, with the legislature blowing bubbles and playing politics week after week. I don't understand how they can trifle with a situation as serious as this, but that apparently is what they are doing.

He also sent a circular letter to ministers of religion and to all persons prominent in voluntary organizations, pointing out that though fifteen weeks of the session had passed the legislature had passed not a single important bill, that relief funds would soon be exhausted, and that the RFC would not help states that would not help themselves.[32]

Pinchot's energetic lobbying for the appropriation had been spurred on by a further warning from the RFC, relayed by Robert Kelso, that all loans would be stopped unless the State did more. He said that all the RFC expected was "reasonable diligence, but with this consideration in mind, the next move was plainly up to Pennslyvania and it would have to be substantial." On March 25, Kelso recommended that Pennsylvania, which had "sound credit and great wealth," should get no more money.[33]

Finally, and after much acrimony, the legislature yielded to pressure and made an appropriation of $40,000,000 for relief, financed mainly by a bond issue. This outcome gave no one full satisfaction but saved everyone's face. The RFC had made its point and stuck to it. The SERB got its money and could distribute it through a reasonably efficient network of county boards. The city council of Philadelphia had weathered the storm without raising more money from its citizens. The voters could congratulate themselves on having given the bond issue (submitted to them as required by the constitution) a handsome majority. The legislature had avoided raising taxes. Gifford Pinchot had at last succeeded in getting adequate relief to those who needed it.

[32] LC Pinchot, Pinchot to de Schweinitz, March 30, 1933.
[33] NA RG 69 (RFC Files), Kelso to Croxton, February 11, March 25, 1933.

The old poor boards were the principal losers, but they still retained a considerable capacity for obstruction.

A lesson to be learned was that townships and poor districts were incapable of handling the social consequences of the depression. Criticized in earlier years, they were now wholly discredited. Counties were in a better position, but experience had shown that they could do little without an effective state board supervising county agencies. As Pinchot said in his final message before leaving office: "The State Government is an efficient operating unit. It compares favorably with the best modern business organizations. The inefficiency lies mainly in the local units of government."[34]

A further lesson was that even a strong state board could not do what was required to meet the crisis. Whether the reason was to be sought in the exhaustion of state and local resources, constitutional restraints, or deeply ingrained attitudes, it was clear that even an old and rich state could not or would not give adequate relief to its able-bodied unemployed. In Philadelphia it was made clear that whatever lip service might be paid to local responsibility, the city would not care for its own.

The many disputes that attended the development of relief policy in Pennsylvania should not obscure the progress made during the troubled governorship of Gifford Pinchot. In a confidential assessment dated March 2, 1933, the SERB rated eleven county boards as good, thirteen as poor, and the remainder as adequate. Even if "adequate" was generous for some boards, it was no mean achievement for this standard to be attained in six months in fifty-four out of the sixty-seven counties. More difficult to assess is the degree to which opinion had shifted, but by 1933 more people than ever before recognized the need to give not merely relief but adequate relief to the unemployed. Pinchot's fight on behalf of the unemployed had not been wholly in vain.

Illinois also made early application to the RFC, but unlike Pennsylvania received quick and favorable consideration. A loan to tide over immediate difficulties was given on July 20, and the State was encour-

---

[34] *Final Message to the General Assembly of the Commonwealth of Pennsylvania by Gifford Pinchot, Governor* (Harrisburg, 1935). The message contained a complete review of social policy and legislation during his administration and indicted the Republican majority for having failed to follow his recommendations. With justice he pointed out that this had led to a resounding Democratic victory in the 1934 state elections.

aged to apply for more in the fall. As the Illinois Emergency Relief Commission (IERC) had been inundated with applications from Chicago, other cities in the state, and depressed mining counties, the first loan came just in time to save it from stopping further aid.

To prepare the ground for a second application, the IERC made a careful survey of needs and available funds, and came to the disturbing conclusion that even without raising the very low prevailing standards or paying rent for the unemployed faced with eviction, $36,000,000 over and above private and local resources would be required. The situation in Chicago and Cook County was alarming, and dire consequences were feared if relief stopped. Armed with this evidence, the IERC requested a further $23,000,000 to see them through until January 1933, and a delegation led by Edward L. Ryerson, chairman of the IERC, came to Washington to present the case and to impress upon the RFC the urgent needs of the metropolitan region.[35]

With good cause, the RFC asked what the State was doing to help itself. The legislature had met on Labor Day but had spent weeks without showing any inclination to vote taxes for relief. Most downstate legislators treated relief as a Chicago problem, argued that wealth in the city was untapped, and made much of alleged waste by profligate social workers. Of the 102 counties in the state, 52 were not interested in getting more money for relief, and if one of their representatives voted to raise taxes, he would, in the words of the state speaker, be "voting his own exit" at the forthcoming election. The RFC saw the difficulty and agreed to give a loan of $3,000,000, but this did no more than meet Chicago's immediate needs. Some further allocations were made in the new year, bringing the grand total from federal funds to $48,463,621.[36]

Illinois did not get all that it had asked for, but it got more than any other state. In March 1933 the RFC said that there would be nothing more until Illinois made a larger contribution, but in spite of this ultimatum no significant sums were appropriated, and from July 1932 to August 1933 federal funds paid for 99 percent of unemployment relief costs in Illinois.[37]

---

[35] For accounts of relief in Illinois, see Frank Z. Glick, *The Illinois Emergency Relief Commission* (Chicago, 1940), and Arthur P. Miles, *Federal Aid and Public Assistance in Illinois* (Chicago, 1941).
[36] FDR Library, Hopkins Papers. Memorandum of the meeting of the Board of the RFC with a delegation from Illinois.
[37] Ibid.

The legislature did agree on a sales tax, but this was promptly invalidated by the Illinois Supreme Court. An amended measure, framed to get around the constitutional objections, scraped through by a bare margin, in the legislature; but it yielded too little to make a serious contribution to relief costs. Although the main thrust of opposition to new taxes came from the rural counties, the state's leading newspapers did not help, and many businessmen continued to resist increases in relief expenditure. As one of them explained:

While it is probably true that we cannot allow anyone to starve (although I personally disagree with this philosophy and the philosophy of the city social worker), we should tighten up relief all along the line, and if relief is to be given it must be on a bare subsistence allowance.[38]

The prevalent view did not go as far as this, and relief was justified provided that someone else paid. Few objections to the principle of federal aid were heard, and wherever distress was severe, more was requested; but lack of contributions from the State kept relief at the bare minimum, and Illinois succeeded in doing less with more federal money than any other state.

There was a contrast between the treatment accorded Illionis and Pennsylvania. In both states, there was evidence of acute distress in the largest cities and of chronic unemployment in coal-mining communities; in both, the legislatures were at first unsympathetic to requests for state aid and opposed to raising taxes. Yet whereas Illinois received a quick allocation from the RFC, Pennsylvania had to wait for over two months, was asked to supply far more detailed information, and received nearly $19,000,000 less in the first twelve months of federal relief.

The discrepancy between the treatment of the two states may be explained in part by Pinchot's unpopularity in Washington, coupled with the hope (which proved to be vain) of getting a Republican elected in Illinois in November 1932. Something may also be due to the careful review of needs and resources prepared by the IERC for the RFC. Pinchot weakened his case by claiming that distress was acute without producing the facts to substantiate his normally correct assessments. The IERC was also able to convince the RFC that it could exer-

---

[38] A. M. Schlesinger, Jr., *The Age of Roosevelt,* Vol. II, *The Coming of the New Deal* (Boston, 1958), 265 (quoting Robert E. Wood of Sears Roebuck, described as a "liberal businessman").

cise effective control over relief administration, but in Pennsylvania the unfortunate results under the first Talbot Act (highlighted by Pinchot's attacks upon it) increased suspicion that federal funds might be drained away into the morass of inefficient local administration. These considerations played their part, but the fact that gave most urgency to the deliberations of the RFC was the explosive situation in Chicago, Mayor Anton Cermak told the RFC in September 1932 that if the relief stations closed, it would be necessary to call out the state militia to deal with the violent disorder that would ensue. Pennsylvania may have suffered because Philadelphia was a more peaceable city than Chicago.[39]

As more states applied for loans, the RFC was called upon to verify the facts and, as most loans were given for very short periods, to inquire whether renewals were justified. Under the terms of the act, the primary responsibility of the RFC was financial; it was not, and was not intended to be, a national department of welfare. Its approach was open to criticism, and in November 1932 Edith Abbott, writing on "the fallacy of local relief," made the point that ability to pay, not need, determined the amount it gave. The issue turned on whether "some financially incompetent local government" could not be made to pay more, and the RFC was compelled to ask "what can a state afford," not "what ought it to afford?" Miss Abbott might have been reassured if she could have inspected the confidential RFC relief files, in which she would have found the field representatives doing a great deal more. Most of them were experienced welfare administrators and, for the first time, local relief administration came under professional scrutiny from men who could not be denied access to even the darkest places and whose reports would regulate the flow of cash.[40]

From different parts of the country the message was the same: Order, planning, uniformity, and knowledge were required; poor administration, needless variety, ignorance, and amateur prejudice were the realities. Distress had been pictured as an urban and industrial problem but was also acute in many depressed rural areas. Local governments

---

[39] Mayor Cermak's remark was made during the meeting with the Board of the RFC (see note 36, this chapter).

[40] Edith Abbott, "The Fallacy of Local Relief," *New Republic,* November 9, 1932, reprinted in Edith Abbott, *Public Assistance,* Vol. I (Chicago, 1940), 730–60.

were collapsing under the burden of relief, but in only a few states were determined efforts being made to provide aid where it was needed.[41]

In Kansas, Sherrard Ewing found an efficient program but little understanding of the human problems created by unemployment. The state committee had done an outstanding job in organizing work projects, but the chairman was obsessed by the idea that most applicants for direct relief were "loafers who don't want to work." It was official policy that only "those who wanted to work" need apply for emergency relief, but local officials who were responsible for vetting applicants had been given no clear instructions on eligibility. Some local officials used the relief program to get the state to pay for work they would have been obliged to undertake in normal times. The Governor was responsible for administering RFC money but was unhappy about the way it might be used and "blurted out his lack of confidence in county commissioners."[42]

In Maine the Governor saw similar difficulties. Robert Kelso found him set against "throwing RFC funds to the poor boards" and doubtful whether more money would make the poor relief system function effectively. He proposed to get around the inefficient town governments by departing from the New England system and organizing relief on a county basis. Meanwhile, relief was not reaching those in distress, and Kelso was shocked to find that conditions in remote Aroostock counties were worse than those that he had encountered anywhere else (with the possible exception of some Pennsylvania coal towns and a few industrial districts with very high unemployment). Even if the Governor succeeded in his reorganization plan, financing relief might still present insuperable difficulties; existing taxes would yield no more, the State had so far refused to raise them or borrow, and it was therefore doubtful whether the conditions for an RFC loan had been met.[43]

---

[41] Disorganization affected others besides the unemployed, and many welfare services were cut back or neglected. The Federal Children's Bureau reported that during the year ending June 30, 1933, there had been "a serious curtailment of services to children, or in some cases the entire abandonment of these services." It said that "reports from many states leave no doubt that in the hysteria of economy there has been a reckless disregard of obligations that the community has assumed toward children." (*Annual Report of the [United States] Secretary of Labor for the Year ending June 30, 1933,* 74–5.)

[42] NA RG 69 (FERA Files, Old Series), Box 2: Reports on visits to Kansas, January 1, February 29, and March 16, 1933.

[43] Ibid. Reports on visits to Maine, November 29, 1932, February 1 and May 14, 1933.

In Texas the RFC field representative was A. W. McMillen, a professor of sociology from the University of Chicago seconded to government service. In Travis County his indignation at what he found spilled over. The relief committee was "the worst encountered anywhere in the United States." The two men running it were "only a degree above illiteracy," and one was rumored to demand two dollars from every Mexican placed on the relief rolls. A successful applicant was given a ticket and told to report to the foreman of the work project, but there was no subsequent check to see whether full-time, part-time, or no work was provided. Direct relief was equally slipshod, and it was alleged that some applicants got both grocery orders and work relief but others in equal need got nothing.[44]

The Travis County relief committee ran a soup kitchen, to which people came with buckets and left with spoonfuls. McMillen's verdict was that "the whole relief set-up is primitive, inefficient, and wasteful." Things were not much better in the state organization. Accounting was unreliable, information was deficient, and any improvement was blocked by a member of the state commission from eastern Texas who talked constantly, made it impossible to consider matters calmly, and was "almost the most disagreeable person . . . ever encountered in a meeting." Decisions when made were the product of ignorance, prejudice, and acrimony.[45]

In Virginia the RFC representative had to insist that federal loans for relief were not intended to finance current programs for highway construction, must be the responsibility of designated agencies, and ought to be allocated according to need. The whole welfare system was outdated. Only twelve counties had public welfare departments, and in all others the whole responsibility for welfare and relief rested with directors of the poor in their separate districts. Despite representations from the RFC, little was done until June 1933, when the Virginia Emergency Relief Administration (VERA) was created, with the Commissioner of Public Welfare at its head. The new law also required counties receiving federal aid to set up relief committees, and existing public welfare departments were strengthened by the appointment of field representatives.[46]

[44] Ibid. McMillen to Croxton, February 13, 1933.
[45] Ibid.
[46] NA RG 69 (FERA Files, Old Series), Box 2 (Virginia), August 19, 1932.

These improvements had some effect and William A. Smith, an engineer and former city manager, proved to be an efficient executive secretary of the VERA; but old poor law principles still ruled in most county districts, and the VERA staff was too small to provide effective supervision over the expenditure of federal money. In addition to being weak at the roots, the Virginia system was defective at the head. The legislature, backed by the Governor and by the powerful U.S. Senator Harry Byrd, steadfastly refused to vote money for relief on the ground that state expenditure on highways should be recognized as the State's contribution to work relief. Thus Virginia followed, on a grand scale, the practice of many small units of local government in claiming that normal public work relieved unemployment.[47]

McMillen's reports on California contained a summary of all that was wrong in relief administration. The State had a formidable problem with migrants arriving in great numbers from all parts of the United States, but there was no comprehensive program for transients. Information was difficult to obtain because no system of reporting by local units had been instituted.[48]

Los Angeles exhibited the worst examples of incompetence and malpractice. An Employment Stabilization Bureau had been set up to cooperate with the POUR and then to distribute money from the RFC loan. Its director, Harvey Fremming, was prominent in organized labor, but McMillen reported that he was "completely lacking in executive capacity" and that the bureau was "the most chaotic organization" he had ever encountered. It had little control over its branch offices, failed to insist upon the investigation of cases, and seemed powerless to prevent the use of RFC money for party political purposes. Under pressure from the RFC, the bureau appointed forty

---

[47] The fullest account of relief in Virginia is still Arthur W. James, *The State Becomes a Social Worker* (Richmond, 1942). He was a long-time official of the State Board of Public Welfare and a great admirer of William Smith; his very favorable judgments must therefore be discounted, but as an insider's story, the book tells a great deal about welfare administration. Robert F. Hunter, "Virginia and the New Deal" in Braeman et al., *The New Deal*, Vol. II, 103–36, describes the political background and Virginian attitudes to relief. Heinemann, *Depression and New Deal in Virginia: The Enduring Dominion* (Charlottesville, 1983), gives more attention to relief administration; on Smith see Heinemann, *Depression and New Deal*, 82, 122.

[48] NA RG 69 (FERA Files), Old Series, Box 2, California: Reporting a visit, October 18–20, 1932.

investigators, but all were taken from the relief rolls, none had qualifications for the job, and their visits were few and perfunctory.[49]

To deal with the flood of applications for relief, Los Angeles had evolved a procedure that opened wide the door for political influence while imposing unnecessary hardship on those in need. Applicants were classed as "on call" or "active." The active got employment only when all on call had been placed. Naturally all men on the active list wanted to transfer to on-call, and though this might be done by waiting in line with 400 others at the central office, a surer way was to seek political help. Every day a list of approved applicants went from party headquarters to the relief office, and work was invariably found for all who were on it. It was said that the mayor's wife managed most of this business. Adverse publicity had brought about a grand jury investigation, but the city authorities had tried to destroy all copies of its report. McMillen was able to obtain one and incorporated it into his report to the RFC. He recommended that the city bureau should no longer be recognized as an efficient agency and that all federal money should be handled by the Bureau of Welfare in Los Angeles County, which, in welcome contrast to the city, had a trained staff and used sound professional methods.[50]

The city of Los Angeles was the worst example of relief maladministration, but matters were not much better in the state. Although Governor "Sunny Jim" Rolph showed little interest in relief problems, he had set up an Unemployment Commission in 1930 (which argued that the "new poor" should be treated differently from normal relief clients), and when federal loans became available, he applied for and received $9,800,000.[51]

The State Department of Welfare was designated as the agency to handle RFC money, and Rolph appointed as its head Mrs. Riva Spivalo. She had been a child evangelist in New York, had since been associated with Aimee Semple McPherson in Los Angeles, and had no perceptible qualifications for the post, which she clearly intended to treat as a personal power base. She dismissed experienced officials and appointed incompetents, but unlike other wayward state officials she made herself unpopular with the legislature, which regularly cut her

---

[49] Ibid.: Visits during April 1933.

[50] Ibid.

[51] *Report of the State Unemployment Commission,* Sacramento, January 1931 (recommendations not acted upon until January 1933).

budget. She was soon at odds with the RFC. McMillen was astonished to hear her announce over the radio that she would use RFC money to help victims of a Long Beach earthquake, and had to remind her sharply that the RFC loan was for the relief of unemployment and nothing else. The Governor professed to know nothing about the matter, or indeed to be aware that the RFC loan had been received. McMillen concluded that Rolph and Mrs. Spivalo were "less competent to do the state's business" than any others in his region. All in all, the record in California provided the strongest possible argument for firm directions in future federal relief policy.[52]

The RFC had little information on two states containing large metropolitan regions. Massachusetts and Maryland embodied very different traditions, but both stood out as long as possible against federal aid, and the RFC field representatives had therefore only a short time to make their assessments. As Maryland represented the last stand of state rights and Massachusetts a partially successful defense of the original system of town self-government, both are worth examination.

The peculiar geography of Maryland meant that the city of Baltimore and the other five regions of the state had few interests in common. In social structure and attitudes, the "eastern shore" of the Chesapeake belonged to the old South. In the central part of the state, south and west of Baltimore, was much arable and grazing county with pleasant small towns. Ringing the District of Columbia were high-class residential communities serving the national capital. To the west the long, narrow projection of the state penetrated Appalachia and included some mining districts. Baltimore itself attracted less attention than other great cities, but it was the second busiest Atlantic port and an enormous volume of midwestern trade was carried by the Baltimore and Ohio Railroad. About one-third of the population was black, there were substantial German and Jewish groups, and Catholicism of the old style (that is, English or German) was strong. The city was a cosmopolitan oasis set in the midst of a state with its roots in a rural, Anglo-Saxon, and slave-owning past.

The southern character of the state was evident in its administrative structure. The counties were the units for all forms of local govern-

[52] James Leiby, "State Welfare Administration in California, 1930–45," *Southern California Quarterly* LIV (1972), 303–18.

ment, including welfare. Traditions of local autonomy were strong, and the legislators, meeting biennially for somewhat leisurely sessions in the pleasant state capital at Annapolis, were little disposed to enlarge their responsibilities.

The State had developed an efficient public health administration concerned mainly with sanitation, water supplies, action against epidemics, and keeping the valuable inshore fishing grounds clear of pollution. Other public services were backward by the standards of the day. Dr. George Walker, of the State Board of Charities, told a meeting of the League of Women Voters that in twenty county almshouses recently visited, the majority of the inmates were physically or mentally sick, medical care was inefficient and infrequent, and food was poor. Most of these dismal "homes" were "oubliettes where unfortunates were shut away and forgotten," and were, in addition, uneconomical to run. In evidence before the Ways and Means Committee of the lower house of the legislature, Dr. Walker said that the average cost per inmate was $400 a year when a centralized system with modern buildings would give humane care at an annual cost of $250 a head. In a state where indigent old people were treated so shabbily, rapid action to relieve distress caused by unemployment was improbable.[53]

In 1930 Albert C. Ritchie was elected governor for a fourth term as an old-line Democrat. He was an honest, fair-minded, and efficient administrator who had been born and bred in the conviction that the best government was that which governed least. In his fourth inaugural address he described Maryland as "a self-governing state, free to settle its own problems in conformity with the needs of its people, who should be unhampered by an excess of government from within and by undue Federal supervision or interference from without." Acting on these principles, he was convinced that neither a centralized state relief administration nor federal intervention was necessary.[54]

Opposing views were most likely to be expressed in Baltimore. The city was unusual in having depended almost wholly on private charity to provide general relief. Though the city government was active in welfare matters – with good institutional care and environmental serv-

---

[53] *Baltimore Sun,* February 25, March 26, 1931. This and the following references to Baltimore newspapers are taken from Ritchie's own extensive collection of newspaper clippings in the Maryland Hall of Records, Annapolis.
[54] January 14, 1931.

ices – it gave no outdoor relief and confined itself to identifying needs to be dealt with by private agencies. The State Department of Charities paid for old-age and widows' pensions but gave no help for general relief. A community chest raised funds for relief, but in 1930 it had met little more than half its target of $2,000,000, and even optimists did not forecast more than $1,500,000 for 1931. An Emergency Unemployment Committee had been set up to promote work projects and work-sharing schemes; its administrative costs were met partly from the proceeds of a state gambling tax and partly by the city, but it had no money to distribute.

Howard T. Jackson, the Mayor of Baltimore, was usually at odds with the Governor, but was at first inclined to accept his view that the city could pull through without outside help. As time went on, he became more and more convinced that state aid or, failing that, federal assistance was necessary. He used his position to make public the plight of the city, but Ritchie stuck firmly to the principle of local responsibility, with exceptions in only the most unusual circumstances.

Ritchie's resistance to federal interference caused him to refuse information when requested or to give it in such general terms that it could be of little use. A representative from the POUR reported that the Governor thought that his State did not need "any attention from Federal sources," and members of his administration would give little help. The State Department of Public Welfare had no figures on the number unemployed or the relief given, and its director "did not think it was necessary to take any special steps to stir the counties to any unusual activity on account of unemployment." The POUR circulated some questions to state governors, but Ritchie ignored repeated requests for replies, and when he finally answered in November 1931, it was to state briefly that the relief organization was satisfactory in all counties, that there was no need to appoint a state chairman to supervise relief, as he did this himself, and that Maryland would take care of its own unemployment. The meticulous way in which Ritchie handled most official business leaves no doubt that the discourtesy was intentional; though within the limits he had set, attention to welfare would be scrupulous.[55]

[55] NA RG 78 (POUR Files): Report by L. A. Halbert to Frank Bane, American Association of Public Welfare Officials, on the Unemployment Relief Situation in Maryland. Copy in files of Assistant Director, POUR. Ritchie's reply to the POUR questions is in ibid., November 11, 1931.

The Governor's reticence was counterproductive because it left Mayor Jackson and other leading Baltimoreans with a clear field to make public their needs and force Ritchie on to the defensive. Because he was a serious contender for the Democratic presidential nomination he had to avoid any appearance of insensitivity to suffering, and, in a public statement following a conference with officials and representatives of city charities, he repeated his view that no state aid was needed in any county but promised that if the city could not handle its own problems, he would call the legislature into special session to authorize a bond issue and a loan to the city in anticipation of its proceeds. "People are not going to be permitted to go unfed, unclothed, or unsheltered anywhere in this state."[56]

There can be no doubt that Ritchie spoke for a majority in the state. In May 1932 the Maryland Conference on Social Work issued a special report on conditions, which it found good in eleven counties and fair in seven. Though distress was severe in five counties, the report made it clear that "the present attitude of the people of the state, as voiced in the twenty-three county reports, is at present almost solidly opposed to state financial aid and in favor of the use of local resources to meet local needs." The conference urged statewide planning to coordinate work projects but neither transfer of funds to the hard-pressed city of Baltimore nor additional taxation.[57]

The passage of the first federal Emergency Relief Act made little difference in Maryland. The State obtained a federal loan for highway construction, but this was something that might have happened at any time; no move was made for an RFC relief loan, and Baltimore struggled along without additional help. In November 1932, Ritchie defended his policy in a letter to an influential Baltimore rabbi, Edward L. Israel. He said that the State had not given Baltimore money because a lend/loan agreement had provided funds to meet the emergency. Although no new taxes had been passed to finance relief, he had decided to submit some proposals to the legislature at their next meeting. No federal aid had been sought because inquiries had shown that there were very few localities unable to handle their own problems, and where this was impossible, the legislature might be persuaded to make special provision.[58]

[56] *Baltimore Sun*, March 18, 1932.
[57] *Baltimore Post*, May 26, 1932.
[58] Maryland Hall of Records, Correspondence of Governor Ritchie, Ritchie to Rabbi Edward L. Israel, November 8, 1932.

The situation changed in March 1933 with the publication of a report by an Advisory Committee on Unemployment Relief, which had been set up on the Governor's own initiative. It found widespread distress in Baltimore, the city of Cumberland, and twelve counties, and it was no longer confined to "low standard white people, the Negroes, and the poor who are always with us." To reconcile local responsibility with state obligations, the committee contributed a fragment of social theory:

We live in an intimate cooperative society. The strong and the weak, rich and poor, intelligent and stupid, the thrifty and the lazy, the generous and selfish are all inextricably bound together.... In the last analysis the State ... pays the bill for the individual and family deterioration which is the inevitable result of misery and want.

The committee argued that a state relief agency was now necessary and suggested that it be modeled on the Board of Health, with the immediate task of securing the appointment of county relief boards, but to remain as a permanent part of the state's administrative structure. It did not make a positive recommendation that federal aid should be sought, but it noted that thirty-seven other states had already done so and wondered what it was in Maryland's situation that made it an exception.[59]

Even with this report on his desk, Ritchie delayed for over two months before finally deciding to apply for an RFC loan. His last-ditch stand in defense of state rights and local reponsibility had been defeated by events. There was an ironic footnote: Less than two years later, the federal government threatened to cut off aid to the state that had proclaimed so long that it could care for its own because it was not doing enough to help itself.[60]

Massachusetts enjoyed the distinction of being the only state with major industries to survive the depression without being forced to

[59] *Report and Recommendations of the Advisory Committee on Unemployment Relief,* Baltimore, March 1932.
[60] NA RG 69, 406.2, Maryland: Aubrey Williams to Arch Mandel, May 29, 1934: "Mr. Hopkins has informed the Maryland crowd that they have got to put some money into the relief pot, as he does not intend to continue to pay the entire bill." Before this the *Baltimore Sun* reported a speech in the city by Hopkins in which he said: "Maryland should not ask the United States to hold the bag.... Cities and States talk about protecting their credit. This gives me a pain."

make radical changes in its system of relief. This was appropriate in the home of the town meeting, and local government in Massachusetts retained features that contributed to its strength. Urban places were usually part of the town in which they were situated and not separately incorporated, as was common in other states. The fragmentation of responsibility and the complexities of overlapping administration were therefore avoided, and the fiscal base of local government was much stronger than in other parts of the country.

The relative efficiency of local finance was particularly important. In 1931 the State Director of Accounts wrote that although Massachusetts had "felt the depression more than anyone could possibly have foretold," its local finances were "in far better condition than [those of] other sections of the country." By 1932 it had become necessary to dip deeply into reserves, but cities and towns had kept their financial structure "in a sane and sound condition." When federal aid finally came, it was limited to work projects and designed to preserve rather than supplant local responsibility.[61]

A major reason for the resilience of Massachusetts during the depression was a strong tradition of public responsibility for welfare, embodied in an active Department of Public Welfare. It had no executive power to control the local administration of relief, but in this and other matters it had long been the custom in Massachusetts to rely upon advisory state agencies without power to coerce but carrying weight with informed opinion. Local governments could ignore advice and improvements were liable to take longer than impatient reformers would wish; but over a long period, events moved in the direction indicated by the Department of Public Welfare. There was also some gain in the fact that the state capital was its greatest city, which fostered close links between government, commerce, and professional life.

The Department of Public Welfare was directly responsible only for the management of state institutions, the care of dependent children, and the administration of a housing act, but it kept in close touch with local welfare problems, compiled statistics, disseminated information, maintained a flow of good advice, and acted upon the assumption that once local officials understood a problem and were made aware of modern methods for dealing with it, they would bring their own practice into line.

[61] *Annual Statistics of Municipal Finance for 1931* (Boston, 1932).

The department's policy was intelligently conservative, and it claimed that its tried and tested methods brought durable results. On the one hand, its reluctance to innovate can be judged from its statement in 1924 opposing statutory pensions for disadvantaged groups: "Any system of old age pensions, pensions for the blind, pensions for the handicapped, or pensions for any particular class of disadvantaged persons would tend to substitute for the present intelligent and modern system of public welfare administration the wholesale method of the dole." On the other hand, the department urged upon towns the need to treat all forms of destitution and dependency under one comprehensive program, to investigate all cases individually, and to fix the level of relief according to need.

Indeed, the Department of Public Welfare went beyond these precepts of social work to argue that welfare must concern itself with the causes as well as the consequences of poverty. In 1925 it said that just as modern medicine was as much concerned with causes as with cures, "so modern philanthropy is bending its efforts toward discovering the causes of poverty and is trying to devise means for its prevention." It also insisted that all forms of welfare called for special skills, and smaller towns were urged to combine in appointing trained social workers – as many already did when appointing school superintendents – for "social service is a profession with at least as many skills as the teaching profession."[62]

The functions of local government increased as the horizons of welfare extended. In 1931 the Department of Public Welfare claimed that a relief crisis had been averted by "the development of strong local boards of public welfare during the last two decades, when each new relief responsibility was placed squarely on the shoulders of existing boards instead of upon new boards created for new forms of relief." Typical of this policy was an Old Age Assistance Act, passed in 1931, that preserved "the important advantage of elasticity" by leaving town officials free to fix the amount of assistance to be given in each case."[63]

Self-congratulation did not mean that all was well. In 1932 a state

---

[62] Massachusetts Department of Public Welfare, *Annual Reports:* 1924, 3; 1925, 8; 1933, 2–3.

[63] Ibid., 1931, 2; Old Age Assistance Law – ibid., 1930, 2. On December 5, 1931, William Phillips (State Commission on Employment) told the POUR that out of 355 communities in Massachusetts, 160 had relief committees, 182 did not need them, and only 12 gave cause for concern (NA RG 73, Massachusetts File: record of a conference between Phillips and Fred Croxton).

committee on mothers' aid deplored the low standards of relief and condemned some towns for ceasing to give an allowance for rent. Sensibly it observed that "if the rent is not paid to the owner he cannot pay taxes, and then where is the money to come from?" Also, as the depression deepened, the larger cities faced catastrophe. In January 1933 the RFC representative noted that one in seven were without work in Boston, and that the outcome of a community chest drive was very doubtful.[64]

Federal aid became imperative but Massachusetts accepted it only for work projects, and insisted that the administration and financing of direct relief remain local responsibilities. The RFC representatives could not pursue their inquiries where federal money was not being used, but early in 1933 one of them reported that all he had heard indicated inadequate relief and outdated methods. In contrast, the State claimed that the towns treated the unemployed as potential wage earners and were advised not to ruin their prospects by driving them to destitution. The truth lay between the two. The average level of relief given was high, some local officials acted upon the good advice they received, and others continued to administer poor relief on traditional lines. There was much to commend, but trust in local government meant that old ways could continue without directives from a state relief agency or critical comments by RFC representatives.[65]

While officials of the RFC found their way into the perplexing land of relief administration, the instigators of federal relief prepared for the next step. In November 1932 the steering committee of the Conference on Federal Action on Unemployment was reconstituted as a committee of the American Association of Social Work, whose journal, *Compass,* became the principal means of communication with social workers interested in further federal action. The American Public Welfare Association set up a separate group, the Conference on the Maintenance of Welfare Standards. In January 1933, when LaFollette reintroduced his bill, an impressive array of witnesses, including twenty-five social workers, had been lined up for hearings.[66]

---

[64] Massachusetts Department of Public Welfare, *Annual Report,* 1932, 11–12; NA RG 73 (POUR Files): Alice F. Stenhold to the RFC, January 22, 23, 1932.
[65] NA RG 69 (RFC Files): Massachusetts.
[66] Colcord, "Social Work and the First Federal Relief Program"; Bremer, *Depression Winters* (see note 4, this chapter).

In 1932 the paramount purpose had been to demonstrate that only the federal government could fill the gap between what was being done and what ought to be done; in 1933 it was to show that the first Emergency Relief Act was a faulted half-measure and that the coming change of administration would certainly mean its supercession. The loss of the bill (in the last lame duck session ever) was of no great moment; what was important was to prepare the ground for legislation after March 4, 1933.

In addition to exploring the limitations of the existing federal law, it was necessary to show that even when states were willing to act they could not bring relief as speedily or at the level that the desperate situation required. Constitutional restraints, the uncertain outcome of referenda on amendments, and the attitude of some state courts meant that it might be a long battle before governments could obtain the necessary powers. It would have been impolitic to reflect on the incompetence of state legislatures, but their delays, obstruction, and muddle were notorious. It had also to be shown that though efficient relief agencies were in operation in several states, the problems of the great cities were beyond the capacity of any state to solve. Finally, national responsibility was most easily demonstrated in the continuing problem of migrants in search of work, and it was decided to hold separate hearings on the relief of transients.

The hearings were conducted in a different spirit from those of the preceding year. Then the purpose had been to persuade a majority in Congress that legislation was necessary and the President that he must recognize the failure of the policy he had backed. In 1933 the question was not whether there would be a new policy but the shape that it would take. The agenda was to demonstrate the harm done by inadequate relief, highlight the special problems of large cities, show that state financial systems were too inflexible to find the money from their own resources, and argue the need for uniformity under federal guidance. A distinction between statutory and discretionary payments must be made, loans must be replaced by grants, and the principle established that a federal agency must have control over the expenditure of federal money.

Frank Bane, a much respected welfare administrator, tackled the inadequacy of relief. Much that was given amounted to no more than the minimum required to avoid starvation, and in many localities no allowance was made for rent, clothing, or medicine. The attempt to survive in these wretched conditions must, he said, "contribute ultimately to the deterioration of family life in the city, State, and Nation." Dr. Isaac Rubinow, a veteran campaigner for social insurance and a member of the Ohio State Unemployment Insurance Commission, said that even in Cincinnati, where finance was sound and government good, there were 120,000 out of a population of 600,000 dependent on relief (which had cost $3,000,000 in 1932 and was expected to cost half as much again in 1933). For Ohio as a whole, a low estimate for the coming year was $45,000,000 to support 225,000 families, and this was typical of the heavily populated states; the sums might seem to be prodigious, but "what we are doing with the 10,000,000 unemployed people in this country is to establish a new American standard of life, and it is on the basis of $200 a year." Rubinow referred scathingly to ignorant clamor about the dole: "What really produces demoralization is not so much the dole as the inadequate amount of the dole."[67]

In some cities, all relief had been stopped for lack of funds. How, then, did people survive (for it was sometimes said that no one starved)? Helen Hall, of the University Settlement in Philadelphia, quoted an answer from a pamphlet recently published in the city:

They did not starve to death when relief stopped. They kept alive from day to day, catch-as-catch can, reduced for actual subsistence to something of the status of a stray cat prowling for food, and for which a kindly soul set out a plate of scraps or a saucer of milk.

Mrs. Helen Tyson of the Pennsylvania Department of Public Welfare emphasized the effects of deprivation on health and described the results of a survey of school districts, covering a total of 800,000 children, of whom 20 to 40 percent were undernourished and no fewer than 75 percent suffered from physical defect.[68]

The experience of one small Pennsylvania town, wholly dependent on a steel mill that had ceased production, gave dramatic warning of

[67] 72nd Congress. 2nd Session. Senate Committee on Manufactures, Subcommittee on Federal Aid for Unemployment Relief, *Hearings, January 3–17, 1933*, Bane, 21ff.; Rubinow, 250–1.

[68] Ibid., Hall, 390; The most publicized examples of relief stoppage were in New York City in January 1932 and in Philadelphia in May to November 1930, April 1932 and June 25 to August 14, 1932. Karl de Schweinitz, Community Council of Philadelphia, described the effects of the stoppage of relief (115ff.); it meant that the administration packed up and that when funds were restored, the waiting list for interviews was very long. Hospitals were in financial difficulties because bills were unpaid, and other welfare services almost came to a halt. For Mrs. Tyson's evidence, see ibid., 411–569.

the contagion of unemployment and inadequate relief. Of its 2,000 people, 1,300 were on such low relief that they could not survive without free flour distributed by the Red Cross. No taxes were collected, no rents were paid, and a man who owned five houses was himself on relief because he had no income. Storekeepers faced bankruptcy, and the one physician attended people without being paid. Over the whole community there had settled a wasting blight. "Men stood around listlessly . . . and had been half-starved for so long that they had no spirit left."[69]

Harry Hopkins gave evidence that carried weight coming as it did from the head of an effective state relief agency and a close adviser of the President-elect. He gave an account of New York expenditure on relief, which had risen from $2,000,000 a month in December 1931 to $8,000,000 twelve months later and was expected to rise to $10,000,000 in the near future. In rebuttal of the frequent assertion that state relief stifled local efforts, Hopkins said that there was no evidence that New York's massive aid had had this result, and in spite or because of it, most localities were working effectively. In a significant statement, which might be interpreted as the keynote on relief for the next administration, he declared that "the unemployment relief problem in its magnitude has expanded beyond the capacity of local and even of State resources."[70]

Why had states reached the limit of their financial resources? Simeon E. Leland, professor of public finance at the University of Chicago, gave an expert analysis of the fiscal situation. States, cities, and other local governments depended heavily on property taxes (which were often excessive); local income and sales taxes were impractical; and though states could and often did levy such taxes, they had borrowed so freely in flush years that the revenue was swallowed up by interest charges on bonds. Thirty-six percent of the country's wealth was concentrated in Massachusetts, New York, Illinois, Pennsylvania, and California; but even these states were unable to cope with their relief problems, and there could be no solution short of a massive injection of federal money derived from equitable taxes. "Those who hold otherwise fail to recognize the very imperfect character of our State governments and their fiscal systems."[71]

[69] Ibid. 415. The description was given by Mrs. Tyson.
[70] Ibid., Hopkins, 79ff.
[71] Ibid., Leland, 216.

Several witnesses stressed the need for greater uniformity and national regulation. One put the problem in a single sentence: "We have forty-eight different ideas of how relief should be administered and forty-eight different ideas of who shall pay for it." The conventional respect for local responsibility was attacked by Helen Hall:

Unfortunately the words are used with more earnestness in combating Federal aid than in facing just how adequately the community itself is meeting that local responsibility. . . . We can well question the right that a community has to say that it is taking care of its own, when what it means by care is little more than payment of a grocery order.

It was no longer enough to provide federal money and leave its use to local or state governments; the way in which it was spent should be a national responsibility. Alex Pomerene, chairman of the RFC, admitted to having had only limited success in persuading states and localities to spend more on relief, and Mrs. Tyson (a state official) pressed for "planning on a nationwide basis."[72]

Nowhere was national responsibility more urgently needed than in tackling the difficulties of the larger cities. Only eight states made major contributions to unemployment relief, and even where they did, the cities carried most of the burden. It was easy to blame state administrations and legislatures for this imbalance, but how could they deal adequately with the economic giants placed by historical accident within their borders? Of the 165 political units with the largest revenues in the United States, 117 were cities. New York city was second only to the federal government; the next six included Chicago, Los Angeles, Detroit, and Philadelphia; only two states – New York and Pennsylvania – were in this league. Further down the list, Boston had a larger income than Massachusetts, Cleveland only slightly less than Ohio, St. Louis more than Missouri, and Baltimore more than Maryland. Other cities in the first thirty were (in order) Pittsburgh, Buffalo, Milwaukee, San Francisco, and Washington, D.C.[73]

[72] Ibid., Paul V. Betters, 209; Pomerene, 308; Tyson, 413. Fred Croxton of the RFC explained that the records often distorted the picture of federal relief because some states applied only for their worst hit counties. A map of Ohio, for instance, showed the greater part of the state not in receipt of federal relief, but in fact the areas receiving federal money covered 60 percent of the state's population (319).

[73] Ibid., 203ff. Paul V. Betters, executive director, American Municipal Association. The figures on expenditure were extracted from the *Annual Report of the Secretary of the Treasury, 1931; Financial Statistics of Cities . . . Over 30,000*, 1930; and *Finance and Statistics of the States*, 1930.

While states and cities argued over the equitable distribution of burdens, conditions in the metropolitan centers deteriorated. In Chicago some employees of the Board of Education (including janitors and clerks, as well as teachers) had not been paid for eight months; some city employees were on relief, though nominally in full employment; policemen preferred to resign and take a small but certain pension rather than wait indefinitely for payment of their salaries. The Chicago *Tribune* reckoned that the city owed its servants over $44,000,000. This situation had been brought on by the crippling responsibility for thousands of unemployed combined with the consequences of an economic disaster for which neither Chicago nor Illinois was responsible.[74]

The hearings on transients revealed the unprecedented scale of the problem, the impossibility of handling it at the local level, and the contradiction between praise for self-help and the treatment given to men traveling in search of work. The inevitable inference was that there must be a complete break with traditional attitudes to people without settlement, which could be achieved only by instituting a national program.

The most dramatic illustration of the difficulties came from California, where 1,200 unemployed men without settlement in the state crossed the borders every day. A state law had prohibited public relief for nonresidents, and the entire responsibility had fallen on private charities and community chests. During 1932 the State, with help from the cities, had tried to tackle the problem by setting up labor camps; however, progress was hampered by extremely hostile local attitudes. Homeless men were not wanted – whether as individuals looking for shelter or as inmates of camps – and the most that many communities would do was to provide a night's shelter and transportation to their place of legal settlement. A man who refused to move on was denied all relief, and in some instances transients from other states were taken to the border and told to walk. In the face of this hostility, many transients had not applied for relief but had set up their own camps and shared the proceeds of casual work for local farmers. There were seventy such camps in the Los Angeles area; in local eyes they were not

[74] Ibid., 270 (from evidence given by Edith Abbott).

praiseworthy experiments in cooperation but hideouts for desperate men preying upon the local communities.[75]

In the Eastern states attitudes were no more tolerant and perhaps more deeply rooted in tradition. Prentice Murphy, the Philadelphia welfare administrator, said that often the principle for local authorities was "if in doubt, call the police and have him arrested." How did this square with American traditions of kindliness and respect for those who were trying to help themselves?

An arrest because of poverty is something we like not to think about. . . . This fear of the stranger who is in need is a primitive one, and yet the chilled and unpleasant looking applicant may be, and very generally is, a person of worth and true appeal.

The common belief was that all transients were hobos, scroungers, and would-be criminals, but they had always included casual workers in search of seasonal employment and now included large numbers of young men eager to settle where they could find work. A check in Atlanta on 5,431 transients found 1,641 high school and 194 college graduates. In Philadelphia a disreputable-looking person, applying to a private charity, explained that three days in a boxcar in zero weather, without water, sleep, or food, would make anyone look like a thug: "But give me three days of heat, food, soap and water, and I will look just as I really am – a graduate of the University of Chicago."[76]

The evidence given by Harry Hopkins had been carefully checked with Roosevelt. On December 19, 1932, Hopkins wrote that he had been invited to testify and wanted to make sure that their views coincided. "It would be an advantage to have the groundwork laid . . . so that if a special session is called . . . a relief bill which will be in substantial accord with your views should be ready for immediate passage." He intended to advocate a federal organization "very similar to the one

---

[75] 72nd Congress, 2nd Sess., Senate Committee on Manufactures, Subcommittee on Relief for Unemployed Transients, *Hearings*, 5, 2–3 (S. Rexford Black), 34 (Grace Abbott). Paul V. Robinson, superintendent of the Wayside Mission, Anderson, Indiana (159), explained that in normal times transients fell into three main categories: migratory workers, especially in lumber, construction, and harvest work; habitual wanderers (the hobos), who made up perhaps 5 percent of the whole; and petty criminals, mentally deficient, and unsettled foreign labor.
[76] Ibid., 86.

you set up in the state, and it seems to me that it would work admirably in Washington."[77]

It was therefore no accident that the major points made by Hopkins provided the framework for future New Deal legislation on relief. He said that federal aid should be given in grants, not loans; the federal agency should be a separate organization, not bound by the rules and procedures of an existing department; and the federal government should deal directly with states through public agencies, and not with cities, counties, or private organization. Part of each grant should be allocated on a formula compounded of population and relief expenditure, but the remainder should be applied where needed at the discretion of the federal administrator.

Hopkins argued for grants, not loans, because federal aid should be regarded as a transfer of income from regions and individuals with a surplus. A state unable to finance relief out of current revenue should not be required to shift the burden from the present to the future. He said that a new federal agency free from existing bureaucratic precedents, would avoid the lengthy inquiries the RFC had made to ensure that a state's resources were exhausted. When distress was so severe, a "quick and discriminating decision" was essential. The federal government should deal only with states and public agencies because the chain of responsibility must be fixed precisely, and a working relationship would be easier to establish with a single state relief administrator than with numerous political subdivisions and private organizations, each with its own conventions and methods. The use of a substantial portion of the grants for discretionary payments would give the federal administrator the power to allocate where need was proven and on conditions laid down by himself.

Though the new agency would deal only with states, it would have to be aware of what was being done by local governments and maintain continuous pressure upon them to do their share and improve their methods. Hopkins told the subcommittee.

I believe ... that it is extremely important in any federal bill to fully protect the gains we have made in encouraging towns, cities, counties and state governments to meet their fair share of the load.

[77] N.Y.St.A.: Governor's Correspondence (TERA Files), Hopkins to Roosevelt, December 14, 1932. For the four following paragraphs, see his evidence to the subcommittee, 80ff.

He said that in New York the TERA had contributed very large sums to help local governments but had never relieved them of any of their own responsibilities.

When the hearings were complete, the next task was to prepare a bill, and at Roosevelt's suggestion, Hopkins was added to the unofficial drafting committee. The bill that emerged followed the lines proposed by Hopkins and informally endorsed by Roosevelt. Possible dissension in Democratic ranks was averted when Senator Wagner was persuaded that grants were preferable to loans and agreed to sponsor the bill in the new Congress. Immediately after his inauguration, Roosevelt called Congress into special session and on March 21 declared that it was "essential to the recovery program that measures immediately be enacted aimed at unemployment relief." On March 27 Wagner introduced the emergency relief bill.

The bill passed through its various stages without alteration in substance, but two important clauses were amended. The Senate voted to place the new relief administration under Civil Service rules; but this was struck out in the House and not revived by the Senate. This left it open for the new agency – the Federal Emergency Relief Administration – to employ hundreds of social workers without previous government employment and without the normal examination. The other matter concerned the treatment of recalcitrant states. The bill gave the federal administrator the right to appoint a state administrator if this was the only way to carry out the intentions of Congress; an amendment gave him the right, under rules and regulations prescribed by the President, to assume entire control of unemployment relief in any state.

The threat to place relief under federal control was to be a powerful weapon, but of greater importance for normal operation was the implied right of the federal administrator to inquire into the details of relief management in any part of the nation. During the debate, LaFollette defended the principle of discretionary grants because they could be used by the federal administrator as a lever to raise the standards of local relief. "This means," declared a critic of the bill, "that through his agents he has to go into every city of the land and determine whether the sad charges of graft and corruption, appearing in the very meanest type of political manipulation, are justified." Of greater significance was his right to demand improvements in state and local practice and to refuse money if the response was unsatisfactory. For social workers this was precisely the kind of investigatory power for which they had hoped; it opened a door through which they might advance to reform relief methods and principles, and ultimately to destroy the poor law that they had condemned for so long.

Appendix: The Unemployment Relief Census, 1933

The FERA made a survey of unemployed persons on relief in the late summer of 1933 and revealed the following facts.

1. There were wide variations, from region to region, in the number on relief. The average for the United States was 10 percent of the able-bodied population, but in some states it was as high as 25 percent.
2. Pennsylvania, New York, Ohio and Illinois accounted for about one-third of the total.
3. Other badly affected states were (in order of proportionate numbers on relief) Florida, South Carolina, West Virginia, Arizona, and Kentucky.
4. Three-fifths of those on relief lived in urban places of over 2,500.
5. The proportion of blacks on relief was higher than their proportion of the whole population. In cities with a significant number of blacks, the blacks on relief greatly exceeded the whites.
6. Large families dominated in the total number on relief, but among blacks there was little difference in family size between those on relief and those supporting themselves.

The census enumerated the people on relief as a result of unemployment. It therefore underestimated distress among farm owners or tenants who were suffering as a result of lost markets, loss of casual earnings, or drought.

Source: FERA, *Unemployment Relief Census,* Reports 1 and 2 (October 1933).

5

PARALLEL GOVERNMENT

The New Deal carried federal administration to the roots of American society. Activities that had never before been the concern of the national government came under federal scrutiny and local autonomy contracted. Although federal officials seldom possessed executive power in the states and formal respect was paid to local responsibility, a system of parallel government developed in which traditional authorities continued to function but the most important decisions were made in Washington. Nowhere was parallel government so clearly illustrated as in relief administration.

The new act followed closely the original LaFollette-Costigan bill, but with the modifications suggested by Hopkins and endorsed by Roosevelt. The RFC was authorized to borrow $500,000,000 for relief, but expenditure from this fund was the exclusive responsibility of a new Federal Emergency Relief Administration (FERA). A grant of $200,000,000 was allocated to the states, each receiving a grant equal to one-third of its expenditure on relief during the preceding three months. The allocation by population had been dropped and relief expenditure emerged as the basic measure of need. Subsequent interpretation of this section made it clear that only the expenditure of public money could be taken into account, but that loans received from the RFC could be included. The remaining $300,000,000 (significantly, it was now the larger portion) formed a fund at the disposal of the federal relief administrator from which he could make discretionary grants "sufficient to provide an adequate standard of relief."[1]

[1] For authoritative accounts of legislation and policy, see the historical introduction to *The Final Statistical Report of the Federal Emergency Relief Administration,* prepared for the WPA under the direction of Theodore E. Whiting (Washington, D.C., 1942; rpt. New York, 1972); Josephine Chapin Brown, *Public Relief 1929–1939* (New York, 1940; rpt. 1971); Edward Ainsworth Williams, *Federal Aid for Relief,* Columbia (University

The administration of the discretionary grants was the key to the new policy, and social workers hoped that the federal agency would use this powerful lever to improve relief standards. They were dismayed when Roosevelt, after signing the bill, emphasized the principle of local responsibility in words that Hoover might have used. Nothing in the act, he said, was intended to absolve the states and local communities of their obligation to ensure that destitute people were given the necessities of life. This was fair enough because, however comprehensive the federal relief program might be, it would have to rely upon local people to operate it; but Roosevelt went on to say:

> The principle which I have explained is that the first obligation is on the locality; if it is absolutely clear that the locality has done its utmost but that more must be done, then the State must do its utmost. Only then can the Federal Government add its contribution to those of the locality and the State.

Was it, then, the function of the federal government to provide no more than a backup for relief policies decided and directed by state and local authorities?[2]

Writing in the *Nation* five months later, Edith Abbott described Roosevelt's statement as "probably the most reactionary pronouncement that has come from the White House since the New Deal was inaugurated." The act had clearly recognized national responsibility; the President had plainly declared that it did not mean what it said:

> No matter how many excellent new rules are announced, can they ever be carried out if thousands of the old "poor masters," "overseers of the poor," "county agents," "township trustees," and various local officials are to be allowed to continue their wasteful activities?[3]

This read more than was warranted into Roosevelt's statement. He spoken of effort and money, not methods. He knew from the New York experience that a vigorous state agency could do much to raise

---

Studies in History and Economics 5, No. 452) (New York, 1929). Josephine Brown was a staff member of the FERA and assistant administrator, WPA. E. A. Williams joined the headquarter staff of the FERA in 1935, and his work is based on confidential files and conversations with leading personalities in the administration.

[2] Samuel I. Rosenman, ed., *The Public Papers and Addresses of Franklin Delano Roosevelt,* (New York, 1938–50), Vol. 2, 183. At a conference of governors called to explain the relief program, Roosevelt emphasized strongly the need for reasonable contributions from the states.

[3] *The Nation,* October 11, 1933; reprinted in Edith Abbott, *Public Assistance,* (Chicago, 1940), 752–8.

relief standards, and he was fully aware that the discretionary grant was a powerful weapon in the hands of the FERA. Yet the President's statement launching the FERA, and the somewhat hysterical reaction to it from some social workers, exposes an ambiguity that ran through the whole federal relief program.

In its final report, the FERA chose to play down national responsibility in relief policies and to claim:

> The emergency relief program in which the FERA participated was not a Federal program. It was a state and local program in which the Federal Government cooperated by making grants in aid.[4]

Yet the confidential reports in the FERA files, and many of its regulations and executive orders, tell a different story. The central office was kept fully informed through formal and informal channels of everything that went on in relief administration: the field representatives dealt with governors of states as equals; state relief administrators looked to Washington for directions; and county administrators knew that they operated within a federal framwork.

In the operation of parallel government, personal ties and assumptions were more important than official relationships. Many of the key officials in state and county relief agencies were trained social workers. Shared experience and identical sympathies bound them to their federal counterparts and separated them from the old breed of locally elected poor law officials.

This social work network was knotted together at the top when Roosevelt appointed Harry Hopkins to head the FERA and social workers knew that a man of their own breed was in charge. Their confidence was reinforced when Hopkins showed that he was equally ready to bypass normal bureaucratic delays and to bring pressure to bear upon the states. In an intentionally symbolic gesture, he disbursed millions of dollars to hard-pressed states within a few hours of taking office and while the administrative machinery of his agency was still rudimentary. Within a few weeks he would make it clear that states wanting federal money would have to conform to federal standards, and though the FERA was in existence for little more than two years he would, during that time, take complete control of relief administration in no fewer than six states.

---

[4] *Final Statistical Report of the Federal Emergency Relief Administration*, 5.

The new system was without precedent in American history. It was government by experts at the expense of elected amateurs. It was government by outsiders: outside the political system, outside the bureaucratic establishment, and belonging to a profession that had yet to win public recognition. Social workers had no national body comparable to the governing bodies of other professions, no power to deny employment to unqualified persons, and no means of disciplining their members. With a few exceptions, the men who occupied the leading positions in the FERA – the heads of divisions in Washington and the field representatives – had not been educated at prestigious universities, and many came from midwestern or southwestern states and rural or small-town backgrounds. They had not held public office except in welfare organizations, had never been elected to any post, and owed nothing to party affiliation. It was natural that their authority was resented by men who were fighting their way up the political ladder, and suspicion was often mutual. In their dealings with state governments, relief administrators ignored political claims to office, and though outwardly respectful did not conceal in private their low opinion of legislators and elected officials.[5]

In the lower echelons of the new relief army, the trained social workers (upon whose employment the FERA insisted wherever possible) had no standing in local politics or public life. Many were young and a very large number were women. County relief administrators were often without previous experience in public life and had nothing in common with the normal type of county commissioner or township official. Local relief committees of prominent citizens were encouraged by the FERA in the expectation that in relief administration they would supplant the men who were accustomed to running local government. A county commissioner might be a member of such a county relief committee, but most of his colleagues would be appointed on account of their experience in business or charitable work. Political activity was a positive disqualification.

Hopkins lost no time in making it clear that a new style in government had been launched. Three weeks after his appointment he explained its objectives to a meeting of social workers gathered in Detroit. He said that under the former relief act, both the states and the federal government had assumed that it was none of Washington's

---

[5] Searle F. Charles, *Minister for Relief: Harry Hopkins and the Depression* (Syracuse, N.Y.), 1963. There are notes on the staff of the FERA in the appendix to this chapter.

business to lay down conditions for the expenditure of federal loans. "All that is changed. They are grants now and I have to sign my name to every one of them." He stressed the opportunity for all who wished to improve the relief system, and said that he was tired of hearing of hardships that no one tried to cure.

Here is the chance of a lifetime to do something about some of these things if we have any brains at all. I am for experimenting with this fund in various parts of the country, trying out schemes which are supported by reasonable people and seeing if they work.

Although the overriding purpose was to get relief to those who needed it, this should not be achieved at the expense of other social objectives. For instance, the FERA would not supplement miserably low wages or permit the depression of living standards to unacceptably low levels. "We are not going to allow relief agencies to starve people to death with our money."[6]

At the same time Hopkins cautioned social workers against attempting too much and allowing ideals to hinder practical achievement. "Our job is to see that the unemployed get relief, not to develop a great social work organization throughout the United States." Thus, at the outset, Hopkins brought out alternatives that would be presented throughout the whole history of federal relief policy: Was the new agency to use its undoubted power within the existing system or work to change it?[7]

Among the early regulations issued by the FERA, the most important was a ruling that federal money should be handled only by public agencies. If a state found it expedient to employ a private agency, it must be placed under state authority and its staff taken into public employment. The FERA also insisted that each state must have a central agency in charge of relief. If none existed, it must be created before federal grants were handed over; alternatively, if a state designated an existing welfare department for this duty, the FERA had to be satisfied that it had sufficient independence to do the job effectively. State relief directors were to be approved by the FERA; in the event of a deadlock, the federal administrator could step in and make his own appoint-

---

[6] F.D.R. Library, Hopkins Papers, Box 49, Records of Staff Conferences, December 6, 1933.
[7] "The Developing National Program of Relief," *NCSW 1933*, 65–71.

ment. Another condition was that the state agency must set up county relief agencies that were independent of the existing poor law authorities and not subject to their control. States were expected to pay their fair share of relief, and federal agents would study resources, taxes, and financial management in each state to determine what this should be. A reluctant legislature could not be compelled to tax and appropriate, but if it failed to do so, the consequences were clear: Either the state would lose its grant or the federal administrator would exercise his power to place the whole operation under federal control.[8]

The relationship between the FERA and the governors of the states was certain to be difficult. Even the requirement for FERA approval could not alter the governor's right to appoint and dismiss state directors, and it was frequently more convenient to agree to an appointment that was not wholly suitable than to engage in a prolonged dispute while nothing got done. Insistence that relief was a state program meant that a governor was legally responsible and could be held to account if things went wrong. When state authority was responsible but federal authority claimed the right to say what should be done, friction was inevitable.

Other problems surrounded relief in metropolitan centers. By its own rules the FERA could not deal directly with any city, county, township, or other subordinate units; yet the temptation to deal directly with mayors of large cities was strong if it seemed that a governor was blocking the relief that was plainly needed. It did not, of course, escape the notice of New Dealers that leaders in big cities played a vital part in national politics, and that favorable consideration of their relief problems might pay better dividends than deference to a governor whose political base was in rural counties.

Another area of friction developed from the remaining poor law responsibilities of local governments. By law FERA money was intended to relieve distress caused by unemployment resulting from the depression; and local governments were to continue their traditional care for those who were destitute for other reasons. In practice the line was difficult to draw, and became more difficult as the depression lengthened. There were old or partially disabled people who would have got by with casual labor in normal times; there were middle-aged men formerly engaged in heavy manual labor who would be

[8] FERA, *Rules and Regulations*, No. 3, July 11, 1933.

unsuitable for reemployment when good times returned; there were old people who would normally have been supported by sons and daughters, but whom the depression had deprived of family aid; there were young people who had never been employed; and there were actors, artists, and musicians who might have been short of cash in the best of times. Thus the opportunities for argument over doubtful cases were frequent, and various cross-currents made the situation more confused. Some local governments did not hesitate to unload as many cases as possible on to relief agencies using federal funds, and some keen county administrators, seeing the poor standards adopted by local poor boards, were only too ready to take on more. The next stage would be a demand from the FERA or state agency that the local governments resume responsibility for persons classified as unemployable. A logical conclusion was that all argument should be resolved by the adoption of a national assistance program for all types of dependents, but this lay beyond the limits of anything that could be achieved in 1933.

At an early stage, the FERA laid down restrictions on the use of federal funds. They might be used to pay for medical attention, but not for hospital bills; they could be used to assist families, but not mothers eligible for aid under existing laws; nor could they pay boarding fees for orphaned, abandoned, or neglected children. "These necessary services to the destitute should be made available through state or local funds." At first, the FERA opposed cash relief except as wages for approved work projects; but in some areas there was growing pressure to give cash rather than grocery orders, and many relief administrators regarded resistance to cash relief as a survival from the times when it was assumed that a poor person was incapable of managing his own domestic affairs. The FERA came to accept cash relief when local relief administrators favored it, and then to give it positive endorsement.[9]

In other respects, the FERA guidelines were in advance of the practice in most states. Relief was to be given to all the needy unemployed and their dependents, and might also be given to employed men whose wages were too low to provide their families with the necessities of life. The ruling that the unemployed deserved relief without first establishing that they were deserving was a welcome emphasis upon need rather than moral character, but it would sometimes clash with the favorite

[9] Ibid., No. 8.

principle of all social workers that every case should be investigated. The rule that relief should be sufficient "to prevent physical suffering and to maintain minimum living standards" was a radical departure from the idea that relief was adequate if it prevented starvation. Estimates of need should be based on family budgets, taking into account shelter, heating, fuel for cooking, clothing, medical care, and other necessities. Relief might include payment of rent or mortgage interest. Work on relief projects should be paid at the going rate, and, so far as possible, skilled men should be given appropriate work and wages.

Transient relief was the only problem treated from the beginning on a national scale, and the FERA Rules and Regulations No. 8 went into great detail in describing the new arrangements. Each state was required to set up a transient bureau under a director appointed by the state relief agency and approved by the FERA. The state bureau was to set up local centers to provide food, shelter, training, and education, and, where appropriate, work camps, farms, and rehabilitation units. The whole operation would be paid for from federal funds. This was an important innovation at a time when Hopkins claimed that only two or three states had done "a serious job in caring for transients."[10]

The problem of settlement had to be faced when dealing with transients. The first hurdle was surmounted by reimbursing states in full for the relief of persons with no legal settlement. The perennial difficulties created by variations in state law were overridden by the rule that settlement meant a year's continuous residence; if this was established, transients were to be treated as normal relief clients. Unhappily, this did not end the trials of indigent men and women – not wanderers in search of work or habitual vagrants – who were taken ill in places where they had no settlement; they were still likely to be consigned to the last place where they had resided for any length of time or to become subjects of lengthy litigation between communities.

Hopkins sketched out his ideas for the organization of his administration when he spoke to the National Conference of Social Work. He envisaged a comparatively small central staff of between thirty-five and fifty, and ten or twelve field representatives who would "go out to the various states trying to interpret the policies of the Federal Relief Administration." His modest expectations for the size of the head-

[10] *NCSW 1933*, 69.

quarters staff were soon overtaken by its expansion, and the field representatives soon ceased to be missionaries and became regional directors with their own staff of experts. In the early days, they were based in Washington and visited states for routine inquiries or when special difficulties arose; but by May 1934 they had their own regional offices, with five divisions responsible for social work, engineering, financial scrutiny and statistics, rural rehabilitation, and research. By this time, they were giving continuous surveillance to the states assigned to them, and though without executive authority, most of them exercised a decisive influence upon state relief policy. All general instructions were issued through them, and they also had control over any agents sent from Washington with special duties.[11]

Although the primary function of a field representative was to serve as the eyes, ears, and voice of the FERA, most of them came to interpret their task more broadly. The authority that they exercised varied with circumstances and personalities, but most of them established an informal ascendancy over relief administration in their states. They used this power to improve local practice and, so far as possible, to inculcate new attitudes toward the relief of distress. This often meant reviewing state and local methods, as well as the use of federal money. These positive attitudes were reinforced by the men in Washington and (in the words of one who joined them in 1935):

The federal relief officials were not satisfied with attempting to establish safeguards for the honest expenditure of federal money by the states; a further objective was to channel state and local spending in such a manner as to carry out definite social policies.

Among other things, they reviewed state programs in advance, insisted on the employment of qualified persons, demanded comprehensive state reports, and maintained running statistical checks. Their efforts were always restrained by uncertainty about the future prospects of the FERA, but they were effective in securing special programs with defined objectives – such as transient relief, student aid, and rural rehabilitation – and in insisting on professional administration.[12]

The rule that federal money went only to public agencies did not mean that private effort was ignored. In September 1933 Hopkins

[11] 73rd Congress 2nd Sess., House Appropriations Committee, Hearings by Subcommittee, January 30, 1934, 1–4.
[12] E. A. Williams, *Federal Aid Relief*, 71–4.

reminded a meeting of community chest officials that he had spent most of his working life with private agencies, insisted that the success of the FERA would depend on their support and cooperation, and that old barriers had broken down. "The people that administer public relief . . . are the people that have been conducting the private agencies of the country, whether they are chairmen of local or state committees or on the board of directors or executives of those agencies." He might have added that a majority of the FERA field representatives had also been trained in private charitable work.

There was therefore a natural alliance between the FERA and all men and women who had labored long to improve the treatment of the poor, and the campaign on which this alliance was engaged resembled a military operation. Strategy was determined at headquarters, tactics were left to field representatives and their allies in the states, and the enemy was often the local political hierarchy. The confidential reports of the field representatives provided the intelligence on which strategic decisions were based, and they derived much of their information from members of state or county agencies who had little faith in the goodwill or competence of their own governments.[13]

The FERA administration grew but procedures remained speedy and informal. An army officer, investigating the possible employment of army engineers to supervise work projects, was impressed and a little puzzled. Hopkins showed little interest in permanent organization, but was "concerned rather with the utmost rapidity of widespread operation. Every day was important." The young members of the staff were on first-name terms with each other and with their chief, staff meetings were informal but no time was wasted, and decisions arrived at verbally were executed without waiting for confirmation in writing. It was all very different from the way in which the Army conducted its affairs in peacetime but might be compared to operations at a battle headquarters.[14]

Harry Hopkins was forty-three years old when he was appointed to head the FERA. He was born in Iowa and graduated from Grinnell College, but made his career entirely in New York except for a spell (1917–22) with the Red Cross in New Orleans. From 1922 until he

---

[13] "The Relation of Federal Relief to Local Welfare Responsibilities," an address to The Community Chests and Councils, Inc., September 8, 1933. Mimeographed copy in F.D.R. Library, Hopkins Papers.

[14] Report by Lt. Col. John C. R. Lee, Corps of Engineers. Copy in F.D.R. Library, Hopkins Papers, 49.

joined the TERA, he was director of the New York Tuberculosis and Health Association. The historian William Luchtenberg observes that "for a social worker he was a very odd sort," and, according to a much quoted characterization, he "had the purity of St. Francis of Assisi combined with the sharp shrewdness of a race track tout." In office he was brusque, impatient with administrative delays, and suffered no fools gladly. Never physically robust, he seemed often to be straining toward the breaking point, with his energy fueled only by cigarettes and strong coffee. One contemporary wrote:

Always direct in his language, Hopkins probably uses "lousy" more often than anyone else in the Administration. He is a pretty good phrase-maker and bawler out . . . [and] his bite is much worse than his bark. . . . In Hopkins the fire of social justice burns intensely but not foolishly. He is a shrewd fellow, but too loyal to his ideals to compromise in matters of principle, and as many Governors and politicians know he is a "tar baby" in a fight.

Hopkins was the ideal person to launch a great new venture into unexplored territory. He made up his mind quickly, left no one in doubt, and insisted that everyone come straight to the point. He won devoted loyalty from all who worked under him but had little patience with state politicians who seemed to be dragging their feet. There would be occasions when relief in some states might have gone more smoothly if their governors had been handled more gently; Aubrey Williams, Hopkin's right-hand man, was even less adept at soft speech and turning away wrath. He was the same age as Hopkins and, coming from an impoverished Alabama family, had had little formal education. He had worked as a child in various full-time jobs in Birmingham, but enrolled in a small Tennessee college and then at the University of Cincinnati with some idea of joining the Presbyterian ministry; but before graduating he went to the war front in Europe with the YMCA, joined the French Foreign Legion, and transferred to the U.S. Army in 1918. After the war was over, he took a degree at the University of Bordeaux before returning to Cincinnati for training in social work.

In 1922 Williams became director of the Wisconsin Conference on Social Work and taught part-time at the University of Wisconsin. In 1932 he joined the American Public Welfare Association as a field representative in Mississippi and Texas, where, at the request of the governors, he set up effective organizations for work relief. Hopkins recruited him for the FERA, first as field representative in the Southwest and then at Washington as administrator of the Civil Works Administration and deputy administrator of the FERA. He also became one of Mrs. Eleanor Roosevelt's correspondents on welfare questions, and from 1934 spoke every year at the National Conference of Social Work to explain and defend government policy. His virtues were shining; all that he lacked was tact and a sense of humor.

Almost all of the other men and women on the headquarters staff and in the field had considerable experience in social work. They shared common assumptions, defined the problems in much the same way, and did not require lengthy explanations. This shared experience was an asset of enormous strength when things had to be done in a hurry.[15]

The achievement was impressive. In little more than a year the FERA built up a powerful central agency, ensured that relief reached those in need, and developed several ancillary programs for artists, writers, actors, musicians, rural education, and college students who would otherwise have been compelled to cut short their studies. Investigations revealed hitherto unsuspected depths of rural poverty, and as a consequence an ambitious program of rural resettlement was launched. It would soon be separated from the main body and function as a separate agency.

During the grim winter of 1933–4 the Civil Works Administration (CWA) – linked with the FERA but run as a distinct and wholly federal operation – organized a crash program of work relief that brought temporary employment to almost four million. It was ended in the spring of 1933 (much to the disappointment of many social workers), but the FERA took over its unfinished projects, and during the summer approved and funded many new work plans submitted by the states.

In addition, in November 1933, Roosevelt issued an executive order allowing unclaimed matching grants to be used as discretionary grants to states where the need was greatest. This proved to be of special benefit to poor states that had not been able to afford heavy relief expenditure and thus qualified only for small matching grants. The new order put a reserve in the hands of the federal administrator to help these states, particularly those hit by drought or where rural relief had been at abysmally low levels.[16]

[15] William E. Leuchtenberg, *Franklin D. Roosevelt and The New Deal* (New York, 1963); "Unofficial Observer" [John F. Carter], *The New Dealers* (New York, 1934).
[16] Williams, *Federal Aid for Relief*, 214.

The FERA was always handicapped by being tagged as "emergency." This inhibited long-term planning and cast doubt on hopes that the future would bring a permanent relief program nationally administered. To some extent, these fears were allayed by the sheer size, strength, range, and sophistication of the FERA administration. Its statistical service took over the best of tried methods and went on to break new ground in social investigation. A Municipal Finance Section, set up to measure a states's fair share, abandoned the crude yardstick of previous expenditure and tried to discover the point at which a state could meet its relief commitment without cutting expenditure on education or other social services and without leaving resources untapped. Statistical series were compiled to measure production, retail and wholesale sales, money income, savings, deposits, automobile registrations, and taxable income. Other series recorded demographic data, federal tax revenue, property values, and factors such as drought, debt, and tax arrears. States were then placed in order in each series, and a combined order was obtained. The final order, determined after further modifications, was then used as the basis for negotiation with each state. In the words of one writer in close contact with FERA administration, the whole complex operation was "by far the most extensive inquiry" ever made by a federal agency with the object of finding "an equitable and objective basis for sharing the financial burden of states and localities."[17]

Another new departure was a Division of Investigation, set up in July 1934, to look into complaints, initiate its own inquiries, and pass on the findings to the states for action. The most common allegations were political favoritism by relief officials; discrimination against applicants on political, religious, or racial grounds; bribery, kickbacks, embezzlement, forgery; and collusion with contractors on work relief projects and payroll padding. Given the size and ramifications of the relief operation, proven cases were remarkably few, but every complaint was investigated. The most difficult situations were found not when a dishonest individual got his hand into the relief till but when a whole county government or party organization was involved. In these cases, what was called into question might be practices that the community had never regarded as unethical, and conspiracies of silence might shelter the accused. Even so, investigation was salutory;

[17] Ibid., 167–8.

the murky waters of long accepted public mores might be disturbed, but continued inquiries and accumulating evidence of the seamy side of local administration served insensibly to improve public ethics.

State officials might fail to respond with appropriate action, particularly when political or racial discrimination was alleged, and the FERA often had to be content with an assurance of better practice and greater vigilance for the future; but federal pressure, even if not irresistible, could not be ignored. A major sanction was the power to withhold matching grants, for though the amount due was determined by a statutory formula, it was not paid until the FERA was satisfied with the arrangements for handling it. This power, though threatened on a few occasions, was hardly ever used; but the same well-informed observer believed that without it "the agency could not have gained the degree of control which it came to possess over state and local relief administration."[18]

A second major sanction was to place the whole state relief operation under federal control. Examples occurred in Oklahoma in February 1934, when the Governor refused to accept federal aid unless exempted from FERA rules and regulations; in Massachusetts in March 1934, ostensibly because the state constitution would not permit the distribution of funds to towns except on a population basis, but also because of continued disagreements between state and federal officials over relief policy; and in Georgia in April 1935, when the state government persistently failed to cooperate with its own state relief administration in raising standards. In Louisiana relief was federalized in the same month for similar reasons. Relief was federalized in North Dakota because Governor William Langer was indicted by a grand jury and convicted of soliciting political contributions from employees of the relief administration. The last case of federalization was in Ohio, where the Governor was accused of trying to annex the relief organization to his personal political machine.[19]

Normally, federalization meant little change in personnel, because former state relief officials became federal employees unless there was ground for their removal; but once the critical step had been taken, the state governments might cease to cooperate, cut back on appropria-

---

[18] Ibid., 175ff. See 238–41 (Georgia), 243–7 (Oklahoma), 253–7 (North Dakota), 261–5 (Ohio). For Louisiana see John Robert Moore, "The New Deal in Louisiana," in John Braeman, Robert H. Bremner, and David Brody, eds., *The New Deal,* Vol. II. (Columbus, Ohio, 1975), 137–65.

[19] 73rd Congress 2nd Sess., House Appropriations Committee, Hearings on Emergency Relief and Civil Works Program, January 30, 1934; evidence by Hopkins, 7.

tions, and transfer as much of the relief burden as they could to the federal payroll. Thus federalization was a powerful threat but carried no assurance that relief operations would be permanently improved. There were therefore sound reasons for avoiding this drastic remedy as long as possible, and for returning responsibility to the state as soon as there was a prospect of fair and efficient administration.

At the time, the discretionary power vested in the federal relief administrator attracted little attention from constitutional lawyers, but in retrospect it can be seen as a striking departure from the traditions of legislative control and public accountability. Very large sums of money were allocated without public hearings and without the right of appeal by those who thought that they had been unfairly treated. Decisions by state and county relief agencies were invariably subject to review by lay boards, but there was no independent commission with power to review actions taken by the relief administrator.

Hopkins was a man of manifest integrity, but he did not suffer fools gladly, readily forgive state governors who obstructed FERA policy, or exercise patience when state legislatures failed to contribute their fair share of relief costs. When so much was at stake, there were inevitable allegations that he was influenced by animosity or political considerations, but there was no way of conducting an independent review. Criticism could only be expressed by political action, and those who felt themselves aggrieved made their complaints to Congress because they had nowhere else to go. Thus legislators opposed to the FERA were constantly supplied with fresh ammunition, and extreme centralization proved to be an element of weakness rather than strength.

Attacks on deep-seated political and social mores would require years, not months, to show results, but some of the innovative programs fostered by the FERA had immediate and lasting effects. The most ambitious was the Rural Rehabilitation program, which aimed to revive whole communities sunk in apparently incurable poverty. In June 1935 this program became independent, with rural rehabilitation placed under a new Resettlement Administration, but it had been planned and initiated by the FERA. Another ambitious project was the Land Program, launched in June 1934, to cooperate with other agencies in acquiring land for forestation, grazing, recreation, and wildlife protection. In the same period, the Drought Relief program was initiated with a special appropriation from Congress. The Educational program recruited unemployed teachers to reopen rural schools or avert their closure. The Federal Surplus Relief Corporation was an independent agency, but it worked in close cooperation with the FERA. Thus the FERA, created to counter the ills of industrial society, became a powerful force for change in rural America.

Of all the programs the Federal Transient Administration was the most successful in tackling an ancient evil. For the first time, a nationwide organization brought uniformity and humane principles to bear upon the age-old problem of migratory labor, vagrants, tramps, hobos, and men wandering in search of work. The program guaranteed shelter for all, assisted the wanderers to find work, and set up labor camps in regions where there was no regular work to be found.

Within the FERA there was a small Division of Self-Help Cooperation, which planned, fostered, and helped to finance cooperative enterprises, but the results were not impressive. Of far greater significance was the College Student Aid program, which recognized, for the first time, a national interest in the availability of higher education. Grants were made to colleges to provide part-time work for students who lacked money to complete their studies. Nominally limited to the children of parents on relief, it was interpreted broadly to include those who remained independent but with nothing to spare.

Although these programs employed a large staff and explored many innovative possibilities, by far the largest group of state relief employees were engaged in the routine tasks of investigation. They accounted for 47 percent of the personnel and 45 percent of the salary bill. As Hopkins explained to the House Appropriations Committee:

> Every application has to be investigated; we have to send investigators out to visit families, to look up the bank accounts, and look up insurance, and to see whether the relatives can take care of these applicants or not.

With the number on relief reaching more than 10 percent of the population in forty states and more than 17 percent in eight of them, the number of families affected by these investigations was very large. Because some were on relief for short periods and new applications were constantly received, the actual number investigated each month was much larger than the twelve-month average. Although the FERA insisted upon the most modern methods of investigation, it clung to the old belief that it was better to spend a great deal of time and money than to pay a pittance to one unworthy person.[20]

[20] North Carolina State Board of Charities and Public Welfare, *Biennial Report, 1934–6,* 6.

The FERA affected social attitudes and policies in many ways. Although first priority was always given to work relief, there was a growing realization that the provision of jobs did not weaken the case for direct relief in the home. When work relief was scarce and its rewards were meager, families required additional support, and there was a growing realization that the different kinds of relief should be the components of a single policy. Experience also pushed social workers beyond the immediate task of relieving distress caused by unemployment to review the causes and character of long-term poverty. Nowhere was this more apparent than in backward rural areas, where returning prosperity would not raise many small farmers, tenants, and sharecroppers above bare subsistence. For them relief should not be an end in itself but the first step toward rehabilitation.

Other circumstances also demonstrated the need for a comprehensive welfare policy. In cities there had been a traditional separation between permanently dependent paupers, who were usually left to public welfare, and the victims of temporary misfortune who normally looked for help from private charities. Care of the aged had been arbitrarily divided between public welfare for the improvident and private help for the worthy poor. Welfare had been further fragmented by the responsibility of private agencies for selected religious, ethnic, and occupational groups, or for destitution resulting from a single identifiable cause (such as blindness, mental deficiency, or physical disablement). The relief of the able-bodied unemployed cut across these lines of demarcation and reinforced the case for unified welfare administration.

Under the aegis of the FERA, public welfare replaced private charity as the dominant force in social administration. The rule that the FERA would deal only with state agencies, the amount of money distributed through these channels, and recruitment of the best social work talent by national and state agencies pushed charities into second place. Indeed, this development was welcomed by many who remained with private agencies and had deplored the way in which unemployment relief drained their funds and impoverished more constructive programs.

Relief work also brought the federal and state agencies into contact with a wide range of entrepreneurs – contractors, merchants, storekeepers – and lawyers, physicians, and bankers. No government activity had ever before touched so many lives or affected so broadly the social fabric. Decisions made in the state relief agencies, by the field representatives of the FERA, and ultimately by Hopkins in Washington carried with them direct consequences for thousands of individuals in every state of the Union.

The impact on state and local government was clear. Before June 1933 there had been relief agencies in eight states; a year later, they were found in the remaining forty. Relief commissions had been set up in the great majority of counties and salaried directors appointed; the old practice of amateur relief administration had given way to the appointment of professional social workers to key positions, and workers without formal training learned to observe professional standards. The research and statistical work conducted in Washington created constant demands for accurate information from the field and led to marked improvements in local recordkeeping and reporting. This great body of ordered information was to have enormous influence upon the future evolution of social policy, and not least upon the plans for social security maturing behind closed doors in Washington.

Local authorities retained responsibility for what were coming to be known as the "unemployables," and the emergency relief agencies were legally responsible only for dealing with distress that resulted from unemployment, but the distinction became blurred as the depression continued. Local authorities were anxious to transfer to emergency relief every case that could be remotely linked with the effects of depression, and, in any event, it became increasingly difficult to distinguish among the unemployed between those who remained eligible for work and those whom age, illness, or loss of skill had put out of the labor market. Even among the residual and chronic cases remaining as charges on local funds, the example of new methods and professional social work prompted steady improvement.

These developments brought the ideals of the social work movement within sight of realization: uniform standards, professional methods, local administration under national supervision, and the fusion of all types of welfare into a comprehensive national policy. Experience had also brought important modifications to the conventional wisdom of social work. The emphasis on work relief as the preferred form of help for the able-bodied caused some to speak of a "right to work" to be preserved by government along with the other basic rights. At the same time, experience taught that home relief must supplement work relief. The temporarily unemployed were better helped in their homes than placed in unsuitable work, and work relief might fail to provide enough income for a family.

The old principle that no one should starve – with the implication that public duty ended when life was preserved – was being replaced by the idea that a man reduced to poverty through no fault of his own should be helped to maintain his home, provide clothing for his children, receive necessary medical care, and preserve the decencies of life. Beyond this the conviction gained ground that society, rather than personal deficiency, was responsible for most forms of poverty. One practical aspect of this change was the gradual shift from relief by grocery orders to cash payments, which were cheaper to administer and preserved the self-respect of recipients. The oft-repeated assertion that a dole corrupted character ceased to be an axiom of social policy.

The pressure exerted by the FERA did more than influence administrators and professionals; silently but unmistakably, it helped to transform public attitudes toward poverty. In a typical comment, the North Carolina Commissioner of Public Welfare, Mrs. W. T. Bond, declared in 1936 that the two preceding years had "witnessed the greatest advancement in public welfare work" since the reorganization of the State Board in 1917 and had produced "unmistakably an aggressive awareness of the social needs of the people on the part of local communities and county officials."[21]

Though relief was centralized in state agencies and the FERA held the purse strings, the humblest workers in the field were called upon to make important decisions on individual cases and might have a direct influence on policymaking at higher levels. The preponderance of trained social workers in state and federal hierarchies meant that reports were evaluated by people familiar with the problems of social work and with the vocabulary used to describe them. The county administrators could be confident that professional criteria would prevail over local objections, and this encouraged a willingness to make decisions, provided that they were compatible with the received wisdom of social work.

Sometimes contempt for the opinion of local officials and advisory committees was misplaced, and relief administration might have won a more secure place in public esteem if more regard had been shown for lay opinion; but professional harmony meant respect for those who

[21] *NCSW 1934*, 158 (see note 35, this chapter).

directed policy and confidence among those who executed it. Everyone engaged in relief administration was aware of authoritative direction from above, but initiative could thrive when men and women in the lower ranks expected support from their superiors. Dedication to the task, personal commitment, determination to succeed, firm guidelines, clearly defined objectives, and willingness to accept responsibility in the field meant that the relief administration was quite unlike the conventional picture of bureaucratic government.

Experience with the unemployed tended to alter conventional attitudes toward cash relief. At the outset, most social workers shared the common dislike of cash payments except in return for work; cash relief might become a dole and was condemned without much examination of the facts. Although official attitudes continued to endorse this view, the case against relief by grocery order gathered strength.

Cash relief was cheaper to administer, encouraged self-reliance, and refuted the notion that with lost employment went the capacity to handle money. Why should men and women who had always been independent suddenly have others determine what they should eat? Though relief in kind became more sophisticated, with greater reliance on family budgets and nutrition studies, there was growing reluctance to place in tutelage men and women who had always managed their own affairs. In 1934 no less an authority than Aubrey Williams, by then assistant administrator of the FERA, reminded the National Conference of Social Work that they should not claim too much power to decide how people ordered their lives:

We have to rely on people, many of them very young, whose major qualification is that they have good ordinary intelligence and a desire to be helpful . . . [and] I have more confidence in what Mrs. Smith can do with a five dollar bill than in the plan of centralized control.

In practice, the elaboration of technique in the compilation of family budgets was of greater use in persuading states that their standards were too low than in fixing amounts for relief in kind.[22]

Successful operation of a relief program depended primarily upon a close relationship between the FERA field representative and the state relief director, and then upon having experienced county administrators who were in tune with the aims of federal policy. The FERA deter-

---

[22] 74th Congress, 1st Sess., House Appropriations Committee, Hearings on First Deficiency Appropriation. Bill, 1936, 153.

mined the minimum number of trained social workers to be employed by the state agencies, but it was not always possible at first to recruit the right number. The difficulty of getting qualified men and women for the job was compounded in some states by insistence that only citizens of the state (and, in some instances, residents of the county) should be employed, and in others by the demands for trained workers by city departments of welfare, with consequent shortages in rural districts.

Field representatives were always overworked. They made regular visits to the states in their regions, but these were likely to be short if things seemed to be working well. In these states, the relief directors were left to get on with the job until such time as a special problem attracted attention from Washington. Conversely, field representatives had to spend a disproportionate amount of time in states where the relief administration was weak, standards abnormally low, or political interference rampant. Most of them evolved routine methods for checking efficiency in states that they had no time to examine in depth. In many states, locally prepared family budgets occupied much of their office time, with further time spent in assessing the explanations when the budgets – and levels of relief based on them – were abnormally low.

The FERA always insisted that it would not be responsible for inadequate relief. Hopkins told the Appropriation Committee of the House of Representatives that if states wanted to give a family two dollars per month, which was starvation relief, "they could continue to do that with their own money, but not with federal money." This was a perennial problem in the rural South, with the added difficulty of relating relief levels to wages for low-paid seasonal work. The frequent demand that federal policy respect local customs usually meant holding wages on work projects below the minimum paid to the least skilled laborers and refusing relief to able-bodied men at harvest time (though local employers were happy to see them supported for the rest of the year).[23]

In the summer of 1933, Harper Gatton, relief director in Kentucky, told Hopkins that the FERA work relief rate of 30 cents an hour was too high when employers were already protesting at having to pay $1.59 a day. Hopkins replied that "the best thing that can happen to the South is a substantial increase in the wage rates because I do not

---

[23] Paul E. Mertz, *New Deal Policy and Southern Rural Poverty* (Baton Rouge, La., 1978), 50.

see how we are ever going to get any purchasing power into our new economy on a dollar a day." All over the South relief failed to reach the levels recommended by the FERA, and it was a common complaint, as in Alabama in September 1933, that relief was "far from adequate by any decent standards."[24]

There was further trouble with Kentucky when the legislature made no appropriation for relief and, in defiance of FERA policy, voted to give no relief to miners on strike. Aubrey Williams, acting for Hopkins, threatened to stop all federal aid and leave the state and localities wholly responsible for the 22 percent of the population dependent on relief. His only concession was to agree to suspend relief for those who were offered but refused harvest work. Similar difficulties were experienced in Louisiana, where the state relief director refused work relief to farmers, tenants, and sharecroppers and objected to CWA wage rates. In the South the FERA faced the fact that the depression was not the sole cause of distress. Endemic poverty, and income that had been falling in the 1920s, made short-term remedies irrelevant. Relief was needed immediately, but rehabilitation must be the long-term goal.[25]

Another problem for the FERA in the South was to ensure that local authorities fulfilled their responsibility for relieving the old, infirm, and disabled. In many parts of the South, the paternalist tradition imposed on plantation owners a moral obligation to help tenants and sharecroppers to survive in hard times; but once state or federal money became available, no time was lost in transferring distressed people to public relief. Employers and county officials assumed that the purpose of federal policy was to shift the burden of relief from individuals and communities, and saw no reason to distinguish between different kinds of poverty. The FERA was often in the ambiguous position of pressing states to raise the standard of relief while protesting that the number of persons benefitting from federal funds should be reduced.

In some states, where the administration was unsatisfactory but not sufficiently so to justify complete federalization, the FERA required governors to appoint one if its field representatives (or a member of his staff) as the state administrator. This happened in Maine for a short time, in Tennessee for several weeks, and in California for a considerable period in 1934. It was also necessary to resist attempts by

[24] Ibid.
[25] Ibid., 59.

politicians to get rid of efficient relief officials. The leading case, which attracted national attention, was the unsuccessful attempt by Senator William McAdoo of California to secure the dismissal of Ralph Branion, the state administrator.[26]

With so much federal money passing through the hands of state and county relief administrators, there was always a danger that their influence might be used for political ends. In evidence before a House committee, Hopkins was able to cite several letters on this topic, of which the earliest, written by Aubrey Williams in August 1934, directed that "employees of relief administrations shall in no way use their official positions in attempts to control political movements." It was a standing order that a relief employee who ran for political office must resign, and anyone who allowed political partisanship to influence relief distribution was dismissed.[27]

There were always limits to what could be accomplished. Hopkins admitted that "it was never possible to achieve living standards of minimum decency for the entire unemployed population in need of relief." Although a good deal of money was spent in grants to the states for training social workers, there were never enough of them, and too many of those who received training lacked expereince. Nor could FERA influence extend to the large number of elected local government officials – county commissioners, superintendents, overseers, township trustees, and the like – who could obstruct where they could no longer direct. For them the guideline was still the old poor law, and despite the infusion of trained social workers, many of those who administered emergency relief came from the old school. The eye of the FERA was not all-seeing, and many local officials could continue in their old ways, provided that they avoided open scandal.[28]

Some radical critics fastened upon these deficiencies. As early as May 1934, Gertrude Springer, writing in *Survey,* asked, "why have we to go on with this devastating fumbling with human misery . . . we could wipe out our poor laws and stop pinning the legal stigma of "pauper" [on the unemployed]. . . . We could abolish the miserable system of grocery orders." She thought that the new work program of

[26] For California, see pp. 238–43.
[27] 74th Congress, 2nd Sess., House Committee on Appropriations, Hearings on First Deficiency Appropriations Bill, 1936, 161.
[28] Harry Hopkins, *Spending to Save: the Complete Story of Relief* (Seattle, 1936), 99.

the FERA was no more than old work relief by another name. "Only the stipulation of wages in cash and not in kind changed the doubtful sweetness of its smell." Home relief continued on the "old dollar stretching basis," and though work relief depended on federal funds, it was often local custom to spread the benefits so thinly that wages had to be supplemented by home relief. In January 1935 another critic wrote that "whatever has so far been achieved, and at what cost, insufficient money has been available adequately to provide even the rudimentary requirements of food, clothing, and shelter. The availability of funds, not the needs of the unemployed, controlled relief payments, and when not enough money was available the necessary cuts reduced relief below the level that experienced social workers regarded as irreducible."[29]

The view from the top might reveal little of what went on in the valleys. The difficulties faced by county administrators and young social workers must often be imagined rather than described, but there exist two revealing accounts of county relief. The first is a narrative account by a trained but inexperienced young social worker in a remote Michigan county; the second is a contemporary research project on three rural counties in Maryland, Alabama, and Minnesota. They are notable not only for their implicit agreement on some basic problems but also for their disagreement over the quality of local government, thus demonstrating the folly of generalizing too broadly.

Mrs. Louise Armstrong was appointed as relief administrator in a Michigan county. She was a local resident, but her previous experience of social work had been in Chicago, and she had to learn from the beginning the facts of life in a very different environment. The county contained one small city, much forest land worked hard by timber companies and then abandoned, and a large number of small and very poor farms. The population was old stock American, with a large number of more recent immigrants from Scandinavia and Poland.[30]

A public meeting, called to explain the aims of the relief program, was almost a disaster. The need to find more money for relief was not questioned, but there were violent objections to state supervision. "They wanted a blank check handed over to them to spend as they saw

---

[29] Gertrude Springer, "X equals?" *Survey Graphic* 22 (May 1934), 250.
[30] Louise V. Armstrong, *We Too Are the People* (Boston, 1938; rpt. New York, 1971). For the following paragraph, see 73–5, 181–5.

fit." Their first priority was to pay off old debts, and the second was to push on to emergency relief the chronic cases for whom they were legally responsible. Worse was to come because the county relief commission shared these views, condemned Mrs. Armstrong's attempt to control the administration of unemployment relief, petitioned the state agency to remove her, and threatened to resign if she was retained. They reckoned without a tough state relief administrator who accepted with alacrity their offered resignation and appointed a new county relief commission in their place. In the new commission the dominant personality proved to be a tower of strength and gave Mrs. Armstrong good advice and consistent support.

She needed all the support that she could get because there were constant difficulties with local government officials. Most members of the county board of supervisors had no education beyond grade school and little administrative experience. Even worse was the situation in the townships. Mrs. Armstrong wrote:

The township supervisors, not only in our county but all over the state . . . waged a ceaseless battle against the Emergency Relief set-up, and had used every means of political pressure in their power to gain control of it.

She blamed public attitudes rather than individual failings and drew the conclusion that whatever plans for social betterment might be advanced, "real progress toward social justice cannot be achieved as long as the ethical standards of our people remain unchanged."[31]

The alliance between a strong state director, a determined, though perhaps tactless, county administrator, and a sympathetic chairman of the new county relief commission made emergency relief function according to plan in this Michigan county. One could hardly expect to find such a combination everywhere, and the inference is that emergency relief policy would have been ineffective if the same refusal to cooperate had prevailed in most localities. The normal response must have been more cooperative, more willing to innovate, and better prepared to adapt national and state policy to local conditions. This inference is confirmed by the study of emergency relief policy in three rural counties carried out by federal investigators and published in 1936.[32]

[31] Ibid., 297, 465. In her conclusion she wrote: "I must admit that I did find myself face to face with social conditions which were, and still are, a disgrace to any social order which placidly assumes itself to be civilized" (470).
[32] Elizabeth McCord, Wilma Van Dusseldorp, and Sybil Pearse, *Social Work and Practice in Three Rural Counties* (Washington, D.C., 1936) (study for the Social Services Division, FERA).

The three counties were located in different parts of the country and were given fictitious names: "Brightwood" in Minnesota, "Estabrook" in Alabama, and "Wallingford" in Maryland. In all three, people without training in social work dominated local relief administration, but the study took a far more tolerant view of nonprofessional direction than was common among social workers. "The money spent on social work was their own money, and it was being spent for persons who were often their own neighbors." County commissioners, lay members of relief boards, and relief clients "were all part of a closely knit community," and once a problem had been explained, leading citizens were usually ready to accept responsibility. They invariably preferred work to home relief, but there was "a decided tendency toward accepting more adequate standards . . . than was the rule before the coming of state and federal aid."[33]

Nearly all social workers in the three counties were citizens of their states; in two, nearly all were local residents, and in the third, where state policy opposed the employment of local people, it was difficult to recruit or retain staff. Cooperation with the local relief board and with the county commissioners was not a matter of choice but a requirement for the job. The salaried relief director had to have a clear idea of the aims to be achieved, but also had to be tactful, make allowance for local opinion, and be ready to spend much time in explaining issues to the relief board in a way that would win them over. The county administrator who could not carry his board with him, became impatient when progress was slow, or demanded clear-cut responsibilities would "find great difficulty in doing rural social work." In all three counties, the commissioners took an active interest in relief and liked to keep in close touch with the public agencies, and because not all of them were members of the relief board, the county director might find himself obliged to do the job of explanation twice.[34]

Despite the slow pace of rural administration, there were important changes. In all three counties the state agency was successful in pressing for higher standards, the investigation of all cases became normal, and local contributions did not diminish but increased with the coming of federal aid. In "Estabrook," Alabama, state and federal aid was

---

[33] Ibid., 10–11.
[34] The authors pointed out that the record in the three counties was probably well above average. They were regarded as doing well by the relief agencies in states that had a reputation for good social work.

eagerly sought as soon as it became available, the local people anticipated state requirements by setting up their own relief administration,
and the program was popular with local businessmen because it
brought money into the county.

In "Brightwood," Minnesota, unwieldy administration and confused responsibilities invited conflict between the county commissioners, the child welfare board, and the county relief committee; but in
practice, they worked as committees of a single organization rather
than as independent units. The commissioners consistently resisted
any attempt to take relief administration out of their hands, but three
of them had considerable experience and were committed to improving standards; only one commissioner (representing the Farmer–Labor
party) normally opposed change. There was general recognition that a
trained staff was needed and that the commission must have professional advice available.

In "Wallingford," Maryland, all relief before the depression had
been in the hands of two private agencies, and the absence of any public welfare program was a disadvantage when emergency relief had to
be provided. Fortunately the people who had managed the charities or
contributed regularly to them were well informed on welfare matters
and provided experience on the county relief board. Tradition in the
private agencies had been paternalistic, and it had been customary to
give immediate relief to applicants with good local recommendations,
but to take a hard line with people thought to be idle or incorrigible
even if their families suffered. The need to relieve men and women
who were destitute through no fault of their own but who lacked local
sponsorship created a great deal of hard investigatory work for the
trained relief supervisor. Though this work was never fully appreciated
by the board members, they were, nevertheless, proud of their record
in bringing relief to those in need.

What emerged from this study was therefore a far more favorable
picture of local administration than was common among professional
social workers; giving credit to local participants, it also recorded a
willing response to state and federal pressure. Methods were improved,
more generous standards were accepted, and there was a perceptible
shift from the maxim that no one should starve to the hope that those
who had had the misfortune to lose employment would not be reduced
to subsistence level. The study also implied that vigor in emergency
relief administration had had a tonic effect on other public and private

welfare agencies. The most notable finding was that traditional local government had worked closely with the new agencies once their aims had been understood. Lay control was compatible with respect for professional advice. The study is therefore a useful corrective to the prevalent condemnation of local government by most social scientists. It also suggests that the FERA left a permanent imprint upon welfare policy and practice by slow penetration of the social fabric rather than by dramatic confrontation.

When the National Conference of Social Work assembled in 1934, cheering reports of progress toward rational and humane relief policies were clouded by doubts about the future. Aubrey Williams described the resistance offered by conventional beliefs and practice. Too many public officials still acted as though a destitute man was "individually and morally at fault." Too many people in authority still resented the appointment of trained social workers and clung to the notion that an unqualified resident would do a better job than a professionally trained outsider.[35]

On the bright side, Williams thought that it was possible to do business with politicians, who were usually "fair and decent ... straight shooters and for the most part played with their cards face up." The same could not be said for "some powerful board members of private agencies, chambers of commerce, and the like ... who pass the word quietly down the line that such and such a person is dangerous and not to be supported." He said that niggardly finance was a continuing obstacle to sensible policy, but voter resistance to taxes should be blamed. The politicians would have spent quickly enough if they thought that it would be popular, but lacking this assurance they usually backed local officials in wishing "all social dependency to be dumped on the federal government."[36]

Some speakers drew attention to the lack of cohesion in welfare policy. Fred R. Johnson, superintendent of the Michigan Children's Aid Society, said that in his state the Department of Welfare looked after state institutions, the Director of State Welfare was responsible for care outside institutions, and the probate judges, acting with a commis-

---

[35] Aubrey Williams, "A Year of Relief," *NCSW 1934*, 157–65, 161.
[36] Ibid., 162.

sioner for the care of crippled children, distributed mothers' aid without any state supervision. A commissioner for pardons and paroles was responsible for the welfare of ex-prisoners and their families, and the fire commission looked after sufferers from fire. Several cities had their own departments of welfare, and counties had their superintendents of the poor. There had been no attempt to coordinate the welfare responsibilities of all the officials and agencies, and now, side by side with them and equally independent, were county relief committees, county directors of relief, and the State Emergency Relief Administration. The speaker's prescription for a cure was greater centralization. The fragmentation of responsibility bred worse evils because "a fundamental weakness of American government is lack of administrative capacity ... [which is] frequently at lowest ebb in counties and local units of government." Only in the federal and state governments could be found the necessary knowledge, integrity, and capability, and in them must be vested authority to impose uniform standards.[37]

Joseph P. Chamberlain of Columbia University saw another compelling reason for centralization. The local unit was "the weakest link in the chain of government," and it would be folly to entrust its officers with control of very large sums of money when "political war chests were never so empty, and it was never so difficult to get places for those who would do most good to the party and, at the same time, the least good to the needy." The local politicians might be amenable to argument, as Aubrey Williams suggested, but they could not be trusted with state or federal money.[38]

William Hodson was president of the conference for the year, and his address was the most thoughtful and in some ways the most radical contribution. His title was "The Social Worker and the New Deal," and he began by claiming that important innovations had been treated as temporary expedients because governments had refused to face the facts. Experience in the depression had led social workers to "recognize the absolute necessity of establishing relief administration as a permanent function of government"; but states and cities had borrowed rather than taxed, paid their relief workers poorly, and offered them

[37] Fred R. Johnson, "The Integration of Emergency Relief with State and Local Departments of Public Welfare," *NCSW 1934*, 406–11, 410.

[38] Joseph E. Chamberlain, "Social Legislation," 272, *NCSW 1934*, 263–83.

no prospects of long-term careers. There were few examples of plans for the future based on the need for permanently enlarged and professionally managed welfare agencies.[39]

Hodson argued that improved organization would not produce the desired results unless accompanied by profound changes in the attitudes toward poverty. He had seen the CWA as a hope for the future, with its federal management and new approach to poverty. "The adoption of this splendidly conceived program of work and wages ... was a historic moment in the history of government, its abandonment a tragedy." It had demanded a decent wage for useful work and relief "adequate to maintain a decent minimum standard of living," and had thus reversed the principles of the old poor law, which made humiliating work the penalty for dependency and gave sufficient relief to prevent starvation, but no more.

C. M. Bookman, the respected secretary of the Cincinnati Community Chest and a spokesman for organized private charities, followed with an emphatic plea for federal responsibility:

Relief is more than a local question and never can be solved satisfactorily except by national action. Some states and some counties within the states have always been too poor and too lacking in leadership to solve their own problems. Every social worker knows how unfortunate and backward areas add to the social problems of the cities, and how adversely they affect our entire national life.

Distress might be local but its consequences were national. Hodson agreed, but reminded the conference that decisions must often be local. The remedy lay in a national code of practice to govern local relief administration.[40]

Other speakers also had reservations about centralization. One of them went over familiar ground in sketching the weakness of local finance and admitted that only the federal government could reach the pockets of those who ought to pay, but he also asked what assurance there was that the federal government would not itself become enmeshed in the spoils system. He argued that the logic of the quest for efficiency must not be carried too far and that some local check upon central authority must be retained. Following a similar line of

---

[39] William Hodson, "The Social Worker and the New Deal," *NCSW 1934*, 3–12.
[40] C. M. Bookman, "The Federal Emergency Relief Administration: Its Problems and Significance," 29, *NCSW 1934*, 13–31; Hodson, "Social Worker and the New Deal."

thought, Peter Kasius, general manager of the Provident Association of St. Louis, asked a question that can well stand as the tailpiece of this chapter:

Have we reached a point in our political experience when we must admit that the further government is removed from the people, the better government we will have?[41]

Appendix: Notes on Members of the FERA Staff

The names are in alphabetical order, with information (when known) on age in 1933, college education, role when appointed to the FERA, earlier professional career, and other posts held during the FERA period).

For Harry Hopkins and Aubrey Williams see p. 180–2.

JACOB BAKER (38). Staff member with special interest in planning for social security. Colorado Teachers and Agricultural College, University of California. Taught science and agriculture in rural high schools; obtained employment as personnel expert with Birmingham Steel and San Joaquin Light and Power; consultant to other companies on personnel management.

FRANK W. BANE (41). Consultant. Randolph Macon College. Director, American Public Welfare Association.

PAUL V. BETTERS (27). Consultant on urban problems. University of Minnesota. Staff member, Brookings Institution, 1930; executive director, National Institute of Municipal Law Officers, 1933; executive director of the United States Conference of Mayors, 1933.

CHARLES J. BIRT (35). Field representative in southwestern states, University of Cincinnati.

CHARLES M. BOOKMAN (52). Assistant administrator (temporary). Otterbein College. Associate director, Council of Social Agencies,

[41] Joseph P. Harris, "Public Support of Social Work through Taxation, Federal Grants in Aid, and State Participation," *NCSW 1934,* 412–23; Peter Kasius, "Promotion of Local Public Welfare Programs," 499; ibid., 5, 495–503.

1914–16; executive director, Community Chest of Cincinnati, since 1917.

JOSEPHINE C. BROWN (40?). Member of research division; assistant director, Works Progress Administration, 1935; author of *Public Relief, 1929–39*.

H. JACKSON DAVIS (37). Medical consultant. Harvard; graduate work and staff posts at Stanford, Johns Hopkins, and Yale universities.

TREVOR J. EDMONDS (46). Field representative, midwestern states. Formerly a staff member of the Red Cross.

SHERRARD EWING (45?). Field representative. Formerly director, National Association of Travelers' Aid Societies; field representative, RFC, 1932–3.

EDITH FOSTER (46). Field representative in southern states. Northwestern University.

CORRINGTON GILL (35). Head of Statistical and Research Division. University of Wisconsin, U.S. Navy, 1917–19; independent economic research analyst, Washington D.C., 1927–30.

BEN GLASBERG (44). Field representative, Rocky Mountain states. City College of New York. Author of *Across the Desk of a Relief Administrator* (Chicago, 1938).

ROWLAND HAYNES (55). Field representative, north central states. Williams College. Academic posts at the universities of Chicago and Minnesota. Left FERA to become state relief administrator, Nebraska (1933).

HOWARD O. HUNTER (37). Field representative, Indiana, Illinois, and Michigan. Louisiana State University. Director of the community chest, Bridgeport, Connecticut, 1925–33.

ALAN JOHNSTONE (43). Field representative, southeastern states. University of South Carolina and Harvard Law School. Director of South Carolina relief administration, 1932–3.

ROBERT W. KELSO (53). Field representative, Pennsylvania and Maryland. See Chapter 1, Appendix 2.

ROBERT T. LANSDALE (34). Field representative at large. Oberlin College.

ARCH MANDEL (45). Field representative, New York and New Jersey. City College of New York.

JULIAN F. STONE (32). Director of federal work projects. Ohio State and Harvard universities. Airplane pilot; employed by TERA, New York, before joining FERA.

LAWRENCE WESTBROOK (colonel) (44). Assistant administrator; director, National Relief and Rehabilitation program (1935). University of Texas. Army Signal Corps, 1917–19; director of Texas Relief Commission, 1933–4.

ELLEN WOODWARD (46). Assistant administrator in charge of the women's division. San Souci Women's College. Daughter of U.S. Senator N. V. Murray; married to Judge Albert Woodward of Mississippi; before joining FERA, participated in many public activities in Mississippi.

Sources: Who Was Who in America; Searle F. Charles, *Minister for Relief: Harry Hopkins and the Depression* (Syracuse, N.Y., 1963); *New York Times* (obituaries); *Social Science Review* (in memoriam notices); Lt. Colonel Lee's report on the FERA staff (see p. 180).

6

TO AID THE STATES

Despite all the pressure that the FERA could exert, the bottom line was that it existed to give grants to the states. Once a state had received a grant, it controlled expenditure; state law defined the authority of relief agencies, executive orders were issued by the governor or by the relief director he had appointed; the legislature decided what money should be appropriated from state resources. Members of a state relief administration and county directors might tacitly acknowledge the FERA as their real superior; but they were servants of the state, derived their authority from its law, were bound to observe the authority of the governor, and might find their operations curtailed if the legislature failed to make an adequate appropriation.

This situation made the relationship between the FERA and state authorities uneasy and possibly hostile. Field representatives had to spend a great deal of time conciliating governors, finding ways of circumventing those who were unsympathetic or obstructive, or working out the best way of backing those who were cooperative but who faced opposition. State relief directors were usually ready to follow the FERA guidelines, but if disputes arose they were fully entitled, as state officials, to resist federal directives. County commissions and township boards might have failed in the task of providing adequate relief, but they retained powers derived from state laws or constitutions. Most frustrating of all, for the FERA and its local allies, was inaction or obstructive action by majorities in the state legislatures.

The path of relief administration would be strewn with misunderstandings and with arguments, which could become acrimonious. The FERA had money, influence, support in Congress, and backing from the President, but there were limits to what it could do, and its representatives had to exercise constant vigilance against unwelcome interference by duly constituted local and state governments. Even more damaging were unofficial attempts to bring relief administration under party control. On the side of the states, there were many occasions for complaint (sometimes justified) of high-handed behavior by federal agents and failure to understand local conditions.

In the summer of 1933, the first task was to assess the situation, and there were questions in every state that required immediate answers. What were the existing arrangements and how were they financed? Was there an efficient state relief agency, and was its director up to the job? If there was no state agency, what steps were being taken to create one? Once these basic facts had been settled, there were other matters that would affect the allocation of federal grants. Had county agencies been set up, how many trained social workers were employed, and was adequate relief being given? How many were unemployed and how many others were in distress? Was there evidence that relief administration was being manipulated for party purposes, or was lax administration causing waste? The starting point, in finding the answers, was the information collected in the relief files of the RFC; but it was patchy, with voluminous correspondence about the conditions in some states and nothing but formal reports on others. The FERA field representative had to get into action and produce reports without delay.[1]

No state had given the RFC more trouble than Pennsylvania, and it soon presented the FERA with critical decisions on involvement in local affairs. Fortunately, the energetic Robert Kelso, who had represented the RFC, continued as the FERA field representative. On file was a report, which he himself had written for the RFC in June 1933, alleging that people who did not need relief were being employed on projects financed by federal money and that individual cases were not being investigated. He had cited Delaware County, where the relief load had risen in 1932 from 1,615 to 7,044, as an example. Alarmed at the escalating cost, the State Emergency Relief Board had appointed a trained social worker as county supervisor, and within seven weeks 818 families were taken off the relief rolls without denying assistance to anyone in need. Similar action in twelve other counties had reduced the total number of relief cases by 22,000. This action by the state

---

[1] An early task was to discover the facts. The FERA carried out a comprehensive unemployment relief census. See Appendix to this chapter.

agency had been welcome, but the fact that it had been necessary meant that local administration would have to be scrutinized with great care.[2]

In August 1933, when Kelso made his first report to the FERA, the change in the climate in Washington led to a shift in emphasis from cost to effectiveness. He had encouraged the SERB to rationalize and simplify the system. "The County Boards are for it and the poor boards are not objecting. The politicians who have been dividing up federal money do object." He also advised that in two coal-mining counties – Lackawanna and Luzerne – it was essential to get relief out of the hands of the local poor boards.[3]

The strategy to be pursued by the FERA was clear. It must give all support possible to a state board that was acting on the right lines but encountering local and political opposition. This meant that the field representative must concern himself with the details of local management and take sides in the struggle for the control of money intended for relief. The other side of the coin was that many poor boards were in acute financial difficulties and were doing all they could to transfer cases to federally financed relief funds. The state board normally took the line that it was responsible for the relief of distress caused by unemployment but not of destitution from other causes. Local officials were soon appealing to the FERA against rulings by their own state board, and questions that had once been the exclusive concern of the State were being settled in Washington.

A dispute in Fayette County illustrated the difficulties that could arise. The county poor directors stated that until August 1933 all relief had been given by the county emergency relief board, but that the SERB then ruled that distress not caused by unemployment was the responsibility of local poor boards. The county board proposed to transfer 2,000 cases, but the poor boards being near bankruptcy, it agreed to retain temporarily about half the chronic cases; however, the poor boards found themselves unable to handle even this diminished burden.

The county board then proposed to take over two-thirds of the local cases, classify all outdoor relief as emergency relief (thus qualifying it

[2] The reports to the RFC are in F.D.R. Library, Hopkins Papers, Box 59. Kelso reported on a visit on June 23–5.
[3] Ibid.; reports: August 9 and 24.

for federal aid), and ask the state board for an increased allocation of federal money to handle cases for which it was not legally responsible. There was little hope of raising more money in the county, some large employers had intimated that they might close down and move out if taxes were raised, and it was said that if the Frick Coal Company stopped paying taxes, the county government "would have to fold up completely." With reluctance Harry Hopkins agreed not to question the county board's classification and to provide the necessary funds on the condition that relief per family was raised from $5.35 to $16 a month. Thus Hopkins and his staff were drawn deeply into the jungle of local affairs, and, faced with evidence of desperate distress, connived at actions contravening the letter, if not the spirit, of federal law.[4]

Whereas Pennsylvania was trying to attract more federal money, Massachusetts was trying to keep it within strict bounds. The State had deferred application for an RFC loan and refused to certify that all state and local resources were exhausted. The official argument was that the towns were fully capable of fulfilling their traditional responsibilities and that their finances were sound enough to carry the additional burdens imposed by the depression. Under the new law it was necessary only to demonstrate need, and Massachusetts applied for a grant but for work projects only. Kelso thought that the matter was being handled very casually. When he asked the Governor who would handle relief he was told that the State Emergency Finance Board would do it; the chairman of the board, who was present, "seemed surprised" and said that if the job was "merely to act as a channel for funds," he was not interested, but would accept if it implied "power to jack up the standard . . . and set the relief machinery completely aside where sound organization demanded it." In the event, the Finance Board was soon bogged down in detail, whatever the intention of its chairman, and accomplished little. In the opinion of the FERA representatives, the failure of Massachusetts to set up a separate emergency relief agency remained a major obstacle to good relief administration.[5]

---

[4] L. C. Pinchot, Fayette County File, 1934; NA RG 69. 406.2, Reports by Haynes, July 21, September 17–18, 1933; by Hunter, January 7, February 12, April 6, 1934.
[5] NA RG 69, Kelso to Hopkins, September 17, 1933.

When Kelso made his second visit, in September 1933, the prevailing attitude was that the federal government had no business inquiring into the way that the state spent its money, even though some of it originated with the FERA. He reported that the towns were paying their bills with federal money to avoid raising taxes. John Scully, the State Relief Director, had been given no separate office or staff and seemed to believe that Washington would not sanction expenditure on such items. More disturbing was the official failure or refusal to understand the aims of the relief program:

> There seems to be an ingrained feeling in the mind of Scully and local relief administrators that the money should be used to pay tax on properties which would otherwise be subject to tax sales. In this way the town expects to be paid for forcing its own citizens into dependency. This is deadly serious in Massachusetts. I hope it seems like a job in Washington.[6]

The difficulty of conducting a large relief operation without a separate state agency soon became apparent. In January 1934, Kelso telegraphed Hopkins that there were "inexcusable complications with every chance of discredit arising from the mistake of handling FERA funds through the Massachusetts state treasury." The state constitution required the Governor and the Council to approve every disbursement from the treasury, and this gave men with neither experience nor responsibility an opportunity to question and delay every payment. In February Kelso insisted that "the system was completely past its usefulness," and that relief policy was becoming embroiled in political rivalries. What was required was a single agency under a responsible director, although the ineffective Scully might continue as his deputy.[7]

Kelso was succeeded by Robert T. Lansdale, who reported that he had great difficulty in finding out anything about relief administration and that what he had learned was "fragmentary and not very illuminating." However, he had discovered that the law in Massachusetts would have to be changed before an independent relief agency could be set up; that even then the state treasurer would retain power to veto the settlement of relief accounts; and that the legal position would be doubtful, because the constitution forbade the state from making payments to the towns for poor relief. These legal obstacles gave Hopkins

---

[6] Ibid., Kelso to Hopkins, September 17, 1933.
[7] Ibid., Kelso to Hopkins, telegram Jan. 13, 1935; letters, January 17, February 15, 1935.

a plausible excuse for breaking through all the barriers to effective relief administration, and in March he placed emergency relief under federal control.

Massachusetts refused to hand over direct relief – which remained the exclusive responsibility of the towns – and federal operations were limited to work relief. This division of responsibility avoided the disputes over gray areas that occurred in Pennsylvania, but local government was inoculated against the pressures exerted elsewhere by the FERA to improve standards and methods. If local responsibility is the bedrock of American democracy, Massachusetts deserves credit for defending it, and the able commissioner of public welfare, Richard K. Conant, expressed his hope for gradual improvement in his report for 1934:

Peering through the clouds of depression, unable to guess how long bad weather may last, driven by the hurricane of Federal activities, all we can see tells us to keep our little craft headed as it was, away from the old pauper laws and toward a modern system of public welfare.

The FERA field representatives could see only an opportunity missed – and missed for the wrong reasons – while the assumptions of the old poor law remained embedded in Massachusetts town government.[8]

Other New England states clung to the principle of local responsibility, but the towns were often too weak to resist federal aid. In Vermont, town government was still primitive (and perhaps happy), and in its rural communities the authority of the neighbors assembled in the town meeting and serving their turn as selectmen or in other local offices was still the natural and unquestioned mode of government. Some offices changed hands frequently, but continuity was often assured by a few hard-working and respected citizens who were reelected time after time. Local government might lack vision, but it was well suited to close-knit communities in which everyone knew everyone else and families had lived in close association for generations.[9]

Unfortunately town government was being weakened even before the depression. Standards of life on the small farms were low, many had a hard struggle to survive, and younger people – many from fam-

---

[8] Ibid., Lansdale to Aubrey Williams, March 26.
[9] Richard M. Judd, *The New Deal in Vermont: Its Impact and Aftermath* (New York, 1979), 17ff (and for the following paragraphs).

ilies settled for generations – left the state in large numbers. As depression tightened its grip, shrinking yields from taxes and rising demands for relief pressed many towns and small cities toward bankruptcy. The first instinct of every Vermonter was that the towns must nevertheless look after their own, but resistance to federal help crumbled as conditions worsened.

By August 1932, 12 of the 13 largest cities in Vermont had taken the first step by voting to support RFC loans for highway construction; by June 1933, 172 towns had applied for federal help, and an Emergency Relief Administration (ERA) was created. With the coming of the FERA, field representatives began inquiring into relief administration and pressed for improvement. Friction soon developed. Vermont was poorly equipped to manage any kind of centralized system; large work projects were difficult to launch and manage because the ERA staff was too small and town resources were too slender. Many towns could not or would not comply with the FERA rules for regular reports and statistical records. It went without saying that a Vermont overseer of the poor would continue in his accustomed ways, with scant attention to anything that a city-bred social worker might say. A program of rural rehabilitation began in the spring of 1934 but encountered much resistance from the hill farmers whom it intended to benefit.

Though local standards remained well below those recommended by the FERA, state officials were reluctant to break the time-honored conventions of local autonomy. As late as February 1935, the FERA field representative reported that the State Director of the Social Service Division favored cooperation with the overseers (rather than direct operation by the State), believing that "within *a few years* the Overseers may adopt a more liberal policy." There were happier days ahead, and after 1935 Vermont would operate successful programs under the Works Progress Administration; but in 1933 and 1934 it remained a problem area in which the modern methods advocated by the FERA made slow progress against rural poverty and conservatism.[10]

Massachusetts attempted to modernize within a traditional framework and Pennsylvania moved, uncertainly but surely, toward centralized administration and adequate relief; but New Jersey resisted change or

---

[10] Ibid., 45 (quoting from NA RG 69, Branion to Hopkins, February 1, 1935), 50–6.

accepted it grudgingly and incompletely. There was a State Emergency Relief Administration already in operation when the FERA appeared, and it seemed at first that there would be close cooperation between state and federal agencies. John Colt, the State Director, told Hopkins that the localities were not contributing enough to relief and suggested that a strong letter from the FERA might do the trick. In the history of the FERA, it was not uncommon for a state relief director to call for federal action against those who were nominally subject to his authority, but events would show that Colt's anxiety over finance did not extend to the improvement of relief methods. Relief administration in New Jersey continued on principles that were being abandoned or modified elsewhere.[11]

The system was unusual because relief was given first and the recipient was then required to earn it by doing work. This tended to perpetuate the idea that physically demanding but psychologically unrewarding labor was a penalty for destitution at a time when the FERA was insisting that wages at the going rate should be paid for useful work projects. It also required cumbersome accounting to keep track of relief given and the "work credits" to be set against it. Even though the State adopted the FERA policy of promoting useful work projects to employ people from the relief rolls, the field representative, Arch Mandel, found that in June 1934 clients were still being given relief and then offered an "opportunity" to work for it. He made it clear that this plan should be stopped as quickly as possible, and recommended that the State switch to the straightforward system of paying wages for work relief projects and giving direct relief without imposing conditions. Though the State complied, it remained optional for counties to adopt the new system, and five of the twenty-one did not do so.

At the end of 1934, Mandel was close to admitting defeat when he said that it was "not a question of maladministration and . . . not altogether inefficient administration . . . [but] it is inept." Relief clients were restive, the peculiar arrangements for work relief were unpopular, cash wages were not paid for work on many relief projects, and the state administration regarded unsympathetically the efforts of its social work division to promote "the humane objectives of relief." His verdict was that "The New Jersey Administration, and in this it reflects I believe the state at large, has a more hard-boiled attitude in the matter

[11] NA RG 69 406.2, New Jersey, C. Louis Knight to Corrington Gill, July 18, 1933.

of relief than we like to see." Methods were outdated but not economical; and in April 1935, 311 people were still employed in the finance division of the state relief administration.[12]

The weakness of the FERA in New Jersey was that no one in the state was prepared to work energetically for improvement. Where constructive results were achieved in other states, it was because a governor, state relief director, or state relief commission was ready to welcome the assistance of federal officials in breaking down barriers and overcoming obstacles. Lacking this kind of cooperation, the FERA could do little but complain or occasionally threaten. The truth behind the claim that federal emergency relief was not a federal but a state program was that the wider objectives of improving relief administration could not be achieved without an ally in high places.

Resistance to centralization was expected in Maryland, where an old-line Democratic governor presided over a bastion of state rights. Although Governor Ritchie had shown his dislike of federal aid by delaying application for an RFC loan until the deteriorating situation in Baltimore forced his hand, he moved with surprising rapidity to set up an effective state administration. Ritchie had strong common sense, and he realized that once the crucial decisions had been made, nothing would be gained by delay. Immediately after the passage of an emergency relief act he designated the Board of State Aid and Charities as the relief agency and appointed Harry Greenstein, an able and experienced social administrator, as relief director. But he also insisted that wide discretion must be left to the counties in administering relief.[13]

Later Ritchie explained that it would have been possible to set up a strong central agency to determine policy and control local units, but that he had preferred to encourage the development of autonomous county welfare boards (and a special commission for Baltimore) to meet regularly, employ trained personnel, and set "the whole tone of the local programs." The state agency received federal directives, modified them as necessary, and sent them on to the county units, where they might again be adjusted to local conditions. Later it would be claimed that the relief program in each locality had "taken on a char-

[12] Ibid., Mandel to Hopkins, June 30, December 17, 1934.
[13] Maryland Hall of Records, Annapolis, Ritchie Papers, "Review of the Relief Situation in Maryland."

acter which the official administrative body there has determined in its best judgment to be desirable."[14]

When Kelso first encountered this decentralized system, he did not like it. He reported that the central agency exercised no control and assumed that it had no power to regulate relief in the localities. Rejecting this pattern of delegated power, he argued that "control by the public body of the actual disposition of Federal money must be real in every sense."[15]

Greenstein persevered, acting as an adviser on local policy rather than as its director, and was able to exert much influence upon the way things were done. Government was limited but not inert. One danger in local autonomy was rule by a clique, and in November 1933 Greenstein called the county chairmen together for a meeting in Baltimore and urged upon them the need to ensure wide participation in the relief program. The local boards should be enlarged to provide as broad a representation as possible. He suggested that each member of a county board become chairman of a district committee, with the power to coopt nonmembers of the board. This would leave the ruling group intact but encourage broader participation at the grass roots. He made no reference to black membership, but it might be inferred that this would be welcome in districts where blacks were numerous. The chairmen seemed impressed and agreed that the idea should be pursued.[16]

Greenstein explained and defended the Maryland system in a pamphlet published in 1934. He argued that the Relief Administration had acted upon the assumption that "the more remote the control of relief, the less effective and less responsive it would be to the best interests of all concerned." The policy had been to encourage "the greatest degree of autonomy on the part of each local unit," though (unsaid but understood) the decisive influence on local choice was exercised by the man who controlled the flow of cash. Greenstein did not overstate the case when he said that the first federal grant meant "the beginning of state administration of unemployment relief in Maryland; the launching of a new venture in social welfare; the inception of a new issue in the State's financial, social, and political life."[17]

[14] Maryland Relief Administration, *Relief . . . a Challenge to Maryland* (Baltimore, 1934), 4.
[15] NA RG 69 406.2, Maryland, Kelso to Hopkins, June 26, 1933.
[16] Maryland Hall of Records, Ritchie Papers, Minutes of the State Emergency Relief Committee.
[17] Maryland Relief Administration, *Relief . . . a Challenge to Maryland,* 7.

There were a number of difficulties in West Virginia, where extreme distress was notorious in mining districts and real but concealed in many of the mountain communities; but the state was dominated by a small oligarchy of large employers, supported by legislators from rural districts and small cities, opposed to higher taxes and state regulation. Governor William G. Canley had called the legislature into special session in July 1932 and recommended legislation that would make it possible to accept a modest RFC loan. The legislature refused, but the Governor used his executive authority to accept a loan and appoint an Unemployment Relief Administration. The first act of the new agency was to order the formation of county relief committees, but enormous difficulties had to be overcome. Although federal funds made it possible to keep relief at subsistence level, no county gave adequate relief and state and local contributions were far short of what was required.[18]

When the FERA began operations, Hopkins, after receiving a report on the state's finances, concluded that there was "no reason whatever why it should not assume its share." The state had no income tax, a sales tax of only 0.75 percent, and sound credit, but low taxes had left most of the local units "pretty well broke." In 1932 H. G. Kump, a Democrat, had broken Republican ascendancy in West Virginia by winning the governorship. Hopkins told him that no more federal funds would be available unless the legislature took action to improve revenues, but if a reasonable effort was made, he promised to pay a generous 60 percent of the relief costs. Roosevelt also sent the Governor an abbreviated version of the report on state finances with a note saying, "I do hope you can do something about it." Under this pressure the legislature reluctantly agreed to make an appropriation for relief, but standards remained very low.[19]

The state director of relief, Francis W. Turner, claimed that his administration had been kept "absolutely free from personal or partisan political influence" and that the counties had "refrained from making a political football of the relief program." Lorena Hickok, an energetic newspaper reporter, friend of Mrs. Roosevelt, and Hopkins's

[18] *Organization and Activities of the State of West Virginia Department of Public Welfare, July 1931 to January 1, 1933, and of the Unemployment Relief Administration, August 19, 1932, to January 1, 1933* (Charleston, W. Va., 1933), 72–8.

[19] F.D.R. Library, Roosevelt Papers, FERA Misc., Hopkins to Roosevelt, August 16, 1933.

unofficial investigator, took a gloomier view in August 1933. She thought that political interference was as prevalent as it was in Pennsylvania. Privately, Turner was equally pessimistic and told Miss Hickok: "Here you've got our whole civilization built on rotten foundations – and a lot of damned fool capitalists and petty politicians are fiddling away while the thing collapses." Hickok agreed that "All the little petty politicians are trying to get their fingers in the pocket book."[20]

In Charleston, Turner reinstated a good but Republican county relief administrator who had been fired by the Democratic county committee. In Wheeling he was forced to take over and appoint a board of his own choice. There was constant friction with local officials, with consequences that were as petty as they were irritating. In Wheeling, center of a region in which distress was rampant, the county commission removed all typewriters from the relief headquarters in a gesture that was only the most striking example of malice matched by incompetence. The intransigence of the legislature and local government in West Virginia remained to plague the FERA and the state's unemployed. In an extreme form, it presented the FERA with the choice between conniving at penurious and callous local attitudes or coercing the state by cutting off funds – penalizing the unemployed whose relief was the primary purpose of its existence.[21]

Difficulties also multiplied in the midwestern states. In Ohio the struggle for control of the relief program did not come to a head until 1935 and will be described in the next chapter. Elsewhere the FERA encountered formidable problems but achieved some major successes during its first twelve months.

In Indiana there was a complex and inefficient system of local government, disputed interpretation of the federal law, and a weak bargaining position for the FERA because the State made no request for a discretionary grant. The first issue raised was control of personnel. Governor Harry Leslie had appointed county relief committees before setting up a state administration in compliance with the federal act, and the county committees claimed control over the people whom

[20] *Organization and Activities . . . of the Unemployment Relief Administration,* 73; Richard Lowitt and Maurine Beasley, eds., *One Third of a Nation: Lorena Hickok Reports on the Great Depression* (Urbana, Ill., 1981), 15.
[21] Lowitt and Beasley, *One Third of a Nation,* 16.

they had appointed. In September 1933 the FERA field representative, Rowland Haynes, insisted that the state agency must have exclusive control over relief workers. The Governor agreed, and the FERA policy carried the day despite intense pressure to leave appointments to the counties.[22]

Relief finance was another issue. Townships were the tax authorities but counties were responsible for ensuring that revenue was sufficient to meet public needs. Some counties were selling bonds to make up the deficiency in the tax revenue, but their market prospects were doubtful. In Green county the auditor refused to levy additional county taxes, merchants refused to accept orders payable by the county, and the FERA refused to grant more than 50 percent of the actual revenue.

Howard Hunter, who took over as field representative late in 1933, found an ally in Governor Paul McNutt, who was "unusually strong in impressing the different units that they must put up a share of the money." However, in January, Hunter said that there was continuous trouble with the local authorities and that this would continue "until they get rid of their atrocious township system." On the credit side, Center Township, including the city of Indianapolis, was under "our" control, although the trustees "still throw bricks at us constantly."[23]

In March 1934, Hunter pressed for action to solve the problem of local government in Indiana:

I am convinced we are going to have to take quick and drastic action on the township trustee system in this State. It is bad enough under ordinary conditions, but the political township trustee set-up is going to be too inefficient and cumbersome to handle the show.

Hunter complained that after nine months of effort the 1,100 trustees were still in charge of relief and were performing very badly. He proposed that the county committees be given power to eliminate township control. Again the Governor backed him and required signed agreements from the trustees to accept the authority of the county committees. By October 1934, all the counties and townships had been persuaded or coerced into putting up adequate funds for relief.[24]

---

[22] NA RG 69, 406.2, Indiana, Rowland Haynes to Hopkins, September (?) 1933.

[23] Ibid., memo by Hunter, November 25, 1933.

[24] Ibid., Hunter to Hopkins, November 18, 1933; January 19, October 4, 1934. Hunter told Hopkins that the county committees would "put the Township Trustees delicately on the shelf" (F.D.R. Library, Hopkins Papers, Box 57).

Thus was forged an alliance between the FERA, the Governor, and the State Relief Board against the elected representatives in local governments. Locally, the instruments of central control were the appointed county committees. This was the most complete example of such an alliance in operation, and won strong endorsement from the FERA. In addition to praising the Governor, Hunter commended the State Relief Board, and in June 1934 told Hopkins that it had "run along so nicely against such odds"; in October it was still operating "in an orderly manner and with about as little trouble to us as in any State I know of."[25]

In Illinois too there was recovery from a bad start caused by chaotic local government. When the FERA first appeared on the scene, there were 1,500 units responsible for relief and no regular reporting to any central agency. There was an efficient audit of federal and state relief funds, but in the fall of 1933 it still seemed impossible to make headway with the local units. In the legislature, members from rural counties allied with some business interests insisted that Chicago and Cook county must look after their own and opposed new taxes for relief.

Governor Henry Horner, a Democrat inaugurated in January 1933 after many years of Republican domination, proposed a sales tax, which secured a bare two-thirds majority (required to bring it into immediate operation) but was then voided on a technicality by the Illinois Supreme Court. A substitute bill was defeated in the state senate. The very large sums already received by Illinois from the RFC persuaded Hopkins to adopt a tough line: A grant of $4,000,000 in July 1933 was to be an advance payment of the matching grant due in October, and further grants would be conditional upon the state and localities providing two-thirds of the relief costs.[26]

Relations with the FERA got off to a bad start. In July 1933, Horner objected to submitting his appointments to the Relief Commission for approval by Hopkins, and a contest was averted only because the field representative, Rowland Haynes, thought that the appointments were satisfactory. His successor, Howard Hunter, found the commission

[25] Ibid., Hunter to Hopkins, June 1, 1934.

[26] For a sympathetic account of Horner's administration, see Thomas B. Littlewood, *Horner of Illinois* (Evanston, Ill., Chap. 7, passim). General studies are Frank Z. Glick, *The Illinois Emergency Relief Commission* (Chicago, 1940); Arthur P. Miles, *Federal Aid and Public Assistance in Illinois* (Chicago, 1941); David J. Mawer, "Unemployment in Illinois during the Great Depression" in Donald F. Tingley, ed., *Essays in Illinois History* (Carbondale, Ill., 1968, 120–32); IERC, *Biennial Report, 1934–6*.

"weak and very political" and said that Robert Dunham, the State Relief Administrator, tried "to dodge all important issues," with "constant confusion, indecision, and uncertainty" as a consequence. He thought that neither the Governor nor the commission was strong enough to control the county relief committees and suggested that Hopkins get rid of Dunham, put in "an administrator for the whole show," and find "a very high-class man . . . as our direct representative" in Chicago. There should be a firm agreement on the allocation of grants to the counties, strict financial control, state supervision of all work projects, and the reorganization of the relief committees in about thirty counties. Fortunately these drastic proposals, which would have brought on a first-class political row, were not accepted.[27]

On a visit in March 1934, Hunter found most members of the commission "not very sympathetic to our progress." The Governor was not helpful "and pretty successfully dodged committing himself on anything important." The only good man on the commission was a Republican, and no Democrat showed "guts or intelligence." At the same time, Hunter agreed that there were real difficulties. Relief alone was costing $5,000,000 a month, and with the end of the CWA, the commission would become responsible for a further 100,000 cases. Unless they got more federal money, they would have to choose between cutting relief to unacceptable levels or maintaining standards and starting "another wrangle with the legislature." This report probably reinforced Hopkins's distrust of Horner, and personal communication between them ceased. Hopkins corresponded on relief directly with Mayor Kelly of Chicago. Horner ignored Hopkins and appealed to the President. There is no record of action by Roosevelt, but the master politician must have wished to avert an open quarrel with the Democratic governor of a state, which might be crucial in the 1936 election.[28]

Members of the Illinois Relief Commission had grounds for complaint. They believed that they had done a good job under very difficult circumstances, and an investigation by the FERA staff into their

---

[27] F.D.R. Library, Hopkins Papers, Box 57, Haynes to Hopkins, 20 July 1933 and report on a visit, July 25–August 1; memo by Hunter, November 1933.

[28] NA RG 406, Hunter to Hopkins, March 20, 1934. On May 7, Hunter wrote: "I may say that the rumor has been definitely disproved that John Dillinger is hiding out in the accounting department of the Illinois CWA." Dillinger was a Chicago gangster and currently Public Enemy No. 1.

administrative costs proved to be a triumphant vindication. In November 1934 Hunter took back his earlier criticism and wrote:

It is fair to add that in our opinion the administration of relief in Illinois, since the organization of the Commission, has been handled in a most effective manner. In our opinion there are few States, indeed, which have handled the relief problem in as orderly and adequate manner as has Illinois.

He went on to say that "the operation of relief in Illinois has developed into a highly centralized system" for disbursing public funds, but the Relief Commission had gradually strengthened its control by exercising its right to approve or reject key appointments.[29]

The major remaining difficulty was the State's failure to pay its share. In February 1935, Horner called a special session of the legislature to vote new taxes, but it was soon apparent that members intended to talk the session out without taking action. In April, Hopkins cut off all federal aid until the State contributed $3,000,000 a month. In other states, governors sympathetic to relief had welcomed similar pressure on reluctant legislators, but it was deeply resented by Horner. At last a sales tax was passed to finance relief, and though it was not expected to yield the $3,000,000 demanded by Hopkins (and would produce even less than the estimated revenue), it allowed everyone to escape from an impossible situation. At the end of May the FERA transferred $5,000,000 to the Relief Commission, which had almost ceased to function.

No one could claim much credit, but the FERA had made a serious error in not working wholeheartedly with the Governor and the Illinois Emergency Relief Commission. The whole episode illustrated the truth of a maxim that ought to have been grasped at the outset: If the FERA had a firm ally in a state, it could work wonders, but endless difficulties ensued if it antagonized all who were legally responsible for relief. The real losers, with everyone at odds, were the unemployed.

When Rowland Haynes first visited Michigan as the FERA field representative in July 1933, he complained of political favoritism in relief administration. The Governor refused to appoint anyone to a county

---

[29] NA RG 69 406.2, Howard Hunter, report to the IERC, November 1934; Lee G. Lauck to Corrington Gill, September 15, 1933. Hunter's change of heart probably began with a conference in June when the Governor told the IERC that though it had been set up to conduct a short-term operation, it was now time "for consideration of a more permanent welfare and relief plan."

relief committee who had not been approved by the county Democratic committee. The State Relief Commission could not resist, but was fighting for the right to veto unsuitable appointments. There were also financial difficulties. The State had benefited during the first flush of FERA spending and had received a grant of $1,500,000; but the yield from a sales tax, intended to finance relief, would not come in for several months and a further discretionary grant was requested from the FERA. Even when the tax yielded revenue, it was estimated that it would not produce enough.

An experienced and active State Relief Commission and tactful assistance by the FERA field representatives succeeded, somewhat surprisingly, in overcoming most of these difficulties. In February 1934, Howard Hunter reported that the state commission was one of the best of its kind in the country, had won exclusive power to appoint members of county committees, and was conducting a "lean and efficient" operation. He said that they did not "clutter up the State office with a highly centralized organization," but that it was nevertheless easy to get an overall view of what was being done. Rejecting attempts by Detroit to establish direct communication with the FERA, Hunter wrote that it would be "exceedingly poor policy to issue orders to any county except through the State Administration."[30]

An efficient state agency backed by the FERA was able to pursue an energetic policy. Alarmed by the rising relief costs, it put every county on a budget and pressed the legislature to provide enough money, though with little success. Hunter told Hopkins that the Michigan legislature, "with all its weaknesses and lack of leadership, . . . has no clear idea of its relief responsibilities." Money was voted, but always less than was needed.[31]

Although the state agency won high praise from Hunter, he found plenty to complain of in local relief administration. He described the Wayne County Relief Commission as "a particularly inefficient outfit," and working closely with the newly appointed state director, William Haber, a young professor of social administration turned public servant, he conducted an energetic campaign against local inefficiency:

We kicked the Mayor of Albion very squarely in the middle of the pants and changed the entire commission in that place. Several Aldermen in the attractive village of Grand Haven, who had placed themselves on the Civil Works

[30] NA RG 69 406.2, Michigan, Haynes, reports, July 21, September 17, 1933; Hunter to Hopkins, February 12, 1934.
[31] Ibid., Hunter to Hopkins, January 7, 1934.

Administration payroll, were very forcibly kicked off. In a very few places, notably Ann Arbor, Grand Rapids, Muskegon, etc., we had to force the local boys to obey our rules on the payment of proper wages to skilled labor.[32]

This episode in Michigan history is a striking example of parallel government, with the two experts – federal and state – describing what "we" had done to clean up the mess made by local politicians.

The background to the situation in Minnesota was described by Mrs. Blanche La Du, chairman of the State Board of Control, in an address to the National Conference of Social Work in 1933. At the close of 1932, distress had been severe in the larger cities and northern counties, but sixty-one counties in the southern and western parts of the state were still able to carry their own relief load. Governor Floyd Olsen had designated the Board of Control, hitherto concerned with management of the state charitable institutions and with child welfare, as a State Relief Administration, with authority to investigate, establish standards, and distribute RFC funds. Fortunately, since 1917, the State Board of Control had appointed child welfare boards in each county, and there were therefore some experienced people ready to accept responsibility, but in thirty-four counties where townships existed, "the task of administering poor relief [was] a most difficult and unsatisfactory one."[33]

Mrs. La Du went on to describe an attempt to set up a new system of county welfare boards. A bill was drafted for the legislative session beginning in January 1933; though it was strongly backed by the Governor and by representatives from all counties receiving RFC funds, bad management squeezed it out of the legislative timetable. When the FERA was established, relief administration was still chaotic; county welfare boards existed in some counties but not in others, and where townships existed, relief administration remained primitive. Many counties had been lightly touched by the depression and were unlikely to respond to proposals for heavy taxes to aid the hard-pressed counties and cities. There was more sympathy for the farmers, in counties where drought had worsened the situation, but readiness to help in this quarter would reduce the funds available for unemployment relief in other parts of the state.

---

[32] Ibid.
[33] Blanche La Du, "Coordination of State and Local Units of Welfare," *NCSW 1933,* 494–505.

The first reaction of Sherrard Ewing, the FERA field representative, was that the State Board of Control was not up to the job. Its members were two elderly men "who didn't know what it was all about," and "a fine capable woman" (Mrs. La Du). The State Relief Administrator, Ralph Rarig, did not know how little he knew about relief and was not making proper use of his trained staff. Some experienced social administrators, such as Pierce Atwater of the St. Paul Community Chest (recently appointed as a field representative for the FERA), thought that Rarig ought to go; but Ewing preferred to keep him, giving his assistant, Miss Guildford, more responsibility as director of the field staff. Local administration also caused concern. Minnesota had been given a special federal grant for road construction in the areas stricken by drought, but Ewing reported that county officials were trying to grab it "to get a lot of free roads built, if possible, before any relief set-up is made."[34]

Whatever Ewing might report or the FERA decide, the outcome was likely to be determined by Floyd Olsen, the charismatic Governor, whom Rarig described as "looking like a Viking with a personality plus." In the summer of 1933, Olsen decided that the relief situation was so important and so difficult to handle that he would have to assume personal control. Mrs. La Du might be approved by the FERA, but Olsen was not prepared to trust anyone who might dispute his authority. When one of the men on the Board of Control died, he appointed one of his own supporters, and, as the other old man did what he was told, Mrs. La Du was in a difficult position.[35]

In some states this situation would have been a prelude to restraints on the central agency; but Olsen did not want a weak board, and once in control, he demanded strong action to bring local governments into line. On November 29, 1933 he summoned the Board of Control and made "quite a speech in which he said that [the board] was allowing too much freedom to local units, that authority should be centralized, and that a number of local people should be turned off relief committees." The function of the board was to advise the Governor, which meant, in effect, that he would act upon its advice when it suited him to do so. He intended to keep a tight rein on the Civil Works program,

---

[34] NA RG 69 406.2, Minnesota, Ewing, reports, July 1, 23, 1933; Ewing to Hopkins, October 7, 1933.

[35] Ibid., Ewing to Hopkins, October 13, 1933; Edmonds to Hopkins, November 25, 29, 1933; telegram, Edmonds to Hopkins, December 14; letter, December 16.

even though this came under direct federal control. He told the new FERA representative, T. J. Edmonds, that "the Governor is the boy who will have to stand the heat if anything in this civil works game goes wrong." State relief administrators normally directed the civil works program as federal officials, and in December, in a move that caught the field representative by surprise. Olsen appointed himself State Relief Administrator, though retaining Mrs. La Du as a member of the board and appointing Rarig as secretary.

From that time on, what happened to relief in Minnesota would depend on Olsen and no one else. The FERA officials had to stand on the sidelines, but after recovering from the initial shock, they usually liked what they saw. In October 1934 Edmonds told Hopkins that "Governor Olsen deserves a great deal of credit for his attitude all the way through on the subject of relief."[36]

The success of the relief operation in Minnesota depended upon a Governor who was ready to take personal responsibility for ensuring that relief did what it was intended to do, had the capacity to master details, and was strong enough politically to override local obstruction. The FERA field representative was treated as an adviser, with neither the opportunity nor the need to assume the authority that his colleague exercised in Michigan. No state better fulfilled the prescription that the FERA was not a federal program but a state program with federal aid.

Southern states offered similar problems in a different context. Politics were controlled by tightly knit ruling groups of the Democratic party, though their ascendancy might be challenged, from time to time, by rival factions. The rhetoric of state rights was deeply embedded in popular political conscience, as were localism, suspicion of all government, and reluctance to put taxpayers' money into the hands of politicians. Low expenditure on poor relief was justified by the belief that in a rural society men could fend for themselves and support their families even if they had no regular employment. Especially prevalent was the belief that poor whites and blacks, being accustomed to a low level of subsistence, needed little or no help in bad times. In some southern

---

[36] Ibid., Edmonds to Hopkins, October 17, 1934. Among other points praised by Edmonds was Olsen's condemnation of politics in relief – he issued a public statement that "I'll drum any Farmer–Laborite playing politics with the CWA out of the party" (February 17, 1934) – and his appointments to relief posts were "excellent and non-political" (October 17, 1934).

states, child welfare was an exception to this rule and had been successfully developed.

Provided that the existing social order was preserved, complacency usually prevailed; but depression and distress could not be ignored. When the first LaFollette bill was introduced in the Senate, several southern Democrats had been ready to accept federal money, provided that control of grants remained with the state authorities and no conditions requiring state actions were attached. The Emergency Relief Act of July 1933 went far beyond what they had been ready to accept in the spring of 1932, but within the new framework there was still room to play for maximum federal aid, minimum increases in state taxes, retention of local responsibility, and assurance that relief rates set by a national agency would not disturb the normal pattern of southern earnings.

It was appropriate that Virginia proved to be the most successful defender of state rights while drawing heavily on federal aid. The powerful United States Senator and former Governor, Harry F. Byrd, dominated the state and was well placed to resist encroachment by any federal agency. Throughout the period of federal relief, the State maintained that it had fulfilled its obligations by making increased appropriations for highways to provide employment, and that direct relief must be paid for by the counties and the federal government. Looking back over eighteen months of emergency relief, the Richmond *Times Dispatch* noted:

[Political leaders in the state] were determined not to spend any of the State's money for the neediest unemployed.... They are great advocates of State rights when such advocacy meets their convenience, but when it doesn't, they believe in letting Uncle Sam hold the bag.[37]

Virginia had an able and conscientious state relief administrator in William A. Smith. He was ready to put pressure on the counties to pay their share and spend federal money honestly. A field representative accorded him grudging praise when he said:

[Mr. Smith] has the characteristic traditional attitude of the Southern person toward the negro and the less fortunate white person, which expresses itself in

[37] Quoted by Ronald L. Heinmann, *Depression and the New Deal in Virginia: The Enduring Dominion* (Charlottesville, Va., 1983), 80. This work gives an overall account of relief in Virginia; see also Robert F. Hunter, "Virginia and the New Deal," in John Braeman, Robert H. Bremner, and David Brody, *The New Deal*, Vol. II (Columbus, Ohio, 1975), 103–36.

a paternalistic concern for their welfare. It is a real interest and concern, and should not be confused with the distaste and in instances dislike one finds in some persons and in certain sections of the South and Southwest toward the negro and the poor white Southerner.

However, Smith had little sympathy with the FERA's insistence that the State must make a contribution, or with bolder plans for administrative reorganization.[38]

Virginia had an old established Department of Public Welfare, with broad responsibilities, but it pulled out of unemployment relief when the Virginia Emergency Relief Administration (VERA) was set up in June 1933 and left it to carry most of the cost of relief. Local units applying for assistance were expected to assume responsibility for its administration and might be willing to do so when a work project was of evident benefit to their communities; it might be more difficult to obtain when the unemployed were the prinicpal beneficiaries.[39]

As in other states, the VERA had the right to appoint relief personnel, but exercised it with an exaggerated respect for local opinion. A person with strong local backing was normally appointed. Engineers for work relief projects were nearly always local people and were invariably continued in office until their incompetence or dishonesty became blatant. Favoritism by local officials was not condemned but regarded as a reasonable desire to ensure that local people in good standing were suitably rewarded. One result of the system was that administrative costs were high and levels of relief low. Between 15 and 18 percent of relief expenditure went on administrative costs at a time when 10 percent was the national average, but unemployment relief was given at about half the national figure. Local leaders welcomed federal money but not the social philosophy that went with it, and late in 1934, after the FERA had been in operation for nearly eighteen months, a field representative told Hopkins:

Local participation consists largely in accepting funds for the local emergency relief administration. The local communities are putting in as little as they can because they are fundamentally opposed to the whole relief program, and their contributions are almost entirely for materials and supervision of work projects.[40]

---

[38] NA RG 69 406, Virginia, report on a special study by Gertrude S. Gates, Federal relief supervisor, February 1935.
[39] Ibid.
[40] Ibid.

These shortcomings did not prevent Virginians from claiming special virtues for their system. A speaker at the 1934 meeting of the Social Science Association of Virginia expressed a widely held view when he claimed that it was a model of "centralized policy in decentralized administration." If a critic had been present he might have pointed out that as relief was being paid for largely by the federal government, the function of the FERA, as interpreted in Virginia, was to keep alive a system that competent observers regarded as mean, costly, and archaic.[41]

Tension between Virginia and the FERA was inevitable. On October 20, 1923, Allan Johnstone of the FERA, addressing a meeting of county officials, stressed the imperative need for them to contribute. Local responsibility was, he said, an essential element of southern society:

I happen to be a Southerner and I know that we feel a person is first a citizen of his county and city and State before he is a citizen of the United States – we fought a war about it once – and we still have that idea.

But rights could not be preserved unless duties were performed and it was an obligation for counties to do all that they could, do the job properly, and not reduce the unemployed to the lowest level of subsistence. He warned that he was "not interested in going into cooperation with a state or locality on that sort of basis."[42]

Johnstone sent Hopkins a memorandum of a meeting with Governor John Pollard, who agreed to put two propositions to a meeting of prominent legislators: first, that the FERA would be responsible for three-quarters of the unemployment relief costs until 1 February 1934, with local governments providing one-quarter; and second, that the legislature should provide sufficient money when it met in January to raise the State's total contribution to three-quarters. Hopkins annotated the memo: "First thing is conditional provided that the second is done."[43]

---

[41] Frank W. Hoffer, "Address to the Social Science Association of Virginia," quoted in Arthur W. James, *The State Becomes a Social Worker* (Richmond, Va., 1942), 33. This is a firsthand but uncritical account of relief administration in Virginia. The author was for many years director of the educational program of the Department of Social Welfare.

[42] NA RG 69 406, Virginia, report on a meeting, October 20, 1933; Johnstone to Hopkins, October 13.

[43] Ibid., reports on meeting and discussion, October 13, 1933.

The meeting with the legislators was a failure because "no one was present except a few frightened social workers." Johnstone then had a meeting with Senator Byrd and Governor-elect George Peery in which the two Virginians said that the State (already in deficit and committed to a program of improving schools and insane asylums) could not raise money for relief. Johnstone then suggested that the VERA should be strengthened. He also insisted that the FERA must approve all staff appointments, expected to be consulted on relief standards, and would not contribute unless both were acceptable. The response was clearly unsatisfactory because on October 28 Johnstone telegraphed Hopkins that no FERA money should be advanced to Virginia because it would be used "to prosecute a program of relief so inadequate as to be absolutely indefensible." By November he had relented a little and recommended disbursing $300,000 a month because the localities were providing materials and supervision for CWA projects, though the legislature was unlikely to make an appropriation. In January this amount was raised to $500,000.[44]

The situation as viewed by the FERA remained unsatisfactory. In March 1934 Johnstone estimated that $7,000,000 would be needed following the end of the CWA. He suggested $2,000,000 from the State, $4,000,000 from the FERA, and the balance from the counties (mainly in materials and supervision). He thought that the State could easily meet this target but added:

What is known as the "Machine" in Virginia headed by the able and astute Senator Byrd has, however, complete control of the situation and will resist an appropriation for relief even to the extent of abandoning a relief program.

He asked whether Roosevelt could influence Byrd. The President was unwilling or unsuccessful, and Virginia continued to receive FERA money without making any state contribution to relief.[45]

At the close of 1934, Mrs. Gertrude Gates of the FERA, who had been sent to report on conditions in Virginia, wrote informally to Aubrey Williams:

The conservative element, which predominates . . . in this state, does not . . . want to help in meeting its relief cost, because it does not believe relief is nec-

---

[44] Ibid., Johnstone to Hopkins; telegram, October 28; letters, November 24, 1933, January 3, 1934.
[45] Ibid., Johnstone to Hopkins, March 7, 1934.

essary but there is a willingness to accept FERA funds as long as they can get funds without putting up money themselves.

She said that rural legislators, who filled three-quarters of the seats in the General Assembly, would not appropriate money for relief in the cities, and that the cities wanted money but were "playing poker with Washington."[46]

Mrs. Gates recommended a reorganization of the state into thirty-five districts under direct control by the VERA, a state work relief program to meet minimum needs, no supplementary relief, and all clients in rural counties to be treated as rural rehabilitation cases. William Smith rejected this advice on the ground that the VERA program should not be divorced from local government, that counties would object so strongly that it would be impossible to get any cooperation on work projects, and that there were other ways of cutting administrative costs. Hopkins approved the recommendations and directed that they be put into effect immediately, but Virginians were adept at resisting directives from Washington and nothing was done.

Virginia's assessment of William Smith's work was very different from that of the FERA representatives. A close associate, writing Smith's obituary in 1940, claimed:

His greatest and lasting contribution was the impetus and assistance he gave . . . to the extension and development of the statutory welfare organization in the counties and cities. . . . He often told his staff that the welfare program would go on long after the FERA was forgotten. In every possible way he made the emergency effort a supplement rather than a substitute for local welfare effort. Frequently, where no local welfare machinery was to be found, he financed its development as such rather than as an emergency organization.

There was a clear conflict between the attempt to provide emergency relief as quickly and efficiently as possible and long-term plans to root welfare agencies firmly in local soil. Given Virginian traditions, the political complexion of the state, and the lack of experience in welfare administration, Smith was right to plan for the future; but in the meantime, many humble citizens paid the price in inadequate relief.[47]

In North Carolina the welfare record was patchy. It was mandatory for cities and counties to have public welfare departments, but the State

[46] Ibid., Mrs. Gates to Aubrey Williams, December 14, 1934.
[47] James, *The State Becomes a Social Worker*, 265.

exercised no control over appointments. Welfare was usually combined with other functions, so that welfare officers might also serve as managers of county institutions, school attendance officers, or poor law officials. State appropriations for local welfare were small and almost ceased during the depression, when they were most needed. A feeble beginning had been made with mothers' aid, but only Confederate veterans and their widows received old-age pensions. With this background, the state legislature was unlikely to respond to demands for new taxes to pay for unemployment relief.

Governor John Ehringhaus had won election as a reformer. He was to carry through notable improvements in the state's educational system, and in 1935 promoted a permanent system of unemployment relief; but he was also committed to balancing the state's budget and reducing its large debt. In this he would be remarkably successful, leaving a surplus of $5,000,000 when he left office in 1937; but to achieve this he resisted increased expenditure and was unwilling to see taxes poured into the bottomless pit of relief. So far as possible, relief would be provided on the cheap and would utilize existing machinery.

Relations between the state and the FERA got off to a bad start with a disagreement over the appointment of a state relief administrator in August 1933. The Governor wanted Mrs. Thomas O'Berry, a prominent local citizen with experience in private charitable work; but Allan Johnstone thought that she was unsuitable and refused to approve her appointment. Robert B. Watson was then appointed, but Mrs. O'Berry, a formidable and opinionated woman, became a member of the State Relief Commission. A point gained was that Professor Howard Odum, a leading authority on public welfare, was to be its chairman.[48]

Letters from Watson to Corrington Gill (head of the FERA's statistical division) described conditions in North Carolina and gave an insight into relief administration in the rural South. The local governments controlled relief expenditure, and though state money could be disbursed only by the State Treasurer and Auditor, they normally accepted local accounts. The Auditor did little more than check vouchers without further inquiry. "The Auditor," wrote Watson, "trusts the Relief Director and the Treasurer hopes that the other two are honest."

---

[48] NA RG 69 406, North Carolina, telegrams, Johnstone to Hopkins, August 8, 12; letter, August 12. Johnstone thought that Watson's appointment had been agreed to in July.

There was no uniform system of relief administration and could be none "with local government supreme."[49]

Watson described some of his visits to counties. In Raleigh the relief office seemed to be in good order, but in passing accounts the county auditor – working in a drab, dingy, and cluttered office – admitted that "all I can do is to see if 2 + 2 = 4." In Vance County the superintendent of welfare was also the relief director. She kept records by checking vouchers against bank statements. The county treasurer, who was president of one of the banks, was interested only in ensuring that payments were made in accordance with the law. The county auditor refused to keep bills and vouchers, so they remained with the relief director. No books were kept and no records of anything except payrolls, vouchers, orders, warrants, and payments for direct relief. "The Relief Director thinks the plan is working fine and hopes no one requires her to do anything more complicated."[50]

In October 1933 Watson wrote about a forthcoming census of unemployment in the state. The chief obstacle was lack of interest on the part of the administration (which "was not confined to the census"), but he believed that it could be a success, provided that "1. Mrs. O'Berry keeps her hands off and does not interfere. 2. Brinton [the state statistician] is hard-boiled enough to carry out his excellent plans and organization in spite of hell, high water, and Mrs. O'Berry."[51]

As in other states, a major difficulty was reluctance by the legislature to vote money for relief. In February 1934, Hopkins issued an ultimatum: no appropriation, no discretionary grants. Johnstone, though holding no brief for the State, questioned this decision and pointed out that North Carolina was very poor, had carried a deficit of $15,000,000 in 1933, and was $151,000,000 in debt. He said that taxes were already so high that further increases would be unproductive, that almost the only thing that the State did not tax was tobacco (the state's major product), and that a 3 percent sales tax was not producing the expected revenue. Was the State required to borrow more or impose a higher sales tax (with doubtful prospects of yielding more revenue) in order to qualify for further aid from the FERA? Johnstone calculated that the needs were incontrovertible: $1,200,000 for relief, $300,000 for rural rehabilitation, and $46,000 for transients. As in other similar sit-

---

[49] Ibid., Watson to Corrington Gill, August 3, 4, 1933.
[50] Ibid., October 25, 1933.
[51] Ibid., Johnstone to Williams, February 15, 1934.

uations, when the choice was between a tough line on finance and cutting relief to those in need, generous counsels prevailed. In spite of the ultimatum, discretionary grants continued, as did exhortations to the State to pay its share.

Toward the close of 1934 and early in 1935, Johnstone reviewed a situation that was still unsatisfactory. The state relief director lacked authority, the director of rural rehabilitation was inept, the state engineer was not an engineer but a contractor, and only the state auditor earned some praise. There was a good state statistician but not enough reliable information to allow him to function effectively. A plan for reorganization proposed by the FERA was promising, but in working out the details, "it should be taken into account that county lines are a part of the North Carolina scene, whether we like it or not." The social service division was improving, thanks to the replacement of a director "who retarded its progress for eighteen months." The transient service was poor. Rural rehabilitation was making some progress, though a lack of understanding of its aims had been "somewhat conditioned by the philosophy of Dr. Howard Odum who has not been sufficiently clear in the bulletins issued from our Administration."[52]

Johnstone thought that there was still "an undue feeling of dependence on federal grants" and that the State could at least put some money into the works program and "should not be permitted to escape it." These comments bring out the salient points in the North Carolina story. Improvement had come about as a consequence of federal initiative, but within limits set by state parsimony and ramshackle local administration. The push from Washington had not achieved all that the FERA administrators hoped for, yet had begun a transformation of the welfare system.[53]

Governor Eugene Talmadge of Georgia moved quickly to set up a Relief Administration, but its head, Dr. Herman De La Perriere, has been described as "the archetype of the rotund, southern politician who had absolutely no knowledge or ability in the fields of either relief or administration," and his clear intention was to organize relief as part of the Governor's personal patronage machine. All the appointments in the relief administration were political, and few trained work-

---

[52] Ibid., Johnstone to Mrs. Gates, December 11, 1933.
[53] Ibid., Johnstone to Hopkins, January 19, 1934.

ers were employed; but Talmadge had no intention of antagonizing his supporters in local party organizations, and once money had been allocated for relief, the counties were left to dispose of it as they wished. With Talmadge dominant in the state and in the Democratic party, the problem for the FERA representatives was to find an ally within the state who would work with them to break the system.[54]

Fortunately for the FERA, there was no doubt about the solution. Miss Gay Shepperson, head of the State Department of Welfare, had much experience, a strong will, and little respect for Talmadge. She was "a diminutive, slight woman, with a squeaky voice," but there was not doubt about her determination, and she quickly established a close working relationship with the FERA and especially with Allan Johnstone, the field representative.

The first step – designed to effect change without wholly antagonizing the Governor – was to convert the Relief Administration under De La Perriere into a five-member commission with control over relief policy, but giving Miss Shepperson, as executive secretary, power to hire and fire relief employees. The commission retained the right to approve but not to initiate appointments. Miss Shepperson immediately dismissed all persons already appointed by the Relief Administration and told the commission that, in future, she intended to employ trained social workers wherever possible. Aware that she had the backing of the FERA and that discretionary grants might depend upon the outcome, the commission agreed. Working closely with Allan Johnstone, she then began to reorganize the county relief agencies.

Governor Talmadge was not a man to allow himself to be outflanked. By law all federal grants were made through him, and he retained the right to sign all checks. He used this power to refuse to sign salary checks for a number of new appointees. However, the FERA held a trump card: Continued aid would be conditional upon the establishment of a satisfactory state relief organization. Talmadge was forced to yield, but he continued to interfere (especially in the sensitive matter of appointments). In this he could count on support from local politicians and might exploit popular suspicion of federal interference. Miss Shepperson was able to counter this opposition by giving

---

[54] Michael S. Holmes, *The New Deal in Georgia: An Administrative History* (Westport, Conn., 1975), 22; see also Chap. 1 of this excellent study for other information in this and the following paragraphs.

publicity to aims and needs in relief, and in September 1933 Johnstone secured her appointment as Relief Administrator.

Tension remained and came to a head in December 1933 when the commission, instructed by the Governor, voted to dismiss a Miss Van De Vrede who had been appointed by Miss Shepperson. It so happened that Hopkins knew Miss Van De Vrede as a well-qualified social worker, and thought the case clear enough to justify drastic action. He also wanted to head off threats by the Governor to set up a purchasing agency in order to control supplies for work projects, or to free himself from federal pressure by refusing federal money (making those in distress suffer to vindicate the rights of states). In January 1934 Hopkins announced that the Georgia Emergency Relief Administration would be placed under federal control, with Miss Shepperson as administrator.

Faced with this threat, Talmadge capitulated and agreed to cease attempts to control the commission or to interfere with appointments. The outcome was that Georgia came to have one of the most professional relief organizations in the country. This did not mean that all went smoothly, but the battle between the professionals and the politicians shifted from the capital to the counties. Relief administrators were often at odds with county commissioners or county relief committees; but there was no doubt that the state administration, now virtually autonomous within the state and backed by Hopkins, had the upper hand.

In a state where much difficulty had been anticipated, the FERA had won a famous victory. This result had been brought about partly by the Governor's blundering tactic, but mainly because there was an effective ally within the state. Miss Shepperson had shown determination and a natural political dexterity. She could not have done it without FERA support, but without her the FERA could have achieved very little.

In July 1933 Aubrey Williams, the field representative, found the situation in Alabama "difficult and full of contradictions." The Child Welfare Bureau had been for some years under the direction of a Mrs. Tunstall, who had made it one of the best in the country, with an experienced staff that could provide the nucleus for a relief organization; but there was tension between her and the relief director, Thad Holt, who had ambitious plans to "put into effect a strong clear-cut State organization and county system . . . but never gets it done." Mrs. Tunstall was irked by the director's inexperience and ignored his instructions. Williams thought that too much depended upon her assistant, Miss Loula Dunn, who got on with the job and held things together but was "unquestionably . . . taking more punishment than we have a right to ask any human being to absorb."[55]

At least Alabama had men and women who were committed to making a success of relief. In September, Williams was still impatient with Holt for not getting things done but also described him as "an excellent promoter, full of new and generally good ideas." In December a new field representative, Miss Edith Foster, was impressed by the Alabama relief staff: "a fine group, earnest and enthusiastic.[56]

The relief staff needed all the enthusiasm and skill that they could muster, for conditions in rural Alabama could hardly have been worse. Tenant farmers and sharecroppers were living in such poverty that they had been trying to get CWA work. There were many stories of local politicians making what they could out of relief, and Miss Foster thought that one account was worth passing on to her superiors. A judge of a county juvenile court and an ex officio chairman of the local CWA board had resigned in order to give himself a job as timekeeper on a CWA project; but this was less reprehensible than it seemed, for, with his court fees yielding only $200 a year and no other employment available, his family would have needed relief in any event. The level of relief given was very low, but rural families, accustomed to scraping a subsistence living, might get by on relief that would be hopelessly inadequate elsewhere.[57]

Acute distress was found among both races and in both rural and urban areas. In Alabama 35.7 percent of the population were black, but their share of those on relief was only slightly larger, at 39.5 percent. Urban places of over 2,500 contained 28.1 percent of the total population and 25.2 percent of the relief population. Black unemployment was much higher in towns than in rural areas (24 against 17.7 percent). Whites were better off in the towns (only 11.4 percent were on relief), but in rural areas there was actually a higher proportion of whites than blacks on relief. Although blacks were generally slightly worse off than

[55] NA RG 69 406, Alabama, Aubrey Williams to Hopkins, July 24, 1933.
[56] Ibid., Williams to Hopkins, September 13, 1933; Edith Foster, private letter to Williams, December 5, 1933.
[57] Ibid., Report by Edith Foster, December 21, 1934.

whites, over 60 percent of those on relief were white and belonged, for the most part, to families long resident in the state.[58]

In October 1934 Loula Dunn, promoted to the position of regional social worker, said that in Birmingham federal and even state supervision was still resented, and she doubted whether much progress could be made. "The old private agency attitudes and methods still prevail." It was clear that Alabama was not going to be in the vanguard of the movement to modernize social work; but within limitations, the record in Alabama was better than early critics feared. In January only twenty one counties were ready to administer federal funds, but sixty two were doing so by May and only five remained outside the system by the late summer. The relief load rose from $171,000 in January 1933 to a peak of over $1,000,000 a month in October and November, and by August 1934 it reached nearly $1,500,000. Handling sums of this order was no mean feat for a state where administrative skills were in short supply.[59]

The other side of the coin was that almost all of the money was federal: From January 1933 to December 1934, the federal government paid for 96 percent of unemployment relief and rural rehabilitation, local governments contributed just 4 percent, and the state gave nothing at all. Federal grants enabled the leaders in social work to carry through a program that would have been impossible if they had had to depend upon state resources and upon backing from state and local authorities. Thus the Alabama story provided a striking example of parallel government in action.[60]

When the first FERA representative visited Oklahoma, his immediate reaction was that no one in an official position knew anything about the problems. There was no state department of public welfare, and no county had a welfare agency. It was assumed that anyone could administer relief and that all appointments would be political; but even if public opinion had been better informed, there was an acute shortage of trained social workers because only one private agency had had a professional staff. The Governor, W. H. ("Alfalfa Bill") Murray, was domineering, erratic, and determined to control the relief operation.

[58] Ibid., Loula Dunn to Williams, October, 1934.
[59] State Emergency Relief Administration, *Two Years of Federal Relief in Alabama* (Montgomery, 1935).
[60] Ibid.

Until the fall of 1933, he attempted to administer both state and federal funds from a single small office.[61]

This situation was intolerable because the state's relief problems were urgent and perplexing. There were some small coal-mining communities that had been set up by railroad companies to provide fuel for their long-distance trains but were put out of business by the switch to oil-burning locomotives. No alternative work had been provided, three-quarters of the miners were unemployed, and few in work earned more than $200 a year. There were some very large lead and zinc mines, but falling demand had cut the work force from 10,000 to 4,500. The oil industry was in better shape, but there had been some fall in employment. Agriculture had been tragically hit by drought, with cattle dead and former wheat fields deep in dust. Drought, the boll weevil, and a fall in demand had brought cotton growing to a standstill.[62]

Leflore County provided an example of everything that was wrong. The population was recorded in the 1930 census as 42,896. In December 1934 27,472 persons were on relief, of whom 60 percent were said to be unemployable. The county had the worst record in the state for insanity, silicosis, tuberculosis, pellagra, and malaria; 6.3 percent of the adults were illiterate, and school attendance was not compulsory. On top of all the ills produced by undernourishment, abject poverty, and ignorance, the county had a very high incidence of venereal disease, which was traceable to widespread prostitution in the prosperous period around 1926. Public health was rudimentary, and even if anyone had the will to do something about disease and dirt, there was no money available. County taxes were unpaid and probably irrecoverable. A gloomy FERA report concluded:

Under such conditions rural rehabilitation is impossible. There are no resources of food, feed, or fuel upon which to build. There is nothing to sell from which revenue can be derived.[63]

Though distress was extreme in Oklahoma, relief operations were sluggish, officials obstructive, and money blatantly misused. On December 15, 1933, Charles Birt, the FERA field representative, had an "extremely unpleasant" interview with Governor Murray. The following day, the Governor was calmer and ready to discuss the general

---

[61] NA RG 69 406, Oklahoma, Report on special problems (1933).
[62] Ibid.
[63] Ibid.

situation, rather than resorting to abuse, but he insisted on retaining control over all funds and on the right to appoint personnel. In a third interview, Murray said that if the FERA did not like the way things were being done, it had better run the show and take responsibility. Birt suggested that he should write to Hopkins on these lines.[64]

On December 31 Birt wrote privately to Aubrey Williams, now assistant director of FERA:

I have come to the conclusion that possibly something can be done with the old boy. . . . Yesterday when he had finished talking, I got down to brass tacks with him. I told him what some of his loyal political friends were doing in his name around the State in the relief administration. In substance I told him most of his friends were really his worst enemies. Naturally he just about hit the ceiling.

Birt thought that given sufficient support he could "re-vamp this setup," but that it would take time and Washington must either be patient or decide upon more drastic action.[65]

With this evidence before him, Hopkins decided against playing a waiting game, and on February 23, 1934, he took control of the whole operation in Oklahoma. Birt was now in charge, and his first step was to recommend the removal of the state relief administrator, Colonel Carl Giles, whom he described as incompetent, ignorant of relief methods, and unwilling to support more experienced subordinates. Hopkins, feeling perhaps that Birt was too closely involved in personal rivalries within the state, moved him to another area and sent John Lane to replace him.[66]

Lane took a less drastic view of what should be done. He recommended that Giles be given at least three months to show what he could do under new direction; his lack of experience and administrative skill was outweighed by the respect he enjoyed and his support among nonpartisan and honest people. There was a real danger of throwing away what little had been accomplished by acting too quickly. Lane confessed:

Oklahoma is an extraordinary and puzzling state. . . . It will never sustain a relief administration, or a social service, operated by highly trained social workers from cities, especially from cities outside Oklahoma.

[64] Ibid., Birt to Williams, December 15, 1933.
[65] Ibid., December 31, 1933.
[66] Ibid., report by Birt to Williams on steps taken March 1–22 to bring relief under federal control.

There was resentment because Washington was thought to interfere too much, and (with obvious reference to Lane's predecessor) the conduct of some federal representatives had caused great offence. An attempt to replace Giles by a federal administrator brought in from outside would "produce a revolution" and lead to general sabotage of the relief program.[67]

On April 1, Colonel Giles had an interview with Hopkins and, in Lane's opinion, the assurances that he received produced a great improvement in morale. He wrote that the state administration was "developing a program as intelligent as Oklahoma can sustain, and . . . that is all that can be expected of Oklahoma." In 1935 the replacement of Murray by E. W. Marland led to quieter and more productive times. The new Governor was keenly interested in relief and determined to make the state increase its financial contribution. A new relief administrator, John Eddelman, was described as "a first rate official," and in February 1935 another FERA field representative, M. J. Miller, found "a fine spirit in the entire relief organization."[68]

Although the relief program was "as intelligent as Oklahoma could sustain," the extent of the achievement should not be minimized. From a poor start, in primitive and chaotic conditions, the FERA had built the structure of a modern relief system in little more than a year. Problems on the ground multiplied as drought continued and the migration of the "Okies" began; but without the constructive work of 1934, a disaster might have been a catastrophe.

California is the next exhibit in this gallery of states. The State Emergency Relief Administration (SERA) was not created until March 1933, when the situation was already desperate. In addition to unemployment, California had to cope with the tremendous inrush of transients arriving from all parts of the nation. Long-standing disputes between the State and its two large cities, between city and county jurisdictions, and between northern and southern sections of the state made it difficult to formulate and carry through a policy for the state as a whole. In addition, the FERA was plunged into personal and partisan quarrels over control of the relief program.

---

[67] Ibid., Lane to Hopkins, May 1, 1934.
[68] Ibid., Miller to Hopkins, December 8, 1934, February 7, 1935.

The great figure in the state Democratic party was United States Senator William McAdoo, who intended to use the FERA program to build up his party in a state where Republicans usually had the edge. He claimed to have been responsible for inserting into the federal act the clause permitting the FERA administrator to nominate a state relief director, and expected this authority to be used to prevent Republican appointments. On July 11, 1933, Pierce Williams, the FERA field representative, reported to Hopkins an interview with the Senator. "He could not believe it, when I said that the Federal Emergency Relief Administrator would appoint the State Administrator only if he found that the present system failed to provide the relief which the law intended should be provided." From this time McAdoo was no friend to the FERA and began systematically to discredit Williams and the State Relief Director, Ralph Branion, who was a Republican though not a partisan. This would culminate in a public dispute in which the principles of old-style political management would be arrayed against those of new-style social administration.[69]

Nor could the FERA expect much help from the state government under the Republican Governor, John Rolph. In July, Pierce Williams corrected a rumor that the Governor was trying to control the Relief Commission. "On the contrary, his indifference to the relief job is almost complete." By December indifference had become obstruction. Williams wrote that a major difficulty in handling local situations was that all FERA grants became state funds, and "Governor Rolph and his officials try to tie us up every time we want to do something with federal money."[70]

The main reliance for sensible direction of the relief program rested upon the State Relief Administration. Williams thought it a strong body, which was gaining control over appointments. County supervisors submitted a list of names from which the commission could choose, but if none on the list were suitable, the commission could make its own appointments without local concurrence.[71]

[69] NA RG69 406, California, Williams to Hopkins, July 11, 1933; for an account of McAdoo's feud with Williams and Branion and the social controversy that ensued, see Bonnie Fox Schwartz, "Social Workers and New Deal Politicians in Conflict: California's Branion–Williams Case, 1933–1934," *Pacific Historical Review* 42 (1973), 53–73.
[70] Williams to Hopkins, July 11, December 16, 1933.
[71] Williams to Hopkins July 11, 1933.

Circumstances in California caused the FERA agents to become much more involved in the affairs of the large cities than in other states. In San Francisco, relief funds had been distributed exclusively through the Associated Charities, which acted on behalf of numerous private charities. Its head was Miss Katharine Felton, who had never drawn a salary and who "typified to many San Franciscans devoted and unselfish social work." Unfortunately, she was also autocratic and unwilling to accept changes unless she had initiated them.[72]

The ruling by the FERA that federal funds must be administered by public agencies meant that the Associated Charities could no longer act as the city relief agency. It would have been easy to bring it under public control, with its staff enrolled as state employees, but the Citizens Relief Committee wanted to use the order as the basis for a complete reorganization, including the displacement of Miss Felton. Pierce Williams reported that the committee was very good but that three of its members would resign unless changes were made. Following his advice, the committee was recognized as a public relief agency, with a free hand to reorganize the city's relief system. This brought to an end Miss Felton's domination and gave San Francisco a relief organization that won the confidence of the FERA.[73]

Los Angeles had given the RFC a great deal of trouble, and the FERA inherited a situation that was difficult, if not impossible. Affairs were so tangled that in November 1933 Hopkins sent a personal letter to Louis Howe, Roosevelt's confidential aide, with information to pass on to the President. He said that field representatives had repeatedly drawn attention to the inefficiency of the relief administration and that much of the blame rested upon the county supervisors. He pointed out that California was the only state in which control over relief policy had not been vested in nonpartisan committees.

All of our efforts are being concentrated on taking the administration of relief away from the county supervisors in Los Angeles and putting full control in the citizens committee which has been set up there for this purpose.

A point was gained when John Quinn, the new chairman of the Board of Supervisors, agreed that relief should be handled as the FERA wished, and Hopkins thought that the Bureau of County Welfare was

---

[72] Williams to Hopkins, July 28, 1933.
[73] Ibid; NA RG 69 406, California, memo by Eva Hance, July 30, 1934.

at last operating under the direction of the Los Angeles Citizens Emergency Relief Committee.[74]

This forecast was too optimistic. Even while the citizens committee was trying to establish a service to certify all relief cases professionally, the Superintendant of Charities, who been appointed by the board of supervisors, made his own appointments and placed them on the federal payroll. Cooperation between the two agencies became impossible, and, unable to thread its way between these competing local interests, SERA was thwarted. A report of July 1934 concluded that "at no time has it ever been possible for the SERA to determine the legitimate unemployment relief load in Los Angeles County."[75]

In other parts of the state the relief program developed more smoothly. Until May 1934 the SERA struggled with local authorities who were setting their own standards and tried – with varying degrees of success – to divorce relief administration from local politics. Every county was required to set up an emergency relief committee, but its members were appointed by the board of supervisors, and though approved by the SERA might still reflect local prejudices. The degree of authority exercised by the local committees varied from county to county; in some, they controlled policy subject to state and federal law, approved the county directors of relief and other personnel, set standards for investigation and casework, and approved the sums claimed for reimbursement. In other counties the board of supervisors claimed authority over relief personnel, and in some the committee itself was uncooperative.

In May 1934 the SERA was strong enough and impatient enough to cut through the tangle of local authorities and establish its own county relief offices for work programs. A year later these offices were handling both work and direct relief. An official report described the SERA as "a fully integrated organization," divided into five divisions (work projects, social service, field service, accounts and statistics, and spe-

---

[74] F.D.R. Library, Hopkins Papers, Hopkins to Louis Howe, November 13, 1933, and the report by Eva Hance (note 75, this chapter). The letter to Howe was occasioned by an allegation, made to the President by Representative J. H. Hoeppel, that FERA funds were being used to build up a Republican machine in Los Angeles. Hopkins denied this but admitted that federal funds had been used by at least one former member of the board of supervisors for personal political purposes. He also described the county welfare officer (Earl E. Jensen), who had been reappointed by the Board of Supervisors, as "inefficient, unsympathetic, and incompetent."
[75] F.D.R. Library, Hopkins Papers, memo by Eva Hance, July 30, 1934.

cial activities including transients, homeless people, and rural rehabilitation). There were similar administrative structures in the larger counties. The administrative staff of the SERA was a few hundred in 1933 but grew to nearly 9,700 by 1935, with a further 1,800 employed as directors and inspectors of work projects. The SERA was running under its own power by 1935, but it would never have got off the ground if the FERA had not begun by insisting that it must be the sole channel for federal aid and by backing its efforts to set up efficient agencies in all the counties. Thus the major legacy of the FERA in California was an administrative revolution that would have been impossible without federal pressure.[76]

The success was real but concealed some dangers that lay ahead. The great changes promoted by federal relief inevitably produced a crop of bureaucratic problems. In states with simpler social organization or with masterful governors their growth was restrained, but in California they proliferated.

The state was large and diverse, its government was usually uncooperative, its welfare services were keen to preserve their independence, and local autonomy had been the rule in carrying out many tasks of government. The superimposition of centralized relief therefore added another network of authority to an already complex system. The superintendent of a work project had to make regular reports to the county committee and to each division of the SERA; on many questions he had to deal with the county board of supervisors, and on others with a state welfare agency. The SERA would not release federal money until its officials had received full documentation and perhaps carried out separate investigations. If a county supplied materials, the county treasurer would not disburse funds unless the application was made in proper form and double-checked; the auditor would want to know how every penny of local money had been spent. Every applicant for work relief had first to be certified as eligible by the local authority, investigated a second time by officials of the county committee, and subsequently reviewed once more by the SERA. Before certification individuals had to be classified, and this took time and effort. Was unemployment the cause of distress? Was the person a transient? Should a person with settlement in the state be relieved on the spot,

[76] *Review of the Activities of the State Relief Administration of California, 1933–35* (Sacramento, 1936), 23–4.

or should another county be told to take responsibility? Was home relief or work relief more appropriate, and should it be given by the county or by the SERA? The administrative problems multiplied, paperwork grew from month to month, and critics could rely on finding abundant evidence of bureaucratic waste.

In North Dakota the FERA confronted agrarian radicalism mixed with political farce, threats of mob violence, and personal tragedy for farmers reduced to abject poverty. The Non-Partisan League was a major political force advocating a debt moratorium and curbs on the money power but lacking a practical program for rural relief. In the fall of 1933, Lorena Hickok, traveling through the country as an unofficial observer for Hopkins, reported on conditions in one North Dakota county (said to be the worst in the state, but several others were little better off):

They haven't had a decent crop there in something like four years. Last summer the grasshoppers ate up just about everything. The most urgent needs are clothing, bedding, and fuel. Those people have not been able to buy a thing for four years. Their houses have gone to ruins. No repairs for years. Their furniture, dishes, cooking utensils – no replacements in years. No bed linen. And quilts and blankets all gone. A year ago their clothing was in rags. This year they hardly have rags.

There were 800 families on relief and 50 more approved but without relief because there was no money. From twelve to twenty-five new applications were coming in every day. In one township of 196 families, all but one were on relief; in another, only two were not.[77]

In Burleigh County (including Bismarck, the state capital), there was a different story. The county relief commission could not resist demands from an unemployed council; too many people were getting too much relief, and too much of the state's FERA grant was being absorbed at the expense of others whose need was greater.

Poor relief administration was a local responsibility, with state and county financial assistance, but as the demand increased, many townships preferred to cut relief rather than find their statutory one-quarter of the costs. During the depression, county commissioners had been given greater responsibilities, but the effects of this change were not yet

---

[77] Lowitt and Beasley, *One Third of a Nation*, 55–76; the county was Bottineau (68–9).

apparent. Except in Bismarck, professional social work was almost unknown.[78]

Much would depend upon the flamboyant Governor, William Langer, elected in the fall of 1932 as a Republican with Non-Partisan support. A State Relief Committee had been set up to handle RFC loans, but its influence was indecisive. Langer promised energetic and radical action, but in March and again in April 1933, Sherrard Ewing, the RFC field representative, reported that little was being done. He thought that there was a good state committee with an excellent chairman (Judge Adolph Christianson of the State Supreme Court), but Langer did not support it and sometimes countermanded its orders. In Burleigh County, anyone could get relief who made enough noise and one-third of the families on relief had not been investigated; others were in real distress but got nothing. Ewing described the county as "an exceptionally bad example of poor work," with bad organization, a weak policy, and unqualified staff. "A little painter out of work, who probably had never handled over $100 at one time in his life, was given responsibility for paying out large sums each month."[79]

When the FERA was set up, Ewing continued as field representative and submitted a gloomy report. The state committee was embarrassed by Langer's appointments and reluctant to set up a field staff for fear that it would be filled by his political appointees. Under pressure from the FERA, Langer agreed not to interfere with the committee, which was then able to replace an uncooperative secretary with a more suitable person. From another source, Hopkins learned that very little relief was getting through to the northern counties, where it was urgently needed, and that unrest was growing in counties where the people still had some spirit left.[80]

In December, Trevor Edmonds took over from Ewing and reported that the situation was still unsatisfactory but that Judge Christianson would do well if his hand could be strengthened. To achieve this, he told the Governor that the FERA would deal directly with the state administrator; but in January 1934, Aubrey Williams telephoned

---

[78] For a general account, see Elwyn B. Robinson, *History of North Dakota*, (Lincoln, Neb., 1966), 399ff.; NA RG 73, Ewing to Croxton, March 2, 1933. Ewing wrote: "In no other state have I encountered indications of such absolute destitution as in North Dakota."

[79] NA RG 73, Ewing to Croxton, April 9, May 3, 1933; for Langer, see Agnes Geelan, *The Dakota Maverick: The Political Life of William Langer* (Fargo, N.D., 1975).

[80] NA RG 69 406.2, North Dakota, Ewing to Hopkins, July 23, 1933.

Edmonds that "they were getting an awful lot of complaints about the North Dakota situation." Edmonds replied that things were not so bad as reported, but this was followed by the news that Governor Langer was to be investigated by a grand jury for soliciting and collecting political contributions from federal employees. On March 1, 1934, by telephone from Washington, Hopkins ordered Edmonds to put the whole relief operation under federal control. Because the position of Judge Christianson was delicate, E. A. Willson was appointed state administrator.[81]

Federalization was a drastic measure but proved to be no more than a prelude to a time of troubles. The grand jury duly indicted Langer; he was convicted on June 17 and sentenced to eighteen months' imprisonment and a fine of $10,000. He was released pending appeal, campaigned vigorously for reelection, and won easily against an alliance of dissident Leaguers, independents, and Democrats. The State Supreme Court then ruled that a convicted felon could not serve and ordered a new election. Lieutenant-Governor Ole Olsen prepared to take over for the interim; but Langer, having obtained an opinion from the state attorney general that conviction was stayed by a pending appeal, refused to allow Olsen to take office. The State Supreme Court again ruled against him but claiming that politics, not law, ruled the court, Langer called out the National Guard to prevent Olsen from taking office. The ugly situation was saved only by the good sense of the National Guard commander, who recognized Olsen's authority and saw him installed in office.

Mrs. Langer then took her husband's place in the election but was defeated by a Democrat, Thomas Moodie. This did not end the affair, for Moodie was then disqualified from holding office on the ground that he had previously voted in Minnesota and had lost his status as a resident of North Dakota. Walter Welford, elected as Lieutenant-Governor, then took his place and provided North Dakota with a short period of calm government until 1936, when Langer (having had his conviction squashed on appeal) was reelected, though with only 36 percent of the vote.

---

[81] Ibid., December 27–29, 1933, January 15, 1934. Williams had heard that "this man Langer is running wild with Willson." Edmonds replied that his informant, Miss Sallsbury, was "a fine person but not always well-informed." Williams said that he had heard the same story from the U.S. District Attorney in Fargo.

Political turmoil prevented the development of constructive relief policies. The situation of North Dakota's farmers remained deplorable, and the federalized relief administration bore the brunt of their anger. On July 11 a large crowd of relief clients presented themselves at the Governor's office, and Langer was reported to have advised them "to turn the heat on the Federal Government and on the State Relief Administration, and to stick to their demands." On the same afternoon that he called out the National Guard, Langer told a crowd of relief clients that Washington was fully able to meet their demands and urged them "to raise hell until they got them." Willson had been threatened with tarring and feathering, but Langer suggested that he should be given ten days to go to Washington and get the money before action was taken. The principal demands were for work at 50 cents for thirty hours a week and payment of rent, clothing, medical care, and hospital expenses without calling on local funds.

Excessive heat – the temperature in Bismarck was 105° F – did not encourage calm deliberation, and when Edmonds arrived in Bismarck to see what could be done, he encountered a large and angry meeting of relief clients. One of Langer's adherents declared that the federal government spent billions on battleships but spared nothing for starving families, and was much applauded when he declared that this meant war between the rich and the poor. Edmonds intervened, promising to forward their demands to Washington if a committee could formulate them, and this cooled the meeting down. Edmonds excused his conciliatory offer by telling Hopkins that "he had decided not to get an interesting story for the files at Washington at the expense of a coat of tar and feathers in this hot weather for Mr. Willson, who is really a nice, harmless, and very efficient person, and we need him. I understand that it takes a long time and a lot of kerosene to remove tar from a nude body."[82]

After this tense moment, the weather and tempers cooled down and realistic steps were taken to get relief to the farmers who needed it. In September, Willson thought that it would be safe to return relief administration to state control. Governor Ole Olsen was cooperative, and Willson thought that he could handle the relief situation even if Mrs. Langer was elected. When Governor Welford was eventually installed after the Moodie episode he proved to be helpful, but it was

---

[82] Ibid., Edmonds to Williams, July 23, 1934, for this and the following paragraphs.

not until December 1935 that Hopkins decided to return relief to the state.

The FERA had taken the knocks in the summer of 1934, but from that time it won support for its relief efforts. In April 1934, immediately after relief was brought under federal control, 148,000 persons, or about a fifth of the population, were on relief. During the year their number increased as more farmers became destitute and unemployment spread to white-collar workers in the towns; but relief operations expanded to meet the demand. Willson later wrote:

The program . . . was the biggest business in the state and affected every one of its citizens, directly or indirectly. . . . It promoted business that would otherwise never have existed, repaired and built new roads, buildings, and residential facilities; provided immunization and corrective care for thousands of children, gave the state the beginnings of a permanent program of water conservation through dam building as well as the beginnings of a permanent program of public welfare.[83]

Without this extended federal program, North Dakota would have faced a mammoth catastrophe and perhaps political anarchy. The State had shown neither the will nor the ability to handle the crisis on its own. Acting under federal direction, modern methods were introduced and large sums of money were applied where they were needed; but the State did very little to help itself. Until 1935 the state legislature made no appropriation for relief, the localities paid one-tenth of the relief costs, and the FERA found the remaining 90 percent. In spite of earlier recrimination federal generosity did go unrewarded. In 1936 Roosevelt carried every precinct in North Dakota and ran far ahead of Langer in the popular vote.

This review of FERA operations in selected states has revealed similarities and sharp differences. No state solved its relief problems without federal aid, and once the first step had been taken there was little hesitation in accepting federal money for a function that had been exclusively local. The precept that a community must care for its own had gone by default, and many local governments were eager to hand over to federally funded programs cases that were not the result of the depression and unemployment. The appendix to this chapter shows that in 1934 the FERA paid a high proportion of the relief costs.

[83] E. A. Willson, *Relief in Review in North Dakota through December 15, 1935* (Bismarck, N.D., 1936) 26.

In executing relief policy the balance of responsibility varied from state to state. In some, the FERA was content to leave administration to state and county agencies; in others, it felt obliged to concern itself with detail. The relationship between federal and state authority depended much on personalities. In some states the FERA put its confidence in a strong state agency or the governor proved to be an effective and willing ally; in others the field representative had to play a lone hand. All state legislatures were reluctant to take their share of financial responsibility, and some ended by appropriating little or nothing for relief. When more was given it was likely to be borrowed rather than raised by taxation, with the implication that state funding of unemployment relief was a temporary expedient, not a permanent commitment. This inaction on the part of state legislatures had implications that were little understood at the time. The Fourteenth Amendment had empowered the federal government to protect individual rights against state injustice; events were now pressing it to accept responsibility for individual welfare when states failed to meet the standards set by humane concern and civilized practice. The conclusion was hard to accept, and the New Deal soon drew back from the brink of the national welfare system demanded by this logic.

Appendix: Federal relief in twenty-four states

	1	2	3	4	5
Alabama	337	13	18,990	18,097	95.1
California	803	14	66,830	48,434	72.5
Connecticut	183	11	18,504	9,841	53.0
Florida	307	21	18,038	18,027	99.9
Georgia	389	13	20,550	19,588	95.1
Illinois	1,129	15	106,984	72,282	67.6
Kansas	316	17	19,882	14,570	73.4
Kentucky	483	19	15,590	13,307	65.3
Maryland	175	11	19,843	14,713	74.2
Massachusetts	690	16	72,960	40,191	55.1
Michigan	866	18	60,760	41,190	67.8
Minnesota	568	22	35,218	28,573	81.3
New Jersey	658	16	49,798	42,631	85.5
New York	2,077	17	274,379	152,496	55.6
North Carolina	328	10	13,993	13,804	98.6
North Dakota	196	29	12,471	11,469	92.0
Ohio	1,193	18	77,334	57,237	74.0
Oklahoma	677	28	19,642	16,409	83.7
Pennsylvania	1,738	18	146,092	105,575	72.8
South Dakota	286	41	20,886	19,559	93.8
Vermont	27	8	1,980	1,191	60.1
Virginia	194	8	7,697	6,750	87.7
West Virginia	396	23	19,176	16,683	87.0
Wisconsin	432	15	39,206	30,787	78.8

1. Total on relief in December 1934 (000s).
2. Percentage of total population on relief.
3. Total cost of relief in 1934 ($, 000s).
4. Federal contribution ($, 000s).
5. Percentage of total paid by the federal government.

In addition to those listed, the states with a very high percentage of their people on relief in December 1934 were Idaho (24) and New Mexico (31), and those with 10 percent or less were Delaware (8), New Hampshire (9), and Maine (10).

Source: Statistical Abstract of the United States, 1935.

7

RETREAT

In January 1935 Howard Hunter, the able and vigorous field representative in Michigan, ran into trouble. Frank D. Fitzgerald, the newly elected Governor, proposed to abolish the State Relief Commission, transfer its powers to the Department of Public Welfare, wind up the county relief committees, and restore all relief responsibilities to county poor directors and township supervisors. Hunter told him that the FERA could not possibly agree to these changes. In an interview, Fitzgerald promised to make no move without notifying Hunter and admitted that he was less interested in changing the relief machinery than in replacing the people who were running it. He also denied any commitment to the old order and hinted that he might consider alternative modernization plans.

Hunter had no faith in conciliatory moves by a Governor who was, as he told Hopkins, "unbelievably reactionary," opposed to the whole relief operation, and intent only on getting control of federal relief funds. Hunter took it upon himself to assure members of the State Relief Commission that the FERA would not allow their "really fine program" to be ruined by permitting relief "to be kicked back into the hands of the township supervisors and reactionary politicians." He asked Hopkins to back his stand and "when it is necessary to state very emphatically, that in the event of attempts to transfer the Relief Administration to the political Welfare Department . . . we will grant our funds to a specifically appointed Federal agency in the State."[1]

The reply from Washington, written by Aubrey Williams, came as a brutal shock to a man who had believed that he was acting in accordance with the FERA precedents when dealing with refractory states. Williams said that the request to Hopkins "put the whole question of

[1] NA RG 60 406.2, Hunter to Hopkins, January 20, 1935.

the future relationship of the FERA and the States fairly on the kitchen stove." Clearly, Hunter had failed to understand how matters stood.

> We should keep on fighting for everything that we have gained. . . . Yet you must be told that the Federal authorities are checking relief back to the several states.

In other words, the "unbelievably reactionary" Governor was only one step ahead of federal policy. Williams went on to refer in general terms to plans for a federal works program and social insurance, but made it clear that there would be no more pressure on states to adopt approved methods of relief administration. The FERA would neither withdraw federal funds nor override a state government by direct action:

> We want to hold what we have got, but it has not got to be done through threats. . . . All that is frankly out. We have got to do it through working back and forth from Harry and persuading these people what we feel is the best thing to do.

This implied that in future the only way to get things done would be by the kind of political trading normally used to win over reluctant states.[2]

What Hunter had not read or understood was a passage in Roosevelt's State of the Union Message delivered a few days earlier. In it the President had said that "the federal government . . . must and shall quit this business of relief." The rapid progress of the FERA had encouraged its friends to believe that the day of permanent federal welfare administration had dawned; the President's message meant that what they were witnessing was the brief high noon of a short-lived experiment.

The sudden announcement of the decision to end the FERA created alarm among the keenest advocates of welfare reform. "Don't do it Mr. Hopkins!," wrote Edith Abbott in an article in the *Nation*.

> All who have recognized the miserable incompetence of the old system know that returning to local relief authorities means returning to everything that is reactionary in the field of social welfare . . . local politicians temporarily banished by the resolute orders of the Federal Relief Administration, will return to the welfare controls.

---

[2] Ibid., Aubrey Williams to Hunter, January 26.

The FERA had initiated programs never been considered before, but few would continue without federal supervision.[3]

The warning was well judged, but other reactions were muted. The decision to return general relief to the states might be seen as a declaration of intent – to be carried out as the depression receded – and not as an immediate end to federal relief. The appropriation to the FERA was not suddenly cut, and it would spend more in 1935 than in any preceding year. Nor was it possible to consider realistically the future of relief policy until the Social Security bill completed its long passage through Congress (it did not pass the Senate until June). The Emergency Relief Appropriations Act, which set up the new federal works program (the Works Progress Administration), passed in March, did not preclude further appropriations for direct relief.

An even stronger argument for suspending judgment on federal relief policy was the decision of the Supreme Court in *Schecter Poultry Corporation v. The United States* on May 27, 1935, declaring the National Industrial Recovery Act to be unconstitutional and casting doubt over the future of all New Deal laws. The opinion of the Court was delivered by the Chief Justice, two justices concurred in a separate opinion, and there was no dissent. For New Dealers the ominous threat lay not in the detailed argument over the right to make and approve codes for industry but in one sentence from Chief Justice Hughes's opinion: "Extraordinary conditions do not create or enlarge constitutional power." What would the courts make of many other state and federal laws in which the word "emergency" justified the use of unprecedented government power?[4]

During this period of doubt, friends of the FERA were encouraged by the way in which Roosevelt and Hopkins handled a dispute with Ohio. After a highly publicized controversy the President placed the state's relief administration under federal control, and this drastic treatment of a large, complex, and important state, under a Democratic governor, encouraged the belief that federal relief was safe for the time being.

---

[3] Edith Abbott, "Don't Do It Mr. Hopkins," *The Nation*, January 9, 1935.
[4] *Schechter Poultry Corporation v. United States*, 295 U.S. 495. Chief Justice Hughes spoke for seven judges; Mr. Justice Cardozo concurred in a separate opinion joined by Mr. Justice Stone. An important fact (often glossed over in accounts of the Supreme Court and the New Deal) was that the "liberal" justices joined their "conservative" colleagues in finding the NRA to be unconstitutional.

Politics in Ohio were intensely partisan, and within each party were factions that represented in part the natural divisions and conflicts in the state. Cleveland had little in common with Cincinnati, and the other industrial centers had interests that differed from those of the two largest cities. Farmers were often arrayed against manufacturers. There were strong cultural differences between the northern counties, with traditions derived from New England, and the southern counties, where many families traced their roots to the South.

Faced with the depression they had clung to the idea of local responsibility, but a State Relief Commission was set up in 1932 to handle RFC loans and continued under the FERA. By May 1933 there were county relief commissions in thirty counties and in all eighty-eight by the fall. During the winter of 1933–4 the State Relief Commission also administered the CWA program under federal direction. With county relief commissions uncertain of their powers, townships still going their own ways, the relationship between the state and the cities often obscure, and the State Relief Commission acting as both a state and a federal agency, confusion was certain to arise. "Any attempt to describe the administrative chaos of this period," wrote a future state relief administrator, "would be futile."[5]

The state commission was vigorous, had considerable success in the face of difficulties, and soon won the confidence of the FERA. A firmly controlled though complex relief organization was being developed when progress was checked by the unwillingness of the state legislature to provide financial support. In the spring of 1934 a special session refused to appropriate more money for relief or to impose new taxes, and local and federal funds were left to carry the burden.[6]

George White, the Democratic Governor, backed the relief commission and pressed unsuccessfully for relief appropriations; but in 1935 he was succeeded by Martin L. Davey, a businessman who made adroit use of the radio in campaigning and publicity. Davey was also a Democrat, but of a different school; he had compaigned on promises to restore relief administration to local officials and oppose tax

---

[5] For a general account, see Dayton H. Frost, *Emergency Relief Administration in Ohio, 1931–5* (Columbus, 1936).

[6] Ibid., 69. The "trend was the slow but definite centralization of control of organization to meet immediate demands requiring immediate action." For this and the following paragraphs, see David J. Maurer, "Relief Problems and Politics in Ohio," Braeman, Bremner and Brody, *The New Deal*, Vol. 2, pp. 77–102.

increases. After scoring a narrow electoral victory, Davey reaffirmed his commitment to these policies and made it clear that he intended to put the relief commission under political control.

Shortly after his inauguration, the new Governor fired the state relief director, Frank D. Henderson, and replaced him with William A. Walls. On February 24, 1935, he dismissed Mary Atkinson, superintendent of the State Division of Charities, who then alleged that she had been fired for refusing to reveal the political affiliations of sixty-five departmental employees. Worse was to follow when the legislature adjourned, with Davey's blessing, without renewing the State Relief Commission Law, which was due to expire on 1 March. When protests came from the FERA, Davey wrote to Hopkins, suggesting that the federal government assume complete responsibility for relief in Ohio.[7]

The ostensible reason for this request was that the state's share of relief costs had been assessed at $24,000,000 when the people of Ohio were "already groaning under a multiplicity of taxes." Davey also charged that the existing relief administration was costly and inefficient, and that in Cleveland "the average case worker spent half the time writing reports and did not have time to visit." He also said that the qualifications required for case workers had been framed to exclude all but graduates from college social welfare programs, and as a result, there were "many young, immature, though no doubt well-meaning, so-called case workers," who lacked experience of life and approached problems "from a purely theoretical standpoint." It was not possible to remedy these faults by state action because, as Davey told Hopkins, "all the policies for the relief program of this state are determined in Washington and supervised by your agents in Columbus."[8]

Hopkins was in no mood to conciliate. He replied publicly with a scathing attack in a press interview and insisted that Ohio must pay its share. Open recrimination continued as Davey appealed to the people in a radio address on March 12 and claimed that with a free hand he could save $5,000,000 on relief. Meanwhile, a secret investigation initiated by Hopkins produced evidence of political discrimination in relief appointments and of attempts to control money from firms seeking business with the Relief Administration, to pay off debts incurred

[7] F.D.R. Library, FERA File, Davey to HH, March 4, 1935.
[8] Ibid.

during the Governor's campaign. Hopkins laid this evidence before the President and was assured that "corrupt interference with relief in the state of Ohio" made it imperative for him to continue his investigations; "let the chips fall where they may." Concurrently, 200 civic leaders in Cleveland launched a campaign to get the legislature to pay its share of relief and to discredit Davey. On March 15 two members of the Cuyahoga County relief commission carried their complaints to Washington, and on the following day Roosevelt ordered Hopkins to take over relief administration in Ohio. An action that had been sharply rejected when requested by Davey was adopted twelve days later as a punitive measure.[9]

Open war continued when Hopkins sent an open letter to the press claiming that the evidence "not only establishes the utter unfitness of some of the men who are now in high position in the relief administration; but it demonstrates the necessity of safeguarding the expenditure of federal funds in Ohio." He added that federal action did not relieve the State from the obligation to contribute its share. Davey replied by swearing out a warrant for Hopkins's arrest on a charge of criminal libel and challenging him to come to Ohio and face trial. In a message to the legislature, he said that he had no knowledge of the finances of the State Democratic Committee, that every appointed official in the relief administration was hostile to him, and that it was "wasteful, inefficient, and inhuman." With greater accuracy, he said that the federal takeover was doing what he had asked, but with "contemptible methods, involving character assassination."[10]

In this message, Davey also publicly attacked the relief administration for violating "the sacred right of American citizens . . . [to] the inviolability of private family affairs" by sending young professional social workers into their homes "as a pack of inquisitors . . . with a grocery order in one hand, and their inexcusable intrusion into the pri-

[9] Maurer, "Relief Problems and Politics in Ohio," 92. Roosevelt received many letters from Ohio protesting against the treatment of Davey (F.D.R. Library, Roosevelt Papers, OF 444a, March 1935). The most significant came from Robert F. Kaser, a Democratic member of Ohio's House of Representatives; he said that under Henderson the relief administration had been built up as part of Governor White's personal organization. Change was essential because "the relief situation in each of the eighty eight counties of this state has already reached the riot stage." Earlier Henderson had accused both parties of trying to use the Relief Administration politically. In Youngstown there were many political factions, all wanting to run the show but all united to oppose the relief director he had appointed.

[10] Martin Davey, Message to the 91st General Assembly, March 18, 1935, 5.

vate affairs of helpless people in the other." He accused the commission of sending strangers "to take charge of a great humanitarian program among people they do not know," and said that a principal aim of these social workers was to create jobs for others of their own kind. "When this relief program was taken away from the township trustees and from the respected citizens and local officials in most of the counties it was a colossal blunder."[11]

Here the matter ended, with the Governor claiming points in the verbal war and the state relief administration free to get on with its work under federal control. Once again, the FERA had shown itself capable of defeating local opposition and organizing relief in a state with the agency that it approved. Once again the federal taxpayer paid the price of victory as Ohio continued to contribute only a small amount to relief.

Howard Hunter's attempt to prevent the Governor of Michigan from taking control of relief administration and changing its character had been rebuffed, yet decisive action had been taken against Governor Davey in Ohio. The inconsistency was apparent rather than real, for the issues in the two cases were different. Hunter's complaint was that Governor Fitzgerald was attempting to abolish a state agency approved by the FERA and to restore local responsibility. The offence of Governor Davey was his attempt to use relief, paid for largely by federal money, for party and personal patronage. The Governor of Michigan was a little premature in adopting what was to be federal policy; the Governor of Ohio was accused of trying to drag a federally funded program into the net of state patronage. The Ohio incident was a confrontation in the familiar field of spoils and influence, not a commitment to continue federal control over state relief.

Future policy had been the subject of diligent planning behind closed doors in Washington. It was intended to provide a rounded and comprehensive strategy that would meet the needs of all who required public assistance and spread responsibility over national, state, and local governments. By drawing lines clearly between the different types of people in distress, it was hoped that arguments over who should pay

---

[11] Ibid.

for what would be avoided. The authors were not, of course, completely satisfied with their work. It had been necessary to reconcile the best with what was possible, but the men who planned the new policy, and persuaded the President to adopt it, were convinced that it would provide a framework for future development.

The national responsibility for relieving unemployment was recognized by a great program of public works to provide jobs. The national government would also help a state in caring for certain categories of people in need – the old, blind, physically disabled, insane and mentally retarded, orphans and other children in need – provided that the state presented schemes that were satisfactory. An entirely new Social Security program would protect wage earners against unemployment and destitution in old age by mandating compulsory insurance against these hazards. These were the plans unfolded by the President and his advisers in the early months of 1935, discussed at length in Congress, and enacted during the "second hundred days" from May through July 1935.

There remained the people who were unable to work but did not belong to one of the categories. These were the unemployables, and for them the federal government accepted no responsibility. They might be relieved by state agencies, counties, local government, or by a combination of all three under whatever laws a state chose to adopt. Relief of the unemployables was usually described as general relief, and was intended mainly for those who were temporarily or permanently out of the labor market: old people, chronic invalids, and persons who were partially disabled, sick but not hospitalized, or psychologically incapable of holding down a job.

By May 1935, when social workers met for their annual conference, the act establishing the Works Progress Administration (WPA) had been passed, but there was no definite word about the future of general relief, and the social security bills were still under consideration by Congress. Naturally, it was the prospect for social security that attracted attention. A paper by Aubrey Williams to review and explain federal policy concentrated on what the New Deal had achieved in relief and, for the future, what social insurance would mean. The way in which Williams explained what had been done left the impression that a federal commitment to general relief would continue for some time. He said that the first point gained by the New Deal had been to establish national responsibility for distress caused by economic failure, and the second had been to identify those in need and, in doing so, to reveal new dimensions of destitution:

We have not only turned up a large volume of chronic poverty to which even the best of us in the past have been willing to close our eyes, but we have also learned in detail just who these people are, where they are, and some of the many causes which have brought them to such dire straits.

Looking to the future, he admitted that the coming social security legislation would not be perfect "but a very substantial beginning." He asked those who believed that it was not going far enough to realize that it was going as far as was politically possible. "An attempt to introduce a complete and final program of social insurance at this time would be self-defeating." This was fair enough, but a reasonable inference was that the federal government would continue to assist in relieving those who were going to be left out.[12]

It was not until Congress had adjourned, after the exhausting second hundred days, that it became clear that federal withdrawal from general relief was imminent and that the last FERA grant would be made in November. The realization stirred people, many of whom had never been particularly friendly to federal relief, to deplore the consequences of its sudden cessation. In November the White House was getting four or five telegrams of protest every day, and on November 16 Congressman Fred H. Hildebrandt of South Dakota wrote a long letter to the President making a plea for the unemployables, especially the old. What was to be done with them when poorhouses were full, county treasuries empty, and the harvest poor? The reply, drafted by Hopkins, pointed out that the distress of many unemployables could not be attributed entirely to the depression. Local communities had always been responsible for the care of their own poor, and it would be all the easier for them to resume this responsibility with the new social security laws taking some chronic cases off their hands.[13]

[12] Aubrey Williams, "Organization for Social Security in the United States," 460 *NCSW 1935*, 457–65.
[13] F.D.R. Library, Roosevelt Papers (OF 444a), F. H. Hildebrandt to FDR, November 16, 1935. Hopkins's draft reply, ibid. On November 7 Steven Early, the President's White House secretary, told Hopkins that there had been four or five telegrams a day protesting the end of federal grants for direct relief. Among other letters on the subject in Roosevelt's FERA files is one from Herbert F. Goodrich, dean of the University of Pennsylvania Law School, expressing concern over the cessation of direct relief in Philadelphia County; FDR's reply is in 444 Misc.

The return to local responsibility might have been easier if there had been a significant fall in the number of unemployed; in fact, the number remained obstinately high, in spite of better business conditions, and the federal work projects were still in low gear. In *Survey* Paul Kellogg voiced the dismay of rank-and-file social workers: "The liquidation of federal relief made this seventh winter of our discontent, these months when talk of recovery has been in the air, one of the most excruciating spans of the depression." Even if the states took up the burden with good will, rudimentary fiscal systems would make adequate relief and effective administration impossible in most of them.[14]

Edith Abbott deplored the fulfillment of her prophecy and wrote that "the bitter truth has gradually dawned upon social workers that we are doomed to drift back to the old days of pauper relief." This was the real complaint. It was not so much a question of who was responsible or how much money was available, as a conviction that only the federal government could continue the work of improving relief methods. Grace Abbott, then still head of the Federal Children's Bureau, would later remark that "federal aid for relief . . . might have served as a lever for building up a permanent federal–state relief program. But wisely or unwisely, this objective has been sacrificed to other ends."[15]

How can the decision to return general relief to the localities be explained? At the National Conference of Social Work in 1936 Aubrey Williams defended it as a necessary political choice. Congress had found the money for an enormously increased program of public works and was asked to swallow the huge (and, for some, indigestible) morsel of social insurance. It was unlikely, Williams argued, that the majority would have also agreed to continue support for direct relief. The government, realizing that it could not have everything, had been forced to decide its priorities, and (correctly, he believed) had chosen work over direct relief. The latter could be carried on by the states; only the federal government could finance and manage the former.[16]

Aubrey Williams referred in general terms to the political opposition without describing it. Jacob Fisher, radical secretary of the National Coordinating Committee of Social Service Employees, had no doubt

---

[14] Paul Kellogg, "Employment Planning," 455, *NCSW 1936,* 454–69.
[15] Edith Abbott, *Public Assistance* (Chicago, 1940), 763 (reprinted from *The Nation,* March 18, 1936). Grace Abbott, *From Relief to Social Security* (Chicago, 1941), 37.
[16] *NCSW 1936,* 452.

that it was the result of a successful counterattack by business interests. "The engineers of defeat for the social work program have been the American Manufacturers Association, the United States Chamber of Commerce, and the Liberty League." This diagnosis was imaginative but misleading. Members of these organizations might welcome the dilution of any part of the New Deal policies, but there is no evidence that they had mustered their forces to end the FERA. Edith Abbott was nearer the mark when she said that the FERA was destroyed in the house of its friends.[17]

The momentum of the New Deal had faltered in the spring of 1935, but by the summer Roosevelt had reasserted his leadership, and the continuation of the FERA, at least for a limited period, would have won the necessary support if demanded by the President. What killed the FERA was not the Liberty League and its allies but determination on the part of the administration to end it. When Harry Hopkins drafted the letter for Roosevelt to send to Congressman Hildebrandt, he wrote: "I am firmly convinced that the basic responsibility should remain in the hands of the states and localities, as it has in the past." The federal abandonment of general relief was not dictated by political necessity or hostile pressure but was a freely determined choice to resurrect local responsibility.[18]

There were indeed some features in the FERA program that caused reasonable concern. Expenditure was rising and was explicable in several ways. The savings of individuals became exhausted as the depression lengthened, and there was a growing number of white-collar workers among the unemployed, including young graduates without jobs, actors, musicians, writers, and artists. Middle-aged men who had been unemployed for some time were increasingly unlikely to be offered work. Other explanations for rising costs were found in the enlarged dimensions of rural poverty and the need to rehabilitate and resettle, as well as to relieve; in new programs such as college student aid and rural education; and in the expensive transient program.

Rising costs were evidence of rising demand, and might be adduced to support the expansion of the FERA rather than its abandonment; but in Washington they were seen as an argument for cutting direct relief and concentrating on rehabilitation. From this the next step was

---

[17] Ibid., 437.
[18] See note 13, this chapter.

to argue that federal relief must be limited to the victims of depression and, that people who could not work must not be a charge on federal funds; but the figures seemed to show that federal relief was merging into general relief. It had often been asserted that the FERA was not intended to take responsibility for unemployables, who should be (as they always had been) cared for by their own communities. Yet a detailed report from the FERA to the National Economic Council in November 1934 showed that in eighty cities 20 percent of the FERA cases consisted of adults too old to work, handicapped persons unable to support their families even when employed, and families in which the only able-bodied person was a mother with dependent children. If this trend continued, the federal government might find itself responsible not only for the unemployed but for all who had worked at some time in the past.[19]

One suggestion for limiting costs was for the federal government to agree to pay a fixed proportion (say, 50 percent) of all unemployment relief costs and allow the states to decide how it should be distributed among those in distress. Hopkins was much opposed to any plan based on invariable formulas and abandoning the discretionary principle. When the idea was put to him by a congressional committee, he rejected it flatly and pointed out that "if the Congress starts paying that 50 percent for unemployment relief, it will be a very difficult thing ever to stop."[20]

There was also concern about the increasing cost and complexity of FERA administration. Hopkins had begun the FERA with a promise to employ only a small central staff, but even in the short time that it had been in existence, it had grown alarmingly and become more complex. Each new program required a separate division; in addition, there were central offices for statistics, investigation, and relations with the states. Elaboration at the center generated similar growth in the states.

---

[19] Mimeographed copy in F.D.R. Library, Hopkins Papers, Box 47, Dated November 10, 1934. The *Final Statistical Report of the FERA* gives the following figures on costs and direct relief. The total federal expenditure rose from $50,000,000/$70,000,000 per month in 1933 and was $148,000,000 per month in January 1935. The number of persons receiving general relief from all sources was over 20,000,000 in April 1933. Work relief programs cut this number to just over 11,000,000 early in 1934, but by the beginning of 1935 it was over 20,000,000. The average monthly benefit per individual was $14 early in 1933 and $28 by the beginning of 1935.

[20] 74th Congress, 1st Sess., House Appropriations Committee, Hearings on First Deficiency Appropriation Bill, 160.

In November 1934 Howard Hunter, reporting to Hopkins on what seemed to be the high administrative cost of relief in Illinois, added:

I have a strong conviction that a considerable number, of what I think are unnecessary administrative costs, is directly attributable to our own FERA office in Washington. The large number of departments and specialists in the Washington office which have been in the habit of dealing on direct lines with the States have caused a great deal of administrative cost which could have been avoided.

On the basis of the Illinois study (and a similar one in Kentucky), Hunter believed that between two and three million dollars a month could be saved. Yet the field representatives had to bear their share of the blame for bureaucratic growth. They had begun as individual advisers and emissaries, but had found it necessary to establish their own regional offices with counterparts to each division of the central administration.[21]

If cost was one consideration, the strain of battle with recalcitrant states was another. Few states were contributing what Hopkins regarded as their fair share, and several had contributed little or nothing to unemployment relief. Attempts by state politicians to gain control of relief were persistent, and the dispute with Ohio was only the most violent of several. Hardly a month went by without Hopkins being forced to intervene, either to bring pressure to bear on a state to increase its appropriations or to ward off attempts to gain control of relief for political purposes. Hopkins and Aubrey Williams (who was in charge of federal–state relations) were not men to run away from a fight, but the continual difficulties must have made them wonder whether it would not be better to allow the states to make their own errors and hope that their voters would soon set them on the right road.

These arguments might support the case for putting the FERA on a tighter rein rather than for abolishing it. The real argument for bringing it to an end drew upon traditional ideas rather than current problems. Hopkins told a congressional committee:

I came to believe more and more that we should not undertake to take care of unemployed people by means of the dole or grocery order while the heads of

---

[21] F.D.R. Library, Hopkins Papers, FERA Files, Howard Hunter to Hopkins, November 7, 1934. The administrative costs of the FERA rose from $25,800,000 in the second half of 1933 to $101,700,000 in the second half of 1934 and from 6.9 to 10.9 percent of the total expenditure.

families remained at home in idleness. It was an extremely demoralizing thing. . . . [It encouraged] an unwholesome attitude toward the Nation and the States. . . . It was creating a dependent class in America.

Fears of the dole and demoralization were invoked to explain the end of the FERA, just as they had provided slogans for those who had opposed its inception.[22]

This mood had been reinforced by confidential reports reaching Hopkins during the fall of 1934 and forwarded by him to the President on December 10. Hopkins had selected trained observers, not previously involved in front-line relief, and (as he told Roosevelt) "sent them out to see what the relief and employment prospects for the winter looked like; whether the relief load seemed to be going up or down and why; [and] the physical condition and morale of the unemployed."[23]

Wayne Parish, a journalist who had covered relief for the *Literary Digest,* reported on the New York and New Jersey metropolitan areas. He found that relief rolls were increasing, that there were no prospects of private jobs, and that among the unemployed there was no longer any hope of regular work. This gloomy assessment was, he said, endorsed by everyone connected with relief, from William Hodson down to humble field workers.[24]

For Parish it was even more disturbing to find that, for a growing number, relief was regarded as a way of life that the government had a duty to sustain. He wrote:

Relief is regarded as permanent by both clients and relief workers. Clients are assuming that the government has a responsibility to provide. The stigma of relief has almost disappeared except among white-collar groups.

Relief workers all reported a belief among their clients that government had an obligation to provide everyone with minimum subsistence, and many went further to claim a right to live comfortably. Men on relief were more truculent, "more critical, more complaining, more ready to react," and increasingly resentful of investigation and surveillance by social workers. Though the poorest people were getting

---

[22] 74th Congress, 1st Sess., House Appropriations Committee, Hearings on First Deficiency Appropriation Bill, 154.

[23] On December 10, 1934 Hopkins sent the reports to Missy Lehand with a covering note saying that "the President was anxious to go over them." The reports are in FDR Library, Roosevelt Papers, FERA Files.

[24] For this and the following paragraphs, see the report by Wayne Parish on New York.

more help than ever before, Parish found much evidence of "mental deterioration." There were young people who had never been employed and had grown up "in a world of government subsidy." Older men saw nothing before them but dependence on relief, and complained more and more of the level at which it was given. William Hodson told Parish that they could not go on for another year "without being forced to bring in a new social order."

Bruce McClure, a FERA staff member, reported more briefly but in a similar vein from Lawrence County, Pennsylvania. He found that relief, particularly work relief, was "regarded by a great proportion of our clients as a regular and accepted way of life" and that acceptance of government assistance no longer carried any stigma.

Lincoln Colcord, another FERA staff member, reported from Detroit that he was constantly asked: "How can relief go at the present pace? Where is it leading? What sort of citizenry is it creating?" It was also disturbing to find that when things went wrong, the federal rather than the state or local government was invariably blamed. Whether the federal government was right or wrong, it won little praise and much criticism.[25]

Colcord devoted a good deal of his report to the the views of businessmen. He recorded at length the views of William Knudson, a leading executive with General Motors and a splendid example of the American success story – a man from a poor immigrant family who had risen to the top. Knudson supported the New Deal but not its relief policy. Relief, he said, was being too easy; it "should be unattractive" and "entail hardships that a man would lift himself out of by getting a job." He agreed that there would always be unemployables, but it was essential not to increase their number or to make them feel that they had the same privileges as more favored citizens. "The differentials between work and relief should be kept alive."

These confidential reports recorded no interviews with unemployed persons; demoralization was assumed rather than tested, and was attributed to familiarity with relief rather than to lack of regular work. Social workers were quoted mainly to demonstrate that relief had become a way of life and was regarded as a right. Complaints by the unemployed were deplored, but low standards of relief were not condemned. These flaws must have been evident to Harry Hopkins, but he took the reports seriously and believed them worthy of considera-

---

[25] Ibid., reports by McClure and Lincoln Colcord.

tion by Roosevelt. Their record of widely felt anxieties could not be ignored, but they provided no evidence that anyone would be better, more satisfied, or less demoralized if the federal government withdrew from general relief.

A very different assessment was made by Lorena Hickok, who had been acting as an unofficial observer for Hopkins since the beginning of the FERA. Miss Hickok was not a social scientist, and her letters, usually describing observations and conversations during the preceding twelve hours, were impressionistic rather than systematic. She admitted that when she began she knew nothing of relief, and that after eighteen months she was learning every day; but she was an extremely good reporter, with a keen eye for humbug and a warm sympathy for people in distress. In August 1934 she endorsed the separate treatment for employables and unemployables:

The more I travel around, the more convinced I am that what we're going to have to do is to separate the employables from the unemployables, set up a real work program for the employables, giving them enough to live on, apply a means test if we have to, and cut out all this infernal nonsense about case work and so on. We're getting top heavy.

What she wanted, therefore, was a straightforward work program, separated from general relief and administered differently; but she did not suggest that the FERA should be ended and she would later argue that nationwide relief must be indispensable, at least throughout 1935.[26]

Later in the year, Miss Hickok made a close study of conditions in Baltimore and came up with more radical suggestions. She found that demoralization was not caused by relief, but by the very low wages paid by employers:

Their big idea – their WHOLE idea – is this: "There are a lot of people out of work. Therefore, we ought to get help for very low wages." And they get resentful as the devil because relief makes it possible – however little it may amount to – for people to refuse to take jobs at less than a living wage. . . . They are trying to make the relief budget, which was never supposed to be anything more than a temporary, minimum subsistence budget, the actual BASIS for wages.

Montgomery Ward had applied to the employment service for waitresses to work three hours a day for 25 cents an hour. There were ste-

[26] Richard Lowitt and Maurine Beasley, *One Third of a Nation: Lorena Hickok Reports on the Great Depression* (Urbana, Ill., 1981). Lorena Hickok to A. Williams, August 23, 1934, 315–16.

nographers working in Baltimore at $3 a week and the best for no more than $13. A chemical company paid crane operators 40 cents an hour and complained because they were not skilled enough. Only one hotel paid maids as much as $9 a week to look after fifteen or twenty rooms with no tips. At these rates, an employed person either had to live below subsistence level or apply for supplementary public relief. Baltimore was notorious as a low-wage town, but Miss Hickok did not believe that the attitude of employers was very different elsewhere.

In Detroit, Lincoln Colcord was equally skeptical of the good will or even the common sense of many business leaders. Some favored company welfare schemes but refused to recognize their dependence upon public relief to maintain a pool of labor. The motor manufacturers looked after temporarily laid-off skilled workers, but unskilled labor was "left out of the reckoning and fell on the community as a relief problem." Company executives would not admit that public relief was "holding the bag for them in the general labor market." Hordes of black workers, brought in by Ford and other companies in prosperous years, were on relief, and because they were unlikely to return to the rural poverty from which they had fled, the effect was to maintain unskilled labor for private employers at public expense.[27]

Colcord found that the personnel officers of large companies, who were supposed to understand labor problems, were usually men of narrow vision and stereotyped views. None showed any understanding of social security, and many were ignorant of conditions in their own neighborhood. A typical example of their confident ignorance was displayed at a meeting when one of them asserted that relief increased radicalism. Colcord intervened to say that radicalism was not increasing, that relief was a major factor in preventing it, and that real dangers would arise if relief was suddenly halted. Others agreed, but the original statement, if unchallenged, would have been accepted as true by the men who were employed by their companies to understand labor.

What was the remedy? Miss Hickok confessed that she had not always been clear in her mind about the proper relationship between relief and wages:

But now, dammit, I am wondering if the only way to get employers to pay people enough to live on won't have to be for the government to treat the unemployed as labor surplus, take them all out of the market, pay them living wages, and let industry howl.

[27] Ibid., Hickok to Hopkins, November 13, December 6, 341–51.

The point was worth considering, even though it had an uncomfortable likeness to the dreaded dole, but this was never the way the federal works program functioned or was intended to function. For the most part it aimed to provide low-grade employment for able-bodied people unable to find private employment, not to improve the standards and conditions of labor.[28]

What of the unemployables? Miss Hickok now emphasized that they were no longer confined to the old, the handicapped, and habitual paupers. There were those who could not afford to relinquish relief (poor as it was) and work for abysmally low wages; there were many more who "through loss of skill, through mental and physical deterioration due to long enforced idleness . . . [were] gradually being forced into the class of unemployables – rusty tools, abandoned, not worth using any more." This was the reality to set beside facile generalizations about relief becoming a way of life. Relief was not easy money, but it was taken when no other hope was offered.

And so they go on – the gaunt, ragged legion of the industrially damned. Bewildered, apathetic, many of them terrifyingly patient. Protest groups have made little headway among them.

There was little organized protest, but Miss Hickok, quoting a FERA investigator in Pennsylvania, told Hopkins that "there seems to be a general acceptance of the fact that leadership will develop among the educated young people who are mingling on the only jobs they can get with embittered unskilled laborers and absorbing their point of view."

A telling point in favor of the new policy was that the federal government was being blamed for the mistakes of others. Corrington Gill, of the FERA central office, observed that demands from unemployed councils (for work or adequate relief) were usually reasonable, and that if trouble followed, it was "chiefly as a result of the lack of tact and the mishandling of the situation by local authorities." Nevertheless it was usually the FERA that came under fire and incurred the hostility of those whom it most wished to help. For Hopkins, one cogent reason for getting the federal government out of relief was to ensure that those who were most responsible for shortcomings in relief – parsimonious state legislatures, obstructive governors, inefficient local officials, or

---

[28] Ibid., 351, and for the next paragraph, 361–4.

politicians trying to get control of the money – should carry the blame.[29]

Two years of running battle with states for not paying their share or for interfering unwisely with relief administration might not inspire confidence in their will or efficiency, but the architects of the new federal policy set store by the good will of the state welfare agencies. Edward Ainsworth Williams, who joined the FERA in 1935, learned from his superiors that "the rapidity and comparative success with which the FERA raised the personnel standards and improved the administrative practices of the state and local agencies . . . was notable in federal grant history." Most state agencies had followed its advice so closely that they had virtually become operating divisions of the FERA, and though their position would not be the same once the flow of federal money ceased, they would be strong enough to hold their own and find useful allies among the politicians. The scale of relief operations had given many people a stake in their efficient performance, and substantial political groups favored sound relief policies for reasons ranging from humanitarian concern to fear of social disorder or simple determination to get their districts a fair share of whatever aid was available. These facts may have persuaded Hopkins and Roosevelt that withdrawal of the federal government would not mean a return to the old order.[30]

Preparations for the new policy had been going ahead during the fall of 1934. Aubrey Williams, assisted by Corrington Gill (the FERA's chief statistician), prepared a memorandum. He argued that it would be possible to put 3,000,000 of the able-bodied unemployed to work on useful and socially desirable projects, which would be supervised by state work agencies but approved and wholly financed by the federal government. The earnings would be sufficient to provide adequate support for families but held at a level below that paid by private employers. Almost 2,000,000 able-bodied unemployed would remain on relief, but some would be absorbed by the Rural Rehabilitation progam, and the states would be able to relieve the rest if they received federal grants to help with old-age assistance and mothers' aid.[31]

---

[29] Gill's comment is in F.D.R. Library, Hopkins Papers, Box 49, from a memo dated September 6, 1934.

[30] Edward Ainsworth Williams, *Federal Aid for Relief* (New York, 1939), 233.

[31] F.D.R. Library, Hopkins Papers, Box 49, memo dated November 30, 1934, by Aubrey Williams (revised by Corrington Gill).

Williams said that it would be essential to continue federal grants for general relief during the transition period, but that this should be complete within a year. The financial arrangements would also have to convince those concerned that no one would lose:

There must be absolute certainty that those families and individuals who qualify on the basis of need for relief be provided for in any arrangement replacing the present system. If this is not done, no plan can long withstand the pressure and demand both of those who are in need and of the communities in which they live.

On the other hand, it would be equally necessary to regulate the demand for federal work by imposing realistic means tests. The applicants must demonstrate that they faced destitution without relief. This might appear to be the pauper's oath revived, but Williams believed that the test could be effective but carry "little in the way of stigma for those to whom it is applied."

These suggestions were incorporated into the final plan for what became the Works Progress Administration (WPA), with three important exceptions. First, the program became wholly federal, with agencies in the states appointed by the federal government. Second, the arrangements for the transition were never spelled out with sufficient clarity, and states and local governments were not able to forecast how many on relief would be absorbed by the federal plan or what burden would fall upon local communities. The third modification was intended to meet this difficulty by adopting the distinction between employables and unemployables, with the implication that the former would be looked after by the WPA and the latter by a charge on state or local funds. In theory a locality would know precisely what its relief commitment would be by counting the number of unemployables. This attempt to create a new category of unemployables (too easily identified as those who were not on WPA projects) proved to be most unfortunate. Few localities would know far in advance how many on relief would be accepted by the WPA, and many who were capable of work found themselves labeled as unemployable and classed with those who were physically, mentally, or temperamentally unable to hold steady jobs.

A different approach to the problem of unemployables was manifest in drafts of the plans for social security found in the Hopkins papers. The common features of the various proposals were that unemployment was a permanent problem, that "hard times bring little or nothing that is not with us in good times," and that the effect of the depression was not to create but to magnify the difficulties. There would always be unemployable people in society – typically, the aged, disabled, mentally deficient or diseased, victims of tuberculosis or other wasting diseases, and social or psychological misfits – and recent experience had shown that they were more numerous than had hitherto been supposed. They were "the orphans of society" and should not be left to private charity; government had an additional responsibility for preventing the social consequences of neglecting those unable to help themselves. This statement involved a logical, precise, and workable definition of the unemployables, and the concept should never have been introduced into proposals for general relief.[32]

In fact, it had never been the intention to find work on federal projects for all of the unemployed. Harry Hopkins was explicit on this point at a later date when he told the House Appropriations Committee:

The purpose of the Works Progress Administration is to provide useful work for particular groups of people in their particular skills. It was not our purpose to provide work for everybody.

It was soon realized that when the FERA grants ended, many people capable of work would be applicants for general relief. The danger was that they would fall between two stools: unable to get WPA employment but not eligible for general relief because they were on WPA waiting lists as employable.[33]

Whatever the arguments for changing relief policy, Hopkins could not have moved without approval from Roosevelt; but there could have been little doubt in his mind that this would be given. From his earliest days as Governor of New York, Roosevelt had consistently maintained that relief was normally a local responsibility and had expressed his dislike of anything approaching a dole. He knew that the longer federal subsidies for general relief continued, the more difficult it would be to end them, and that increasing pressure for paying relief in cash was pushing the country toward something that would be indistinguishable from a dole. On November 27, 1934, two letters showed

[32] F.D.R. Library, Hopkins Papers, Box 49. The second draft is dated June 13, 1934. The others are not dated.
[33] 74th Congress, 1st Sess., House Appropriations Committee, Hearings on First Deficiency Appropriation Bill; Hopkins, p. 155.

that his mind was made up. In a private letter to Colonel E. M. House (to whom he wrote frequently and in confidence) Roosevelt said that he intended to seek an end to federal relief. The second letter was to Louis Ludlow, a Congressman from Indiana who had pressed for cuts in federal expenditure, and though sent by one of his secretaries was approved by the President. It said that the major obstacle to reducing expenditure was that relief must continue, either by cash payments or by providing work. "The first method costs less but the President does not approve it, and says that the Representative would have a revolution in his district if he tried it." The works program would be more expensive, but the price was worth paying to escape from the cheaper but deplorable and unpopular dole.[34]

The act establishing the WPA was approved in May 1935, and an unprecedented $4,000,000,000 appropriated for relief. Of this, $940,000,000 went to the FERA to complete its commitments for 1935, about half of the remainder was for heavy construction work by the Public Works Administration, and the WPA got $1,360,000,000. With this it hoped to provide employment for 3,500,000 persons out of the 11,000,000 to 12,000,000 unemployed.

It was a rule from the start that, with the exception of a small number with special skills necessary for a project, WPA employees must come from the relief rolls. This was to ensure that the principal beneficiaries would be the long-term unemployed, who would not be forced to compete with men recently out of work. To encourage widespread employment, projects were limited to $800 per man-year, and in order to spread the work, only one member of each family could be employed. These provisions were designed to help as many as possible of the long-term unemployed, but the inevitable results were that much of the labor was of poor quality, projects were sometimes of limited value, and the weekly earnings could not always support a family. It was also unfortunate that a skilled man out of work had to go through the indignity of applying for relief before he could become eligible for WPA employment. Fortunately different rules were applied when the WPA launched projects for writers, artists, actors, and musicians.

---

[34] Copies of F.D.R.'s letters to House and Ludlow are in F.D.R. Library, Hopkins Papers, November 1934.

In the early months of 1936 the WPA came under fire from three sides. Some conservative Republicans opposed federal relief in any form; a group drawn from both parties, but including some leading southern Democrats, wanted to cut the federal works program and resume grants to the states for direct relief; and a number of liberal New Dealers (and, outside Congress, most social workers) supported the WPA but as an addition to a restored FERA.

The conservative opposition was easily voted down, but its exploitation of defects in the works program could be highly embarrassing to the government. Inevitably, when so much was done so quickly, some projects proved to be fiascos, some supervision was incompetent, and some workers gave the impression of doing nothing but filling in time. All provided evidence that could be used to discredit the whole program, and the word "boondoggling" entered the language.[35]

A particularly damaging criticism was that the WPA was being used to strengthen Democratic party machines in cities and states. Roosevelt had repeatedly condemned political interference with relief administration and attempts to bring it under party control; yet it was difficult to separate an activity, touching so many aspects of social life and spending so much money, from politics. Appointments to WPA posts were not made as rewards for political services, but they were not likely to go to known critics of the New Deal or to persons unacceptable to state Democratic leaders. Hopkins was reported to have made an off-the-record remark that "no one would suppose him foolish enough to name state or municipal administrators who were not agreeable to the Democratic leaders." There had been highly publicized conflicts with prominent Democrats in some southern states, in California, and most recently in Ohio under the FERA, but most disputes were avoided by the discreet exercise of "political clearance" with politicians in good standing with the government. The act establishing the WPA gave this open recognition by requiring approval by the Senate for appointments to the top positions. It was commonly said that the new policy had given direct relief to the governors and work relief to the senators. Open evidence of political influence could easily be supplemented by allegations that were difficult to disprove.[36]

---

[35] The word "boondoggling" was known before 1935 but rarely used. It passed into general use to describe useless, time-wasting public work.
[36] Edith Abbott, "Public Welfare and Politics," 37–40, *NCSW 1936*, 27–45.

Opponents of federal relief in all forms could also rely on support from much of the press and from some orthodox economists. Typical of those advocating a return to the free market was emeritus professor Irving Fisher of Yale, who told a New York business audience that recovery would be hastened by an end to all forms of federal relief. A reduction of taxes on business, and federal loans without security to encourage industrial expansion, would do far more to reduce unemployment than programs that "put a premium on not working."[37]

Critics opposed to the WPA but in favor of aid for direct relief drew upon evidence of shortcomings in the works program, but their main contention was that it was far more expensive than direct relief. Many of them also objected to federal control, wages paid above the local rate, and lack of consideration by state administrators for the interests of local employers. They also cited the hostile reaction by social workers to the end of the FERA without endorsing their further demand that a restored program of federal relief should be subject to even tighter federal control.

Joanna Colcord, of the Russell Sage Foundation, explained the real attitude of the American Association of Social Workers to the WPA. It gave credit for what had been done for those whom it employed, welcomed the indirect stimulus given to state and local governments to provide improved services, and was fully committed to the principle of a federal works program:

What it does not want is a work program which is so set up that it can become the football of politics; which forces the unemployed through relief channels in order to obtain public employment; which fails to pay going wage rates; which decries and disparages direct relief; or which monopolizes the interest and the funds of the federal government and excludes it from any participation in the general relief program necessary as an underpinning to work relief and categorical home relief alike.

Criticisms in this style were, of course, accompanied by frequent regrets about federal withdrawal from general relief and by alarming reports of the disintegration that followed the restoration of local responsibility.[38]

Social workers carried little political weight, and their criticism of federal policy meant that they could no longer expect Harry Hopkins

---

[37] *New York Times,* May 22, 1936.
[38] Joanna Colcord, "Relief, Style 1936," 295. *NCSW 1936,* 291–8.

to fight their battles in the administration; but they were the people who had to make any program – federal, state, or local – work, so their opposition had to be taken seriously. This explains the unusual efforts made to win them over at the 1936 meeting of the National Conference of Social Work. Aubrey Williams's explanation and defense of government policy had become an annual event, but this year the WPA was also represented by its assistant administrator, Josephine Brown. It was also significant that Roosevelt sent an anodyne message to the conference expressing his good wishes and his appreciation of "the efforts of social workers to make this country a more neighborly place in which to live." In spite of these special efforts, the conference witnessed a furious row between Aubrey Williams and prominent social workers.

With conspicuous lack of tact, Williams accused social workers, and particularly members of the American Association of Social Workers, of aiding those who wished to destroy the WPA. Their literature had been cited three times by hostile senators in support of the argument that appropriations for aid to the unemployed could be cut:

You who insist upon federal relief find yourselves in the company not only of our political opposition but also, and more serious, of all those who favor the form of assistance that can be stretched to the thinnest possible point, to that fine point of adjustment which costs the least to their pocket-books and still does not endanger their loss by revolt.

This was not calculated to win over the men and women who believed that progress in social work had been set back by the change in policy.[39]

Jacob Fisher, chairman of the National Coordinating Committee of Social Service Employee Groups and spokesman for politically radical social workers, asked:

Is it not time for us to know something of the dark forces controlling the destiny of America? Is it not time for us to surrender the illusion that the public

---

[39] *New York Times,* May 27, 1936. The clash reported on this date was at a meeting of the American Association of Social Workers (AASW); Aubrey Williams did not give his address to the full conference until May 29. His paper was probably circulated in advance. In *Survey Graphic* XXV, no. 8 (August 8, 1936 – "The Biggest Issue Is Unemployment"), Paul Kellogg wrote: "In May the National Conference of Social Work . . . broke into the headlines with the Works Progress Administration and the American Association of Social Workers at loggerheads over direct relief versus work relief for the unemployed." Williams's speech is in *NCSW 1936* and his attack on the AASW is at 452–3.

services are an expression of good-will on the part of government, and the illusion that sweetness and light will give us that kind of public welfare program the times demand?

He declared that political action resulted from conflict, and the prizes went to those who were best armed and most ruthless. The FERA had been abandoned as the result of pressure from businessmen who realized that adequate relief kept up wages. "Analyze the process carefully and you will find two trends: the hourly rate on work relief has dropped, and the former bottom to the wage income of America's workers has been pulled out from under them." He urged social workers to ally with organized labor in a united front against business manipulation of government. Political action was essential. "It means our emergence from the semi-darkness of a healing cult into the broad stream of the progressive forces in American life."[40]

Walter West, executive secretary of the American Association of Social Workers, was less emotive but equally scathing in his analysis of current policy. He said that the federal work program was succeeding where wages were adequate, but that it must be judged as well by its failures. It left out a very large number of people, set up a cruel and unworkable category of unemployables, and so multiplied the difficulties of the states that relief standards had declined disastrously.

Saddest of all the effects of the new program is that the federal government, which for two years gave to the nation a very fine interpretation of the needs of those vitally affected by the depression, has discontinued doing that.

In a clumsy but telling phrase, he declared that "since we quit this business of relief . . . the interpretation is for a program under fire rather than for the needs of the people."[41]

In the course of a paper arguing the need for the adoption of civil service rules in public welfare appointments, Edith Abbott deplored the relaxation of the pressure formerly exerted by Hopkins and his aides. "Now again the poor law services are drifting back to the old system of petty incompetence and are becoming more political and more unskilled almost day by day." Social workers had reason to know that political influence ruled once more in all matters concerned with

---

[40] Jacob Fisher, "The Present Status of Relief in the United States," *NSCW 1936*, 434–8.
[41] Walter West, "The Present Relief Situation," *NCSW 1936*, 440–1.

poor relief administration. "The old theory of local responsibility invited irresponsibility."[42]

Apart from Aubrey Williams, Josephine Brown was the only speaker to defend government policy. She admitted that the pendulum, which had swung far in the direction of federal control under the FERA, was now in danger of swinging too far toward state control, and that she had at first shared the "intense regret" of social workers at this development. However, she went on to say:

On second thought, I have wondered if after all it is not a pretty wholesome thing – to test our performance, to face reality, to find out whether or not public welfare can stand on its own feet after this two-year demonstration, and whether state governments will meet their share of the financial burden. Our fiscal studies show that all but two or three of them can do this.

She believed that the imprint made by social work could not be erased, that it had won acceptance as an arm of government, but that it must now strike roots in the community. "Permanent public welfare programs must be indigenous. . . . They must be wanted if they are to endure . . . and this could never have come to pass under such a centralized program as that of the F.E.R.A."[43]

Aubrey Williams would continue to defend the WPA in future years and to treat it as the desirable alternative to general relief. The case for a fully integrated relief system under federal direction went by the board; yet, in a sense, Williams was more radical than his critics. In 1938 he asserted:

From the point of view of social justice and economic efficiency the proper way to deal with the unemployed is for government to provide everyone with socially useful work at his regular occupation, or as near as possible to it, and at his regular rate of pay.

In essence, this was the right-to-work doctrine and a proposition that governments had an obligation to provide work if private employers could not do so. It was coupled with a version of Keynesian economics in which recognition of the right to work was not visionary idealism but "the quickest and cheapest way to attain full economic recovery." The argument would have been more convincing, as a defense of gov-

---

[42] Abbott, "Public Welfare and Politics," *NCSW 1936*, 32, 37, 40.
[43] Josephine Brown, "The Present Relief Situation in the United States," 432, *NCSW 1936*, 423–3.

ernment policy, if the level of unemployment had not still been so high and if so many of those who could work had not been dependent on general relief administered by local government.[44]

Josephine Brown had rested her case mainly on the need to root relief programs in the communities and on the capacity of the states to maintain the standards formerly imposed by the FERA. The way in which the states took up the challenge was therefore vital if progress in relief policy was to maintain its momentum. Could the states build up successful relief administrations within the framework of their existing welfare systems? It is to the states that this inquiry must now turn, and take a road that will also lead back to the starting point, to progress in welfare deflected by the depression and to the crisis in local government.

[44] Aubrey Williams, "The Federal Unemployment Program," *NCSW 1938,* 481.

8

DISARRAY

The new situation created by the end of the FERA called for decisions and action at every level. The federal government had to bring the new WPA into operation, identify and place as many employables as possible, approve new work projects, and deal with complaints if states were unhappy about the transition. In a separate operation the federal government had to approve arrangements made by the states for categorical relief. The states had to decide whether to return all responsibility for relief to local units, give control to counties, retain (at least for a period) their emergency relief agencies, or consolidate all public assistance in one department of welfare. Final action in local units would depend upon state policy, but they would immediately be called upon to certify the eligibility of individuals for WPA employment or categorical assistance.

The central machinery for WPA administration presented few problems. The staff of the FERA was transferred to the new agency, and what remained of the FERA became a division of the WPA. Once the FERA had made its last grant in November 1935, its residual duties were to account for what had been spent and prepare statistical reports. In the states the WPA administration was almost as easy to establish. In most cases, the state emergency relief director was appointed as the WPA administrator, and though he might experience some awkwardness in reconciling his state and federal duties, most states cooperated eagerly in the expectation that they would be relieved of responsibility for employables. In the localities county relief directors became field representatives for the WPA or transferred to county welfare boards. At this level the difficulties were not the result of federal action, but arose from the long periods of uncertainty before new state laws were enacted.

Starting the work program was easy on paper but difficult in practice. Some projects could be taken over from the FERA, but the WPA was more ambitious. Hundreds of new projects had to be approved and proposals solicited in areas where unemployment was high; suitable work had to be found for trained and professional people, and the right skills had to be matched to the right projects. All work was supposed to be socially useful, but where unemployment was high, there was a temptation to accept any projects that promised to keep men occupied. A perennial problem was selection for projects when the number eligible exceeded the jobs offered. Many WPA administrators pushed this problem on to local authorities and told them to choose from among those whom they themselves had certified as eligible.

The WPA usually refused to take action when states complained that their relief burdens had been increased. The official attitude was that unemployables had always been state and local responsibilities, that nothing more was being asked, and that if there were employables for whom the WPA could not provide, the cost was offset by federal assistance for care of the categories. Although it was admitted that some difficulties might arise, it was argued that the states had had plenty of time to prepare for the new situation, and it was assumed that because few had paid their fair share of relief, most of them had untapped sources of revenue on which they could draw. All this was true, but disputes were numerous and often acrimonious. The answer from the WPA was that there had been no promise to take all employables, to which states might reply that they had been given no intimation that so many would be left out in the cold.

The arrangements for assistance in the categories presented fewer problems. The formulas for reckoning the federal contributions were clear, though complex, and (once indigent persons eligible for relief had been correctly identified) left little room for argument. The weakness in the system was not normally found at state level, but rather with the local officials who investigated cases and certified their eligibility for assistance. The federal law required state supervision of all programs for categorical aid, but it was never clear whether this was intended to cover investigation. In some cases the state agencies did little more than satisfy themselves that correct procedures had been followed, and there were wide variations between states in which a central agency issued firm rules and frequently inspected and others where local officials were undisturbed so long as there was no scandal.

A survey carried out by the FERA in the latter part of 1934 provided a statistical basis for the new policy. It estimated that there were 3,450,000 people capable of working but unemployed. Of these, 93 percent had been previously employed, and most of the remainder were under twenty-five. A substantial number had had relief work during 1933 and 1934 and were therefore capable of working again. Of the people on relief but capable of work, 20 percent were skilled and 15 percent clerical or professional; the remainder were semiskilled or unskilled. With 3,500,000 as the target for WPA employment, it should be possible to provide work for all who were able to work, especially if some special programs for the minority of skilled and professional people were included.[1]

The figures seemed to be convincing, but a number of questions were unanswered. The most important was whether Congress could be persuaded to appropriate the money to employ so many people at wages sufficient to support themselves and their families. If the funds fell short, who would look after the employables who could not be employed? If the wages were too low, who would make up the difference? What was to be done with people who had supported themselves in the past but were unsuitable for the work that was offered?

A simple but basic problem was the definition of an unemployable. In December 1934 the new policy had not been announced, but for some time the FERA had been trying to limit the number of cases for which it was responsible. Having tried and failed to draw a firm line between distress resulting from unemployment and from other causes, it was attempting to distinguish between employables and unemployables (for whom the states must be responsible). At a press conference on December 17 Hopkins described the unemployables as "old people, widows, persons who were breadwinners but are now in T.B. institutions, insane asylums, the crippled, and handicapped." He said that the local people were responsible for classifying employables, but if they included persons who were unfit for work, the FERA would reject them.[2]

The proportion of unemployables out of the total population, as defined by Hopkins, was more or less constant, and because the states

---

[1] FDR Library, Hopkins Papers, Box 47, November 1934.
[2] Press Conference, December 27, 1935. Verbatim record in FDR Library, Roosevelt Papers, Emergency Relief File.

had cared for them before the depression, it seemed reasonable that they should continue to do so; but this clear distinction had become blurred as the depression lengthened. A questioner at the December press conference asked how the "psychological unemployment" – of persons who had lost the will or aptitude for work as a result of prolonged idleness – was to be classified. Hopkins replied that this got "into a very debatable field." The question was not pursued, but it would become urgent when classification was not a matter of bookkeeping between federal and state agencies, but of assignment to entirely different programs offering work for some and old-style poor relief for others. In addition to the "psychologically" disabled there were aging unskilled men who were no longer fit for physically exhausting labor, men with skills that were obsolete or in little demand, and others with minor disabilities but still capable of supporting themselves if offered light work. Other difficulties would arise when employables could not be found work or when a project could not be launched for lack of men with the right skill. Was the WPA committed to provide relief for all employables, whether or not they could offer them work? If not, who was?

Even without these problems of classification and responsibility, there were formidable organizational and logistic obstacles. The imaginative WPA plans for artists, writers, actors, and musicians were relatively inexpensive, the persons employed were usually prepared to move to projects wherever located, and close supervision was not required. It was far more difficult to move large numbers of unskilled workers, lay on materials and equipment, and provide management. There were, in addition, the inevitable delays when local projects did not satisfy federal requirements and when reasonable projects wanted by communities did not provide enough employment. There would always be some employables who could not be offered work; there would always be some local officials who would try to push their chronic cases into federal employment; and there would always be some classified as employable to whom local officials would deny relief. In 1938 Edith Abbott reckoned that there were a million people on WPA waiting lists, and the majority of them were getting no relief from any source.[3]

[3] Edith Abbott, "Relief, the No Man's Land and How to Reclaim It," *NCSW 1940*, 187–98 at 187; other effects are discussed by Grace Abbott, *From Relief to Social Security*, (Chicago, 1941), 37.

These difficulties tested the managerial and diplomatic skills of all who were engaged in running the WPA. Enthusiasm and determination carried things along, but there was one insuperable obstacle to success. There was never enough money. In Congress the pressure was always to cut rather than increase, and each compromise between the administration and its critics lowered the level of funding. The first relief appropriation of 1935 seemed enormous, but much of it went to complete FERA commitments, and the WPA's share was not large enough to meet its target by the end of the year. Funds were cut by Congress in 1936, by executive order in the summer of 1937, and again by Congress in subsequent years.

The architects of the new policy claimed that it was never their intention to provide work for every able-bodied unemployed person, and most of them knew that no reliance could be placed upon Congress to continue WPA appropriations at the optimum level. From the beginning, it was therefore a tacit assumption that the states must and could do more. In a lengthy report to the National Economic Council in January 1935, the FERA pointed out that though state and local relief expenditure had risen by nearly 30 percent in two years, about 80 percent of the money had been raised by the sale of bonds, and few taxes had been imposed or increased. The inference was that many states could raise more revenue if willing to do so.[4]

The report also argued that most states could manage without greatly increased expenditure. Twenty-three of them already paid 20 percent or more of the emergency relief costs, and for them the transfer of unemployables to state or local responsibility would mean little more than bookkeeping changes. Not much more was necessary in ten states paying between 10 and 20 percent of their emergency relief costs. In addition, federal help for categorical assistance would free part of their normal welfare budgets for general relief.

The figures might be encouraging but could be read in a different way. The federal government was meeting over 80 percent of emergency relief costs in fifteen states and between 70 and 80 percent in ten more. Even if the WPA was able to employ a very large number, would these states be able to meet the increased burden? And even if it could be shown that they had the financial capacity, would they be willing to provide relief at an acceptable level?

[4] FDR Library, Hopkins Papers, Box 47, weekly reports of FERA to NEC, January 7, 1935.

Pressure from the FERA had gone far in raising standards (though not far enough in the opinion of many social workers). There had been increasingly sophisticated assessments of need, careful studies of family budgets, and agreement on desirable minimum levels of relief. As Hopkins had said on one occasion, the states might starve their people if they wished, but they were not going to do it on federal money. When the FERA withdrew it was certain that some states would abandon statistical studies, discharge their social workers, and drop their level of relief. The offending states would include some that could well afford to be professional and generous. States would also be free to abolish their state and county emergency relief agencies and rely once more on local officials. It seemed incredible to social workers that men who had dedicated so much effort to raising relief standards should abandon the task when it was beginning to show solid results.

What did all this mean for social workers and destitute people in the relief front line? A speaker at the 1937 National Conference of Social Work illustrated the situation in an imagined conversation with a public welfare official. After commenting on the very low level of relief being given, he said that it was at least some satisfaction that all who needed relief were getting it. The conversation continued:

— Now, wait a minute. I haven't said that. We are not giving help to all; only to those that meet our eligibility tests.
— Are there many who don't?
— Yes, a lot.
— What's the trouble? Is something wrong with them – or with the eligibility tests?
— Well, they're "employables" or think they are, but the W.P.A. is trying to cut down.
— Well, if they're employable, why don't they register with the employment service?
— They do, but these men are no good at private jobs.
— I see. Private industry has eligibility tests, too. So what happens to them?
— Well, to tell the truth, we don't exactly know.
  Perhaps the private agencies . . .

The imaginary questioner then visited a private agency and began by saying that it must have few applications for relief since the WPA came into operation. The following conversation ensued:

— Oh, don't we? Do you think those people can live on the W.P.A. wage? Those with large families?

— I suppose not. And what allowance do you give them?
— We don't give them any. It isn't sound practice for a private agency to subsidize public agencies.

The private agency then claimed that it gave counseling and service, first compiling a case history and then referring the applicant to a psychiatrist ("He's quite wonderful really") if there were signs of emotional disturbance, or to a medical clinic ("But then it's usually nothing more than malnutrition or anaemia so we have to close the case").[5]

Most states expected more from the WPA than it was able to deliver. Failure to provide for those who were genuinely unemployable was inexcusable, but there was good reason for complaint when they were suddenly called upon to give relief to able-bodied people who had been on projects funded by the FERA but for whom no WPA work was available.

In Massachusetts the transition should have been easy. The towns had continued to provide general relief. The FERA was responsible for work relief, and its administration was already under federal control. A transfer of FERA projects to the WPA, followed by new federal projects in due course, would have satisfied everyone, including the unemployed. What happened was very different. The FERA projects ran out of funds and were forced to close down before WPA projects were ready to begin; even when fully operational the WPA employed fewer men than the FERA, and the numbers fell as Congress cut appropriations; the towns ended by carrying a heavier burden than they had done in 1932. The outcome was particularly unfortunate because most towns had maintained standards of relief well above the national average.

In August 1935 Arthur G. Rotch, the FERA administrator who would also be responsible for the WPA, told Aubrey Williams that the FERA funds would run out before WPA money was available and asked for eight million dollars to fill the gap. He got six million. Rotch then made a personal appeal to Hopkins, saying that complaints were flooding in, the state government was very dissatisfied, and the situation was "making a bad impression for the administration." All he got was an additional $500,000 because August was a month with five pay

[5] Sidney Hollander, "A Layman Takes Stock of Public and Private Agency Functions," *NCSW 1937*, 174–190 at 176–7.

days. Work projects were reduced and relief rolls in the towns expanded.[6]

Under pressure to keep men off general relief, Rotch overran his budget, and by December WPA wages were in arrears. On December 19 Governor James Curley wrote angrily to Hopkins that because some men on WPA projects had had no pay since 21 November, there was "a possibility of riots and bloodshed." He regarded Rotch as an "abject failure." Rotch might have objected that he had done all that was possible, but he could not deny that the WPA was providing less work in December than the FERA in July and could not keep pace with wages for those who remained.[7]

A strenuous effort to close the gap pushed the WPA total to a peak of 120,267 in April 1936; but it then receded, and by August 1937 was just over 60,000. There was a negative correlation with the number in receipt of local general relief, which rose from 55,436 in October 1936 to over 60,000 at the end of the year and, after a dip in the summer of 1937, climbed steeply to 81,460 at the end of the year, with well over half classed as employable. Nor was it simply an urban problem; the proportion of the population on relief was higher in rural towns (28.9 against 25.5 percent). In all, local relief costs rose from just under $1,750,000 to over $2,540,000 during 1937, and Massachusetts had reason to complain that efforts to keep up the standard of relief had been shabbily rewarded. Far from providing work for the employables, the WPA was doing much worse than the defunct FERA.[8]

Things were even more alarming in Illinois, especially in Chicago and Cook County, where relief fell to a dangerously low level. There is no doubt that the state legislature was largely to blame for its refusal to vote adequate sums for relief; but at the end of 1935 a crisis was brought on by the failure of the WPA to provide work for all employ-

---

[6] NA RG 69 460, Massachusetts, Rotch to A. Williams, August 5; Rotch to Hopkins, August 7; Williams to Rotch, August 9, 1935.

[7] Curley to Hopkins, December 19, 1935.

[8] For this and the following paragraphs, see William Haber, "The Public Welfare Problem in Massachusetts" and William Haber and Herman M. Somers, "The Administration of Public Assistance in Massachusetts," *Social Service Review* 12 (1938), 179–204, 397–416. Haber was a professor of economics at the University of Michigan and former emergency relief administrator for Michigan; Somers was chief statistician for the Wisconsin Public Welfare Department. Both men were members of the research staff of the Massachusetts Commission on Taxation and Public Expenditure in 1938.

ables. The bad personal relations between Hopkins and Governor
Henry Horner made a bad situation worse.

In April 1935 a revenue bill passed the state senate by the bare two-
thirds majority necessary to bring it into immediate operation, but its
fate in the lower house was doubtful. Howard Hunter told Hopkins
that the opposition in the legislature had shown "an unbelievable
unwillingness to face the relief situation realistically." It had been
known since December that the FERA would not continue grants
unless the State contributed more, but opponents of relief continued
to play "the dirtiest kind of politics" on the presumption that the
FERA was bluffing. Hunter urged Hopkins to yield nothing – not even
to extend funds for a further fifteen days – and the relief commission
prepared to close down at the end of the month except for emergency
medical relief.[9]

Under this pressure, the legislature finally agreed to tax the gross
receipts of public utilities and to apply one-third of a 3 percent sales
tax to relief. The yield was not enough to provide the state's fair share,
but the FERA resumed grants in May and for the remainder of the year
accounted for well over three-quarters of relief expenditure. The rolls
included many who were unable to work, so even if the WPA looked
after all employables, Illinois was going to have difficulties.

In November, Hopkins told Robert J. Dunham, the state director of
relief and WPA administrator, that the aim was to employ 183,000 in
Illinois, with an allocation of $62,000,000 to last until March. The fig-
ures might be revised up or down, but this was the basis on which
Dunham should plan his operations. The total looked high but was not
high enough to absorb all the able-bodied unemployed; by December
it was clear that many employables would have to be given general
relief and that the federal government was not going to plug the gap
created by the low level of state funding. For people on relief, the quarrel over responsibility was irrelevant; the reality was less assistance
and more rejected applications.[10]

In December 1935 Governor Horner made a personal appeal to the
President for additional funds. This was followed on December 28 by
a telegram requesting $2,500,000 a month until the end of April 1936
and an immediate guarantee from the WPA to take 265,000 employ-

[9] FDR Library, Hopkins Papers, Box 57, Howard to Hopkins, April 27, 1935.
[10] NA RG 69, Hopkins to Dunham, November 2, 1935.

ables off the state's relief rolls. Commenting on Horner's letter, Hopkins told Roosevelt that Illinois was better able to provide direct relief than almost any other state. In July the Governor had agreed that the State should contribute $3,000,000 a month, but only half this sum had been appropriated. In spite of this, the FERA had continued to make substantial grants to Illinois. Hopkins said that the State now had $20,000,000 of unappropriated general revenue and could perfectly well afford to pay its share of relief.[11]

On Sunday, December 29, 1935, the Illinois Emergency Relief Commission (IERC) met at 5 P.M. to consider the crisis and continued until after 2 A.M. The principal business was to consider and adopt a statement, dictated by the Governor, declaring that the State was confronted with its worst crisis since 1932, but that if the federal government had fulfilled its promise to remove all employables from the IERC rolls, Illinois would have had no difficulty in meeting its relief commitments. Earlier the residual load had been reckoned at 65,000; but in January it would be 150,000 and, in addition, 30,000 on WPA projects would require supplementary assistance to maintain their families. The IERC would require $5,700,000 in January but had less than half that sum available. A further $2,000,000 was expected from state taxes in February, but even this would mean a drastic reduction in relief unless additional federal funds were available. The Governor argued that the federal government must either assume responsibility for all employables or give Illinois a grant of $10,000,000 spread over four months. After a discussion, which was certainly long and must have been agonizing, the meeting adopted the Governor's statement by a vote of 4–2. Robert J. Dunham, the WPA administrator, and two other members of the commission were not present.[12]

On January 2, 1936, Roosevelt sent an unequivocal reply to Horner's letter and telegram: No further grants would be made to Illinois; the WPA was employing 200,000 in the state and would shortly raise this total by 25,000; this was the federal government's fair share of relief responsibilities. The letter crossed with a copy of the IERC's resolution sent to Washington, and it may be surmised that urgent tele-

[11] FDR Library, Roosevelt File, OFF 444, Hopkins to FDR, December 21; Horner to FDR, telegram, December 28.
[12] The minutes of this meeting were sent to Washington, and there is an annotated copy in WPA File 610 (NA RG 69) 2. There are also minutes of the meeting on January 6.

phone conversations followed between Hopkins and the WPA administrator.

On January 6, 1936, the commission met again, with the first item on the agenda a motion by Dunham that the Governor's statement did not represent the views of the majority. He said that the IERC had never expected the WPA to take all employables, but only those eligible for employment on November 1; that the majority had never anticipated that the load would be only 65,000 and did not now accept a figure as high as 150,000 for January; and that WPA employees did not need additional assistance, except in a few instances in Cook County, where living costs were unusually high. He went on to say that the cause of the relief crisis did not lie with the federal government but in the failure of the State to appropriate adequate funds. Finally, Dunham asked the commission to affirm that the federal government had done all that could be expected when state and local contributions over a three-year period had been 4 percent below the national ratio and less than half that of New York and Massachusetts. After a discussion that must have been heated, Dunham's motion was carried 5-4, with himself and the other two members absent on December 29 in the majority.

This left the Governor with no option but to press the legislature once more, and (in order to meet constitutional objections to an emergency appropriation in the regular January session) he called a concurrent special session, which voted $2,500,000 a month from general revenues for relief. But to indicate its displeasure, the legislature also voted to end the IERC and restore all responsibility for general relief to the townships or counties. Thus the controversy solved nothing: The support given to federal policy by the IERC had led to its demise, the WPA did not take more employables, and the grossly inadequate standards for relief declined still further. Worse was to follow.

Maryland was another state to experience a crisis in relief when FERA grants ceased. Since the summer of 1933, the federal government had paid about three-quarters of the cost of general relief. Over the whole period of federal relief, the contribution totaled $33,350,000 against $10,105,000 from the State and only $1,080,000 from the counties. The withdrawal of federal funds from general relief would leave an enormous void and there were no plans to fill it.

The state relief agency was the old established Board of State Aid and Charities, but the key units in relief administration were the county boards, which were described in a report of 1934 as setting "the whole tone of the local program." When FERA grants came to an end, these county boards were left with the whole duty of providing general relief and the added responsibility of preparing lists of persons eligible for WPA employment.

Things got off to a very bad start when the newly appointed WPA administrator, John Maskall, resigned in August 1935 and then attacked federal policy. He claimed that he had accepted office on the understanding that he would control all funds for federal work projects coming into the state, but that the Public Works Administration (PWA) was dealing with the State Road Commission, which was "directly and absolutely antagonistic" and offered no cooperation in launching WPA projects. After resigning, he made a public statement saying that Hopkins and Harold Ickes (of the PWA) squabbled while 30,000 employables in Maryland were without work, that Ickes had put no one to work, although he had fifty million dollars available for construction, and that Hopkins talked about giving 5,500,000 employables jobs within twelve weeks but did little. Maskall predicted that by November fewer than 10 percent of the employables in the state would be at work.[13]

Maskall's sour prophecy proved to be all too true. There was no possibility that the WPA would find work for all able-bodied unemployed, and the transition was made more difficult by the slow-moving state administration. True to the traditions of Maryland, Francis Dryden, who had succeeded Maskall as WPA administrator, was reluctant to put pressure on the counties to produce their lists and suggest projects, and it was soon the turn of the WPA headquarters to express concern about the small number of employables who were being taken up.

In September 1935, reports reaching Washington indicated that only about 100 men were on WPA projects. Corrington Gill wrote to Dryden on October 1, telling him that there must be 33,000 on federal jobs in Maryland in a month's time. There were 4,300 in Civilian Conservation Corps camps and 2,800 on federal construction work; the WPA must find work for 25,800. Dryden replied that the funds already

---

[13] NA RG 69 610, Maryland, May 21, 31, 1935. Note on his resignation, August 1935.

assigned to Maryland, being earmarked for heavy construction projects, were not suitable for providing quick employment for large numbers. On October 22 Dryden telegraphed the WPA, saying that he could provide 6,200 jobs by November 1 and another 5,600 by the middle of the month. Hopkins replied by telegram that he expected no less than 15,000 to be at work by November 4 and 20,900 by November 18, and that responsibility for reaching these targets rested squarely upon Dryden.[14]

After this goading there was some acceleration in the program, but with little hope of providing for all or even a majority of the employables. The counties were faced with burdens far beyond their resources, and the State Board of Charities reported retrospectively:

In most local units there was a period between January and April [1936] when relief had to be arbitrarily withdrawn from many persons in need, and assistance could be given only in the most emergent situations

Even after April, when the legislature had made an appropriation to assist the counties, no money was available until October, and there was nothing for general assistance unless the county commissioners were willing and able to make advances in anticipation.[15]

Roosevelt and Hopkins received many protests against the ending of federal grants for general relief. Some complained that the WPA was not providing enough jobs; others alleged that they could not relieve their unemployables even if all employables were found work. The legislature of Texas passed a concurrent resolution declaring that as the state had recently created an old-age assistance program, it could not afford to relieve all unemployables. When this action was taken, the Texas senate passed a resolution condemning federal policy, and several counties followed suit. A Pennsylvania congressman sent the White House a resolution from a local board of supervisors claiming the WPA had failed to provide work and that thousands who had been on FERA projects had been dropped. In Philadelphia a Committee for the Continuation of Federal Relief was active in organizing petitions, and similar communications came in from all parts of the country.[16]

---

[14] NA RG 69 610, Maryland, Gill to Dryden, October 1, 1935.
[15] Maryland Board of State Aid and Charities, *18th Biennial Report, 1934–6*, 57.
[16] FDR Library, Roosevelt File, OFF 444, November 14, and (for the following paragraph) Congressman C. Murray Tarpin forwarding a resolution from the Board of Supervisors of Mountain Top, Pennsylvania. See also the appendix to this chapter.

When WPA jobs were in short supply, there were inevitable accusations that the lucky ones were chosen on political grounds, and when it seemed that these matters were decided by remote officials unfamiliar with local needs, there were demands for strong local control. The resolution from the Pennsylvania County Board of Supervisors claimed:

The administration of the works program and funds by locally elected officials would save millions of dollars in the cost of administration, wipe out partisan politics as the dominant factor in employing men, put an end to red tape and delay in getting projects under way, and result in better projects and better use of money.

Anyone familiar with local government (particularly in Pennsylvania) would be suspicious of the suggestion that it would be less partisan and more efficient, but the dismay about the future of relief was genuine.

Even where there was no immediate crisis in relief brought on by the end of the FERA, there is abundant evidence that relief standards declined and in some states fell far below the minimum required for adequate nutrition, clothing, and shelter. An unhappy report from the Texas Social Welfare Association claimed:

With the return of the relief burden to local governments plans for meeting human needs in Texas were partially paralyzed. . . . [The consequences] may be found by all who seek them in hovels beneath viaducts, in early deaths encouraged by the diseases of hunger, in high infant mortality rates, in juvenile delinquency, in crowded hospitals for the insane, and in the degradation of the body and spirit among our neighbors – the men, women, and children whom we keep alive but to whom we deny an opportunity to live.

With bitter irony, a contributor to the *Atlantic Monthly* wrote that children, like monkeys in zoos, needed fresh lettuce, bananas, oranges, and spinach, but only the monkeys were "assured of these necessities."[17]

In 1937 Edith Abbott was president of the National Conference of Social Work and chose as the theme of her address "Public Assistance – Whither Bound?". Her survey was wide-ranging but hinged on the following proposition:

The federal government's withdrawal from the home assistance program led to the chaos in which we now find ourselves. The whole relief program has

---

[17] Both items are quoted by Donald S. Howard, *The Works Progress Administration and Federal Relief Policy* (New York, 1943), 92, 95.

collapsed in many areas. Competent workers have been dismissed and those people who were our clients are now nobody's clients and nobody's responsibility.[18]

To counter this pessimism, optimists in the federal administration claimed that two years of federal relief had left an indelible mark and, as proof, pointed to the retention by a majority of states of some form of central agency with relief responsibilities, to the shift from small and inefficient units to county welfare and relief departments, and to evidence that the trend was set toward comprehensive and professional state welfare systems. Uniform action could not be expected when conditions varied so much, but the standards demanded by the FERA would not be forgotten.

In a few states these hopes would be fulfilled, but in most of them the forebodings voiced in early responses to the change in policy would be repeated in later years. In 1940 Harry Greenstein, former director of the defunct Maryland relief administration, delivered a gloomy address to the National Conference of Social Work. His theme was that when the Federal Government returned direct relief to the state and local governments, there had followed "a reduction in relief grants, lowering of personnel standards and administrative practices in many parts of the country. Intense suffering and demoralization attendant upon harsh and oppressive relief measures have been the rule for vast numbers of people during the past few years." Cuts in appropriations for the WPA had meant more transfers to general relief, but the federal government accepted no responsibility for this increased burden on the state and local governments.

Greenstein had no criticism of the federal works program as such, but he complained that those whom it could not employ were doomed to "a precarious existence, dependent upon inadequate and often non-existing local resources." The unwillingness of state legislatures to appropriate money or raise taxes, weak fiscal systems in local government, and arbitrary decisions by local officials provided shaky foundations for a national welfare system, and stability was unattainable so long as the federal government refused to accept any responsibility for general relief. At the same meeting, Edith Abbott demanded "a Federal program for the unemployed, Federally financed and Federally administered." It was clear that there would be no response from the

[18] Edith Abbott, "Public Assistance – Whither Bound," *NCSW 1937*, 3–25, at 10.

federal government to these appeals, war demands would shortly end mass unemployment, and it would be left for future generations to reap the bitter harvest.[19]

A more detached account of federal relief policy by Donald S. Howard, sponsored by the Russell Sage Foundation and published in 1943, drew attention to the unhappy consequences of divorcing general relief from work and categorical relief. He wrote that because general relief was regarded in the United States as "the last line of defense against destitution," it would have been logical to make it as strong as possible.

> The nation's program of general relief, like the innermost ring of defense surrounding an important military objective, should be fully organized and strongly fortified against any eventuality. Instead it is the nation's worst organized, most ineptly administered, and least adequate relief program. "Chaotic" and "haphazard" are terms justifiably applied to it.

Howard went over familiar ground when he argued that the units administering relief were often too small for efficient operation and too numerous for effective oversight. Even where state agencies were conscientious, effective supervision was impossible when there were 560 autonomous units in New Jersey, 900 in New York, over 1,000 in Indiana, Wisconsin, and Minnesota, and no fewer than 1,455 in Illinois. The persistence of these weaknesses puzzled political scientists, but Howard believed that of all deficiencies, the most perplexing was the determination of the federal government since 1935 "to pursue, in this important area, a laissez faire policy."[20]

Accompanying this major failure to create a national welfare system were minor anomalies that flew in the face of natural justice. The Social Security Act stated that categorical assistance must be in cash and that no work must be required as a condition, but cash was the exception in general relief (it prevailed in only seventeen states) and overseers of the poor might demand work before relieving distress. Officials in small communities cut their commitments whenever possible, and help was often refused to persons who were single, alien, in need but not destitute, or employable but not employed. In states

---

[19] Harry Greenstein, "General Relief: Another Category or a Basic Foundation for Public Welfare Administration?" *NCSW 1940*, 177–86 at 179; Edith Abbott, "Relief, the No Man's Land and How To Reclaim It," ibid., 187–98, at 196.
[20] Donald S. Howard, *The WPA and Federal Relief Policy* (New York, 1943), 51, 96.

where child labor was common, relief might be denied if the children in a family refused work. Many were victims of the laws of settlement, which, far from being relaxed, had been stiffened in several states during the depression. Sixteen states required more than three years' residence, and many would not count periods on relief. In Massachusetts, New Hampshire, Rhode Island, New Jersey, and Kansas, the minimum was five years.[21]

People classified as employable were often given less than unemployables, and if they found some part-time work were refused all relief. "Employable" was often equated with "able-bodied," and it was rumored that in one southern state a person capable of walking to the relief office was deemed to be employable and thus ineligible for general relief. In Delaware it seemed that everyone in need was classified as employable except those on the waiting list for old-age assistance. Another ground for refusing relief was that a relative was capable of helping, even though no help was given.[22]

The shortcomings of relief policy occasioned surprisingly little comment in Congress. In 1937 there were some discursive comments, but no concerted effort to propose remedies or even to find out the facts. In the House, Louis Ludlow of Indiana declared his faith in local responsibility but argued that some measure of continued federal assistance was "absolutely necessary to prevent intense suffering." Charles A. Wolverton of New Jersey said that without federal aid the burden on local taxpayers would become intolerable. Jerry Voorhis of California claimed that his state was carrying an unfair burden in the care of transients, for whom they were trying to maintain relatively high standards of relief and public health services. He praised the Resettlement Administration for its well-planned labor camps, but its effort was only a "tiny drop in the bucket."[23]

Maury Maverick of Texas complained sharply that they were all feeling their way in the dark. No congressional committee regularly investigated unemployment and relief. "There is no policy making

---

[21] WPA, *General Relief Statistics, January 1936–March 1937* (Washington, D.C., 1936).

[22] Howard, *WPA and Federal Relief Policy*, 65.

[23] *Congressional Record*, 5, 77th Congress, 1st Sess. Ludlow, 4886; Wolverton, Appendix, 1263; Voorhis, Appendix, 1899–1903.

committee," he said, "and we have no policy." In hearings held by the House Committee on Labor Ludlow declared:

Five years have passed without knowing anything about unemployment or the causes of unemployment, without having any long-range plan, or making any preparation to put a long-range plan into operation ... and without knowing how many unemployed there are.

A House committee heard also from William Hodson, speaking with the authority of an experienced welfare administrator, that argument without knowledge led nowhere. "All America is lined up in camps over relief, and most of these camps are organized on bias, misfortune or half-truth."[24]

In the Senate the issues were confused because Senator James F. Byrnes of South Carolina took the initiative with a bill to raise state and local contributions to WPA projects from 25 to 40 percent of the total cost. Byrnes wanted to cut the federal relief budget, encourage restraint in putting up projects, and secure greater state control over what remained. Other senators argued that as states were already finding more than expected for general relief they could not pay more for work projects, and the debate broadened into a general, though diffuse, discussion of relief policy. A vigorous attack on Byrnes's proposal came from Alben W. Barkley, a Tennessee Democrat (and future Vice-President), who produced voluminous statistics to show that with the return of direct relief the communities had been required to do more than they had done in 1929. If they were now asked to pay more for work projects, it would be a breach of "a sort of gentleman's agreement" under which the federal government took responsibility for employables.[25]

In the same debate, Senator Robert LaFollette tried to shift attention to the future of relief and to the insecure foundation of administration policy. He argued that partial economic recovery had not solved the unemployment problem because new recruits had entered the labor force, industry had economized on labor, and hours worked had increased by 2.5 percent; the number of unemployed was not dimin-

---

[24] Ibid., 5., 4890; 77th Congress, First Sess., House Committee on Labor, Subcommittee on a Bill to Provide for a United States Commissioner of Labor, Hearings. Maverick, 5; Hodson, 18.

[25] Ibid., 77th Congress, 1st Sess., Byrnes, 5808; Barkley, 6021.

ishing but growing, the WPA had no hope of providing work for all, and at least 350,000 men certified as employable were on relief.[26]

Government policy was supported by a conference of mayors from one hundred major cities. Reaffirming their opposition to additional appropriations for direct relief, they declared that "the problem of providing adequate aid to the so-called unemployable relief group is a responsibility which we believe rests solely with the localities and the states." This support from spokesmen for urban America was interesting. Their main concern was to prevent any cutback in the WPA program, which was relatively easy to administer in cities where there was much public work to be done, and labor easily moved from project to project. Most city welfare departments were familiar with the problem of unemployables and able to handle it. There was little enthusiasm for renewed intervention by state or federal agencies or for the increased taxes this might entail.[27]

These debates produced no result. Senator Byrnes's proposal to increase local contributions to WPA projects failed. No bill for restoring federal aid for direct relief was seriously considered. Members of Congress close to the administration would not enter into discussions that might embarrass Roosevelt. Thus the federal government held its course, to the intense disappointment of many who had put their faith in the FERA.

Whatever complaints might be levied against the federal government, the onus for action in 1935 and 1936 was upon the states. Whether the end of federal grants for relief came sooner or later, whether the withdrawal from general relief was total or partial, it was certain that the states must carry more responsibility for welfare and relief within their own borders.

The start could not be auspicious because the timetable for change was uncertain and difficult to fit into the normal legislative pattern. By the time the act creating the WPA had been passed by Congress, state legislatures sitting that year were nearing the end of their regular sessions; others were not due to meet until January 1936. Special sessions could be called, but the most that could be expected of them would be emergency appropriations to meet the shortfall in relief and stopgap

[26] Ibid., 1937.
[27] Ibid., Appendix 31.

measures to comply with the federal Social Security Act. Major reforms were not normally considered without ample publicity, hearings by select committees, and lengthy reports. A governor might anticipate events by setting up his own committee, but action on its recommendations would have to await legislative consideration. Prudence would therefore have dictated a two-year interval between the decision to get out of general relief and its implementation.

The attempt to get everything done within a year explains the confusion and frustration in 1935 but does not excuse the way in which so many states failed to put their relief houses in order during the following year. With a few creditable exceptions, it was a melancholy tale of lessons unlearned and prejudice revived. A number of options, each with several variants, were open to the states. General relief could be returned to local units without supervision or financial assistance. Local administration might be restored, but with the counties responsible for finance and supervision. The Emergency Relief Administration could be retained temporarily, perhaps with reduced power but with continued state assistance for general relief. The final option was to create a new agency (or enlarge an old one) and give it responsibility for all forms of relief and public assistance.

In the eighteen months after the last FERA grant, Kentucky, Maryland, Mississippi, and South Dakota withdrew completely from general relief and returned exclusive responsibility to their local governments. Florida, Georgia, Indiana, Kansas, Massachusetts, Nevada, North Carolina, South Carolina, and Vermont voted no funds for general relief but gave some assistance for relief administration. New Jersey and Missouri withdrew completely from general relief, but later had second thoughts and set up state agencies with limited regulatory power. The remaining states retained the emergency relief administrations as permanent agencies or merged them with departments of public welfare; but the powers of the state agencies ranged from effective regulation to advice, which need not be taken, or the allocation of earmarked grants for specific purposes.[28]

Relief administration was centralized in counties, but without state supervision, in Florida, Georgia, Idaho, Nebraska, South Dakota, most parts of Virginia, and seventeen counties of Illinois. In Connecticut, Maine, and Massachusetts it remained exclusively a town respon-

[28] FERA, *Final Statistical Report,* Table XV (251ff.).

sibility, though information and advice were given by the state departments of welfare. In Ohio relief administration was part county and part municipal; in most other states it became a county function, but under state supervision. The preeminent example of this mixed form was New York, where a strong State Department of Public Welfare had ultimate control but left routine decisions to the local authorities.

In Massachusetts the principal failure was not inadequate relief – the State maintained one of the highest standards in the country – but refusal to break out of a welfare system that had remained unchanged in essentials since colonial times. The towns and cities were the final authorities in deciding individual claims for all forms of assistance, their welfare boards were unsupervised by state agencies, and local taxes on real property furnished most of the revenue for relief. It might have been supposed that this system would have the merit of simplicity, but complications had been introduced with the superimposition of state responsibility for some types of public assistance. This had begun when the state assumed responsibility for the relief of persons without legal settlement. A town, believing that an indigent person was in this position, would make a claim for his relief from the state; but before this was granted, the State would carry out its own investigation to ensure that no one else was responsible. When other forms of state assistance became available – mothers' pensions, old-age assistance, and aid for the categories under the federal Social Security Act – the same pattern was adopted. In Massachusetts the supervision required by federal law did not mean merely directives on methods and standards, but a complete reinvestigation of every case in which the state and federal governments had a financial stake. The greatest harm done by this system was not the obvious duplication of effort but the immersion in the detail of individual cases, which deprived the Department of Public Welfare of an opportunity to provide leadership in the general improvement of welfare administration. The conscientious department did a good job in disseminating information, promoting discussion, and keeping the towns abreast of the latest ideas in welfare administration, but it did not issue directives or make regular inspections.[29]

[29] Haber and Somers, "Public Assistance in Massachusetts," passim.

Matters were made worse by tightening the laws of settlement. To assist town officials in their time-honored task of keeping paupers out, the period of residence required to qualify for a legal settlement was raised from four to five years. Settlement was lost after five years' absence or five years on relief, and the depression had increased the number of people who lost settlement by moving from place to place or by going on relief. In 1932 it was reckoned that less than 9 percent of those on relief were without settlement; by 1936 it was over 18 percent. Every case had to be checked locally and again by the Department of Public Welfare, which employed ten staff members to do it. All the cities and towns spent much time in investigating settlement and in litigation to resist responsibility in doubtful cases. Boston employed no fewer than forty persons to check settlement histories and allocate costs. In 1934 the Commissioner of Public Welfare proposed to abolish the laws of settlement and substitute a state contribution of 25 percent to all forms of public assistance, but this was opposed by local boards and the only point gained was to do away with settlement for dependent children.

Massachusetts had refused federal aid for direct relief and the degree of state centralization that would have been required. The end of the FERA did not therefore throw the state into the financial turmoil of a relief crisis, and in the disputes of 1935 and 1936 the competence of the WPA, not the efficiency of the traditional authorities, came under attack. The State might count itself fortunate, but the outcome was the survival of a system that had been severely criticized in earlier years. In 1938 a well-informed observer saw little hope in piecemeal change and declared that "the anomalous situation of one of the most socially progressive states in the union, with one of the most backward administrations of the pressing problem of public assistance, needs more drastic correction."[30]

Another state with a splendid history of social legislation saw mean and inefficient methods win the battle against improvement. Wisconsin had once been the Mecca of Progressives. It was the home state of Senator Robert LaFollette and his brother Philip was Governor, but the State clung to the principles of local responsibility. Some counties

[30] Ibid., 416.

had set up relief agencies, but though the state Emergency Relief Administration (ERA) had recommended their formation, the process was far from complete by 1935. Where county agencies existed, they assisted rather than directed the town boards, village trustees, and city common councils in their traditional duties, and though cities and villages might delegate authority to a commissioner of the poor, the law required town boards to take direct responsibility for relief. The ERA had been set up by the State to comply with federal law, but it was limited to the allocation of funds, accounting, and securing compliance with FERA regulations. Under the direction of the ERA, work relief was handled by the Industrial Commission.

When Philip LaFollette became Governor for the second time in 1935, unemployment was high on his agenda and an ambitious work and relief bill was his major legislative proposal. He proposed a works program to be run entirely by the State and combined with comprehensive plans for relief and welfare. He consulted directly with Hopkins and the President, and secured from them a surprising concession that the WPA would not operate in Wisconsin but that a federal grant of $100,000,000 would be contributed to the state program.[31]

LaFollette's political position was precarious. He had been elected as a Progressive in a three-party contest with 40 percent of the vote. In spite of his understanding with the President, the Democrats regarded him with suspicion and most Republicans opposed him. In June the works bill, which passed the lower house easily, lost in the state senate by 19–14 with Republicans and conservative Democrats in alliance. After bitter personal campaigning by LaFollette, directed against opposing state senators, a resubmitted bill was again defeated in the senate by one vote. From that point on, LaFollette's plans disintegrated, though he attempted to salvage something from the wreck by executive orders.

The last FERA grant was made to Wisconsin on November 28, 1935, and on December 7 the ERA was abolished by executive order and replaced by a Public Welfare Department – planned as the controlling agency for the whole welfare and relief program – but reduced by the unfortunate loss of the public works bill to responsibility for the

[31] Wisconsin Emergency Relief Administration, *Wisconsin Relief Laws* (Madison, 1934), 12. The *Annual Report* of the Wisconsin Public Welfare Department (1935–7) contains a history of relief administration. See also Public Welfare Department, "Development of the Public Assistance Program in Wisconsin, 1848–1948" (mimeographed, 1948).

categories and approval of applications for WPA employment. It had no power to supervise local administration or to determine the qualifications for relief workers. However, the department was staffed by welfare reformers, and its reports and circulated papers constantly attacked the existing system fastened upon the State by a single vote in the senate.

The battle was joined with the establishment of the new department. An article, published in December 1935 by the Wisconsin *Public Welfare Review,* pointed out that since September 1932 the bulk of relief costs had been paid by the federal government: $12,000,000 from the RFC, over $34,500,000 from the CWA, and nearly $73,500,000 from the FERA. Further federal aid had also come to the State through the transients' program, drought relief, and grants for rural education. The *Public Welfare Review* accepted an optimistic forecast that the WPA would take 68,000 cases but estimated that a further 45,000 would remain dependent on local relief. The cost would be $1,350,000 per month and, as the average from state and local sources had been $500,000, a huge gap had to be filled. In addition, 7,000 persons on WPA work projects would probably require additional assistance and 20 percent of the old-age pension costs still had to be found.[32]

Faced with these facts, drastic action might have been expected, but the legislative response was feeble. The Public Welfare Department was authorized to distribute unexpended federal funds, but no steps were taken to anticipate their certain exhaustion. From May 1936 the State made small and irregular grants to the poorest counties, but in spite of readily available evidence to the contrary the majority in the legislature assumed that relief costs would run down, and no provision was made to continue state aid after the spring of 1937. In April and May 1937 emergency appropriations were made for the distressed counties, but thereafter no state money was available until October, when further short-term appropriations were made without any attempt to plan for the future.

Locally the process of passing on the burden to those least able to pay went on apace. Counties closed their relief agencies and the townships took over. By June 1937 the number of units administering relief had risen from 364 to over 1,000, and the smallest and poorest carried the heaviest burdens in proportion to population. The Public Welfare

---

[32] *Public Welfare Review* III, No. 1 (December 1935).

Department drew the obvious conclusion: "Township financing of relief without outside assistance inevitably results in the poor helping the poor, while the well-to-do escape their share of the general responsibility."[33]

After three years' experience with restored local responsibility, the Public Welfare Department disputed the claim that it had reduced relief costs. Where this had happened it was explained by local economic revival, lowered relief standards, or a combination of both; but the department observed that true facts could not be ascertained because local accounting was inaccurate and no one had reckoned the cost of failing to provide services "which might immediately, or over a period of time, bring about a reduction in the total relief cost to the community." By 1939, after nine years of depression, seven of federal relief (pioneered by a Wisconsin Senator), and three of a Governor pledged to reform, the state was in a worse situation than it had been in 1932.

As well as demolishing the financial arguments for local relief, the Wisconsin Public Welfare Department attacked the incoherence of the State's relief policy. In 1936 it complained that there had been no attempt to gather together all the threads of welfare administration. Relief had been dominated by the "emergency concept," and there had been no attempt to take up the challenge of poverty:

Relief has been too greatly isolated on an island of its own, and except for its relationship to the works program it has not sufficiently integrated itself with other welfare activities which might be of assistance in reducing the total of public dependency.

In 1939 the department returned to the same theme when it asserted that at all levels the administration of unemployment relief had proceeded on the assumption that the phenomenon was temporary and did not call for long-term planning.[34]

The department also criticized crude attempts to distinguish employables from unemployables. People were incapable of working for a variety of reasons, and there was no reason why, as a class, they should be given a lower standard of relief. Even though they might

---

[33] Wisconsin Public Welfare Department, *Annual Report,* 1935–6. In 1948 the number of units was given as 1,067.
[34] Ibid., 1937–9, 40.

include some who were responsible for their own misfortunes, they still had families that deserved support to enable them to live decently:

> The children whose father is unemployed are as important to the State as those whose father is dead, and the man of 64 [is] just as much in need as the man who has passed his 65th birthday.

In conclusion, the department declared that "the State cannot turn back from a responsibility for the general welfare of the most needy group of citizens"; but clearly, this was what the state of Wisconsin had done and would continue to do.[35]

Between 1935 and 1938 there were six official and unofficial reports on the future of relief in Illinois. All assumed that the problem of unemployment would not go away, that WPA employment would run down, that a permanent system of state finance was desirable, and that it should be administered by a centralized state agency. All questioned the wisdom of dependence upon local government, and some argued that relief should be centralized in the counties and the State. None of the reports received much attention from the legislators.[36]

After making emergency appropriations in January and April 1936, the legislature spent weeks arguing about relief administration before passing a law that came into effect on July 1. The IERC was reprieved, but with greatly reduced power. It could estimate needs, allocate available funds, and act as the agent for receiving and disbursing federal grants, but it was given no power to supervise relief administration. Full responsibility for investigating cases, deciding on individual applications, and fixing the level of relief was returned to the 1,454 local units. For the first time, Cook County lost control of relief, which was transferred to the city of Chicago and thirty separate townships. These local units would qualify for state aid, provided that they levied a 3 mil relief tax on each dollar of taxable property, but once state money had been granted, it came exclusively under local control. The IERC warned that needs could not be met from available funds, but went unheeded. Relief payments fell from an average of $24.60 to $15.70 a month.[37]

[35] Ibid.
[36] Simeon E. Leland, ed., *State–Local Fiscal Relations in Illinois, (Social Science Studies . . . of the University of Chicago),* Vol. XXXVIII (Chicago 1941), 195.
[37] Illinois Emergency Relief Commission (IERC), *Biennial Report 1936–38,* 33–4.

Almost immediately the folly of these arrangements became clear. When the legislature met in August, widespread distress was reported from the metropolitan, industrial, and mining districts, and a hunger march was moving in on Springfield. Laws were hurriedly passed to increase state aid and authorize state payment of administrative costs (stopped as the result of a ruling by the State Attorney General.)[38]

As soon as the gates were open, other defects in local administration were revealed. The local units rushed to request state grants (538 in August, 1,375 by October), but many of them did so without making an effort to raise their own contributions. A total of 718 were disallowed by the IERC on the ground that they had not made the 3 mil levy (which was intended to raise local contributions up to about one-third of the total cost of relief).

There was also a suspicion that though relief payments were abnormally low, lax administration allowed payments to many who were not in real need. Although the IERC had no power to supervise administration, seventeen counties requested a review of their relief cases. The IERC found that 48.4 percent were justified, 27 percent should not have been allowed (the remainder had come off the relief rolls during the course of the review or could not be traced). The findings did not claim to be accurate because case records in the local units were poor, incomplete, or missing. The IERC also reported that procedures were unsystematic, services duplicated, and controls weak even in the small units. Local officials made their own decisions without supervision or clear instructions. This review covered only the seventeen counties, but the IERC found "considerable evidence" that "effective policies and procedures for control had not been applied in numerous local units throughout the state."[39]

This evidence enabled the IERC to win greater control over accounting and record keeping in 1938, but relief administration remained in the hands of local officials. The perennial fear of rural residents that they might be taxed to pay for Chicago's mistakes, Chicago's long-standing resentment of government from Springfield, and business opposition to increased taxes combined to prevent progress toward an efficient, statewide, and adequately funded relief system.

In the hope of winning greater power, the IERC had stressed cost

[38] Leland, *State–Local Fiscal Relations,* 189–90.
[39] IERC, *Biennial Report 1936–38,* 34–8.

and waste, but it was also acutely aware of the poor standards prevailing in many parts of the state. In 1938 it undertook a study of relief in seven large cities in different parts of the nation, and Chicago emerged badly from the comparison: It was alone in making no allowance for electricity, and it gave relief at 15 percent below the minimum required to maintain health. Things did not improve. The city dropped its relief payments by 20 percent in 1939, and though they were then raised, poor families still went short of food in order to purchase fuel and pay rent. In the state as a whole, there were extraordinary and indefensible variations – from $14.18 to $87.94 a month – and measured against the United States Department of Agriculture's figure for the minimum cost of an adequate diet, Cicero township in Cook County scored 101.5 percent, whereas Moline township in Rock Island did no better than 36.4. An IERC study in 1938 of 107 local units found that their average relief standard was well below the national figure and that 36 of them were far below even this modest level.[40]

The IERC also commissioned a study by Griffenhagen and Associates, which recommended that assistance for the unemployed should no longer be treated as "an escapable or a temporary or emergency function of government," that a state agency ought to be entrusted with power to control relief, and that without it there would be "uncontrolled extravagance ... financial chaos," and "acute social unrest as the result of real suffering." The report went on to say that if local responsibility was "unchangeable for the time being," the IERC must nevertheless have power to control the form of relief organization, determine the qualifications of personnel, and fix the level of relief given. It should also be enabled to insist on regular records, reports, and statistics. In making the case for greater centralization, the report stated: "The principle of State supervision of local government is generally accepted in the United States. It has been the subject of much discussion in Illinois but has not been put into effect."[41]

In Ohio there was the same lack of realistic planning, the same haste to return relief to the localities, the same failure to create a sound

---

[40] Howard, *The WPA and Federal Relief Policy,* 88–9; IERC, "The Relief Problem in Illinois: A Report to His Excellency, Henry Horner, April 15, 1938" (mimeographed for private circulation) and *Biennial Report 1936–37,* 191–2.
[41] Ibid., 9–11. Griffenhagen Associates, a private company, carried out many surveys for states and cities.

financial base for relief, and the same willingness to make the poorest pay the price as in other midwestern states.

Governor Martin Davey had no cause to lament the demise of the FERA and was committed to returning relief administration to local government, but there was little sense of urgency in setting up a new system. It was not until after the passage of the Social Security Act that a committee was appointed to draft state legislation, and the new law did not become operative until April 1936.

The starting point for the new policy was the return of general relief to the townships. There was no intention of continuing the State Emergency Relief Administration or of transferring its functions to a new agency. The new law set up a Division of Public Assistance in the Department of Public Welfare, but its primary function was to supervise and coordinate aid to the old, blind, and children, not to supervise relief administration. County boards of public assistance were created, with the juvenile judge, a county commissioner, and one or two persons appointed by the state division as members. These were advisory boards without power to make or enforce regulations.

The influence that the Department of Public Welfare could exercise over local administration was limited to informal advice, but it seems that at least some of the counties sought its help in imposing order on unregulated local government. The 1936 report of the department noted that "county officials, anxious to do an increasingly better job for their communities, availed themselves of the services of the Public Assistance staff." In 1937 small steps were taken toward centralization when a state Division of Aid for the Aged was set up with exclusive power to appoint local staffs and decide upon applications. County boards also won the right to supervise administration if a township attracted too many complaints. Federal law required supervision over categorical relief, but Ohio got by with the minimum necessary to comply. The state's old-age assistance law required central direction, but general relief remained under the exclusive control of local officials.[42]

As in other states, those in need paid for the revival of local responsibility. In 1938 Carl Watson, the WPA administrator in Ohio, told a committee of the United States Senate that general relief in the state

---

[42] Ohio Department of Public Welfare, *15th Annual Report*, 1936, 190–2; *16th Annual Report*, 362.

was "deplorable." To illustrate the point, he said that since April 1937, hardly any state funds had been used for general relief, although cases had increased from 53,000 to 103,000. The WPA could not offer more jobs, partly because of cuts in the federal appropriation in 1937 but also because many local sponsors could not meet their existing commitments to provide materials, let alone take on new projects.[43]

In the Atlantic states there was a more varied response than in the Midwest. New Jersey destroyed its relief administration and revived local responsibility, but then had second thoughts and restored a measure of state control. Maryland and Virginia both returned general relief to the counties, but whereas Maryland managed without central direction, Virginia retained a professional state agency with power to determine policy. Pennsylvania set up a fully centralized system under a strong Department of Welfare. New York returned relief to the townships but subordinated them to the counties and gave its Department of Public Welfare overriding power to coordinate and, if necessary, direct the counties and townships.

In 1935 New Jersey extended the life of its Emergency Relief Administration (ERA), but placed it under a Relief Council and cut its appropriation to such a ridiculously low figure that it was forced to discontinue all direct relief in 1936. The legislature then abolished the ERA, and as there were no county relief agencies, the local governments were left with sole responsibility.

These actions were taken despite clear warnings of the consequences, and in its 1935 report the ERA had explained the dimensions of the task. Of the families on relief, 75 percent or a little more could support themselves if work were available; in 10 percent there was an employable young person whose earnings could not fully support the other members; about 12.5 percent had no employable member and no means of support other than relief. Nearly one-quarter of the families would therefore need relief even if employment were fully available, and the prospects for three-quarters or more would depend upon the ability of the WPA to start enough projects. Even the most optimistic forecasts for the WPA did not anticipate so much for a single state.[44]

---

[43] 75th Congress, 3rd Sess., Senate Special Committee on Unemployment and Relief, Hearings, 713.
[44] New Jersey ERA, *Annual Report 1935.*

The deterioration after the end of state contributions to general relief caused a reassessment of the situation. In August 1936 a newly established State Financial Assistance Commission took over the remaining assets of the ERA, and state aid was resumed. Administration remained wholly in local hands, but some check was imposed in 1938 when it was made mandatory to set up local assistance boards with power to appoint a relief director (who did not have to be the local overseer of the poor) and supervise relief administration. Concurrently an Unemployment Relief Commission conducted inquiries, issued its first report in October 1938, and initiated a move that led to the overhaul of New Jersey's antiquated relief system.

The commission began by stressing the long-term nature of unemployment. In addition to the depression, economic changes constantly cut demands for labor and rendered some skills obsolete. For the foreseeable future there was likely to be "a reservoir of unemployed" in which the composition would vary but the volume would remain constant. In early 1937 New Jersey had been relatively prosperous, with manufactures running at about 85 percent of the 1929 level; even so it had been necessary to spend $118,983,000 on relief. In a comment on administrative problems, the commission remarked that "perhaps no phase of relief has caused more confusion than the effort to divide the direct relief population into 'employable' and 'unemployable' cases."[45]

The commission was highly critical of local poor relief in New Jersey. The choice of personnel had been haphazard, relief staffs were underpaid, and offices were undermanned. Even where competent workers were employed, they were not chosen by a uniform merit system and there were no safeguards against the appointment of incompetents. The new local assistance boards held little promise of making significant improvements, and confusion was made worse when their officials and overseers of the poor operated independently in the same area. Investigation was often slack, and there were no fixed rules for determining eligibility. In some instances, local criteria were stricter than those used by the WPA, and a man might be eligible for federal employment but denied relief if there were no federal jobs. Finally, New Jersey spent less per capita on direct relief than Massachusetts, New York, or Pennsylvania and was the lowest in the Northeast in categorical relief.

[45] Unemployment Relief Commission, *Report No. 1,* 17 October 1938, 11, 19, 23.

In the light of these severe criticisms, it was surprising that the commission began its second report, in January 1939, by affirming support for local administration. It suggested that financial support for unemployables should be a state responsibility and that the definition should include not only persons permanently unable to work but also those who were temporarily unable to do so, the administration of relief for the unemployables should be local, but the commission suggested supervision by county welfare agencies. The commission admitted that it might not be possible to stop all state aid immediately, but it affirmed "a strong opinion that all costs of relief (except for unemployables) should be borne by the municipalities."[46]

In summarizing the reasons for this conclusion, the commission went over some very old ground. Local responsibility meant proper attention to costs; competition for state aid (with some localities being more successful than others) would be ended; and variations in methods and standards would be acceptable if decided locally. "Much less disturbance is created if the variations are dealt with by the financial operations of individual municipalities than by throwing the effect of them upon the single treasury of the State, with constant uncertainty and confusion in State financial plans." If this sentence meant anything it was that though local finances might be weak they were consistent, whereas legislative appropriations were unpredictable.

One member of the commission, Robert W. Allen, wrote a hard-hitting dissent:

Explicit in such a proposal is the elaboration of technical difficulties already reduced to a minimum by intelligent centralization of administrative functions and uniformity in operative control. Implicit in the suggestion is an invitation to undesirable interference with operative efficiency.

He said that, once confirmed, the powers of local authorities would "too easily assume the character of an unalterable status quo" and thus prevent any fundamental attack on the underlying problems of unemployment. In the immediate future the commission's proposals would lead to an escalation of administrative costs (so drastically reduced by "intelligent centralization") and were therefore indefensible even on narrow grounds of economy.[47]

---

[46] Idem, *Report No. 2*, 16 January 1939, 12–15.
[47] Ibid., 20.

The New Jersey legislature was not prepared to go all the way with this dissent, but the state relief agency was converted into a permanent body with power to determine policy, issue directives, exercise financial control, and use state funds to equalize burdens between local governments. Local responsibility had been tried and had failed, and it was for the professionals in the state agency to take up the burden of imposing modern welfare concepts upon a system in which decision making was still decentralized.

Decentralization had been the keynote of relief administration in Maryland even when federal relief was at its peak. The relationship between the FERA, the State, and the counties was explained by the state director of relief:

> To be sure certain broad directives come from Washington to the state office; these are then in turn modified, interpreted, amplified, and sent on to the local units. On the whole, excepting for the supervision and guidance which has been afforded by a state staff very limited in number, the relief program in each local governmental unit has taken on a character which the official administrative body there has determined in its best judgment to be desirable.

When federal grants ceased, the Board of State Aid closed the office that had dealt with federal grants, the appointment of the state relief director was terminated, and county boards continued as before.[48]

Although administrative reorganization was not contemplated, relief finance soon created a major problem. The way in which the WPA failed to fulfill expectations in Maryland has already been described, but even without this problem the end of federal grants left a void, which was difficult to fill when counties had to rely exclusively on their own resources. The situation was serious enough in the summer of 1935 for the Governor to set up a commission of inquiry and to call the legislature into special session. It was agreed to set up a State Fund, financed from taxes and empowered to make grants to the counties from October 1. In the meantime, there were no funds for relief except insofar as the county commissioners were prepared to borrow in anticipation of what they might get from the new fund.

There was no agreement on long-term measures. Harry Greenstein, the former state relief director, summarized the arguments that were

---

[48] *Review of the Relief Situation in Maryland, June 1933–June 1934,* (Annapolis, 1934).

"repeated over and over again" in the commission report, its hearings, and the legislative debates.

1. Local control and home rule are the most desirable guiding principles. Only by centralizing authority in those closest to the problem can the necessary degree of economy be achieved. Remote control sets up unnatural standards, stimulates demand far beyond need, [and] increases the cost to the point where it is a threat to the taxpayers' security.
2. Federal control is an invasion of state's rights. It leads to the setting up of bureaucratic federal agencies. . . .
3. Even state control should be at an absolute minimum. . . . It makes little difference that the federal government itself does not dictate when it requires that a single state agency shall be put in a position of strategic supervision of local activities.

With these ideas in the ascendant, there was no hope that Maryland would set up a state agency to administer a comprehensive welfare program or even one with the more limited task of supervising relief. Nowhere was local responsibility more strongly entrenched, and those in distress were expected to make their contribution to its defense by going short on relief.[49]

So far, the story has been one of opportunities missed, consequences unforeseen, and lessons unlearned; but there were states that made stouter efforts to provide new answers to the problem of chronic unemployment or underemployment, and among them were three of particular interest. In two there was an element of pleasant surprise, for few would have predicted that Virginia and Pennsylvania would innovate in this field. The third was New York, where a healthy record in welfare policy promised a constructive response to the end of federal relief. In the event, Virginia moved, after a period of uncertainty, to what was probably the best welfare system that could be achieved in a predominantly rural state; Pennsylvania opted for complete centralization; and New York combined central and local functions in a way that served as a model for those who were reluctant to discard the idea of local responsibility.

In February 1935 Gertrude Gates, a field relief supervisor for the FERA, submitted a bleak report on Virginia. The administrative

---

[49] Harry Greenstein, "Problems in Accepting Grants in Aid," *NCSW 1935*, 277–83 at 278.

machinery for relief had made a good first impression. The Virginia Emergency Relief Administration (VERA) had set up local agencies and prescribed the rules under which they operated, and all appointments as city or county relief directors required its approval. The VERA also reimbursed counties for administrative costs and for the salaries of social workers.

So far so good; but in practice, control by the VERA was more apparent than real. Relief directors were nominated locally and hardly ever rejected. The counties were eager to accept federal funds but themselves contributed as little as possible. Gertrude Gates could find no reason to suppose that the VERA's confidence in local responsibility had done anything to encourage the adoption of efficient welfare policies.

The VERA had indeed inherited a system that was accustomed to promises rather than performance in welfare matters. Since 1908 the State Department of Welfare had recommended the formation of county welfare agencies, but only seventeen counties had acted on this advice. William Smith, the VERA administrator, claimed success in persuading the counties to finance 20 percent of the cost of work projects; but the county contribution usually took the form of supplying materials for local work that ought to have been undertaken without outside aid.[50]

The State Department of Welfare had relinquished all responsibility for relief when the VERA was established, and firmly dissociated itself from all attempts to centralize administration. It had, said its director, no intention of becoming "a department of control over local government." The state legislature, backed by Governors Peery and Pollard, had refused to put any money into relief, and public opinion in the state was said to display "definite opposition to relief as such." Except for what Smith could squeeze out of reluctant counties and cities, the whole relief operation had therefore depended on federal funds, and there was no hint that the state would step in when the FERA came to an end. Nor was it in relief alone that Virginia resisted change. In the regular session of 1936 the legislature refused to participate in the federal plans for old-age and unemployment insurance, and by May 1937

---

[50] NA RG 69 406, Virginia, February 1935. For a general account, see Robert F. Hunter, "Virginia and the New Deal," in John Braeman, Robert H. Bremner, and David Brody. *The New Deal,* Vol. II (Columbus, Ohio, 1975), 103–36. Also Virginia Board of Public Welfare, 27th and 28th *Annual Reports,* 1937–75 (in one volume).

Virginia was the only state in the nation without its own old-age assistance program.

Given this gloomy prognosis, surprising progress was made during the next two years. In January 1936 Arthur W. James, who had been a leading official in the Department of Public Welfare since 1922, wrote to Governor George Peery urging state action "to get rid of the abuse of poor relief administration by the overseers of the poor," and with federal pressure removed, the state was more willing to act. For the first time, Virginia contributed to local relief costs (albeit no more than 4 percent of the total) and, more significantly, made it mandatory for cities and counties to create welfare departments. The county superintendents and relief directors were elected by boards of supervisors but had to be approved by the Department of Public Welfare.[51]

When implementing the new law, the Commissioner of Public Welfare told cities and counties that they would be given all the assistance they needed in finding staff, but that he would not approve the appointment of persons without graduate qualifications or acceptable experience in social work. This was, he said, essential if there was to be a real welfare organization, not "a group of office-holders employed for reasons other than their qualifications." In December 1936 a special session of the legislature agreed, with little opposition, to participate in the federal social security program. In July 1938, after prolonged discussion, Virginia set up its own old-age assistance program. At $20 a month it was well below the national average and was given exclusively to old people in need (to avoid any suggestion that it was a pension), but it was a significant move for a state that had seemed to be determined not to move with the times.[52]

The year 1938 was indeed the *annus mirabilis* in Virginia's welfare legislation. A new Public Assistance Act required every city and county to have a welfare department and to provide funds sufficient to support its work. Control was vested in a State Board of Public Welfare, which appointed a commissioner; existing arrangements for the appointment and approval of local staff were confirmed; and county superintendents of public welfare were to be chosen from lists prepared

[51] Arthur W. James, *The State Becomes a Social Worker*, (Richmond, Va., 1942), 267. James was in charge of the educational program of the Board of Public Welfare from 1928 to 1938.
[52] General Letter of the Commissioner of Public Welfare to Boards of County Supervisors, June 5, 1936. James, *The State Becomes a Social Worker*, 288.

by the state board. The state board was authorized to issue rules and regulations, decide the allocation of state funds, require reports and statistics, and take steps to ensure uniform administrative practice. The principle of local responsibility was preserved by giving local boards exclusive power to decide upon applications, fix the level of relief to be given, and appoint lower officers and social workers.

Inevitably, the new law embodied paternalistic assumptions long rooted in Virginia traditions. It was intended to exclude the "unworthy" as well as to relieve the needy. As a member of the state board told an audience of local welfare officers:

> You are going to be amazed at the number of strong healthy men and women who suddenly find themselves unable to support their aged parents who have worn out their lives working for them. You are going to be overwhelmed by the number of persons who think themselves unable to work.

When cash relief was given, it was to be spent on necessities, not squandered, and further help should be refused if relief money was used improperly. Social workers had, therefore, to take a tough line on relief, but it was equally important to resist political pressure. The public had to be convinced that the new program was "not a panacea for all ills, not a pork barrel . . . not a political soft ball."[53]

The traditional warnings against chiselers and corruption went hand in hand with a realization that old principles had to be modified. The same speaker told social workers: "We can no longer indulge in wishful thinking and speak of getting rid of unemployment. We know now that the many problems of the needy and helpless are going to remain with us for many years to come." In facing the future, they would have to insist that public welfare was a "highly complicated task requiring special knowledge and special technique just as the professions of law and medicine require special knowledge and special techniques."[54]

Experience under the FERA, followed by the sudden end to federal grants, had propelled Virginia into a new era of welfare administration. The relief administrator, William Smith, was a Virginian of the old school who understood thoroughly the society in which he operated. He had pressed cautiously but firmly for a system that would be permanent, professional, and efficient. He could not, nor did he wish to,

[53] Commissioner of Public Welfare to Boards of County Supervisors, March 24, 1938; James, *The State Becomes a Social Worker,* 301, 304–9.

[54] James, *The State Becomes a Social Worker,* 311–12 (quoting Dr. Belle Boone Beard).

break with traditions of local autonomy, but central supervision was assured by control over appointments. Although lack of forward planning when the end of the FERA was announced condemned the unemployed to a year of unprecedented distress, Virginia had then moved with surprising speed to establish a state welfare system that was more efficient than that of any other southern state and a welcome contrast to the blundering township system of the Midwest.

No one familiar with the anarchic local government and careless administration of relief in Pennsylvania before the depression would have predicted that within ten years the state would have the most completely centralized welfare system in the country. A major factor was a political revolution leading to the election of a Democratic governor in 1934, the replacement of the ultraconservative David A. Reed as United States Senator by Joseph Guffey, the state Democratic leader, and Democratic capture of the lower house in the assembly for the first time since 1877. If there had been no other motive, the Democrats had the strongest possible incentive to prove that change meant change. The principal obstacle was the state senate, where the Republicans held on to their majority.

George Earle had been a Republican until 1932, but was nominated in 1934 as the Democratic candidate for Governor, with endorsement by Joseph Guffey. He was determined to bring Pennsylvania abreast of the New Deal, and relied upon popular support to get round opposition in the senate. He inherited a long-running quarrel with the FERA over the state's failure to pay what was regarded as its fair share of relief costs, and Harry Hopkins had recently threatened to stop all federal aid. Earle asked the legislature to raise $120,000,000 for relief from new taxes, and Hopkins backed him by making public his determination to cut off federal funds. The measure passed the senate when some Republicans from mining and industrial districts bolted their party to vote for it after the appropriation had been limited to one year.[55]

When the FERA grants ceased, still more money had to be found, and a long battle began with the Republicans in the senate. By March 1936 and in spite of the WPA, there were 192,261 cases (perhaps over

---

[55] Richard C. Keller, "Pennsylvania's Little New Deal," in Braeman et al., *New Deal*, Vol. II, 45–76.

half a million persons) dependent on relief, and the cost was running at $8,000,000 a month. After angry debates at Harrisburg and demonstrations by the unemployed, a compromise resulted in an appropriation of $45,000,000. The controversy and Earle's appeal for popular support boosted Democratic fortunes, and in 1936 they captured eighteen of the twenty-five contested senate seats. The way was now clear for an unemployment compensation law, other acts to comply with the federal Social Security Act, and a reformed and permanent system for the relief of the unemployed.

A commission on public assistance, dominated by Democrats, reported in December 1936 with drastic and unambiguous recommendations. It began by demonstrating the incoherence, duplication, and waste in the system as it was. Nine different types of assistance were administered locally by at least five authorities separately supervised by the Department of Welfare, the State Emergency Relief Board, the WPA, and the Veterans Commission. It was, said the commission, a system of "appalling size, complexity, and diversity," and it recommended the consolidation of all forms of relief in a new Department of Public Assistance.[56]

Looking to local administration, the commission declared:

There is no longer any excuse for perpetuating a wasteful, inefficient, and antiquated method of poor relief, as generally administered under laws and organizations dating in spirit and largely in fact from the seventeenth century.

After considering possible modernization of the poor boards, the commission decided that nothing constructive could be done so long as four hundred separate units perpetuated "the present confusion and diversity." It recommended that local relief administration should be controlled by County Boards of Assistance, the poor boards abolished, and relief financed wholly by the state. Appointment to the new county boards should be made by the county commissioners, but from lists approved by the State Department of Public Assistance.

When proposals based on the report became law in 1937, Pennsylvania abandoned the once revered principle of local responsibility for relief of the poor and chose complete centralization. Modifications of the original recommendations were the addition of an advisory State

---

[56] Commission on Public Assistance and Relief, *First General Report,* December 15, 1936, 12, 55–6. (An abridged version, *A Message to the People of Pennsylvania,* summarized the findings and recommendations.)

Welfare Commission, the adoption of cash payments as the normal form of relief, and a distinction between monetary relief, coming under the new Department of Public Assistance, and institutional care remaining (together with nonrelief programs) under the Department of Public Welfare. After two and a half centuries the poor boards disappeared from history, membership of the new county boards was partially controlled by the State, and finance for all forms of relief came from legislative appropriations and statewide taxes.[57]

New York anticipated the end of federal relief with greater foresight than any other state, and its plans were, in many respects, a logical extension of what had been done in 1931 when a state was still expected to rely on its own resources. It is probable that New York also received early and precise indications of what was in the wind, since neither Roosevelt nor Hopkins would risk a failure in their own state at this critical period.

Governor Herbert Lehman had set up a Commission on Unemployment Relief during 1934, and it was about to issue its first report when Roosevelt announced the withdrawal of the federal government from general relief. The report welcomed the prospect of an enlarged federal work program but warned that there were certain to be difficulties in moving labor to where it was needed and in matching skills with work opportunities. It therefore recommended that existing work projects should be continued until the future became clear and expressed the hope that the FERA would go on for at least a year.[58]

Looking further into the future, the commission rejected the belief that contemporary difficulties were the result of a temporary emergency and recommended the creation of administrative machinery to provide unemployment relief for years to come. Experience had shown that the localities could not do this on their own; funds would have to come from the state; with state money must come state supervision of

---

[57] "One of the most outstanding legislative enactments in the last two hundred years was the passage of Act 396 by the 1937 legislature by which 425 old poor boards, relics of the Elizabethan age, were abolished and Country Institution Districts established. This marked a turning point in the development of community work in Pennsylvania." Pennsylvania Department of Welfare, *Ninth Biennial Report* (1936–8), 7–8. In another astute publicity exercise, the department published in 1938 (Bulletin 76) a booklet entitled *Decades of Welfare in Four Years.*

[58] For New York, see Robert P. Ingalls, *Herbert H. Lehman and New York's Little New Deal,* (New York, 1975).

expenditure, and this was not merely an expedient for bad times. "We are in complete accord," declared the commission, "with the fundamental view that ultimately all state welfare functions should be combined under the direction of one agency."[59]

This first report was followed by a study of welfare in 112 of New York's 826 townships. It found that the average number of relief cases was sixty-five and that nearly two-thirds of the townships had fewer than fifty families on relief. These light burdens had persuaded many townships that no special administrative arrangements were required; in seventy-six there were no relief offices, and claims were received in the home or business of the welfare officers, of whom over two-thirds served part-time. Yet these apparent economies in small townships had not prevented the cost per case from being higher than it would have been in larger units.

The commission did not question the honesty of township officials but commented severely on their quality. Many of them had "little formal education or native ability and few, if any . . . special training or experience for their jobs." Only 13 percent were high school graduates, and only 8 percent had had any further education. Many were farmers and most of them older men. Only 10 out of 108 were under forty, 12 were over seventy and 3 over eighty. The commission gave about half of them credit for conscientious work; thought that another quarter meant well but were so limited in experience or native ability that their work was unsatisfactory; and condemned the remaining quarter as "inefficient, prejudiced, narrow, opinionated, and resentful of suggestions from the County welfare officers." In most places the salaries offered were too low to attract better-qualified or more able men, though some ran as high as $1,800 a year, with no clear correlation between salary and case load.[60]

Regular home visits were not made in about half of the townships studied. In over a third of them no use was made of family budgets in fixing relief, although the information was readily available from the TERA. Few kept or used systematic case histories. One might have

[59] N.Y. St. A., Reports and papers of the Governor's Commission on Unemployment Relief; *First Report* (Albany, 1936), 12.
[60] Ibid. Confidential Draft of a Report on the Town Relief System; Legislative Document 56 (1936), *State and Local Welfare Organization*, 72–5. This is an exceptionally clear, able, and well-informed report. The confidential draft includes some comments on the caliber of local officials that may have been thought too offensive to include in the printed version.

expected that experience during the depression and guidance offered by the state would have led to marked improvements, but the report concluded that in a large majority of townships, relief administration remained "inequitable, casual, and unsystematic." Social workers and political scientists had been saying this for years, but now it was said by an official body to a sympathetic governor and a legislature disposed to act.[61]

Fortunately, the commission found a happier state of affairs in the counties and improvements that pointed the way to reform. Six counties had already taken welfare administration away from the townships; in nine the township officers still had nominal responsibilities but control was in the hands of County Relief Bureaus; in many others, where there were no county agencies, county officials were directed by the TERA.

During the summer of 1935, the problem of unemployed "employables" came to the fore. Hopkins had estimated that 80 percent of those on relief in New York were employable and would be taken on by the WPA; but it soon became clear that this was hopelessly optimistic, and the target was cut to 70 percent of the relief rolls. Hopkins agreed informally to cover the cost of the employables remaining on relief, but by September the number employed by the WPA was far short of the revised estimate and there was no certainty about future responsibility for the able-bodied unemployed.

Governor Lehman then urged Hopkins to give a public undertaking to accept responsibility for 70 percent of those on relief, whether employed or not, and to continue federal grants for both home and work relief until all employables had work with the WPA. If this were done, Lehman estimated that the State could support 40 percent and the localities 60 percent of those remaining on relief. The reply gave no such assurances, and Lehman then took Mayor Fiorello La Guardia of New York and a representative from the TERA to meet Roosevelt and Hopkins at Hyde Park. They left under the impression that they had an undertaking that the target figure for the WPA would be 396,000 and that the federal government would cover the relief costs for this number, whether or not they got employment. Under this

---

[61] Ibid. The commission was, however, equally critical of some TERA appointments. Although possessing formal qualifications in social work, "the majority . . . have little professional competence" and in many districts were inferior in training and experience to the supervisors who worked under them (Legislative Document No. 55, 47).

agreement, New York claimed $14,000,000, but only $9,000,000 was allowed; Hopkins argued (neither credibly nor creditably) that the 396,000 must include all those employed on construction under the Public Works Administration (PWA), the Civilian Conservation Corps, and other federal projects even though many of them had never been on relief. After a protest from Lehman a further $2,700,000 was allocated, but relations between the state and the federal government had deteriorated to the point at which only formal communication was possible. In this unhappy situation there was one compensation. Clear evidence that large numbers of employables would remain a burden on the state hastened consideration of the report presented by the Commission on Unemployment Relief in December 1935.[62]

The commission recommended that the State should initiate and supervise "a continuing and permanent policy for home relief." The cost should be shared between the state, counties, and cities; but control should be vested in a single department of social welfare to supervise local welfare departments, pay part of the salary of qualified employees, and withhold funds if its regulations were ignored. A commissioner of public welfare should be appointed by the Governor and responsible to him for all executive matters pertaining to the department of social welfare, but policy should be directed by a board of social welfare appointed with the consent of the state senate. The board would issue rules and regulations, fix the qualifications for officers in local welfare departments, inspect all state institutions, and advise the Governor and legislature on all welfare questions. The TERA should be ended and its duties transferred to the new department. In the counties and cities, commissioners of public welfare would no longer be elected but appointed by the County Board of Supervisors or the mayor.[63]

The commission came out in favor of cash relief. It also agreed unanimously that the State should end work relief, arguing that it was no longer necessary to sustain morale, did little to preserve skills, and competed with private employers when communities wanted work to be done. It thought that federal employment ought to be given on the

[62] N.Y. St. A., Governor's correspondence, Lehman to Hopkins, September 11, 1935; Ingalls, *Herbert Lehman*, 54–5.

[63] Legislative Document 56 (1936); Governor's Committee on Unemployment Relief, *Resume of the Report on State and Local Welfare* (Albany, 1935), Recommendations 1–10; Legislative Document 52 (1936).

basis of skill, not need, and that men whose work was unsatisfactory ought to be discharged. Five members of the commission thought that work relief ought to be continued as a local option but did not dissent from the main recommendations.[64]

During 1936 the TERA collected more evidence to support the need for change and a comprehensive plan for all welfare services. In May Frederick J. Daniels, chairman of the TERA, reporting to the Governor on a chaotic situation that had developed in Buffalo, described it as "an excellent example of why our administration feels so strongly about the need for good local administration of relief, which can be arrived at only if there are proper state controls exercised by a state department which has both vision and guts."[65]

With some amendments in detail the commission's recommendations became law, and in July 1937 the TERA transferred its remaining functions to the Department of Social Welfare. In a valedictory note to the Governor, the retiring chairman wrote:

The termination of the T.E.R.A. and the assumption of its activities by the State Department of Social Welfare marks the beginning of a new era in the administration of the State's responsibility towards its socially unfortunate citizens. Lessons from the emergency have brought to us all a new consciousness of responsibility and shown us how to avoid some of the mistakes of the past.

The recognition that relief was a permanent function of government marked the boundary between the primitive and the modern in welfare history.[66]

The act gave the Board of Social Welfare, not the Governor, the right to appoint the commissioner, thus giving it more direct control over administration. The new system was placed on a secure fiscal base, with the current costs of relief to be met from taxation and not by selling bonds. In other respects, the outcome was a little less tidy than the commission had hoped. Aid for dependent children remained the responsibility (in most instances) of County Child Welfare Boards. State reimbursement for local relief expenditure followed the federal law in adopting varying proportions for different forms of assistance: 40 percent for home relief, 25 for old-age assistance and the blind, 50 for the physically handicapped under twenty-one, and 16⅔ for moth-

---

[64] Legislative Document 56 (1936).
[65] N.Y. St. A., Governor's correspondence, May 13, 1936.
[66] Ibid., Lehman Papers, Paul H. Livermore to Lehman, July 2, 1937.

ers' aid. The State contributed 40 percent of most administrative costs, though less for some categories. The federal government reimbursed the localities directly for 50 percent of old-age assistance and a smaller portion for dependent children. Either state or federal contributions or both might be withdrawn if administration was unsatisfactory.

Different levels of assistance in the federal law accounted for some complexities in the state system, and there was always a danger that state plans might be upset by unpredictable changes in federal policy. This was most apparent in the varying amount of work offered by the WPA and in cuts imposed by Congress. As the Board of Social Welfare confessed in its first report: "The inherent complexities of a tripartite governmental responsibility, local, state, and federal, rooted in our very American system, are even greater than might appear." The more the board aimed at precision, the more complex became administration.[67]

Although federal law prevented simplicity in some aspects of relief administration, the root cause of complexity was the freedom still left to the localities, and this was no accident but a deliberate choice on the part of those who made the law. Policy was decided at the center, but detailed administration and part of the cost were left with local government. The qualifications for welfare posts were laid down by the state board, but county commissions and city mayors had a free hand in choosing between qualified persons. The townships were subordinated to the counties, but the division of duties between them was decided locally. The New York system was therefore more centralized than that of Pennsylvania in placing all branches of welfare (with some minor exceptions) under a single state agency, but less centralized in control exercised by the State over local agencies. The respect accorded to local responsibility was counted among the merits of the new system by its architects. David Adie, who became Commissioner of Public Welfare, claimed that "the weight of evidence bears out the wisdom of the New York plan of local administration, in accordance with the traditions of the past, but with state financial participation and state supervision."[68]

In 1937 the immediate problem in New York was to bridge the gap between what the WPA had promised and what it was able to deliver.

[67] New York Board of Social Welfare, *First Report* (Albany, 1937), 8.
[68] Ibid., Adie to Lehman, January 22, 1938.

Faced with an unexpectedly heavy load and the prospect of having to cut relief standards, the Board of Social Welfare made an urgent request asking the Governor to petition Congress "to redeem the often-repeated pledge, never entirely fulfilled to take care of all employables, by allowing a part of federal relief funds [to be used as] grants-in-aid to the States to assist in the financing of direct relief." The plea was rejected and the position worsened by further cuts in the WPA appropriation.[69]

Thus, in the State that had taken the most farsighted and constructive view of the problem, relief lacked funds and faced an uncertain future. Other states were rightly blamed for not tackling problems all could have anticipated; but New York had done all that a state could do, and the federal government was squarely to blame for the continuing difficulties over relief.

Appendix: Correspondence about the WPA[70]

Two letters from Ellery F. Reed, director of the Research Bureau of the Community Chest of Cincinnati, to the President are interesting as a criticism of federal policy from someone not engaged in public welfare administration but with intimate knowledge of the situation in a large city. For further comments on conditions in Cincinnati (based on an article by Reed), see pp. 327–8.

On March 12, 1936, Reed wrote to say that relief policy would be vulnerable in the election campaign because the enormous expense of the WPA could not be justified by the number of people to whom it was giving work.

He said that in May 1935, 2,228,000 out of the 5,169,000 FERA cases were on work relief and that many of the remainder were getting assistance to supplement casual or part-time earnings; a majority receiving FERA aid had therefore been doing some work. Since the introduction of the WPA, the number with no work had increased. Employable men were eligible for WPA work only if they had been on relief in 1935, and a large number of new cases were being assisted from general relief. The measure of the increased burden on local gov-

---

[69] N.Y. St. A., Lehman Papers.
[70] The correspondence is in the FDR Library, Hyde Park; Roosevelt Papers, File OFF 444.

ernment was that in spite of the WPA program, Hamilton County and Cincinnati were carrying a relief load ten times heavier than in 1928, but revenue had not grown proportionately. Property taxes were inelastic, sales taxes were not yielding enough, and the state was poorly equipped to administer an income tax. Cincinnati had made a special levy, but this would run out by midsummer, no other revenue was in sight, and distress was acute.

Reed argued that only the federal government could provide the remedy by giving grants-in-aid for state programs. He suggested matching grants, with the states contributing 30 percent, and a small reserve to give additional assistance to the very poor states. Relief should be locally administered, but with national guidelines for policy and standards.

Marvin McIntyre, one of the President's secretaries, replied on his behalf with a letter drafted by Hopkins. The comparative costs of the FERA and the WPA had been carefully considered. Workers on WPA projects preferred them to FERA work relief. The WPA officials were authorized to take account of local circumstances when assessing eligibility. The tax situation certainly deserved serious study, and this was something that the state authorities should take in hand. The implication of this reply was that the federal government would not assume responsibility for making good the deficiencies in inefficient state fiscal systems.

Reed thought that this anodyne letter had neither answered his points nor stated the facts correctly. He replied that the supposed preference for WPA work was in conflict with the evidence. During the FERA period, people in distress had received (from direct relief, work relief, or a combination of both) enough to live on, but wages for men on WPA projects were often too low to support their families. Whatever discretion was allowed to local WPA officials, the fact was that many employables were not eligible. Indeed, it would be difficult for the WPA officials to take local circumstances into account when they had no way of assessing the family situation, no staff for investigating cases, and were already overburdened. He went on to challenge one of the WPA's basic principles: that the priority in allocating work should be need, not proficiency. He cited the British authorities on the poor law, Sidney and Beatrice Webb, to support the contention that the consequent inefficiency did no one any good. Reed believed that the correct policy would be a public works program organized on PWA principles (i.e., large-scale projects of major importance employing qualified personnel) and a national public assistance program. Locally sponsored but nationally approved small works projects might supplement but not replace the national program.

9

DEBITS AND CREDITS

When the National Conference of Social Work met in 1940, a wide review of the past, present, and future of public relief was on the agenda. Harry Greenstein, the former state relief administrator for Maryland, declared:

When the Federal Government took the position that direct relief was the primary responsibility of state and local governments, something vital was taken out of the relief program.

The result had been "a low grade of pauper treatment over wide areas" and, for those not employed by the WPA, "a precarious existence dependent upon inadequate and often non-existent local resources."[1]

Edith Abbott called her address to the same meeting "Relief, the No Man's Land and How to Reclaim It" but could see no hope of improvement without federal intervention. Using different imagery she spoke to the Illinois Conference on Social Welfare on "the disinherited relief program":

The tenth summer is over – the tenth harvest is gathered – and we are still here – after ten years – with relief never more inadequate than it is at the present time. Things have gone steadily from bad to worse since the fatal decision about "ending this business of relief" was made by the federal government in 1935.

To illustrate the point she cited figures from Chicago. In the early days of the FERA, the average home relief per case had been $32.75 a month; it rose to $40.28 during 1934, then fell to $28.52 in 1937 and to $23.54 by 1939. Moreover a sales tax imposed disproportionately heavy burdens on the poor, so that the real value of relief was about

[1] Harry Greenstein, "General Relief: Another Category or a Basic Foundation for Public Welfare Administration?" 179, *NCSW 1940*, 177–86.

half of what it had been when federal relief was fully operative. A recent report on school attendance had discovered that in "one of the greatest and wealthiest cities in the world" large numbers of children were kept away from school because they had no shoes or lacked proper clothes.[2]

It was generally supposed that families with a member in WPA employment were better off, but this was questioned by Edith Abbott. She told her Illinois audience of a family of two adults and five children living on $65 a month earned by the father from the WPA. A medical examination had shown that all five children suffered from malnutrition, two had rheumatic heart disease, one had a respiratory ailment, the fourth was anemic, and the youngest was seriously underweight. People in this situation could not improve their circumstances because only one member in a family was eligible for WPA employment and he became ineligible if another member of the family obtained private employment.[3]

Earlier in the year C. M. Bookman of Cincinnati, who was not prone to needless alarm, had written an open letter to the President and obtained the signatures of numerous social workers, ministers, educators, and public officials. The letter said that since relief had been returned to the states and localities, it had been so inadequate that the unemployed could expect nothing more than slow starvation. Bookman argued that relief could be neither effective nor economically administered unless "its national nature was recognized." A reappraisal of the whole policy was essential, but in the meantime immediate steps should be taken to deal with transients and "end the passing of these unfortunate people from city to city and state to state."[4]

Bookman's bleak picture was drawn from Hamilton County (including the city of Cincinnati), where the relief organization had won a reputation for efficiency under the FERA. More recently a reduction in relief cost during 1937 had been offered as proof of the success of decentralization in Ohio. In fact, all justifiable reductions had been

[2] Edith Abbott, "Relief, the No Man's Land, and How to Reclaim It," *NCSW 1940*, 187–98; "The Disinherited Relief Program," *The Social Service Review*, XIII, 1940, 688–93.
[3] Abbott, "The Disinherited Relief Program," 691–2.
[4] C. M. Bookman, "Essentials of an Adequate Relief Program," *NCSW 1940*, 158–76. The letter asserted that "The point of view that relief is in all its ramifications a local problem ignores many of the underlying conditions that make relief today a very different and much more serious problem than it once was" (165).

made while the FERA was still in operation; what followed was not the result of prudent administration but of forced cuts that left many needy people without help. In May 1937 there had been 10,224 on relief (excluding transients); the end of the state relief program made necessary a savage cut to 3,440 in June. The desperate distress of so many families soon demonstrated the inhumanity of this reduction and a restoration of some cuts raised the figure to 6,000 by November, but at the expense of other services.[5]

What happened to the unemployed in Cincinnati who were dropped from the relief rolls? No one knew the precise answer to this question, because records and reporting had ended with the cut in funds; but it was clear that they did not get WPA employment (it too was being cut) and that few got help from private agencies (which had neither the will nor the money to assume once more a burden that had almost broken them in 1931). About a quarter had found private employment, but it was suspected that much of it was casual or part-time. The county could not afford to pursue inquiries, but visits by volunteers to families formerly on relief indicated that about 24,400 were "entirely without resources" and unlikely to find employment. Some "had practically nothing to eat, except occasional surplus products, food supplied by friends or neighbors, and fruit salvaged from garbage at the markets." One family relied mainly on scraps from a nearby restaurant, where the proprietor thought that they were being collected to feed a dog.[6]

The FERA had been criticized (justly, in some instances) for developing a top-heavy administrative structure with too many demands upon field representatives and state relief administrators, but greater responsibility for state and local governments did not make for simplicity. The certification of persons on relief for WPA employment, the investigation of families requiring aid in addition to WPA wages, the decisions on persons who might or might not be eligible for categorical assistance, and the complex problems that arose when employables were not employed all took time. These duties became onerous and emotionally demanding when they meant the transfer of responsibility from one authority to another, with each on the defensive against

---

[5] Ellery F. Reed, "What Turning Relief Back to the Local Community Meant in Cincinnati," *The Social Service Review* XII, 1939, 1–20.
[6] Ibid., 18–19.

accepting more demands on their treasuries. The diligent social worker was caught in a web drawn tight in order to satisfy auditors rather than bring quick relief to those in need, and bureaucratic complexity was to be a lasting legacy of the depression. In 1952 the following complaint was typical:

The worker becomes entangled in processes that must be followed through to satisfy the accounts of comptrollers – securing affidavits when checks go through without recipients' signatures, meeting time limits in presenting claims to insure no reduction in reimbursements. . . . We tend to lose sight of the client and his needs as an individual in the pattern of regulations and requirements surrounding our work.

Much of a social worker's time could be absorbed in arguing a case drawn up not to give the client the best deal but to ensure that the community in which he became destitute got someone else to pay.[7]

On the face of it, state responsibility (with federal aid) for people unable to help themselves (categorical assistance) should have been easy to administer; but in the opinion of one experienced social worker, it had "brought more routine and procedures, more rules and regulations – resulting in either higher administrative costs or less staff for vital social services." The requirement that need must be certified before assistance could be given had generated "so vast a machine for checking and counterchecking that the machine itself expends more than it saves." The old principle – that it was better to spend much time and money than to let one person get away with more than his entitlement – was reasserted, with more people and more agencies interested in the outcome.[8]

Local governments were eager to get their permanent poor into one of the categories for which the state was responsible; state officials, in turn, had to satisfy themselves that the claimant was destitute and suffering from a disability that made him their legal responsibility. Difficulties also arose over the certification of eligibility for WPA employment. Some local officials were suspected of certifying anyone able to walk; and WPA administrators were constantly accused of political discrimination and of favoritism in taking more from one community than another. Finally, clients themselves learned the game, played off

---

[7] Ruth Taylor, "Problems Created by Assistance Categories," 203, *NCSW 1940*, 199–205.
[8] Ibid., 200.

one authority against another, and organized their own pressure groups to maximize their benefits.

There was even difficulty in the interpretation of plain evidence. In 1938 Corrington Gill, representing the WPA, told a Senate committee that they were "giving employment to substantially all qualified employable persons on relief," but many well-informed observers believed that thousands of employables were without work or direct relief. The difference arose over the meaning of "qualified." The WPA rule that no more than one person per family could qualify might leave several able-bodied adults unemployed. An applicant had to be on relief before he could qualify, and might be taken off WPA work if he took additional part-time work. In some parts of the country there was a strong demand for seasonal work, but it might be difficult for a man to get back into WPA employment when the private work ended. In addition, there were often delays of several weeks before a qualified person could be offered suitable work. It was normal practice for the state, county, or local authorities to certify people as employable and place them on a waiting list; the WPA would then send a request for labor (specifying special skills, if required) when work was available. The state WPA administrator would have a rough idea of how many employables there were in a district, but he was not likely to have an accurate picture and would have no information about the number of able-bodied who were not qualified.[9]

State relief agencies, where they remained in operation, might know how many were unemployed and what relief was being given; cities with active departments of public welfare might also know the facts; but the FERA's statistical division no longer collected and assessed nationwide figures. The WPA took up the task of collecting statistics on relief and unemployment, but figures from many local units were no longer as reliable as they had been when accurate record keeping had been one condition for FERA grants.

In 1938 the Senate set up a special committee on unemployment and relief under the chairmanship of Senator J. F. Byrnes. It held lengthy hearings, but within well-defined limits. The Democratic majority clearly understood that their task was to give general endorsement to

[9] 75th Congress, 3rd Sess., Senate Special Committee on Unemployment and Relief, Hearings (cited hereafter as Byrnes Committee). Evidence by Corrington Gill, 51–2. Colonel Brendan Somervell, WPA administrator in New York, said that 103,000 employables in the state were not employed by the WPA.

administration policy and to make the case for continuing the WPA with adequate funds. The critical comments in its report were mainly directed to faulty administration, its negative conclusions rejected proposals for alternative relief policies, and its positive recommendations were confined to general points for future guidance. A number of prominent industrialists were called, but mainly to establish that they had no plans of their own that promised results. The mayors of a number of large cities gave evidence to demonstrate the continued need for a federal works program. Little was heard of rural poverty or of remote mining areas. No social workers were called unless they held official positions in the WPA or in state welfare administrations. The Republican minority wished to hear from known critics of WPA administration, but Byrnes refused to call them. The committee failed to press hard on the claim that every qualified employable person on relief was being found work, despite evidence that the WPA rolls had been severely cut since 1935, while unemployment had risen sharply in 1937.[10]

In a minority report, two Republicans (John J. Davis and Henry Cabot Lodge, Jr.) said:

It is clear that the Federal relief system, like every other human undertaking, is susceptible of being improved. The possibility of favoritism, both as to localities and individuals, the opportunities for waste, the apparent unwillingness to face the problem of destitution among those who cannot get into one of the existing programs, makes it imperative that further inquiry, which will hear constructive criticism from persons of standing, be held.

The criticisms were justified, though vitiated by association with a veiled attack on Roosevelt's criticism of business, a rebuke to Democrats for not considering a tariff for recovery, and a plea to Congress to get on with the job and stop wasting time over Supreme Court packing and the like.[11]

---

[10] Byrnes Committee, Hearings, passim. Comments in *The Social Service Review* XII (1938), 319–23, 555–6, reflecting the views of and probably written by Edith Abbott, were unenthusiastic. The committee devoted "perhaps a disproportionate amount of time to the testimony of industrial leaders" (319). Its "greatest defect" was that it took no account of "those who exist below the margin with no relief at all" (320). "What comes of it all? Did they [the witnesses] come to Washington to bring new facts and new programs and policies before the committee or merely to answer questions more or less perfunctorily and to restate a point of view often expressed and expressed better elsewhere?" (556). The committee was given credit for bringing to light a good deal of information in detail about the operation of the WPA.

[11] Byrnes Committee, Minority Report.

The Byrnes committee, in its aims, tone, and methods, was wholly unlike the LaFollette committees of 1932 and 1933, but its work in setting the seal of approval on federal policy was of great importance. The chairman was a key personality among southern Democrats, and the evidence, though unexciting, was weighty. The majority report specifically rejected proposals for change. It considered the plea that relief would be cheaper and less cumbersome if the federal government confined itself to making grants to the states to use as they wished. It argued that some states would use the bulk of the money for direct relief and concluded that "the adoption of this program would mean the abandonment of work relief." While rejecting decentralization, the committee was equally firm in turning down the idea that the WPA should give relief to employables for whom no work could be found; this would be, in effect, a restoration of the FERA policy, which had been abandoned. The central message of the report was far from optimistic, but it was clear: There was no better policy to meet the difficulties ahead than that already adopted.

In one sentence, the Byrnes report closed the door that social workers would try in vain to reopen in 1940: "The committee cannot agree that the Federal Government should again enter the field of direct relief for the able-bodied unemployed people." In this they had the support of several witnesses. A particularly telling contribution came from Harold M. Burton, Mayor of Cleveland. Though stressing the serious situation in his city and blaming, by implication, the inaction of Ohio, he added:

It is not for the Federal Government, itself, to enter the limitless field of direct relief. If the Federal Government should undertake to enter again into this boundless area, it will destroy rather than create confidence in Federal fiscal policies.

He did not want the federal government to be passive, thought that an expansion of the WPA operations was essential, and hoped that the federal government would make the adoption of statewide relief and welfare programs a condition for categorical aid; but he was clear that direct relief must come from state and local resources.[12]

The committee might have felt that this and similar expressions of opinion would be sufficient to justify their rejection of a return to prin-

---

[12] Ibid., Hearings, 598.

ciples of the FERA, but the view was emphatically reinforced by Harry
Hopkins, who had been unwell and gave his evidence late in the hearing. It was an impressive performance – one of his last major public
utterances before leaving the WPA – and was obviously carefully prepared. Among other striking passages was one in which he said:

> It is my conviction, and one of the strongest convictions that I hold, that the
> Federal Government should never return to a direct relief program. It is
> degrading to the individual, it destroys morale and self-respect; it results in no
> increase in wealth of the community; it tends to destroy the ability of the indi-
> vidual to perform useful work in the future; and it tends to establish a per-
> manent body of dependents. We should do away with direct relief in the
> United States.

The President's dislike of "this relief business" was well known, but
there had been suggestions that Hopkins had followed him reluctantly.
Now, with all of his experience as relief administrator, Hopkins
declared that the abolition of direct relief was the ultimate aim and
that the federal government must set an example by refusing to touch
it.[13]

One reason why there was no enthusiasm in Congress to challenge
the decision to keep out of direct relief was the lack of public concern
with the question. There was, of course, much frustration and a good
deal of argument over the return to high levels of unemployment, but
there was no pressure for further government action. Republican critics wanted less, not more, and most Democrats argued that the right
balance had now been struck. Paradoxically this lack of demand for
change was compatible with the growing realization that a high level
of unemployment would continue for some time to come and might
even be a permanent feature of advanced industrial societies.

There were several reasons why pressure for change was limited to
social workers and a few others with firsthand experience of continuing
poverty. It was widely believed that the WPA had fulfilled its intended
function; hopes had been raised that the new social security laws would
meet long-term problems; it was assumed that categorical assistance
would relieve those who were genuinely unable to help themselves and
that the people on general relief were either short-term unemployed or
the hard core of layabouts, dropouts, tramps, and petty criminals. It
was also true that neither centralized relief, nor the social workers who

[13] Ibid., Hearings, 1348.

administered it, had won many friends during the FERA period. Finally, there was no strong movement among the unemployed themselves to demand better treatment.

It was realized that the WPA was not providing work for all who were fit and wanted it, but even at its low point (around a million and a half on its rolls) it was doing a great deal. Many of its projects were highly visible and (despite carping criticism) popular; but there was always a fear that if the WPA simply set out to make work, there would be more of the legendary leaf-raking projects. Generally it was felt that those who could be usefully employed were being provided for. What was also important was that the WPA had given employment to many of the skilled and most of the white-collar unemployed. The fear that unemployment was creeping up the social ladder had been exorcised and – more to the point – men who had led unemployed councils and organized protests were supporting themselves once more, leaving the dispirited long-term unemployed without leaders. Finally, it was a significant but unmentioned fact that a high proportion of those still in distress were black.[14]

There was also a persistent fear of centralization, which was not confined to conservative Democrats and Republicans. In the eyes of many people, one great merit of federal withdrawal from general relief was that state and local officials were no longer threatened with a cut in federal funds if they failed to do what an official in Washington thought they should do. Even Edith Abbott, who was the last person in the world to object to authoritarian handling of public assistance, had always been critical of the amount of discretion allowed to the federal relief administrator. It was perhaps with the record of Governor Horner's quarrel with Hopkins in mind that she asked "whether the method of an omniscient administrator, who supposedly was able by means of promises and threats to make each state contribute its 'fair share,' was a wise, stable, efficient administrative method." She sug-

---

[14] Relief recipients were analyzed in an article in *Scribner's Magazine* for January 1935. The vast majority were poorly educated, in poor health, had always had low incomes, had often lived in houses unfit for habitation, and belonged to large families with an above average number of young children. The great majority were unskilled urban workers, sharecroppers, farm tenants, and laborers. Of those on relief, 9.5 percent were white and 18 percent black, and among those over sixty-five, the proportion of blacks was much higher. Relief had kept them alive but had made no appreciable improvement in their living standards because there had never been enough money "adequately to provide even the rudimentary requirements of food, clothing, and shelter" (C. Hartley Grattan, "Who Is On Relief?").

gested that the system of discretionary grants, far from being the key
to the success of the FERA, had been "a dismal failure." Need should
not be judged by Washington administrators but by "the harassed case
workers, who saw the destitute families pay the cost when one state got
less and some other state got still less than enough to meet their
needs." Following this line of argument, she joined those who wanted
more federal money, but in the form of statutory grants to the states
based on the number in distress. This did not mean a restoration of
local responsibility but a national commitment to fund the needs as
assessed by efficient state agencies. Less well-informed critics simply
repeated the old slogans that locally elected officials could judge best
what relief was required.[15]

Social workers had usually failed to win the popularity that would
have given them a strong local base. The creation of state and federal
relief agencies had given them an opportunity, which many had seized
with professional enthusiasm and personal dedication, but those who
aim to do good too often end by earning reproach from their enemies
for doing too much and from would-be friends for doing too little.
State and local politicians resented the exercise of power by officials,
often young and often women, who ignored their wishes, condemned
their methods, and questioned their integrity. Among the public at
large, social workers were at best tolerated for meaning well and at
worst resented for being officious.

The end of the FERA meant that the channels of communication
that had linked front-line social work with Washington were broken.
Though most of the headquarters staff of the FERA transferred to the
WPA, and other key men and women became state WPA administrators, they were no longer concerned with direct relief; the national network of social work was rent apart, and the best that a field worker
could hope for was a sympathetic hearing at the state capital. The work
continued, but the political influence, which had gone with it, operated
only within states and often ineffectively once the federal heat was off.

A serious deterrent to further change was the revival of traditional
attitudes and assumptions temporarily submerged by depression and

---

[15] The "dismal failure" occurs in a review by Edith Abbott of E. A. Williams, *Federal
Aid for Relief* [*The Social Service Review* XIII (1939)]. Williams stressed discretionary
grants as a major instrument for implementing FERA policy. He was correct in assessing its importance, but Edith Abbott deplored the arbitrary way in which some decisions on discretionary grants were made.

massive federal aid. Among them was the idea that a principal aim of welfare was to prevent the undeserving from enjoying a life of ease on public money; from which it followed that lengthening the certification procedure, checking and rechecking, and lowering benefits to subsistence levels were marks of merit and signs that the system was doing its job.

For thoughtful people familiar with welfare administration the fundamental error had been to tear apart what should have been a single garment. In evidence given to the Byrnes committee, William Hodson uttered an unheeded plea:

I hope very much that this committee will help the American people to visualize the problem of relief and American social security as a whole. . . . The difficulty so far has been that we have put a microscope on each distinct phase of the problem, and we talk about work relief, or we talk about old age assistance, or we discuss unemployment insurance, but we never at any given moment of time, see the whole problem in all its relationships.

He said that general relief must be linked with unemployment insurance because some workers would not be eligible for benefits, some would have to seek supplementary assistance to support their families, and the time during which others were entitled to benefits would run out. General relief was also linked with work and categorical relief because the same officials certified eligibility for WPA employment, old-age assistance, and mothers' aid. If home relief was weak, the whole welfare edifice stood on shaky foundations.[16]

These criticisms have been repeated and reinforced by most subsequent writers on American welfare. J. Douglas Brown, a Princeton University authority on social insurance who had been part of the team that planned the social security program of 1935, wrote in 1972 that "an effective national system of public assistance is greatly needed to undergird the system of contributory social insurance." The two forms of aid could be compared to the two wheels of a cart:

They can effectively support a load if they are reasonably matched in size and strength. If they are not so matched, the cart lunges to the weak side and the stronger wheel cannot save the cart from disaster.

[16] Byrnes Committee, Hearings, 627.

Public assistance, being an essential part of public welfare, should not be left "to sporadic local concern."[17]

Others agreed that the legislation of 1935 set an unhappy precedent by putting different types of poverty in separate compartments. Forty-three years after the launch of the new policy, Kirsten Grønberg, David Street, and Gerald Suttles wrote in their *Poverty and Social Change* that welfare was "addressed through a mixed bag of programs scattered across various public and private institutions and levels of government." The greatest weakness of welfare organization was an "inability to set clear priorities," which resulted from incoherence.[18]

In 1978 Lester M. Salamon, author of an authoritative survey of welfare in America, reckoned that no fewer than sixty-two separate federal programs provided social insurance and aid to the needy, and that to get the full picture, the variations from state to state (including such vital matters as eligibility and levels of benefit) had to be taken into account. Complexity became still more complex when recipients received benefits under more than one program. Looking back to the "grand design" of the New Deal, Salaman wrote:

The programs that ultimately emerged from this critical period of innovation were thus a far cry from a comprehensive, integrated system of income security. What had started out in the emergency as a broad program of assistance to anyone in need had become a work-enforcing insurance system providing old age and temporary unemployment protection only to those actively attached to the industrial labor force, and a series of unconnected cash assistance provisions offering limited benefits to selected segments of the dependent poor on terms defined by the states.

It may be that there never was a "grand design" outside the pages of *Survey* and the *Social Service Review,* but a "comprehensive, integrated system" might nevertheless have developed from the Federal Emergency Relief Administration.[19]

A federal agency in the 1930s might have lacked the experience to carry out the fine tuning necessary for an efficient national system, but

---

[17] John Douglas Brown, *An American Philosophy of Social Security* (Princeton, N.J., 1972), 61.
[18] Kirsten Grønberg, David Street, and Gerald Suttles, *Poverty and Social Change* (Chicago, 1978), 1, 12.
[19] Lester M. Salaman, *Welfare: The Elusive Consensus* (New York, 1978), 80.

it could have been acquired. By 1977 J. Douglas Brown argued that a wrong turn had been taken and that as a result, public welfare administration had not been ready to take advantage of the managerial skills developed by the nation at war and by very large corporate organizations. He wrote, in words echoing those used by Edith Abbott forty years before, that it had "become clearer and clearer that public assistance in the United States should be nationally administered and nationally financed." The federal government should not be content with giving grants to supplement state efforts but ought to replace state and local programs by "a national system cutting across state borders and serving regions and districts of appropriate size." The constitutional germ for such a system was contained in the general welfare clause, and Brown argued that if segregated education denied the equal protection guaranteed by the Fourteenth Amendment, there must be a similar remedy for inequality in welfare. The constitutional logic may have been dubious but not the proposition that inequality was contrary to natural justice.[20]

When the arguments over relief policy were presented between 1935 and 1940, there was little hope of reversing federal policy, and several welfare administrators made the best of the situation and suggested ways in which professional practice could be made compatible with local responsibility. Some went further and suggested that centralized relief itself had been at fault in expecting growth without local roots.

John F. Hall, formerly of the Washington State Department of Social Security, described measures adopted in his state since the end of federal relief as steps on the way to an efficient welfare system. He said that statewide projects stimulated interest, activity, and experimentation but could not succeed without local cooperation. For this reason, their adoption by counties had been made optional. County boards were appointed by the State from locally submitted lists, but once in office they controlled the county welfare director, who was no longer directly responsible to the state department. County advisory committees were charged primarily with the study of social problems in their local environment and with publicizing the plans they favored. Unofficial bodies – such as a State Conference of Social Work – were better suited for the discussion and promotion of new ideas than a gov-

---

[20] J. Douglas Brown, *Essays on Social Security* (Princeton, N.J., 1977), 87–8.

ernment agency. Experience with this system persuaded Hall that a state agency should formulate policy but not force it upon local units, and that all programs should be flexible enough to permit local variations. He agreed that county commissioners would not respond to general arguments, however persuasive, but maintained that they were effective administrators if given practical advice and concrete proposals. In the long run the most useful function for the state was not to demand compliance, but to train local staff and keep them abreast of new developments.[21]

Harry Greenstein, former State Relief Director in Maryland, urged his fellow professionals to come to terms with local sentiment; they might not like it, but nothing could be accomplished by swimming against the tide. Indeed he thought that federal attempts to impose standards had been counterproductive. "The overwhelming evidence of destitution" had been overlooked in "the traditional reaction against being told what to do," and the best way to advance was to give the impression that the initiative came from local people. Impatient professionals had done more harm than good because, in their hurry to get things done, they had rushed to set up new programs rather than go about the slower process of grafting them onto old institutions. In Maryland the not untypical result was that county welfare officers had to draw upon seventeen different funds with different scales and methods of reimbursement. Good will had been smothered in bureaucracy, leaving little scope for local initiative.[22]

There was plenty of other evidence that improvisation had generated bureaucratic confusion. In the fall of 1934, Lorena Hickok had reported that relief in California was "the damnedest mess . . . a wretchedly inefficient business." In many places the emergency relief and county officials duplicated each other's work, refused to cooperate, and wasted their time with bitter rivalries. In San Francisco she was told that *fifty-four* papers had to be signed before a man could be accepted for a relief project, but a local investigator who had studied the county administration claimed that it was only *nineteen.* In New York the excellent report on unemployment relief, prepared by the Governor's commission, criticized the TERA for placing social work-

[21] John H. Hall, "Community Organization and Public Welfare Agencies on a Statewide Basis," *NCSW 1938,* 443–52.
[22] Harry Greenstsein, "Problems in Accepting Grants in Aid," 278, *NCSW 1936,* 277–283.

ers in positions of authority "for which they were not necessarily suited" when county supervisors would have done better on their own.[23]

The criticisms were justified (though much might be said on the other side), but it did not follow that the proper remedy was to abandon federal relief. The FERA had had only two years to learn from its mistakes; in a decade, it might have accumulated wisdom and improved relations between social workers and elected officials without losing sight of essentials. However, Josephine Brown, a FERA insider and assistant director of the WPA, defended the retreat to local responsibility. In 1938 she urged social workers to respect local opinion and reminded them that "in spite of state control and recent experience with federal super-imposition, the fact remains that these county people have a right to tackle their own problems." This was in marked contrast to what had come from the FERA in its honeymoon period, when the message was that unemployment was not a local but a national problem.[24]

David Adie of New York spoke with great authority as Commissioner of Welfare in a state that had made a resolute attempt to evolve a workable system following the end of the FERA. He urged social workers to come to terms with the situation, and their first task was to improve the image of their profession. Social workers fell foul of public opinion in two ways (which might appear to contradict each other); They were "viewed as excellent people who have little of the practical wrapped up in their natures" or as "haughty, dominating people with a self-assurance and self-conceit that arouses resentment in the mind of the average legislator." The way to work with local people was to offer practical advice but respect their opinions. Social workers must "believe in and assist in building local responsibility for the administration of the public welfare." Adie believed that this was the only way to develop "the social judgment . . . which will translate itself into the fabric of the people whom we serve.[25]

[23] Richard Lowitt and Maurine Beasley, *One Third of a Nation: Lorena Hickok Reports on the Great Depression,* (Urbana, Ill., 1981), 315; Lorena Hickok to A. Williams, August 1934.

[24] Josephine Brown, "The Present Relief Situation in the United States," 432, *NCSW 1936,* 423–38; "Principles, Content, and Objectives of Supervision," 535, *NCSW 1938,* 528–40.

[25] David C. Adie, "The Establishment and Maintenance of Standards of Social Work in Public Service," *NCSW 1938,* 67–82.

This advice may have seemed tame to many gathered at the National Conference of Social Work. Relief administration might lack a sound local base, but weakness in the limbs did not mean that the head ought to be cut off. Many leaders in social work – Edith and Grace Abbott above all – believed that the way forward was to keep up the pressure for a comprehensive system. There was no split in the ranks, but practical administrators who wanted to get on with the job under existing conditions were not disposed to give open support to the theorists who continued to press the case for national responsibility.

Renewed trust in local responsibility might have been easier to accept if local government had shown signs of reform. When Lane Lancaster brought out a 1952 edition of his work on rural local government, he found no reason to revise the severe judgment he had made in 1935:

The molders of local opinion have been, for the most part, ignorant of or indifferent to those social changes that have made "home rule" almost ludicrous – and they have commonly resisted with an almost religious fierceness all attempts to organize political power so as to make it able to cope with social and economic realities.

He added that even when state or county agencies were active, the local people were skilled in resisting their authority and regarded this power to nullify as a cornerstone of local self-government.[26]

The picture might be a little brighter in some of the larger cities, but the perennial conflicts between state and city governments, and between rural and urban voters, stood in the way of constructive change. By 1936 the political revolution first observed in 1928 had turned most large cities into Democratic strongholds, whereas Republicans maintained their hold in the smaller urban places and many rural districts. State legislatures often refused to give more autonomy to city authorities, but where they had done so, home rule itself might become an effective obstacle to reforms proposed by the state government.

It would be wrong to attribute the frustration of state and local government reform to special interests and party managers. The voters could have forced change if a majority of them had wished to do so, but the majority were more likely to be enlisted in the battle to pre-

---

[26] Lane Lancaster, *Government in Rural America*. 2nd ed (Princeton, N.J., 1952), 307.

serve existing arrangements. Conservative legislators were assured of support and scored frequent successes. There were numerous examples of popular revolt against reform.

In 1936 in Wisconsin, a movement to reform local government was not strong enough "to overcome the forces of rural conservatism, political inertia and ignorance, and professional office-holding." A bill to allow the consolidation of local government in Milwaukee was narrowly defeated despite overwhelming support in the city. A bill to make counties rather than townships the units for relief administration was lost, as was an effort to introduce the merit system in Dane County, where Madison, the state capital, was the principal city. The State Supreme Court took a hand by finding an act of 1921, allowing counties to adopt a commission form of government, unconstitutional. The sole survivor of the reform movement was an act allowing the consolidation of counties if approved by referendum.[27]

An amendment to the constitution of Michigan was submitted for ratification by popular vote in 1935. Ostensibly it promoted reform by allowing counties to frame home rule charters, but it did not repeal those parts of the constitution that prescribed the form of county government. A student of Michigan local government commented sadly that if the purpose of the amendment was to defeat its declared aims, it had been drafted in masterly fashion.[28]

A striking tale of frustrated reform came from Ohio. A special commission on county government, headed by Charles P. Taft (from one of the state's most respected families), recommended sweeping reforms, which included a reduction of elective offices and rationalization of executive authority. The bill based on these recommendations passed the state senate by a wide margin but was lost in the lower house, where "rural conservatism was the main cause of defeat." Though county government in the state enjoyed little respect, the rural voters still firmly believed that democratic government was not secure without the election of all local officials.[29]

In Ohio a bold attempt to reform welfare administration survived in the legislature, only to be vetoed by the Governor. In most counties at least seven different agencies provided eight different but overlap-

[27] Lee S. Green, "The Progress of County Government Reform in Wisconsin," *APSR 30* (1936), 96.
[28] Arthur W. Bromage, "Recent Trends in Local Government in Michigan," ibid., 104.
[29] R. C. Atkinson, "County Reorganization in Ohio," ibid., 105–6.

ping forms of relief, and it was proposed to bring them together under single county welfare departments. Governor Martin Davey, sensitive on all relief questions after his public quarrel with Hopkins, vetoed it with a message condemning centralization as a dangerous innovation and asserting that things were much better managed by township trustees than by the social workers who would predominate in a county system.[30]

Local relief commissions or boards, consisting of prominent local citizens, had been a feature of the depression years, and there was some hope that they might continue as guardians of public welfare. They were normally expected to protect relief administration from political interference, maintain continuity when elected officials changed, represent different economic and sectional interests, communicate local wishes to the state agency and state policy to the public, and secure the services of experienced people who were unable or unwilling to give their whole time to the job. The weaknesses of these lay agencies were that they had often been created by executive order rather than statute, that their powers were vaguely defined, and that they could normally do no more than give advice. Active men and women might soon become discouraged by the lack of executive authority, and it was difficult to retain their services once initial enthusiasm had been blunted by failure to achieve results.[31]

Before the onset of the depression, political scientists had filled their journals with proposals for enabling local governments to handle more effectively the mass of business demanded by a modern society. The prevalent themes had been the elimination of useless elective posts, clearly defined responsibility, and concentration of authority under democratic control. These efforts were in direct descent from Progressive attempts to improve efficiency and curb corruption by bringing home to the voters exactly what they were voting for. By 1930 reformers had permitted themselves a mild degree of optimism about the future, and were encouraged by reports from all parts of the country of official investigations and, in some instances, of specific proposals.

[30] Ibid., 107–9. The failure of this particular bill was the result of a veto, but "the plain fact is that rural opinion in Ohio is sincerely fearful of centralized administration whatever its form and still firmly believes that popular government requires the election of all administrative officials" (107).

[31] R. Clyde White, *Public Welfare Board and Committee Relationship* (Chicago, 1937).

With a few exceptions, the depression brought this movement to a halt and it never recovered its momentum.

There were many reasons for the abortion of institutional reform in local government, but among them was the vote of confidence in local responsibility when the federal government withdrew from general relief. In addition to removing federal pressure, it permitted several states to dismantle their relief agencies and end the informed criticism of local methods that had occupied so much space in their reports and circulars. Institutional change was put into cold storage, and even the unsound fiscal foundations of local government escaped change.

A favorite target for the reformers had been the huge number of small units and the multiplication of special districts. They had hoped for rational consolidation to provide governments strong enough to handle the problems of modern society, but after twenty years of depression, national mobilization, and postwar consolidation, the situation was little altered.

In the first half of the twentieth century the total number of units and their geographical boundaries changed little. The only result of all the talk about consolidating small counties was the amalgamation of two in Texas and three in Georgia. There were examples of consolidation where a metropolitan authority had been created for a county and its major city, but other administrative reforms had been stalled. No more than sixteen counties in eight states had adopted county manager plans, though a few more had set up single executives. There were examples of shorter ballots, a reduced number of elective officials, and the amalgamation or abolition of old offices, but the overall picture was disappointing. Outside the large cities, there was little incentive for people to make a career in local government. Ninety percent of the counties had no merit system for appointments, and New York was the only state in which it was mandatory. County boards remained excessively large in states where every township was entitled to a member, and too many elected officials were exempt from the authority of the county commissioners. Budgeting and auditing were still rudimentary in a very large number of counties.[32]

What had happened was not a temporary setback but the crystallization of institutions in forms that had won little support from social scientists or, indeed, from anyone who took an active interest in

---

[32] Clyde F. Snider, "American County Government: A Mid-Century Review," *APSR* XLVI (1952), 66–80.

improving the conditions of life. After 1950 there was a fall in the total number of local government units, but this was almost entirely due to the consolidation of school districts. In 1962 the Bureau of the Census counted no fewer than 91,236 units of local government, which included 3,043 counties, 17,997 municipalities, 17,144 towns and townships, 34,678 school districts, and 18,323 special districts. In 1977 another count – with slightly different criteria – recorded a further fall in the number of school districts but a decided increase in the number of special districts. It was significant that rationalization had occurred where the public was most interested in the result – better schools, especially better high schools – whereas welfare was left immersed in the complexity of traditional local government. The increase in the number of special districts followed the old precept that it was easier to create a new unit to do a new job than to persuade existing governments to cooperate.[33]

So far, the balance sheet is heavy on the debit side. In most parts of the country there had been a sharp decline in relief standards, and even those who were fortunate enough to obtain WPA work might not get enough cash to support their families. The rapid development of the FERA had generated a large central bureaucracy, but the breakup of the federal relief system brought no significant improvement. Relief administration could be tied up in knots as officials struggled to apply varying and inconsistent procedures for general relief, categorical relief, and certification of eligibility for the WPA. The familiar problems of settlement did not go away but grew, with more migrants in search of work, more casual laborers reduced to destitution, and no more federal aid for transient programs.

The methods and standards imposed by the FERA had not won acceptance as part of the normal apparatus of social life; social workers remained a group apart, and, if the state ceased to make their employment mandatory, few local authorities would insist upon their retention. Above all there was no FERA, no federal Department of Welfare, to fight the social workers' battle at the highest level.

Under these circumstances prophets of doom can be understood, but the nation cannot go through such an experience without putting something on the credit side. Americans had always been adept at add-

---

[33] Russell W. Maddox and Robert F. Fuquay, *State and Local Government*, 2nd ed. (Princeton, N.J., 1966).

ing new functions to government without making constitutional changes. Experts criticized state governments, found legislatures inefficient, and saw local government as a poor foundation for modern democracy, but the 1930s saw states tackling new tasks with old tools, and there was an impressive increase in government activity. In 1927 the total expenditure by the states was $1,452,000; in 1940 it was $3,555,000. Expenditure by local governments increased from $1,541,000 to $2,263,000. By 1956 V. O. Key, the leading authority on state government, observed that the change since 1930 had been so great "as to be one of kind rather then of degree."[34]

Enough has been said of welfare policy to show the extent to which the satisfaction of present needs had been hampered by past assumptions, but it had nevertheless played a leading part in the growth of government. In the 1920s the total expenditure on welfare by state and local governments never exceeded $100,000,000 a year; between 1932 and 1940 the combined total grew tenfold, adding $453,000,000 and $548,000,000, respectively. In 1932 public welfare accounted for 3.55 percent of state and 18.2 percent of local expenditure; in 1940 the percentages were 14.8 and 27.8. The huge demand for unemployment relief may have starved some other items, but state expenditure on public health (closely linked with welfare) rose by $85,000,000 and local expenditure by $52,000,000. Welfare and health also outstripped all other items in their rate of growth. Education and highways had been favored in the previous decade, but in the 1930s expenditure for education increased modestly and that for highways fell.[35]

In local government, a feature of the times (outside New England) was the parallel growth of county functions and state direction. In 1952 it was claimed that in education, highways, welfare, and finance, state supervision touched "almost every phase of county activity." The danger was not that the counties would retreat but that their dual role – as agents of the state and as institutions representing local opinion – would cause misunderstanding. "The time has come," wrote Lane Lancaster in 1957, "to recognize the fact that the vast majority . . . of rural counties cannot continue to lead a double life."[36]

[34] The figures in this and the following paragraph are extracted from *Historical Statistics of the United States,* (Washington, D.C., 1976). Extracted from Series Y, 682–709; V. O. Key, *American State Politics* (New York, 1956), 8.
[35] *Historical Statistics of the United States,* Series Y.
[36] Snider, "American County Government," 70; Lancaster, *Government in Rural America,* 61.

Lancaster was bothered by the ambivalence of county administration, but he also emphasized the changed nature of local government. It no longer enjoyed its former autonomy but had become part of "a federal–state–local system of financing and administering most of the traditional local functions." It did not follow that local government had been weakened; on the contrary, state and federal aid in welfare and public health had "put new life into units long considered moribund" and brought many local governments, for the first time in their history, into contact with modern standards and modern methods of public administration.[37]

Together with this evidence of greatly increased public concern for private misfortune were examples of constructive efforts to provide a new framework for the future. The examples of Pennsylvania, Virginia, and New York have already been noted, but steps taken in other states also indicated major changes in welfare policy. In 1947 the Illinois Public Aid Commission carried out a survey of the way public assistance was handled in other states. It found that in thirty-six states, covering nearly three-quarters of the people in the United States, public assistance was administered by separate agencies concerned exclusively with welfare; in the other twelve, public assistance was combined with the function traditionally associated with "charities and correction," though in Maine and Missouri public assistance and health had been brought together. The existence of a state agency did not necessarily mean that relief was supervised, and in fifteen states it was administered by local welfare officers either without supervision or supervised only for specific functions for which state funds were available; but in twenty-three states it was supervised by state agencies, and in ten others it might be delegated to county or local welfare officers with conditions prescribed by the State. If change since 1930 had been jerky, spasmodic, and incomplete, it was nevertheless real.[38]

In this as in other matters, New York not only led the way but also advanced to new concepts of public responsibility. The creation of a new welfare system to replace the TERA has been described, but there were concurrent moves for constitutional reform in which local gov-

---

[37] Lancaster, *Government in Rural America*, 158–9.
[38] Illinois Public Aid Commission, *Patterns of State Social Welfare Administration* (Springfield, Ill., 1947).

ernment and the duty to relieve distress played their part. A constitutional convention was called for 1938, and its agenda was prepared by reports from a state commission for the revision of tax laws and from special committees of the convention.

The Sixth Report of the commission, presented in 1935, dealt with local government. In a key passage it asserted:

[The constitution and statutes] prescribe a pattern of local government so contrary to elementary principles of human organization that it is difficult if not impossible for the administration of public affairs to be carried on with efficiency. Every canon of political science that history and experience in public administration has taught us in the last hundred years, and that is now recognized as fundamental in our high schools, colleges, and universities . . . is violated by the organization and form of government in the state of New York.

Local government, as it existed, was nothing more than "the product of a patchwork on a garment" woven in 1683.[39]

The Constitutional Convention published its report on state and local government in 1938 and, amid a great deal of factual material, pointed out that relief during the depression had broken away from earlier practice and "in a new and tremendously magnified fashion the Federal government came into contact with the State and its localities." In addition to grants for relief the State had gained by new roads, bridges, public buildings, and cultural projects. Rather than claim that all this expenditure had been wasted, the report suggested – the logical conclusion – that in earlier days the public authorities had not spent enough on the amenities of civilized life.

The federal government had provided most of the money for these improvements, but direct relief had also imposed unprecedented burdens on local governments. Relief costs had increased tremendously – in the cities by over 1,000 percent since 1928 – and in 1935 accounted for 34 percent of city budgets. Expenditure on this massive scale clearly demanded greater planning and control than the existing system allowed; and if the State wished to continue public works, it must

[39] New York State Commission for the Revision of the Tax Laws, *Sixth Report. Reorganization of Local Government in New York State* (Albany, 1935), 14. A number of very able reports were produced in New York in 1936–8: Legislative Documents, 159th Session (1936), Document No. 56; *Report of the Governor's Commission on State and Local Welfare Organization;* Legislative Document (1936) No. 52. *Summary Report on State and Local Welfare Organization;* Legislative Document No. 7 (1938); *Report of the Committee on Social Welfare* (and see notes 40, 41, and 42, this chapter).

make its own plans rather than rely on a federal agency with an uncertain future.[40]

The cities in New York had powers that were not clearly defined, and the passage of a home rule amendment in 1935 had made matters worse by setting the stage for "a battle between the police powers of the State and the home rule powers of the city." The judges had not helped by narrowing the interpretation of city powers while leaving an area in which the validity of local ordinances depended on the way in which individual judges viewed their relationship to health, safety, or morals. To resolve these difficulties, many cities had taken advantage of the "emergencies" to press the legislature for special acts legalizing specific actions. Of the thousand or more laws affecting the cities passed since 1924, no more than a dozen were justified by real emergencies; most of them dealt with bond issues, municipal credit, and minor charter amendments.[41]

A convention committee on social welfare worked on assumptions that might be commonplace among social scientists but marked a departure from former theory and practice. It declared that the basic principles for welfare policy were that relief for people in need was a state responsibility; that a constitution should be framed to allow protection against the hazards of unemployment, illness, and old age; and that "the promotion of public health is a primary responsibility of government."[42]

The new constitution, approved in 1938, embodied these principles. A new article stated:

The aid, care, and support of the needy are public concerns and shall be provided for by the State and by such of its subdivisions and in such manner and by such means, as the legislature may from time to time determine.

A clause in the old constitution, defining the power to tax and borrow, was amended by inserting a proviso that nothing in the constitution should "prevent any city or town from making . . . provision for the aid, care, and support of the needy." Looking beyond relief to causes

[40] New York Constitutional Convention Committee, *State and Local Government in New York* (Albany, 1938), 430.
[41] New York Constitutional Convention, *Report of the Committee on Problems Relating to Home Rule and Local Government* (Albany, 1938).
[42] New York Constitutional Convention, Document No 7: *Report of the Committee on Social Welfare* (Albany, 1938).

of distress, an entirely new article gave the legislature power to provide "low rent housing for persons of low income . . . or for the clearance, replanning, and rehabilitation of substandard and insanitary areas . . . and for recreational and other facilities incidental or appurtenant thereto." [43]

Thus New York wrote into its constitution a new concept of public responsibility for welfare and swept away restraints on actions intended to relieve the distress, safeguard the health, and improve the quality of life of the poorest people in society. The arguments advanced by the committees and accepted by the convention went far toward establishing a philosophic and legal foundation for the welfare state, but most other states failed to adopt such specific commitments and left the extent of public responsibility clouded by uncertainty.

A philosophy for political action must be concerned with legitimacy, aims, use, checks, and instruments of government. It is normally the product of slow growth, with inherited ideas, group interests, practical needs, and changing moral perceptions as its ingredients; but shifts can be accelerated in great crises when conventional beliefs are suddenly seen as obsolete and new ideas are eagerly grasped. The Great Depression was such a crisis and created the conditions for a revolution in social philosophy, but by the end of the 1930s it had gone less than halfway. When economic disaster threatened not only the unskilled and low-paid but also business and professional men, intellectuals and creative artists, clerical and skilled workers, there was an instinctive move toward the idea of an organic society in which the weakness of some inflicted injury upon all. Ruin on the doorstep was a powerful argument for collective action and, for a time, a large majority was prepared to see the relief of distress as a national obligation.

The implications of this new ideology were not assimilated into popular culture or even into the thinking of many intellectuals whose function it was to explore the frontiers of social thought. An easier choice was to agree that national responsibility was fulfilled by finding work for a minority of those who were destitute, assisting the states to care for certain categories of disabled people, and providing a legal framework for social insurance financed by potential beneficiaries and their employers. The mix of national, state, and local responsibility drew

[43] Constitution of the State of New York, Articles VIII, XVII.

upon a jumble of theories rather than a coherent social philosophy. The relegation of general relief to the states (and, in most states, to the localities) rejected the idea that there was a national obligation to meet the social consequences of national economic failure, and evidence of continuing and desperate poverty was countered by the old belief that most paupers owed their misfortune to defects in character and could be justly treated according to the stringent principles of the old poor law.

A generation later, three social scientists, studying the problems associated with poverty, observed that "the United States lacks a comprehensive theory of welfare and shows a strong resistance to developing one." Slogans of earlier years were still substituted for argument, and well-intentioned efforts to understand the poor ended by treating them as a caste apart:

Alternative ideologies necessary to justify proposals for the welfare state may still be called "un-American," "socialist," or even "communist".... Most importantly the old ideology – even with new terminology – provides a set of ready stereotypes. If no longer characterized as willful failures, the poor are now seen, for example, as creatures of a "culture of poverty" under which it is assumed that they have been taught to be satisfied with being poor.[44]

Some of the men and women closely associated with relief policy attempted to construct a new philosophy of welfare based not on a public obligation to remedy social ills but on an individual's right to work. Though it developed from some traditional ideas about man's duty to labor, the right-to-work philosophy could have radical consequences. Though it was hardly seen in this light, an analysis of the evils of the times given by Harry Hopkins to the Byrnes committee was revolutionary in its implications.[45]

Hodson had asked for an integrated relief program with general relief as its foundation, but Hopkins saw the unhappy paradox of poverty in a rich nation as the heart of the matter. "Of the problems facing the American people at the present time ... the problems of destitution, low incomes, and unemployment are foremost." Poverty meant simply that the national income was not large enough to give one-third of the people a decent standard of living and that the shortfall was made worse by the inequitable distribution of wealth. Was it not pos-

[44] Grønberg et al., *Poverty and Social Change*, 6.
[45] Byrnes Committee, Hearings, 1339ff.

sible to explain economic failure by the waste of skill and labor when so many lived in unsought idleness? In a new version of the frontier thesis, Hopkins said that undeveloped land and its settlement had been the challenge in the past, but poverty and underachievement formed the new wilderness of modern times. The old frontier had called for individual initiative, but the new frontier of "idle men, money, and machines" demanded "tremendous organization of productive forces such as only government can supply when business is in the doldrums." Individualism must yield to collective action on an unprecedented scale.

Having advanced so far toward a theory of public responsibility, Hopkins shifted ground to argue that dynamic action could be justified by the traditional belief that governments were instituted among men to secure rights. To life, liberty, and the pursuit of happiness must now be added the right to work, not as an abstract theory but as a dynamic principle for the well-being of society as a whole. Hopkins believed that great productive forces would be released once the able-bodied unemployed were "entitled to a job as a matter of right." Providing work would become a priority for government before which other considerations must give way. It must be real work at a living wage, not token work and low wages, and the trade unions should be seen as the allies of government in keeping up standards, preventing underconsumption, and sheltering labor from the damage inflicted by falling markets.

This remarkable statement contained four major propositions: unemployment weakened the whole society, not only those without work; the cure for the disease was recognition of the right to work; it was the duty of government to protect this right; and high wages would flatten out business cycles. The important consideration here was not the debatable economic theory but the new vista of federal responsibility: When employers failed to provide enough work, the people as taxpayers must step in to do the job. Public works might be one way of doing it, but what of grants to keep unprofitable businesses afloat? Should an employer with ample reserves be penalized for discharging workers when business was slack or prosecuted for depriving people of work without due process of law?

On a later occasion, Aubrey Williams took up a similar theme when he declared that the right to work was not "visionary social idealism" but simple economic realism and "the quickest and cheapest way to attain full economic recovery." In 1940, in a public lecture, he condemned the "false and archaic concept of work which still exists in our modern world." Work should not, he said, be regarded as "a necessary evil whereby man keeps himself alive" but as an essential component of human personality; and since the essence of democracy was recognition of the intrinsic value of the individual, the right to work should be accepted as part of the national philosophy.[46]

Realizing that this doctrine required some fundamental changes in popular attitudes, Williams went on to stress the role of education in training the young for the world they were about to enter. They must be taught to live in the world of work, machines, and science; of economic organization that was marvelous in its complexity but "appalling in the discrepancy between potential abundance and actual poverty"; and of "social organization whereby citizens living in a high degree of mutual interdependence solve their common problems and provide for their common welfare."

As a short-term program, there was much to be said for the WPA. It gave a small but significant number of talented people an opportunity denied by the economic climate. It restored the morale of a very large number of unskilled and less skilled people; left an abiding legacy in creative arts, entertainment, and scholarship, and, as visible memorials, public buildings, recreational facilities, better roads, and hundreds of environmental improvements. As a long-term remedy for economic dislocation its benefits were more doubtful, and as the basis for a new social philosophy it was flawed by unsystematic thinking.

The philosophy of the right to work could be criticized as being no more than a restatement of the work ethic. It was the individual's function to work, and if private business was unable to provide employment, it was the duty of government to do so. Though WPA administrators often criticized business behavior, it could be argued that their function was to keep the labor force occupied and content until industry was ready to take up the slack. The right to work did not imply a right to refuse work.

It was never clear whether the WPA was providing relief or employment. Nor was it clear whether the priority should be to put men to

---

[46] Aubrey Williams, *Work, Wages, and Education,* Inglis Lecture, Harvard University (Cambridge, Mass., 1940), 12.

work, undertake socially useful projects, submit to normal tests of economic viability, or treat losses as contributions by government to the public good. These were not abstract speculations; they affected the appraisal of every project and fostered misunderstanding when different criteria were adopted by the WPA and by the local community or by different branches of the WPA administration. The dilemmas are illustrated in an exchange between the WPA officials in Washington and Chicago. A project had been criticized by the central administration for its high cost and lack of results. The local administrator, R. W. Wright, protested that material success was surely a secondary consideration and that the moral duty to provide work should be paramount:

> When private business, through monopolistic trends, speculative and unwholesome practices, has failed in its duty to provide employment to those who have been an integral part thereof; and when the mistakes of those at the head of such business have been so gross as to require a long period of reorganization and reconstruction along the paths of equitable progression, then the duty of Government is to foster and protect those who suffer until they can be again absorbed in business and rehabilitated.

Why, he asked, should the project be criticized when it employed 1,800 men without other means of support?[47]

Hopkins and Aubrey Williams were on the side of the angels (as well as being prudent social engineers) when they insisted that it was in the public interest to deal fairly and equitably with the millions who were destitute, that a sound relief policy was not charity but commonsense, and that everyone was injured when some were allowed to rot. Thanks to the experience of federal relief there was wider assent to these propositions than ever before; but the theory behind them was not widely understood. The right to work philosophy was a distraction, and when specific issues had to be faced the public at large and their political representatives often fell back on conventional assumptions and familiar methods of dealing with poverty. This was the reality which welfare administrators had to face when they sought for change. The popular majority was at best apathetic, one political party was normally opposed, conservative elements in the other were inclined to obstruct, and legislators showed reluctance when faced with measures that won them no votes.

---

[47] NA RG 69 610. Copy in WPA files dated 4 Nov. 1935.

The Federal Emergency Relief Administration had made it possible to put direct pressure on the representatives of the people. It was federal power wielded with the express purpose of making legislators do what they did not wish to do. The modest success it achieved had raised hopes among social workers that not only local responsibility but also state legislative supremacy would be subordinated to federal law administered by a permanent, national, and professional agency. Experts would prevail over elected amateurs, and the old poor law would be consigned to the dust heap of history.

With the end of the FERA, state welfare administrators knew only too well how many cards were stacked against them. Local governments had manifestly failed to care for their own, and relief administrators had often found their work impeded by the county commissioners, township trustees, or other elected officials. The members of state relief agencies had been constantly hampered by the refusal of most legislatures (including those in some of the wealthiest states) to vote the money for adequate relief. The best hope might lie in finding a governor who was sympathetic and energetic, but too many had been obstructive and opposed in principle to centralized welfare administration, and the least sympathetic had usually enjoyed majority support among the voters. It was sad but true that in normal times the people who wished to improve the condition of the poor had to swim against the tide of democracy.

A less defeatist view was that welfare reformers were in no worse a position than other reformers or, indeed, corporations, trade unions, and other special interests wanting benefits that the majority might not wish to give. Social reformers, like other minority groups, had to learn the political game and cultivate the art of lobbying.

In 1936 the Social Work Publicity Council of New York thought it worthwhile to publish a pamphlet called *Lobbying for Social Legislation* which explained what had to be done. There were preliminaries before the legislative battle began. Experienced lobbyists advised that a complete bill should first be drafted, and many states had legislative drafting bureaus to advise and assist. Contact should be established with legislators, preferably at their homes, prominent persons should be persuaded to endorse the bill, and newspaper support should be sought.[48]

---

[48] Social Work Publicity Council of New York, *Lobbying for Social Legislation* (New York, 1936).

It was important to select the right legislator to introduce the bill; he should be popular, preferably of the majority party, and, if possible, a member of the committee to which the bill was likely to be referred. It would be necessary to keep in close touch with majority and minority leaders and committee chairmen (some committees hardly ever met and all the business was transacted by the chairmen). It was also wise to get on friendly terms with "the army of assistants who made up the legislative machine."

The next piece of advice was never to request a public hearing if there was any chance of passing the bill without one. If a hearing was held, it was important to stimulate a flood of letters favoring the measure, especially if there was a danger that it would be killed in committee or drowned in the flood of reported bills. Finally, it was wise to remember that though legislators would not expect to win overt support in their election campaigns as a reward for help with a measure, they would like to get some political capital out of it. The prospect of winning the good will of influential people might persuade some, and others might want a tradeoff against measures in which they were especially interested. A legislator who was nervous about the public response might ask the lobbyist to stir up interest in his community "so that he may vote for it without jeopardizing his position with his constituents."

Except in the earliest stages – when broad support was being cultivated – there was little place in this strategy for appeals to the public interest or to compassion for those in distress. Indeed, social legislation usually benefitted minorities (and often very small minorities), and success often depended upon avoiding too much popular debate. This advice did not apply when the proposed beneficiaries belonged to a group that readily aroused public sympathy, such as the blind, widows with dependent children, orphans, or persons suffering from an ailment (such as tuberculosis) that threatened everyone. These were exceptions, and what was normally required was manipulation of democratic processes not an appeal to the public.

The most promising developments occurred in some of the larger cities with good departments of public welfare, trained staff, and professional services. They were handicapped by the fragmentation of political authority in many metropolitan areas and by fiscal restraints preventing them from taxing much of the wealth created within their limits; or, where the tax net had been spread more widely, by resistance in the suburbs to paying for relief in the inner city. The cities with the most modern welfare systems and the highest proportion of trained personnel often presented the most striking contrast between what was ideal and what was possible.

The end of the FERA brought on a relief crisis in Chicago, but its immediate cause was the refusal of the state legislature to make sensible arrangements for relief. Other cities were not driven to suspend relief, but in many the welfare services were stretched to the limit. They did as well as could be expected, but their difficulties were increased by the failure to enforce uniform standards across the nation. Under any circumstances, refugees from rural poverty would have sought a better life in the cities, but this migration was encouraged by the relatively high standards of public assistance in the cities compared with the very low levels of relief in many rural regions, especially in the South. Thus the abandonment of nationwide standards helped to create conditions in inner cities that would plague the future.

One reason why well-organized cities and populous counties were able to provide better than average welfare services was their attraction for trained social workers. In states where relief went back to the localities without state supervision, many social workers found that there was no further use for their services, and even in county departments of welfare their future was precarious except where state law made their employment mandatory. There were therefore strong incentives to look for posts with state or city agencies where tenure was more secure and promotions were based on merit. The unplanned consequence was to emphasize the difference between areas with professional staffs, sheltered to some extent from political pressures, and those in which appointments were made locally, no special qualifications were required, and welfare posts were drawn into the patronage net.

The depression had many other consequences for social workers. At the outset, many of them were trained to investigate cases and to treat relief as a means by which individuals could be helped to adjust themselves to society; circumstances forced them to change course and think of relief as a way of enabling people to live decent lives in a society out of gear. Even more important, for the way in which social workers looked at their task, was that many emerged as persons of consequence with their services eagerly sought by government at all levels. Even before the dimensions of the task were fully understood, many of them were given authority to supervise relief administration, allocate large sums of money, and compile reports, which had a direct influence on future policy.

The new opportunities were offered in public rather than private welfare. The federal program had brought public agencies to the center of the stage and relegated private charities to the wings. There was a straightforward brain drain when many of the people who had played a leading part in directing community chests and other large private organizations joined the FERA or state relief administrations. In these posts, they exercised an influence and enjoyed a status superior even to that of executives in prestigious private charities. The end of the FERA forced some, such as Harry Greenstein in Maryland, back into private work, but the experience of running a relief agency in a state or county remained as a major influence upon their thinking about welfare problems. The altered balance between public and private welfare is evident from the proceedings of the National Conferences of Social Work. In the 1920s and early depression years, most leading speakers were directors of community chests or of large private charities, but by 1936 they were welfare officers in states or large cities or connected with the WPA. In the rising generation, talented and ambitious social workers were likely to prefer public to private employment; their influence would be greater and career prospects brighter. Not every social worker could be a Harry Hopkins – rising within a decade from obscurity to become the President's trusted adviser – but anyone with talent might hope to become a state or county director. Private agencies could not offer similar opportunities.

The prestige won by people at the head of social work had its effect upon the status of the rank-and-file. They were no longer supernumeries in society, performing tasks that might be humane but not essential, but people whose employment was required by law. Except in the minority of states that had reverted wholly to predepression practice, social work had become accepted as part of the normal machinery of government. There were reservations. Even if their function was recognized as socially useful, they were not on a par with physicians, ministers of religion, lawyers, or college professors. On the social map they might be found somewhere between high school teachers and post office clerks. Most of the people in higher positions had been selected early in their careers, and the ceiling for a social worker who spent years in the field was still low. In addition, most of the rank-and-file workers were women, but a majority of the executive posts were held by men.

Qualifications about the position and prospects of social workers do not deny the great gains they had made. The FERA period helped them to find their professional feet, learn from mistakes, and improve their status. Local failure to respect social work came to be seen as a sign of backwardness, not as a natural response to people who interfered with others' private lives. Their conferences and periodicals came to concentrate more and more on broad issues of policy rather than details of case study. A new confidence worked its way back to the schools of social work and molded the views of the rising generation.

Even among nonprofessional welfare officials – overseers of the poor and the like – the clock could not be turned completely back. It was no longer possible to maintain that the job consisted of no more than keeping paupers out and issuing grocery orders to those who had settlement. If they did little else that was new, they had to classify people in distress, divide them into employables and unemployables, and certify eligibility of the former for WPA employment and of the latter for institutional care, categorical assistance, or general relief. Since these classifications would be checked by superior authorities, the local government officer could not afford to be careless or perverse. Mass unemployment had discredited the idea that destitute people were normally responsible for their own misfortunes, and with it went the belief that the same kind of treatment should be handed out to all poor people. If agonized social workers deplored the opportunities missed in 1935, the world had moved, at least a little, in their direction.

Turning from welfare administration to general perceptions of the government's duty to remedy social ills, there are imponderables that cannot be easily assessed. At some point between 1930 and 1950, the American people crossed a watershed in their attitude toward federal responsibility, and it is generally accepted that the New Deal, limited as it was in some respects, was a decisive force in carrying them over. In this transformation, federal relief played a crucial part by insisting upon public responsibility for people to whom society had failed to give a living wage.

Some measure of the change can be obtained by speculating on what intelligent men in the past could not predict because it lay beyond the horizon of possibility. The contributors to *Recent Social Trends,* with which this book began, were certainly intelligent and abreast of the most adventurous thought in their fields. Their work was not published until early in 1933, but most of the chapters must have been in proof a year earlier and were based on data collected in 1929 and 1930. Some brief postscripts referred to the impact of the depression, but its consequences were still hidden in the future. What the contributors said was therefore a reflection of the most advanced thinking around 1930, and what they did not say gives a clue to the great strides taken during the next decade.

The chapters on government, public administration, and social policy showed greater awareness of living in a changing world than those on economics. The latter were mainly descriptive, dominated by classical models, and refused to speculate; the former could see movement, expected it to continue, and invited readers to look ahead. It was possible to anticipate expansion in government regulatory functions because this was in line with everything that had happened since 1890. The highway program had shown what could be done with federal aid, and Prohibition (whatever its merits) had shown how far private inclinations could be forced to yield to public authority. The plight of the farmers made it conceivable that the federal government would be forced to support agriculture. Much of what went into the New Deal was therefore predictable from a study of recent trends; what was not anticipated was the speed and scope of change.

By contrast, federal relief was unpredictable because there were no precedents, no observable trends, and nothing to suggest the form it would take. When *Recent Social Trends* was published, the first Federal Emergency Relief Act had been six months on the statute book; but the contributors probably saw it as temporary and exceptional, and none thought it necessary to revise their chapters in the light of events. The FERA, with its central organization, nationwide scope, coercive power, and far-reaching consequences, could not be foreseen.

Other aspects of welfare policy were a shade more predictable. Federal public works had a long history, and proposals had already been made that they should be stepped up in order to absorb unemployment; a federal program of public works was therefore within the range of possibility if the depression continued, but the furthest flights of imagination could not take in anything of the size and style of the WPA. There had been a good deal of discussion about social insurance, especially in the light of British and European experience, but resistance in America had been so strong that no one could predict that a national system of social security would be launched in 1935. The most that social insurance enthusiasts could hope for was that within a decade of some of the more progressive states would develop old-age insurance (from existing old-age assistance laws) and that others besides Wisconsin would experiment with unemployment insurance. What could not be predicted in 1930 was that five years later the federal government would introduce social security and make regular grants to the states for categorical assistance.

These reflections upon the limits of intelligent anticipation lead to the conclusion that in welfare the New Deal introduced a new order. In 1932, when federal relief came to the top of the political agenda, the argument that first prevailed was that it should not begin; in 1935 the most articulate criticism – not confined to social workers – was that it was being brought to an untimely end. There were numerous letters to the White House deploring the end of federal relief, formal requests by governors for its continuation, and many local protests. This opposition was in vain, but it shows how far opinion had moved. The wall between federal and local responsibility had been breached, and could never again be rebuilt.

This book ends with the abandonment of an experiment that had excited professionals and inspired hopes for a national welfare system. It ends also with the survival of forms of local government that social scientists had judged to be incapable of meeting modern social needs. It has been a case study of the way in which a small group aiming to do good achieved remarkable results in a short time; but also a study of opposition, obstruction, and misunderstanding on the part of elected governors, legislators, and local officials. It therefore raises questions that are abstract but of perennial importance for all societies in which governments derive their just powers from the consent of the governed.

It would be hard to deny the proposition that most significant improvements in the human condition have been initiated by small minorities commanding little popular esteem. In America this was the history of abolitionism, temperance, women's suffrage, humane treatment of the insane, improvements in public health, and late-nineteenth-century efforts to modernize "charities and correction." In the twentieth century the improvement of the condition of the very poor has never commanded mass support, and the poor have done little constructive work to help themselves. Improvement has been achieved by small groups of dedicated people who are often dismissed as do-gooders, elitists, or social engineers acting for the ruling class.

If reform groups lack popular support, at least in the early stage of their movement, their friends in the establishment are also few. The hold on the American intellect of the verities of classical economics, the fatalism of social Darwinism, and the model of a self-regulating society are well understood, but it is sometimes assumed that these attitudes were weakened beyond recovery during the ferment of Progressivism. They had indeed less appeal for young intellectuals, but the men who dominated public and professional life in the third and fourth decades of the twentieth century had been young in 1900, and for many of them, the heart of social wisdom was still William Graham Sumner's ominous question "What do the social classes owe to each other?" and his still more ominous answer – "Nothing."

Charity (properly organized) was a Christian duty, and a vocation to serve others was admirable provided that it did not distort the natural machinery of society; but the good citizen should not be expected to sacrifice liberty (or pay unreasonable taxes) in order to help those who had failed to help themselves. Not until the depression broke were these principles seriously shaken; and even then, many influential people continued to see them as beacons to guide the nation out of stormy seas. Evidence of the survival of these ideas is found in frequent references to "blood letting" as a means of restoring society's well-being, even though it might be difficult to find a physician who still believed that a patient's chance of survival was improved by copious loss of blood.

Reformers who were interested in welfare had learned to live in this climate, and their approach was molded by it. The schools of social work emphasized readjustment of the maladjusted as a reply to the claim that society would be healthier if the natural process of deprivation and disease were allowed to eliminate the obviously unfit. The social work case was that skilled help would restore to the labor market many of those who had failed to support themselves and that society could be strengthened by limiting the damage done by disease or indigent old age. Sickly or delinquent children could also be saved and turned into self-respecting citizens. There were also gains to be made by emphasizing the environmental causes of extreme poverty and the damage this did to a community. Even the prominent citizens most hostile to welfare could see the need for change when a visitor had to pass through urban squalor on his way downtown.

Pressing on these and other sensitive nerves, welfare reformers had won some notable victories in the states, the most recent being mothers' aid and the beginning of old-age assistance. Organized private charity had taken great steps forward with the rise of community chests in the larger cities. An important consequence for the future was that a small but lively nucleus of professional welfare administrators had acquired skills and worked out methods that were ready for wider application when the depression struck. In any emergency it helps to have people who know what ought to be done.

The importance of this trained and experienced corps justifies some generalizations on the way in which reform groups have won points in modern society. There are four ways, not mutually exclusive, in which it has been done. The first has been to develop arguments in professional associations and specialist schools, and then to seek publicity, especially when some incident arouses wider interest. In this way, awareness of the need percolates down, gradually winning support for the remedies proposed and finally leading to political action. Broadly speaking, this was how the contributors to *Recent Social Change* believed that the most durable changes had been achieved in the past and would be achieved in the future. They perceived a long-term shift from a belief that nature could not be defied to a conviction that there was a remedy for every ill, that prevention was often the best cure, and that the coercive power of government might be employed when people were too selfish or too ignorant to act for the public good.

The second method was to infiltrate existing administrative institutions. In America this process had been assisted by the fondness for appointed boards, usually with unpaid members but salaried secretaries and a permanent staff. In this way, leading physicians had been given official standing in the improvement of public health and doctors who wanted administrative responsibilities had served as executive secretaries. Many people who were interested in welfare problems served on state boards caring for the blind, mentally retarded, orphans, delinquent children, handicapped persons, and sufferers from tuberculosis and other wasting diseases. Others served on state boards of charities and correction or welfare. These numerous agencies were filled by unpaid volunteers, but they acted with the stamp of state authority and their executive secretaries were usually men who were making their career in this service. The growing importance of public welfare provided opportunities for people who wished to make it their profession; but the most important training grounds for welfare administration were the great organized charities and community chests, with directors and secretaries who were likely to have had professional training or considerable experience in social work. Thus there was a growing number of opportunities for trained social workers to gain administrative experience and for interested well-wishers to learn from them what was being discussed among the professionals.

The third method was to enlist government authority and use it to carry out needed reforms. Even before the depression, America was, at the state level, a much governed country and, on examination, most of the governing was performed by agencies set up for a single purpose, staffed by experts, and sheltered from arbitrary political interference. The degree to which these agencies might call upon state power to implement change and enforce their regulations varied. In New England the usual preference was for advisory boards or commissions that would make their point by publicity, avoid coercion, leave law making to the legislature, and enforcement to state attorneys and the courts. Outside New England the independent agencies often had power to make regulations, and would themselves prosecute offenders if they were not obeyed. In some instances (food and drug laws were striking examples), the states had set up agencies that were primarily concerned with enforcement. Whatever the character of an agency, it was likely to develop its own momentum, formulate its own code of practice, and press for enlargement of its powers and staff. Agencies might fail, as often as not, to get all they wanted, but with most the trend was toward larger, more efficient, and more professional government. In all, the best that social reformers could hope for was find themselves members of an agency dedicated to their chosen field; the next best was to establish an unofficial but close relationship with it.

The fourth means of winning friends and influencing people was by learning and practicing the arts of lobbying and pressure politics. Enough has already been said of this method to make elaboration unnecessary. It need only be added that it was usually assumed that no initiative could be expected from a state legislature without lobbying. If a legislator was known to favor a particular reform, he would soon find himself recruited as part of the relevant pressure group. Organizations opposed to welfare reform could and did maintain their own lobbies, but although many of them (for instance, chambers of commerce) had a watching brief over a very wide range of legislative activities, they could not match the concentration and expertise with which lobbies organized to promote specific measures played the game.

In this situation the representatives of the people (apart from the rare reformer among them) played a plastic part. If anything was to be got out of a legislature, some way must be found of manipulating it, generating outside pressure, or working through an established state agency that had its own permanent lobby at the state capitol. The role of the legislature was not to initiate but to provide complex channels through which informed opinion from outside its walls could shape policy. But skillful promotion could not guarantee success. Measures could fail because some legislatures talked it out or got it sent back to committee on technical grounds, or the majority could exercise the mighty power of the purse and refuse to levy taxes or make appropriations. In this way, a state legislature was often seen by reformers as a fractious animal that required skillful handling but was never predictable, often troublesome, and capable of wrecking valuable bills that had cost years of preparation and months in the lobbies.

When state relief agencies were created, welfare reformers had agencies that they controlled without the need to infiltrate and from which they could break through into an area hitherto under exclusive local control. The first Federal Emergency Relief Act gave them an opportunity to go further and influence state relief policy itself, though under the authority of the RFC, which was not primarily interested in reform. The FERA gave them a program over which they could exercise complete control, and this opportunity was grasped with enthusiasm. The rapid expansion of the federal agency, the development of "parallel government," the pressure exerted on states to improve their methods and raise their standards, the close relationship between field representatives and state relief administrations, the influence exercised through this channel on county and local relief operations, and the federalization of relief in some states all combined to place unprecedented power in the hands of professional welfare administrators who were also committed to reform the system.

At the local level, relief administration was by law wholly a state responsibility, but the relationship between county relief agencies and the FERA was clear and well understood. The counties took their

orders from the state relief administration, which followed the guidelines fixed by the FERA. Social workers, whose employment was mandatory, controlled the local relief of unemployment, and they knew
where their professional loyalties lay. The poor masters or overseers of
the poor in townships or poor districts were largely ignored, except to
ensure that they did not interfere with the relief of the able-bodied
unemployed.

Never before had a body of reformers enjoyed so much power or
such an opportunity to impose their views upon society. As ever there
was danger that power might be abused. A writer in the *American
Political Science Review* warned:

The real danger ... lies in the fact that once a positivist science becomes the
rule of law, or once a group in our society arrogates to itself the right to judge
or to treat another by the findings of such a science, no end to the process is
in sight. What happens depends entirely on the good will of the self-appointed
"social physician." As the supposed knowledge of this group advances, the
relation of patient and doctor tends inevitably to a benevolent or paternalistic
dictatorship by those who possess the acceptable knowledge.[49]

The "benevolent or paternalistic dictatorship" accomplished great
good. It brought much needed assistance to millions in distress, introduced systematic methods of relief administration to parts of the country where they had never been known, and reinforced the efforts of
state welfare agencies that had hitherto been forced to take slower
roads to improvement. Nevertheless the danger of asking too much in
too authoritarian a manner was real, and it is therefore useful to examine the checks that could be placed upon it.

The courts would, of course, be on their guard against breaches of
the law; but the laws were broadly framed and the courts had offered
little resistance to extended use of the police power. In *Samuels v.
McCurdy* the Supreme Court had declined to interfere even in a case
in which state action had gone further than to impose a reasonable
curb on individual rights. During the depression years no state relief
laws were found unconstitutional. Perhaps the most surprising example of judicial acquiescence was in Pennsylvania, where the court that
had invalidated an old-age pension law (with the same judge delivering
the opinion) approved the use of state funds for the relief of unem-

---

[49] Alan Keith-Lucas, "The Political Theory Implicit in Social Casework Theory," *APSR*
47, 1076–91.

ployment in terms so wide that no subsequent law was likely to be challenged. No comparable case in the United States Supreme Court tested the constitutionality of federal relief, and it seems likely that anyone wishing to contest the law was advised that it was not worth trying. This is not to suggest that the courts were lax but that a legal consensus had been reached that governments were entitled to use all reasonable means to relieve distress.[50]

Checks that were likely to be more effective came from the state and local governments, but the motives were often suspect and were certainly not justified on high constitutional grounds. In theory the FERA did no more than furnish federal aid for state programs, and states were always free to reject the conditions on which it was offered. The FERA then had to decide whether to cut off aid until the state's response was satisfactory – thus penalizing the people in distress – or to continue aid without insisting that the state play its part. Thus friction between welfare administrators who had never been elected to any office and the chosen representatives of the people was certain to generate the greatest amount of ill-feeling without reaching a satisfactory conclusion.

The preceding pages have included examples of obstructive governors, but the most persistent check on federal power was the refusal by state legislatures to appropriate enough or, in some cases, any money for relief. Some states were able to hold their negative position throughout the FERA period; others gave too little and too late. Thus the representatives of the people checked the operations of this powerful federal agency by denying money for the relief of their own people. It was a curious and unsatisfactory arrangement.

---

[50] The principle decided in the Pennsylvania case was accepted elsewhere. There remained some doubt about how much control the FERA could exercise once a grant had been made. In the case of *Wiseman (State Commissioner of Revenue) v. Dyess (State Emergency Relief Administrator)* the Supreme Court of Arkansas found that the funds and property of the ERA belonged to the federal government. "Though the Act of Congress refers to grants to the States, this was not done in a way to pass the title and control from the federal government. They continue to be subject to federal supervision." The Governor acted "merely as the agent or intermediary employed by the federal government in discharge of the beneficient purpose of the congressional act" [72 (2) *Southwestern Reporter* 517]. In *Harris v. Fulp* the Supreme Court of South Carolina decided that FERA grants became funds of the state, but that the administrator's power to disburse funds was similar to that of the state treasurer. The administrator's decision was final, provided that it was in accordance with law and he was not subject to political direction (183 *Southeastern Reporter* 158).

At the county level, the relief administrators often encountered resistance from elected officials. There were not many complaints about failure to provide money or materials, but local officers, resentful of this intrusion into their domain, could make life very difficult for the social workers with responsibility for relief. Alternatively, the social workers had to learn to respect the local people, accept a less efficient or humane administration than they would have wished, or take responsibility for relief cases that ought to have been looked after by the local government.

The relations between the FERA and the states must prompt some sober reflections. Can the power of well-intentioned and well-trained experts be checked only by methods that are often inspired by unworthy motives, offend against civilized concern for social well-being, and injure the weakest members of society? Were reactionary governors, mean legislators, or officials greedy for local power to be praised for resisting efforts to undermine the foundations of American democracy? Or were the efforts of the FERA administrators justified by their generous wish to leave relief administration in better shape than they found it?

The end of the FERA made it unnecessary, for the time being, to answer these questions. The federal administrators and their state appointees retained great power, but of a different kind. The headquarters staff of the FERA moved to the WPA and most of them did so with enthusiasm. It seemed a nobler ideal to provide work rather than a dole. The new program being wholly federal, they were rid of the numerous frustrations that had arisen in relations with the states, and were free to devise and develop programs to improve the quality of life. The advantages were great, but so were the lost opportunities. The WPA required state and local welfare officers to certify eligibility for employment but did not regulate the way in which eligibility was determined; it sometimes rejected certified applicants, but because there were usually more employables than jobs, there was no incentive to go out to the highways and byways and ask whether everyone needing relief had been investigated. The WPA approved locally sponsored projects and might require local contributions in the form of materials and supervision, but it refused to accept any responsibility for relief of employables who could not be employed. The direct link between welfare reform and local administration was broken, to the dismay of all who had looked for a national program of public assistance.

Federal money went into categorical relief and an element of control was maintained, but the states decided their own procedures and the regulation required by federal law might amount to no more than a routine check on record keeping. The day-to-day exposure of public assistance to professional criticism was a thing of the past. This was the reality reflected in complaints by social workers that the whole thing had been handed back to untrained overseers of the poor.

There was, of course, room for development in the more active state agencies and, to some extent, in county welfare departments; but in the latter, the active social worker was under the direction of the county commission. The magic once worked by the flow of federal money was no more.

Strategic planning for welfare shifted from Washington back to unofficial national and state conferences of social workers, public welfare associations, and schools of social work. The authority of these bodies was much greater than it had been in the 1920s and their deliberations benefitted from the advice of people who had wielded real power, but this heightened status did not conceal the fact that once more they were outsiders and that improvement could come about only by getting down to the time-consuming task of lobbying state legislatures.

The rise of federal relief showed how a small group committed to improvement could achieve great results, but its end demonstrated the fragility of their power. The traditional forms of government proved to be more durable even though their competence was doubtful and their structure unsound. The episodes in the story put into sharp focus issues that are common to all democratic societies. These issues concern the role of reformers who can do much good but lack popular support, of people in authority who are not directly responsible to the people, and of those who are elected but lack wisdom. Convincing evidence showed that local responsibility – so much admired by traditional political theorists and by modern critics of centralized government – had failed, but no alternative was offered. Government from the center developed strength and purpose, but without a coherent philosophy to justify its power or define its responsibilities. Thus the record presents a final question. What political institutions can best combine the will to improve the human condition with the consent of the governed who may not wish to be improved?

INDEX